LAW AS SYMBOLIC FORM

Law and Philosophy Library

VOLUME 82

LAW AS SYMBOLIC FORM

Ernst Cassirer and the Anthropocentric View of Law

DENIZ COSKUN
Radboud University of Nijmegen,
The Netherlands

Springer

A C.I.P. Catalogue record for this book is available from the Library of Congress.

ISBN 978-1-4020-6255-1 (HB)
ISBN 978-1-4020-6256-8 (e-book)

Published by Springer,
P.O. Box 17, 3300 AA Dordrecht, The Netherlands.

www.springer.com

Printed on acid-free paper

To the memory of my great-grandmother Meyrem Özcan

ACKNOWLEDGMENTS

My thanks go out to many. From an intellectual and aspirational point of view I want to thank Norman Redlich and Paul Kahn for their support throughout the process. My thanks go out also to Bruce Ackerman and our many interactions during the Justice course at Yale. My advisor Thomas Mertens has teached me a lot, professionally and personally. Paul Cliteur I want to thank for teaching me to write an essay. This book is written on a Netherlands Organization for Scientific Research Scholarship. Furthermore, this book has benefited from my visit to Yale Law School and the Beinecke Rare Book and Manuscript Library of Yale University. In addition, this book has benefited from my stay at Georgetown University Law Center, and my frequent visits to the United States Holocaust Memorial Museum Library (for the Center of Advanced Holocaust Studies) in Washington, D.C., because of a Fulbright Scholarship. Finally, I want to thank my grandfather, Ali, my grandmother, Dilber, my mother, Kezzi, my father, Noman, my brothers, Bilal and Ali, and my sister, Dilber Meyrem, for the emotional structure and sustenance in my life that has made it possible for me to write this book.

I have chosen to leave the citations and references to Cassirer's work unabbreviated, because the Cassirer scholarship is central to this book. Thusly also the separate lists of primary and secondary literature that specifically pertain to Cassirer and his works.

New York, November 6, 2006
Deniz Coskun

TABLE OF CONTENTS

INTRODUCTION

This work introduces and systematically elaborates on Law as Symbolic Form. It is inspired by the philosophy of symbolic forms of Ernst Cassirer (1874–1945). For this reason it must immediately eliminate the barriers that have previously prevented the treatment of law and jurisprudence within the framework of Cassirer's philosophy. Cassirer was not a mere theoretical philosopher. His philosophy not only gives room systematically to ethics and law, but, moreover, it is deeply ethically inspired. It is the level of sophistication – as the title "philosophy of symbolic forms" makes apparent – and the theoretical depth of his works that distinguishes Cassirer from his mentor, Hermann Cohen. Nevertheless, as is the case with Cohen, Cassirer remains firmly bound to a practical commitment, *i.e.*, to that of human dignity, and more specifically for our present purposes: human rights.

As no other age has put human creativity at the center of the universe, the Renaissance spirit also characterizes the development of Ernst Cassirer as the last universal humanist scholar of the twentieth century.[1] Born into a prominent Jewish family of Breslau, Germany (today Wroclaw, Poland) in 1874, he entered the University of Berlin in 1892, where he studied law. He soon changed to literature and philosophy, pursuing further studies in history, languages, and the sciences at the Universities of Leipzig, Heidelberg, and Munich.[2] In Berlin he had been introduced to the works of Hermann Cohen by his philosophical teacher Georg Simmel and, in 1896, he became one of Cohen's students at the University of Marburg. He soon became the most gifted and ablest student of Cohen, and would subsequently write a dissertation under the auspices of Cohen about the philosophy of Leibniz (1902).[3] However, unable to find any official commission to a German University, because he was Jewish,[4] he

---

1 See: Habermas, 1997, pp. 9–40.

2 See: Rudolph, 2002, introduction.

3 See: Ernst Cassirer, *Leibniz' System in seinen wissenschaftlichen Grundlagen*, Gesammelte Werke, Band 1, Felix Meiner Verlag, Hamburg, 1998 (1902).

4 We cannot enter here into the debate of Cassirer's relation to Judaism. Cassirer received a Jewish funeral. After the funeral service the *cortège*

became a Privatdozent (unaccredited teacher) in Berlin. Nevertheless, his multi-volume work on the problem of knowledge and the excellent and refined concentration of his theoretical insights in *Substance and Function*[5] would earn him a widely acclaimed reputation.[6] Weimar marked a definite turning point for Cassirer's career. After First World War, Cassirer left Berlin for the newly founded University of Hamburg, which offered him a position of full professor. He was subsequently elected Rector of the University of Hamburg in 1929.

Although Cassirer started as a philosopher in the Marburg School of neo-Kantianism, he gradually created an original philosophical position, *i.e.*, the philosophy of symbolic forms.[7] Cassirer did not intend his philosophy of symbolic forms to be a new philosophy in itself; rather it was, for him, a new way to approach philosophy. With this approach, Cassirer sought to initiate a transformation of Kant's Critique of Reason into a Critique of Culture, that is to say, a prolegomenon to a future philosophy of culture. Commonly regarded as one of the giants in the philosophy of the first half of the twentieth century, Cassirer more or less disappeared from philosophical discourse after the Second World War. The Davos debate seems to have contributed influentially to the dismemberment of Cassirer's philosophy. However, new and various attempts have been made not only to reassess the Davos debate,[8] but also Cassirer's philosophy in

---

proceeded to a crematorium. Cassirer's relation to his Jewish faith was complicated. As then young rabbi Hertzberg, who was taking Cassirer's philosophy course on Kant at Columbia University and who performed the funeral service, recalls from a personal encounter: "*There was something in the whole tone of his conversations which made him into one recurrent theme: that he regretted not having been throughout his life more involved in Jewish learning and not having his Jewish self more central to his entire being.*" See: Hertzberg, 1970, pp. 245–246; here: p. 246. Cassirer displayed a significant degree of limitation relative to his position as a Jew in pre-war Germany; see: Liebeschütz, 1956, esp. pp. 229–231.

5 Cf. Ernst Cassirer, *Substance and Function & Einstein's Theory of Relativity*, tr. W.C. Swabey and M.C. Swabey, Dover Publications, New York, 1953 (1910).

6 See: Krois, 1987, p. 20.

7 Ernst Cassirer, *Die Philosophie der symbolischen Formen*, 3 Bdn., Bruno Cassirer Verlag, Berlin, 1923–1929.

8 Cf. Hackenesch, 2001; and Kaegi, 2002.

general.[9] The so-called Cassirer Renaissance in philosophy has as its leading theme that Cassirer was not a neo-Kantian philosopher anymore, but maintained an independent position, as was exemplified by Cassirer among others in Davos.

Recently, after decades, interest in the philosophy of Cassirer has increased, not only in philosophy, but also in numerous other disciplines. Furthermore his interdisciplinary prolegomenon to a future philosophy of culture, is promising in that his works include elaborated references to a wide variety of disciplines. This is no different for the discipline of jurisprudence.[10] To be concrete, the natural law tradition of human rights is termed by Cassirer as the "*true connection of philosophy with the world*."[11] Accordingly, Cassirer in the first half of the twentieth century established a philosophical–anthropological justification of human rights through his "Philosophy of Symbolic Forms," by maintaining that the human being as an *animal symbolicum* is a thoroughly expressive and normative being, and that the symbolic nature of man poses certain limits upon every state action. Moreover, man as *animal symbolicum* achieves its individuality first in an ethical community constituted by laws.

Cassirer himself never wrote a philosophy of law, however, on many occasions he addressed, in public and in writing, various topics in the philosophy of law, such as constitutionalism, social contract theory, natural law, human rights, and Law as Symbolic Form. The fact that Cassirer has not written a "legal philosophy," therefore, should not directly lead to the conclusion that Cassirer did not have a "legal philosophy."[12] The current study proceeds from existing material Cassirer produced in jurisprudence to what these require in the way of supportive context from the

---

9 The most important reassessment has been given by: Krois, 1987.

10 See: Ernst Cassirer, *Axel Hägerström- eine Studie zur Schwedischen Philosophie der Gegenwart*, Göteborgs Högskolas Årsskrift, Elanders Boktryckeri Aktiebolag, Göteborg, 1939; cf. Coskun, D., *Law as Symbolic Form. Ernst Cassirer and the anthropocentric view of law*, in: Bankowski, Z. (ed.), *Epistemology and Ontology*, IVR-Symposium Lund 2003, ARSP Beiheft 102, Steiner Verlag, Stuttgart, 2005, pp. 25–37; cf. Part I.

11 Ernst Cassirer, *Symbol, Myth, and Culture. Essays and Lectures of Ernst Cassirer 1935–1945*, edited by D.P. Verene, Yale University Press, New Haven and London, 1979, p. 60.

12 For the discussion of whether and in what way Cassirer has to be reckoned a practical philosopher as well, see: Recki, 2004, and Schwemmer, 1997.

perspective of jurisprudence.[13] Through this archeological method, Cassirer's legal philosophy can be extracted from those instances in which he addressed jurisprudential and practical philosophical issues.[14]

Therefore, this research attempts to reconstruct and to give a compilation of the philosophy of law of Cassirer. Although the inclusion of biographical material serves to clarify and enrich the discussion, this work does not attempt to offer a complete biographical elaboration of the life of Cassirer; his widow Toni Cassirer has done this carefully and in detail.[15] Nor does it attempt to give a complete intellectual biography; in different and various instances, Cassirer-scholars have filled up this lacuna. The readers are encouraged to read these works, most of which are listed in the literature references, for further development of their understanding of Cassirer's works. Nevertheless, where possible and functional for our present purposes, it delivers the relevant data necessary for that understanding. As to biographical data, the investigations are confined to Cassirer's public life, in particular those instances where Cassirer has displayed a jurisprudential commitment. Furthermore, it is beyond the field of this research to explain the Cassirer Renaissance in general.[16] However, it is possible to explain here the same trend in practical philosophy, and jurisprudence in particular, by asking for the motives of this research. What is it that makes research into the jurisprudence of Cassirer useful and rewarding?

Firstly, this work is the first comprehensive attempt to treat the subject of law as a symbolic form. It therefore fills up a lacuna with respect to Cassirer's historical contribution to jurisprudence by reconstructing his philosophy of law and his account of jurisprudence. Second, Cassirer himself had a particular interest in law. As his grandson, Peter Cassirer puts it: "*Ernst Cassirer began to study law – his father needed a solicitor for the business, but he very soon changed to Germanistik, and*

---

13 Cf. Deacon, 1997, pp. 367–368.

14 On the archaeology of law, see: Kahn, 1997; and Kahn, 1999.

15 See: Cassirer, T., *Mein Leben mit Ernst Cassirer*, Gerstenberg Verlag, Hildesheim, 1981.

16 For a systematic and biographical treatment of the philosophy of Ernst Cassirer, see among others: Krois, 1987; Paetzold, 1995; Schwemmer, 1997; Sandkühler, 2003; Ferrari, 2003; Recki, 2004; and Hanson, 2006.

also later, as he had become a philosopher still devoted himself to philosophy of language and the great German poets, above all Goethe, who took a special room in his heart. His father Eduard often complained that his most talented son did not engage himself in the business. It would have been much better if Ernst had taken care of the factory, he used to say, and that the dull Richard had become a scholar."[17]

Furthermore, the subject of law has been an important element from the very first of Cassirer's works; at least as early as his treatment of the philosophy of Leibniz in 1902. It is often underestimated in Cassirer-related literature that his interest in jurisprudence and moral philosophy was significant in relation to his later development. Cassirer's engagement with the study of law and moral philosophy, therefore, was relevant both for his personal as well as for his philosophical life. Cassirer never lost sight of the importance of law. Moreover, his anticipation of the Nazi threat to the German nation demonstrates a true jurisprudential commitment. When Cassirer, in 1933, first heard of the Nazi decree that declared, "*Law is, what suits the Führer,*" he most fervently declared: "*If not tomorrow all legal scholars of Germany rise up as one and object to these phrases, Germany is lost.*"[18] His life in exile is full of examples that refer to and advocate the fundamental principles of the rule of law, and, as a fundamental necessity, the bond between "truth" and "law," or what may be called individual moral judgment. A coherent account of the philosophy of law of Cassirer will have to give that insight of Cassirer the attention that it is due.

In addition, our interest in Cassirer covers his critical idealism and his early acknowledgment of the potential danger

---

[17] See: <http://web.telia.com/~u31252427/ecengl.htm> (last visited: September 17, 2006).

[18] See: Toni Cassirer, 1981, p. 189: "*Recht ist, was dem Führer dient.* (...) *Wenn morgen nicht alle Rechtsgelehrten Deutschlands sich wie ein Man erheben und gegen diesen Phrasen protestieren, ist Deutschland verloren.*" The author has had the opportunity to register Ernst and Toni Cassirer at *The Benjamin and Vladka Meed Registry of Jewish Holocaust Survivors* of the United States Holocaust Memorial Museum (USHMM), Washington, D.C. (last visited: August 4, 2006); with acknowledgements to the Fulbright Program and Georgetown University Law Center. Chapter 1 has benefited importantly from my visits to the USHMM and its Library for the Center of Advanced Holocaust Studies.

of mass media for the individual moral person and for its sense of responsibility and reflectivity. Cassirer was a philosopher who believed in absolute values, for example in the form of human rights, and through his experiences with the problem of scientific knowledge he sought to give his theory of absolute values a theoretical underpinning. Cassirer's public engagement with the values of the Enlightenment started in the Weimar Republic by emphasizing the German contribution to the human rights tradition, and responding to theories in practical philosophy that deny the existence of absolute values, in the form of individual human rights, or subject them to serious doubt. This trend is still prevalent today in the form of ethical or moral relativism and cultural relativism, which deny the existence of absolute or universal values respectively by claiming that values differ from person to person and from culture to culture. Although Cassirer acknowledges the diversity in cultural and ethical life in relation to morality, nevertheless this does not result for him in moral relativism or nihilism. Among the variety and differences in moral views Cassirer distinguishes certain ethical forms or moral archetypes that are common to all viewpoints. Diverse cultures may think differently, for example, about the treatment of their dead, however what remains, according to Cassirer, is their shared and ethical concern for the dead.

In this regard Cassirer provides a philosophical perspective for those who wish to believe in absolute values or individual human rights, without losing sight of the possible and the future. That the latter aspect, through the maintenance and activation of the critical faculties of man, is crucial for the possibility of the former, *i.e.*, human rights, became dramatically apparent for Cassirer with the rise of the Third Reich. Cassirer, though, anticipated the possibility of such a threat through his philosophy of symbolic forms, specifically by his references to mythical thought. Critical thought, Cassirer held, did not defeat myth itself, but only its products and configurations. From the earliest times, *i.e.*, pre-Socratic thought, philosophy opposed Logos to Mythos, and was victorious over it again and again, but myth never seems to recede. Philosophy has an important normative task, according to Cassirer, because only through the maintenance of the equilibrium between the various symbolic forms, by assuring the distinctness of each in this plurality, and hence by retaining their distinct formative powers, can we prevent mythical thought from dominating and emasculating our critical faculties. The cultivation of our critical faculties or culture was the solution for Cassirer to the pertinent crisis in pre-war Germany. The striking feature of the myths of the twentieth century, though, is their technique or method of implementation. "*Myth has always been described as the result of an unconscious activity and as a free product of imagination. But here we find myth made according to plan. The new political myths do not grow up freely;* (...) *They are artificial things fabricated by very skilful and cunning artisans.* (...) *Henceforth myths can be manufactured in the same sense and according to the same methods as any other modern weapon – as machine guns or airplanes. That is a new thing – and a thing of crucial importance. It has changed the form of our social life,*"[19] writes Cassirer.

Myth is not a given thing, according to Cassirer, but a process or state of mind. In mythical thought, the one dissolves in the many, and as such the individual cannot, nay *may not* carry individual responsibility or make moral judgments reflectively. Man dominated by mythical thought loses his sense of individuality or sense of moral personality. Consequently, such a person cannot enter into a social contract or be the subject of rights and obligations. Albert Speer, one of Hitler's henchmen, who read Cassirer's *Myth of the State* after the Nuremberg trials, and was struck by its relevance, stated most tellingly: "*Now I was completely under Hitler's spell, unreservedly and unthinkingly I held by him. I was ready to follow him anywhere. Yet his ostensible interest in me was only to launch me on a glorious career as an architect. Years later, in Spandau, I read Ernst Cassirer's comment on the men who of their own accord threw away man's highest privilege: to be an autonomous person. Now I was one of them.*"[20] According to Cassirer, mass media facilitated the emergence of mythical thought in the form of twentieth century totalitarian politics and the totalitarian state. For Cassirer this entailed more than the mere massive

---

[19] Ernst Cassirer, *The Myth of the State*, Yale University Press, New Haven, 1945, pp. 354–355.

[20] Speer, A., *Inside the Third Reich*, tr. Richard and Clara Winston, Avon, New York, 1970, pp. 84–85, cited in: Cristaudo, W., 1991, p. 478.

spread of propaganda or ideology. In his political pathology or what may here be called his pathology of (passive) obedience, Cassirer explains how mass media initiated and sustained a change in the function of language, and hence in the mentality of the people, by stressing, and appealing to, its common root with myth. A coherent account of the philosophy of law of Cassirer will also have to make clear the relation between law, language, and myth. In this respect, Cassirer provides a context for his view of law through his philosophy of symbolic forms, where he explains that we grasp law first in that (mythical) concatenation.

As indicated, although Cassirer designated law as a symbolic form,[21] he never gave an elaborate exploration of law as a symbolic form in the same way that he did with the symbolic forms of language, myth, and science. It is therefore the specific aim of our research to make a connection between the philosophy of symbolic forms and the discipline of law. It is therefore not our aim to answer the question whether law is a symbolic form – as we rely on the fact that Cassirer considered law a symbolic form and shortly elaborated on it systematically – but rather to investigate how and why law is a symbolic form. The questions of how law is a symbolic form, and why law is a symbolic form, ultimately depend on the question of how law manifests itself in reality, in the lives and minds of people. Law is a phenomenon that shapes human lives, by giving people a particular means to cope with life, *i.e.*, to create objectivity and determinacy in human life and conduct, and forms the expression and configuration of the symbolic nature of the human species.

Accordingly, Law as Symbolic Form is to adopt a certain perspective on law, whereby we investigate the semiotic and symbolic structures that support law. In this respect, Law as Symbolic Form gives a functional answer or perspective to the question of the nature of law. It maintains that law can only be known through its manifestation in our lives and minds. For example, that law is a castle in the air which we experience at the most extreme when our trust in the law or a legal system

---

[21] See: Ernst Cassirer, *The Philosophy of Symbolic Forms*, Volume II, *Myth*, tr. R. Manheim, Yale University Press, New Haven, 1955 (1925), XIV–XV; cf. idem, *Axel Hägerström- eine Studie zur Schwedischen Philosophie der Gegenwart*, Göteborgs Högskolas Årsskrift, Elanders Boktryckeri Aktiebolag, Göteborg, 1939a, especially pp. 84 ff.

results in great disappointment, such as in Nazi Germany or Apartheid South Africa. Nonetheless, law unmistakably plays a useful function in the life of man and is a specifically human product. A life without law would be like living without language; without law we would have to live without that extra dimension, by which we can plan or order our common lives. Without Law as Symbolic Form our existence becomes less humane, or, as Grotius, founder of modern natural law theory and of international law, put it, law is a necessary condition for the "*humanitas ipsa*."[22] Law is a typically human product because our symbolic capacities stand at its foundation.

Moreover, by taking into consideration the symbolic nature of man, Cassirer gives a philosophical and anthropological foundation to human rights supported by the latest scientific developments in the study of man, and that incidentally escapes the latest critiques voiced in relation to the universality of human rights, *i.e.*, from an external as well as from an internal perspective. Through his concept of the *animal symbolicum* Cassirer gives a renewed foundation to human dignity, and hence to human rights. As opposed to the other animals, man lives not only in a single space or habitat, the *vitale Lebensraum*, as Cassirer calls it, but he also lives in a symbolic life-world. The ratio is not the distinguishing factor of man, because animals too display a certain kind of intelligence or rationality. Reason does not exhaust the capabilities of man to intelligently cope with his environment. Cassirer suggests that man is foremost a symbolic being, an *animal symbolicum*. "*Man has, as it were, discovered a new method of adapting himself to his environment. Between the receptor system and the effector system, which are to be found in all animal species, we find in man a third link which we may describe as the symbolic system. This new acquisition transforms the whole of human life. As compared with the other animals man lives not merely in a broader reality; he lives, so to speak, in a new* dimension *of reality.* (...) *No longer can man confront reality immediately; he cannot see it, as it were, face to face. Physical reality seems to recede in proportion as man's symbolic activity advances. Instead of dealing with the things*

22 See: Ernst Cassirer, *Vom Wesen und Werden des Naturrechts*, Zeitschrift für Rechtsphilosophie in Lehre und Praxis, Volume 6, No. 1, 1932, pp. 22–23.

themselves man is in a sense constantly conversing with himself. He has so enveloped himself in linguistic forms, in artistic images, in mythical symbols or religious rites that he cannot see or know anything except by this artificial medium."[23]

To illustrate, likewise, the Cambridge psychologist Craik has put forward the idea that the function of the organism's nervous system is to set up a symbolic model of the external world: "*The brain ... imitates or models external processes. The function of such symbolization is plain. If the organism carries a "small-scale model" of external reality and of its own possible actions within its head, it is able to try out various alternatives, conclude which is the best of them, react to future situations before they arise, utilize the knowledge of past events in dealing with the present of future, and every way to react in a much fuller, safer, and more competent manner to the emergencies which face it.*"[24] Impulses from the environment are no longer directly responded by stimuli, but man finds it necessary to pause and give a symbolic reaction, to give meaning to the outer world. As the twentieth century original thinker Arthur Koestler explains, "*For man is a symbol-making animal. He constructs a symbolic model of outer reality in his brain, and expresses it by a second set of symbols in terms of words, equations, pigment, or stone. All he knows directly are bodily sensations, all he can directly do is to perform bodily motions; the rest of his knowledge and means of expression is symbolical. (...) Any attempt to get a direct grasp at naked reality is self-defeating; Urania, too, like the other muses, always has a last veil left to fold in.*"[25]

To continue, similarly, in a recent study in neurobiology Terrence Deacon in *The Symbolic Species*, has shown that man is a strange phenomenon in nature.[26] Human evolutionary history shows an anomaly, as a result of which humans started to make use of "symbolic meaning giving." According to Deacon,

---

[23] See: Ernst Cassirer, *An Essay on Man: An Introduction to a Philosophy of Human Culture*, Yale University Press, New Haven, 1944, pp. 24–25.

[24] Craik, K.J., *The Nature of Explanation*, Cambridge University Press, Cambridge, 1943, p. 61; cited by Koestler, 1966, pp. 510–511.

[25] Koestler, A., 1966, pp. 344–345; cf. Meerloo, 1968.

[26] See: Deacon, T.W., *The Symbolic Species: The Co-evolution of Language and the Brain*, Norton, New York, 1997.

the transition to a meat-subsistence strategy, which was accompanied by tool-use, posed certain socio-ecological problems for mankind.[27] While female members of the group cannot go hunting because they have to nurse siblings, upon return male members need to have an incentive to share the meat they hunt. A particular male member of the group will "agree" to share the meat with a particular female member only when he is secured that the continuity of his "genes" are taken care of and not that of another. The transition initiated the wish or the necessity to attain a social structure that guaranteed unambiguous and exclusive mating and that was sufficiently egalitarian to sustain cooperation via shared or parallel reproductive interests.[28] This social-reproductive dilemma, according to Deacon, served as the initial impetus for symbol evolution, because it required the ability to share "*common intentions, interests, goals, and emotions*" as "*the most effective means for coordinating behavior, and being able to imagine and anticipate another's mental and emotional responses*" as "*a powerful tool for social manipulation.*"[29]

According to Deacon, man found a solution for the social-reproductive dilemma in the construction of a symbolic agreement that involves a promise by those who are party to the social arrangement and have something to lose if one individual takes advantage of an uncondoned sexual opportunity.[30] Although Deacon may be right in tracing the origin of the symbolic faculties of man to the social-reproductive dilemma, he does make clear why it was imperative for man to represent a social contract and why social contracts are necessarily symbolic in nature.[31] One of the primary functions of symbolization is to build an independent mental representation of the subjective experience of another, so represented as if one were able to trade places with the other.[32] By sharing other people's minds and

---

[27] For the impact of the transition to agriculture on man's symbolic or cultural life, see: Ernst Cassirer, *The Philosophy of Symbolic Forms*, Volume II, *Myth*, tr. R. Manheim, Yale University Press, New Haven, 1955 (1925), pp. 201 ff.

[28] See: Deacon, 1997, pp. 396–397.

[29] Ibid., 1997, p. 428.

[30] Ibid., 1997, pp. 399–400.

[31] Ibid., 1997, pp. 401–405. See: Chapter 8.

[32] See: Deacon, T.W., *The Symbolic Species: The Co-evolution of Language and the Brain*, Norton, New York, 1997, p. 427.

representations of their experiences, man solved the problem of organizing group behavior "*around something as intangible as a desired future habit of behavior*."[33] Through the manipulation of symbols man discovered the ability to create models of other's emotional states, and to exercise restraint or determination with respect to them.[34]

Symbolization enables man to exercise empathy or 'imaginative interchange,' as Edmond Cahn put it. With symbolization, nature has equipped man with an instrument of self-defense, because when each projects himself into the shoes of the other, wrong or injustice to another person will be regarded as personal aggression, which subsequently triggers "*those affections of the viscera and abnormal secretions of the adrenals that prepare the human mind to resist attack*."[35] Consequently, as Eric Gans has said in very different terms in anthropology, because no man wants to invoke the aggression of another, and so disturb the social arrangement that guarantees for him a certain beneficial or egalitarian distribution of goods, he displays "manners" or restraint. Therefore, the prey is not directly torn apart and immediately digested, but man first grasps it in terms of an object.[36] Only man is in the position *to come to terms*, literally, with his fellow being. In social life, mainly through linguistic forms, man discovers his true, *i.e.*, symbolic nature, because as such the symbolic excludes the mere subjective and includes the other. As Cassirer notes, only man is in the position to understand another through the various symbolic forms he has devised for himself. Consequently, his capacity for, what we call in this book, symbolic interchange and perspectival flexibility enables him to establish and maintain a specifically human social life.

However, while the fact that man uses symbols distinguishes him from an animal, it also makes him vulnerable to

---

33 Ibid., 1997, p. 400.

34 Ibid., 1997, pp. 431–432.

35 See: Cahn, E.N., *The Sense of Injustice: An Anthropocentric View of Law*, New York University Press, New York, 1949, chapter 1, section 2, The Sense of Injustice. I regard this text of Edmond Cahn as one of the most important texts in twentieth century legal philosophy.

36 See: Gans, E., *Originary Thinking: Elements of Generative Anthropology*, Stanford University Press, Stanford, 1993.

different dangers. With the acquisition or the availability of symbolic capacities, man can inflict upon his fellow man that which he cannot upon members of other species, as the latter are excluded from the specifically human realm of the symbolic. Not only can one man deprive the life or property of another, moreover, he can be mean, denigrating, even genocidal just because the other is a human, and therefore a symbol-using being, *i.e.*, because the sheer presence of the other impugns upon his symbolic life world. Myth as a mental process or state of mind in this respect can easily become instrumental because of its specific perception of expression. Myth accords to every outward sign a physiognomic quality or meaning. Because myth does not operate dialogically, but rather by the invocation of the authority of seniority, it is inimical to (individual) moral progress. Through its physiognomic perception of expression it can easily lead to the demonization or dehumanization of the other. Myth, as a state of mind, thinks in terms of collectivities instead of individual human persons, and in terms of good and evil instead of human dignity.

Human dignity for Cassirer cannot be given a foundation in some substantial or metaphysical concept, not even in rationality; nor can it rest on distinctly religious grounds. For Cassirer human dignity can only be given a functional foundation and rests in the symbolic nature of man. What makes the human being special and raises him above the rest of nature is its capacity to relate to other human beings symbolically, and only in its relating to the other as a meaningful being through the various symbolic forms, hence the appreciation of the humanity of the other, can the human being appreciate its own individual humanity. By progressively relating to other human beings the individual not only attests to its individual humanity, but also creates its view of the world. Accordingly, the various symbolic forms respectively contribute to the personal outlook of the individual; that is to say, constitute its personality or identity. The many conflicts and tensions between the various symbolic forms are resolved only in the concrete, acting individual.

Furthermore, man has so enveloped himself in symbols and symbolic meanings that they have not only become part and parcel of the very structure of his intellect and feeling, or personality, but that he henceforward also cannot promptly escape from them. As a result of this, Susanne K. Langer has explained, failure or destruction of life-symbols important to any person "*is always felt as the most intolerable injury one man, or group of men, can do to another. Freedom of conscience is the basis of all personal freedom. To constrain a man against his principles* (...) *is to endanger his attitude toward the world, his personal strength and single-mindedness* (...) *the very expression of an alien mythology, incompatible with one's own vision of "fact" or "truth," works to the corruption of that vision. It* (...) *is always felt as an insult exceeding even ridicule and abuse. Common insult is a blow at one's ego; but constraint of conscience strikes at one's ego and super-ego, one's whole world, humanity, and purpose.*"[37]

Law, too, gives rise to "symbolic" perceptions and expectations – *his* or *her* rights make the citizen of a rule of law differ from that of a rule of men. A world without law or rights would be an entirely different one, and the loss or denial of rights, like that of any other communal source of meaning, while disorienting, can in itself be a cause of "suffering," or of felt "injustice." Law's meaning has become part of our perception of the world, *i.e.*, our personal outlook and identity. This pathology of the rule of law makes us see that law too has become a symbolic form, yet at another stage and level.

For Cassirer, law, like all symbolic forms, is a particular way for human beings to create a cosmos out of chaos, to relate to others, and in so doing to create a world of their own. Moreover, law in the form of human rights is a necessary element of human life; it is *a conditio sine qua non* for a characteristically human life. The fundamental human right to the free development of personality stands at the basis of the capability of the human being as an *animal symbolicum* to contribute to the progressive development of culture. Indeed, without due regard to fundamental human rights man is not in the position to contribute in his reflective and symbolic capacities to create culture, which is defined by Cassirer as the process of man's progressive self-liberation. Individual liberty, as we explain in this book, becomes a cultural imperative.

---

[37] See: Langer, 1960 (1942), pp. 290–291.

Without respect for human rights not only is man in danger of losing his culturally constructive "meaning bestowing" capacities, but also, society is in danger of receding into chaos and barbarism. Without the guaranteeing of human rights, law loses its character as a symbolic form, *i.e.*, its function and capacity to create order out of chaos, to give meaning and shape to human life and actions.[38] A systematic denial of fundamental human rights will result in the rule of law no longer governing human life, because it loses its persuasive power. Moreover, when law fails to give meaning and shape to human life, it will give room for other, perhaps more primitive elements to take over; it can give way, according to Cassirer, to the power of *myth*. Through his philosophy of symbolic forms, in particular when he refers to myth, Cassirer sought to countenance the fatalistic trends of his time, which put great if not lethal stress on the new democracy of Weimar, and Western culture in general. In various ways Cassirer tried to uphold his belief in values such as democracy and the rule of law, which necessitated him to give battle with forces that were destructive to the polity of Weimar and the ideals for which it stood, *i.e.*, humanity.

Our narrative therefore starts with the Weimar era, inserts an intermezzo with the Davos debate in 1929, and pursues Cassirer as a public person also when he was in exile. When we have established that Cassirer was not a mere theoretical philosopher, and that significantly, throughout his works, he provides himself with the context through which to understand his philosophy of law, in particular the *a priori* nature of law and its connection to individual moral reason, we thereupon focus on his main systematical work, *i.e.*, the philosophy of symbolic forms, and its relation to the field of law. Cassirer's jurisprudence and view of the social contract take as their starting point a new concept of man. The concept of the *animal symbolicum* leads to the view that law is a symbolic form, and that the social contract is symbolic in nature. Furthermore, we focus on the main source of inspiration for Cassirer. His indebtedness to the jurisprudence of the Marburg School and that of Hermann Cohen in particular,

---

[38] Cf. Unger, 1996, pp. 63–64; I respectfully disagree, though, with his subsequent assignment of the role of the Hegelian Owl of Minerva to legal analysis (Ibid., 1996, p. 69).

is obvious. Therefore, while investigating the commonalities with neo-Kantian philosophy and jurisprudence, due regard is given to the distinguishing elements of Cassirer's philosophy and legal theory. In this book we describe the rule of law as *the reign of persuasion rather than the reign of force*, and democracy as the *reign by persuasion rather than the reign by force*.

Structure

This book consists of nine chapters in two parts and proceeds as follows: In Part I, we focus on and explicate the various efforts of Cassirer as a public person to make people steadfast in their belief in humanity, which stands at the basis of law and society. First, in Chapter 1, we focus on Cassirer's engagement with the Weimar Republic and its Constitution. In a time when nationalism had its sway and reduced, in the words of Albert Schweitzer, the individual to a pathologically disoriented figure, Cassirer offered the individual a point of orientation through the Weimar Constitution and "constitutional patriotism." As opposed to the dominant "patriotic" or "*völkisch*" approach of the general public and mass media in Weimar, Cassirer focused on the *Enlightenment* as a European movement and emphasized the German contribution to this development by referring to Leibniz and Wolff.

Furthermore, in Chapter 2, we focus on the Davos debate (1929). In Davos, Cassirer criticized the defeatist and pessimistic tonality of Heidegger's philosophy and made clear why it cannot contribute to a polity that is inspired by the autonomy of man, *i.e.*, democracy. That is possible only in a polity wherein people become aware of themselves as individuals and become active as such. "*Is the infinite your aspiration?*," quotes Cassirer, "*Traverse all the finite's configurations!*"[39]

In addition, in Chapter 3, we focus on Cassirer's anticipation of his later public stance in matters pertaining to political science and jurisprudence. In Chapter 3 we deal with the significance of individual moral judgment both for the rule of law as well as for democracy. In individual moral judgment, justice, as an *a priori* principle, and truth converge, but it is a

[39] See: Hamburg, 1964, p. 218; cf. Adams, 1991, especially, pp. 152–155.

task for the individual to progressively ask for the *quid iuris* of its surroundings; never a mere given. In Chapter 3 we follow that principle to its origins in ancient Greek culture and its subsequent reformulation by the Cambridge Platonists. Albert Schweitzer, as no other, has warned us of the dangers that collective thought and nationalism pose to our sense of self as a moral person. Cassirer fundamentally agrees with Schweitzer's ethical concern, however, for Cassirer, it is not the materialism of the nineteenth century, but rather the fatalism of the idealistic systems of the nineteenth century that have contributed to the dismemberment of the individual.

Moreover, in Chapter 4, we focus on Cassirer's pathology of the totalitarian state or what may be called the politics of myth. During his exile, Cassirer continued his task as a practical philosopher, now in a more normative fashion by claiming, with and beyond Albert Schweitzer, that philosophy as the watchman of Western culture had not merely slept, but assisted as an interested and supporting bystander in the robbery of Western culture. Philosophy has ignored, for Cassirer, the "*true connection of philosophy with the world*," *i.e.*, human rights.[40] Chapter 4 explains how the cultural crisis in the technological age was sustained and usurped by the state through the employment of artificial myths and the propagation of mythical mentality. The politics of myth had its forebear in the intellectual life of the early twentieth century in the form of life philosophy that emphasized the immediate experience of life which disenfranchised reason through its preference for the mythical. As a result, in practical life, the politics of myth saw itself free of the ethical constraints of reason, and hence could easily take inhumane characteristics, most fatally in genocide.

In Part II, we focus on Law as Symbolic Form. First, in Chapter 5, we explore the philosophy of symbolic forms as the general philosophical theory of Cassirer underpinning his practical philosophy. For that purpose, we answer the questions of what is a symbolic form and what were Cassirer's objectives with his philosophy of symbolic forms. By symbolic form Cassirer

---

40 See: Ernst Cassirer, *Philosophy and Politics (1944)*, in: Ibid., *Symbol, Myth, and Culture. Essays and Lectures of Ernst Cassirer 1935–1945*, edited by D.P. Verene, Yale University Press, New Haven and London, 1979, pp. 219–232; here: p. 60.

means "*every energy of the mind [Energie des Geistes],*" through which "*a mental content of meaning [geistiger Bedeutungsgehalt] is connected to a concrete, sensory sign [konkretes sinnliches Zeichen] and made to adhere internally to it.*"[41] For Cassirer, all knowledge of the world is mediated knowledge through the representation by the various symbolic forms. Step by step, in Chapter 5 we explore and elaborate on the distinctive elements of a symbolic form, its logical structure, and its conceptual demarcations.

Furthermore, in Chapter 5, we introduce in what sense Cassirer's symbolic theory was ethical in import, as Cassirer set out to answer in what ways the human being progressively relates to others. Every intellectual activity of the human person, for Cassirer, is inevitably an activity mediated by meaning. By giving meaning to the actions or works of others we enter into a relationship with them. While we know others through their actions and works, through what they do and make, what they say and write, we know ourselves only in our regard for the other as a meaningful being, and *vice versa*. Accordingly, culture is created by giving this meaning an enduring form in works, for example of art, language, science, law, and so forth; it is a dynamic network of meaningful actions. The "meaning giving" capacity of a human being is inalienable. At the same time it forms the core and stands at the basis of human dignity. Through his philosophy of symbolic forms Cassirer sought to investigate the conditions for the possibility of ethical life. The philosophy of symbolic forms, in this respect, represents the various ways in which the individual human being as an "I" progressively relates to a "Thou."

Next, in Chapter 6, we put Cassirer's philosophy of symbolic forms in its context. In Chapter 6, we explore Cassirer's position relative to neo-Kantianism, so as to explicate the commonalities and disassociations between the philosophy of symbolic forms, on the one hand, and neo-Kantianism, in particular the Marburg School of neo-Kantianism, on the other. We make clear that Cassirer distances himself from neo-Kantianism to the extent that

---

[41] See: Ernst Cassirer, *Der Begriff der symbolischen Form im Aufbau der Geisteswissenschaften*, Vorträge der Bibliothek Warburg, 1921/1922, 6, p. 175; translation by Krois, 1987, p. 50.

he develops a theory of symbolism, and that for that purpose he draws inspiration from the works of Goethe. We explicate his indebtedness to and constructive endeavors beyond the practical philosophy of the Marburg School in Chapter 9. Of course, for Cassirer, the human being who gives meaning to his life through science and the human being who gives meaning to his life, say through law or morality, are the same and engage in the same fundamental activity, *i.e.*, meaning giving or symbolism. Therewith, he has set for himself a new, unifying track.

In Chapter 7, we apply the philosophy of symbolic forms to the discipline of law and make clear how man – through the power of symbolic language, foremost by the discovery of the significance of the sentence, *i.e.*, the legal provision – has detached law from its dependence on myth and has permitted law to constitute an independent and autonomous symbolic form. Chapter 7 elucidates how dynamic and sometimes fragile the relationship or the interdependence between law, language, and myth is. Through law, we manage to have an ordered universe or cosmos of our actions. In effect, the provisions of law, whether they are incorporated in enactments of the legislator or formulated in judicial opinions, are not mere means of communicating a certain ideal content, rather they have formative power in the symbolic sphere themselves. The provisions of law formulated in language directed to the future, give expression to a certain promise and prescribe our action in a certain direction.

In addition Chapter 7 makes clear that, for Cassirer, there are absolute and objective values in the form of individual human rights. It is not correct to deny the existence of absolute concepts of law, according to Cassirer, merely because the concepts of law do not directly refer to tangible objects with a particular substance. Even the natural sciences use inner fictions or symbols that do not bear any direct relation to reality. This makes the natural sciences as well as the humanities, of which jurisprudence is a part, no less objective, according to Cassirer. Analogous to the natural sciences, jurisprudence tries to establish a logical scheme of order for our social experiences in the form of a cosmos of law, which is characterized by a functional unity. As every symbolic form, law undergoes a development from the expressive, the representational, to the symbolic or significative phase. In Chapter 7, we elaborate on the development of law through these various phases, and make clear that law has become a universal referential system, wherein the concepts of law (adopted by the courts) do not directly refer to or constitute a certain substance, but express a relationship with other concepts and the totality of law as a general system of legal concepts.[42] Accordingly, it is the universality of the concepts of law that determine their objectivity. In this respect, legal rules and concepts can no longer be approached merely syllogistically, or analogically, but are foremost characterized by functionality.[43]

Finally, law avoids relapsing into mere formalism and reaches to higher levels of universality and objectivity, because it is propelled and continues to be informed by standards of humaneness or what we may call human rights. Human rights keep law as a symbolic system focused on the individual, *i.e.*, they help maintain the legal system anthropocentric. Therefore, Chapter 7 makes clear that next to a formalistic dimension Law as Symbolic Form offers a thoroughly normative dimension, because of the concept of human nature that is at the basis of law. Man as *animal symbolicum* is a thoroughly expressive and normative being. Chapter 7 makes clear that law is a product of human creativity and personality, and as such it reflects, and needs to take into account, human dignity. Because Cassirer did not believe that any definitive substantial definition could be given of human nature, he did not think a certain substantial view of man underlay the concept of human rights. Through his concept of *animal symbolicum* Cassirer indeed offers a solution to the problem of the multiple (and sometimes contradictory) interpretations given in various fields of knowledge and in different cultures as to what man is. Whether in science, economics, or law, whether in Chinese, Western, or primitive culture, according to Cassirer, man is equally to be considered an *animal*

[42] Due process rights (e.g., the right to personal privacy) are exemplary in this respect. For the role of the Ninth Amendment in this process, see: Norman Redlich, *The Ninth Amendment as a Constitutional Prism*, 12 Harvard Journal of Law and Public Policy 24 (1989); idem, Are *there* "*Certain Rights ... Retained by the People*," 37 New York University Law Review, 787 (1962).

[43] Cf. Ernst Cassirer, *Zur Logik der Symbolbegriffs*, Theoria, A Swedish Journal of Philosophy and Psychology, Volume 4, 1938, pp. 145–175.

symbolicum, *i.e.*, a being that operates through meaning. As a result, every relation between the state and its individual subjects must take into account the symbolic nature of the subjects.

Law is a medium not only between individuals, but also between the individual and the state. Through law we give expression to our moral standards, and as such law reflects the law that is in the minds of people. That is to say, law maintains its character as a symbolic form insofar as it is accompanied by a degree of persuasiveness. Law that is accompanied by persuasiveness considers its subjects as morally and intellectually mature persons. Consequently, the rule of law and democracy intersect at what may be called individual moral judgment. Because democracies take into consideration that they have to persuade their citizens, and derive their efficacy from the level of persuasiveness they exhibit in their actions, the symbolic nature of man poses certain limits upon state power. In this respect, through his philosophy of symbolic forms Cassirer provides an intellectual and cultural framework wherein human rights make sense. More specifically his concept of man as *animal symbollicum* provides a renewed philosophical anthropological foundation for human rights supported by the latest scientific data.

Next, in Chapter 8, we consider the human promissory function that stands at the center of any social activity and rule of law. In order to legislate or issue opinions with value of precedent we make use of the process of the promise, *i.e.*, language directed into the future to which we consider ourselves bound and that aims at the regulation of our conduct. However, before we are able to do so we first have several hurdles to overcome, especially the mythical perception of expression. In Chapter 8 we explicate the linguistic turn Cassirer gives to traditional and Kantian contract theory, and explicate the conditions for the possibility of a promise. For that purpose we follow the linguistic development from mythical to symbolic language that first makes possible a promise. We make clear in what sense the capacity to promise, hence to contract, stands in relation to human dignity.[44] Language in the symbolic sense

[44] Title 42, Sections 1981 and 1982 of the United States Constitution, in this respect, respectively state that the competence and the capacity to contract,

involves an active addressing and responding, and presumes the acceptance of the other as an end in itself, *i.e.*, as part of humanity. By accepting the other into discourse we already presume the equality of that person on the symbolic level, *i.e.*, as capable of grasping and conveying meaning through symbolic forms.

Moreover, in Chapter 9, we put Cassirer's legal theory in its context, *i.e.*, that of neo-Kantian jurisprudence during the first half of the twentieth century, by reconstructing the legal philosophical constellation that informs Cassirer's practical philosophical and jurisprudential outlook. Not only does Chapter 9 explicate the way in which Cassirer's jurisprudence can be regarded as a continuation of the jurisprudence of Hermann Cohen, but also it elucidates the particular direction and specific theoretical perspective of Cassirer's jurisprudence vis-à-vis neo-Kantian jurisprudence, in particular as represented by the Marburg School, but also by Gustav Radbruch and Hans Kelsen. Indeed as Kelsen refers to Cassirer to vindicate his critical position in relation to the jurisprudence of Hermann Cohen, Chapter 9 maintains that, from the perspective of Cassirer, the critical position of Kelsen does not apply. For Cassirer, democracy entails *the reign by persuasion, rather than the reign by force*, and as by an interrelation, law stands for *the reign of persuasion rather than the reign of force.* In accordance with the jurisprudence of Immanuel Kant, Hans Kelsen introduces a physical notion of force in his jurisprudence, whereas Cassirer rather constructively pursues the jurisprudence of Hermann Cohen in maintaining that the concept of force in jurisprudence and moral philosophy cannot take physical characteristics, as with Kant and Kelsen, but can only be of an *a priori* nature, *i.e.*, it must have a foundation in individual moral judgment.[45]

---

and that of the sale or lease of property shall not depend upon race (see: *Jones v. Alfred H. Mayer Co.*, 392 U.S. 409 (1968); cf. *Runyan v. McCrary*, 427 U.S. 160 (1978); and cf. *Goodman v. Lukens Steel* (1987)); sections 1981 and 1982 may give rise to *dignitary damages.* See also: *Domino's Pizza Inc. v. McDonald*, 546 U.S. ___ (2006).

[45] Cf. Edmond Cahn, *The Binding of Isaac: A Case Study*, in: Cahn, 1967, pp. 232–240; especially: pp. 239–240; cf. his famous expression: "*the very first place for grace to shine is within the practical workings of the law*" at p. 240; cf. Cahn, E.N., *The Moral Decision: Right and Wrong in the Light of American Law*, Indiana University Press, Bloomington, 1955.

As a result, we introduce Cassirer as a public person with a true practical and jurisprudential commitment, present Law as Symbolic Form, and put Cassirer's philosophy of law in its intellectual context. Finally, in the end conclusion, we give an assessment of the results of the research that we have faithfully elaborated below.

PART I: CASSIRER AS A PUBLIC PERSON

INTRODUCTION

In this part we focus attention on Ernst Cassirer's public engagement and make clear that Cassirer was not merely a theoretical philosopher, but also had an important contribution to make in the practical sphere, *i.e.*, in moral philosophy, jurisprudence, constitutionalism, and political science. The ensuing chapters elaborate further on the philosophical underpinnings of his practical standpoints, as expressed in different circumstances. The first of these took place during the Weimar Republic, when Cassirer alone, and despite strong protest, sought to defend the values embodied by the Weimar Constitution. Another instance we discuss is his participation to the Davoser Hochschultage of 1929, where he took a stance against the philosophical position of Martin Heidegger; and which has become a landmark in the history of philosophy, known as the Davos debate. Finally, his period in exile, first in England, then in Sweden, and lastly in the U.S.A., marks a decisive turning point in his thought, when Cassirer focuses attention on and gives a diagnosis of the crisis of Western culture. His prescription, though, that we must rediscover the symbolic, is not automatic, but must be pursued by each individual. As is explicated below, the symbolic dimension for Cassirer is intrinsically tied up with human freedom.

Part I proceeds as follows: In Chapter 1 we elaborate on the Weimar Republic as the polity and period in German history in and for which Ernst Cassirer first, in words and deeds expressed his public engagement. In Chapter 2, we reassess the Davos debate which is considered by some to have been an important contribution to the dismemberment of continental humanism in general, and Cassirer's philosophy in particular. Furthermore, in Chapter 3, we explore Cassirer's moral philosophical engagement when in exile in England and Sweden. We reserve Cassirer's critique of Scandinavian realist jurisprudence and his defense of the human rights tradition in his inaugural lecture in Göteborg to Part II. In Chapter 3 we focus specifically on Cassirer's ongoing engagement with the practical philosophy of the Cambridge

Platonists, explicate its interconnectedness with the ancient Greek conception of justice, and elaborate on their contribution to the development of the concept of the *a priori* nature of law. In this respect, we focus on Cassirer's encounter with Albert Schweitzer when in exile in England and explicate the influence of Albert Schweitzer's work upon that of Cassirer. After his encounter with Schweitzer, Cassirer was compelled to express his view of why individual human rights are so important and necessary, especially at times of crises.

In philosophy the crisis of the intellectual era expressed itself by the rise of the so-called 'Life Philosophy' movement. Cassirer holds life philosophy responsible for the failure of philosophy to keep culture alert in upholding its ideals. Life philosophy for Cassirer has contributed to the tutelage of culture and helped to make it defenseless against the rise of barbarism. Moreover, when in the U.S.A., Cassirer writes his *An Essay on Man* and *The Myth of the State*. Therefore, in Chapter 4, we give a contemporary reading of his political pathology and explain the relation between his views of the political with the philosophy of symbolic forms in general. Finally, in the conclusion, we give an assessment of the results of Part I, and allude to the subject of Part II: Law as Symbolic Form.

CHAPTER 1

CASSIRER'S PUBLIC ENGAGEMENT WITH WEIMAR[1]

I. INTRODUCTION

Weimar established a democratic state and gave new opportunities to talented outsiders ineligible for public commission in Wilhelmine Germany. Furthermore, it opened centers of prestige and power among others to progressive professors, such as the newly founded Hamburg University. As democracy also entails the equal access to public offices without (negative) discrimination, outsiders in Wilhelmine Germany, for example Jews and Social Democrats, became insiders of the Weimar Republic.[2] This entailed the establishment of a theoretically favorable (political) climate that stimulated the thriving of Cassirer.[3] Essentially, for Cassirer it consisted of a professorship in Hamburg University, the appointment to rector (the first rector of a German university who was Jewish not only by birth),[4] and the availability of a library such

---

1 This chapter has resulted in the following publications: Coskun, D., *Ernst Cassirer and European Constitutionalism*, in: Nergelius, J., Policastro, P., Urata, K. (eds.), *Challenges of Multi-Level Constitutionalism*, Polpress Publisher, Kraków, 2004, pp. 153–169; and idem, *Constitutioneel Patriottisme voor Europa. Wat Ernst Cassirer Verdedigde in Weimar* (Constitutional Patriotism for Europe. What Ernst Cassirer defended in Weimar), in: Kaars Seijpestijn (ed.), *Het Volk en Europa. Grenzen aan Europa* (The People and Europe. Borders to Europe), Vereniging voor Democratisch Europa, Amsterdam, 2004, pp. 83–93; and idem, *De ethiek van de rechter, Ernst Cassirer, de politiek en de rechterlijke macht in Weimar* ("The ethics of the judge. Ernst Cassirer, politics, and the judiciary in Weimar"), Trema, tijdschrift voor de rechterlijke macht (Trema, journal for the judiciary), March 2005, pp. 108–112.

2 Cf. Ernst Cassirer, *Lecture on Democracy*, Beinecke Rare Book and Manuscripts Library, *Ernst Cassirer Papers*, Lectures, Coll. No. GEN 98, Series No. I, Box No. 38, Folder No. 735.

3 Cf. Brenner, 1996.

4 I would like to thank Moshe Zimmerman (Tel Aviv) for this historic detail.

as that of the Warburg Institute.[5] Moreover, Weimar represented that corpus of fundamental values that were dear to Cassirer. Already in his first publication in 1902, in his treatment of the philosophy of Leibniz, he takes notice of the fundamental and inalienable values in the form of individual human rights, which he later himself was to advocate.

In August 1928, Cassirer defended the Weimar Constitution at the tenth anniversary of the Weimar Republic, in his speech entitled *Die Idee der republikanischen Verfassung*[6] (The Idea of the Republican Constitution). In 1930, as rector of Hamburg University he commemorated the tenth anniversary of the Constitution.[7] Finally, in 1932, Cassirer expressed his appreciation of the natural law tradition for the constitutional state before the Hamburg Society of Lawyers.[8] Although it may seem self-evident and a matter of course now, viewed in the context of the Weimar era, it was special that a public figure as prominent as Cassirer remained the advocate of law (and reason) until the end. Before we turn to Cassirer's public engagement with the Weimar Republic, it is necessary to consider the socio-political predicament wherein the Weimar Republic found itself and functioned, because it provides the context within which Cassirer's actions make sense.

This chapter is structured as follows. In Section I.1, we sketch the scene of the socio-political context that marked the transition from the Wilhelmine Empire to the Weimar Republic, and of the socio-political order that Weimar represented. In

---

5 See: Gay, 1968, pp. 16–17; cf. Moynahan, 2003, pp. 35–75.

6 See: Ernst Cassirer, *Die Idee der republikanischen Verfassung*, Rede zur Verfassungsfeier am 11. August 1928, Friederichsen, De Gruyter & Co. M.B.H., Hamburg, 1929.

7 See: Ernst Cassirer, *Wandlungen der Staatsgesinnung und der Staatstheorie in der deutschen Geistesgeschichte*, in: *Enge Zeit. Spuren Vertriebener und Verfolgter der Hamburger Universität im Auditorium Maximum der Universität, Von-Melle-Park 23. Februar – 4. April 1991*, Hg. von Angela Bottin unter der Mitarbeit von Rainer Nicolaysen, Hamburg, 1991; see: Jasper, 1963, pp. 229–239: the idea and a legislative proposal, for a Constitution Day in Weimar never came from the ground; cf. Waßner, R., *Zur Philosophie des Staates. Zwei Reden Ernst Cassirers aus seiner Hamburger* Zeit, in: Carstens, 1998, pp. 219–233; here: pp. 221–222.

8 See: Ernst Cassirer, *Vom Wesen und Werden des Naturrechts*, Zeitschrift für Rechtsphilosophie in Lehre und Praxis, Volume 6, No. 1, 1932, pp. 1–27.

Section I.2, we focus more specifically on the Weimar Constitution in its politico-historical context, because Cassirer's efforts are primarily directed to that document and the ideals it represents. Moreover, in Section I.3, we focus on Cassirer's engagement with the Weimar Constitution and the idea of human rights that it represented. Finally, in the conclusion, we not only give an assessment of Cassirer's endeavors, but also allude to the subject of the next chapter: the Davos debate.

I. 1. What was the Socio-Political Context that Marked the Transition to Weimar?

Although the years following the First World War are known as the Interbellum, Cassirer adhered to the view that the war had never ended. Although the arms in Western Europe were silent, the war still continued, according to Cassirer, but only in different form, *i.e.*, in the production of propaganda through mass media. Furthermore, in Europe and the world at large even the arms were not silent, *i.e.*, there was still some serious fighting on the European Continent. Furthermore, whereas the ally of the German and Austrian-Hungarian Empires the Ottoman Empire suffered devastating defeat in First World War, the newly proclaimed Turkish Republic under the leadership of Mustafa Kemal Atatürk, during the years 1919–1922, fought for and won its independence at the cost of hundreds of thousands of lives.[9] For the first time in human history, humankind witnessed the phenomenon of total war.

Total war entailed the mobilization of the totality of society and the annulment of the international legal distinction between civilians and soldiers. Furthermore, war adopted the cha-

---

[9] For an overview of these events from a biographical perspective, see: Mango, A., *Atatürk*, John Murray, London, 1999. For an overview of Turkey's role in the Second World War, cf. Deringil, S., *Turkey's Foreign Policy during the Second World War: An 'Active' Neutrality*, Cambridge University Press, Cambridge, 1989. For a critique of Turkey's role in the Second World War, see: Weber, F.G., *The Evasive Neutral: Germany, Britain, and the Quest for a Turkish Alliance in the Second World War*, University of Missouri Press, Columbia, 1979. See also: Shaw, S.J., *Turkey and the Holocaust: Turkey's Role in Rescuing Turkish and European Jewry from Nazi Persecution, 1933–1945*, New York University Press, New York, 1993.

racteristics of a crusade by the reintroduction of the phenomenon of the "just" religious war that had been partly relinquished during the seventeenth and eighteenth centuries. The battlefield from now on did not exclude any particular area, and included whatever was necessary for the "fast" achievement of victory. Not only were the enemy's steel and chemical industries targeted, but also the psychological condition, or the morale, of the enemy population through mass propaganda. In addition, the belligerents also subjected their domestic populations to mass propaganda and lies, in order to secure public order and support for the war effort. The modern machinery of press publicity ground into action on a massive scale before the economic and military apparatus began their "conquest."[10] Moreover, modern warfare introduced the mechanization of killing for example in the form of toxic gas or aerial bombing which, to a large extent, cancelled any individual choice and feelings of guilt in the soldier. Individual courage and hand-to-hand combat became less relevant, due to the growing importance the army attached to the development of the mastery of technological skills. From now on, killing became an anonymous and a purportedly clinical matter.[11] In many ways, the First World War was a definitive turning point in world history: it had destroyed all old (political) orders, but did not put in its place a new order in a stable and enduring form. It had ended with the defeat of the German Empire and the dissolution of its allies; however, a lasting peace was still not achieved, despite the fact that its successor, the Weimar Republic, was supported internationally.

During the Weimar Republic, two documents constituted the new order under which the Germans were to live: the *Treaty of Versailles* and the *Weimar Constitution.*[12] The Treaty of Versailles was signed on 28 June, 1919 and marked the (international) legal conclusion of the First World War. It regulated the relations of the new republic with its former enemies, *i.e.*, its relations with the outside world. However, instead of bringing a solution, the Treaty of Versailles made the problems more complex, because it made the peace a matter of winners and

---

10 See: Jaeger, 1945, p. 80, who contrasts the predicament of the "warring" states and their methods with the political balance achieved by the Hellenic city-states.

11 See: Stolleis, 1999, pp. 37–38.

12 See: Mann, 1961, p. 10.

losers, and was a careful compromise between the victorious powers.[13] While it was reasonable for the victors, *i.e.*, the Allies, to demand retribution and to impose this or that condition on Germany, they also, quite incorrectly, put all the blame for the war on Germany. Furthermore, the Allies excluded Germany, now in the form of the Weimar Republic, from the material part of the negotiations of the Treaty. The negotiations for the material conditions of the peace took place between (only some of) the Allies, who literally dictated the terms of the Peace Treaty of Versailles to the Weimar Republic. This was not perceived differently by the population at large; the Peace Treaty was predominantly experienced as a dictate. And, the new republic of Weimar, burdened by the "peace" would feel its negative consequences harshly.

The end of the German Empire began in the early summer of 1917, when the Reichstag passed a resolution calling for a peace of understanding, and subsequently when Prince Max von Baden, the successor to Chancellor Hertling, appealed to President Woodrow Wilson for an armistice based on his Fourteen Points. On October 3, 1918, it was announced as follows: "*To avoid further bloodshed the German government requests immediate conclusion of an armistice on land, at sea and in the air.*"[14] The sight of defeat made it obvious that the old regime of the Empire would not remain unchanged or even survive.[15] The general populace welcomed democratic changes, but they also preferred the continuation of the constitutional monarchy in one form or the other.[16] For that purpose on October 28, the two Bills 'for the amendment of the Reich constitution' were introduced that would make the Reich into a parliamentary monarchy.[17] However, internal and external events in the first months of 1917 had already set the road for a *revolution.* There were several causes for the overthrow of the established constitutional order. First, there was the winter famine, which caused the moral bonds of society to give way: while the rich secretly fed themselves, the poor and exhausted

---

13 See: Vries, 1976, pp. 11–12.
14 See: Kolb, 2005, p. 5.
15 Gay, 1968, p. 147.
16 Mann, 1974, pp. 332–333.
17 See: Kolb, 2005, p. 6.

people, among them returning front-soldiers, had to struggle for their food waiting in line in the front of food stores. Second, in addition to the military, the populace at large conceived the unrestricted submarine warfare as an uncommon method of warfare, and hence as a symptom of exhaustion of the normal methods of combat, that in addition had brought America into the war. Third, the Russian Revolution weakened the perceived absolute authority of government and increased the expectation that a revolution might be forthcoming also in Germany. Finally, and importantly, there were the "Wilson notes," through which the Allies seemed to have made explicit that they would not negotiate with the Emperor, or, if the Emperor remained in office, this would seriously worsen the prospects for an armistice and peace.

All of these factors taken together reached a climax, when on October 29, 1918 sailors at the Kiel Naval Base refused to carry out a last and decisive offensive, and mutinied. The mutiny succeeded in that the State was not able to crush the uprising, and many soldiers and citizens refused to oppose it actively.[18] Henceforth, some kind of revolution seemed inescapable, as the uprisings gradually spread through the country in the direction of Berlin.[19] Already on October 29, the Emperor definitively departed from Berlin to Spa; he was to remain there until his exile to The Netherlands. When the request from the government to abdicate reached the Emperor, he made a final desperate attempt to stay in power by proposing to remain King of Prussia, but it was of no avail. Having received an ultimatum, on November 9, the Emperor decided to abdicate, and subsequently the monarchy collapsed. "*Not hand-grenades and machine guns have destroyed the German Empire, but the lack of belief in the justification of its existence.*"[20]

The same day, hurried by the rumor that the Spartacists were ready to proclaim a Soviet republic, Friedrich Ebert and Philipp Scheidemann, who had assumed leadership of the insurgent forces, proclaimed a social-democratic republic. Again anticipating communist initiatives, on November 10, a first

---

18 Eyck, 1957, pp. 63–66.

19 Meinecke, F., *Unfortunate Collapse – A Liberal View*, in: Hunt, 1969, pp. 6–10.

20 Eyck, 1957, pp. 67–68.

provisional government was installed; the first in the series of many governments with an equally short life span: in the 15 years of its existence the Weimar Republic had in total 17 governments. Five days later, the provisional government declared Hugo Preuß Secretary of State and gave him the task of framing a constitution. Within a period of two months, on January 19, 1919, the provisional government organized national elections for deputies to a constitutional convention that was to convene in Weimar. Subsequently, on February 9, 1919, the Weimar Assembly solemnly opened and two days later, the Assembly elected Friedrich Ebert as President. Ebert on his part, asked Scheidemann to form a cabinet, and, in a relatively short span of time, on July 31, the Weimar Coalition, the majority supporting the government, established agreement on the Constitution in the Assembly. As a result, the second document under which Weimar was to stand, *i.e.*, the Weimar Constitution, became effective as from August 11, 1919, when it was signed by the President.[21] Contrary to the expectations that might rise from the relatively short span of time involved in the framing of the Constitution, the Weimar Constitution was not a dictate pure and simple, imposed by foreign forces. Cassirer was the most prominent voice in Weimar that proclaimed that neither the Weimar Constitution, nor democracy itself was alien to German culture but, as is shown below, stronger still, that both were profoundly influenced by German ideals.

Effectively, the Weimar Republic had an operative constitution less than a year after the "November Revolution" of 1918 that disposed of the *Kaiser* (Emperor) and the *Kaiserreich* (Empire). But, as is known, it saw an abrupt ending with the seizure of the political power by the Nazi's in 1933. Clearly the constitutive document in question and hence the Republic itself demonstrated a decisive weakness. This weakness did not primarily consist of the judges deviating from the letter or spirit of the democratic constitution, this was merely a consequence. The fatal weakness followed from the lenient attitude of the judicial system toward the dominant "patriotic" or "*völkisch*" approach of

21 See: Kolb, 2005, p. 19.

the public and mass media.[22] In opposition to this approach, Cassirer advocated the attitude of *Verfassungspatriotismus* or constitutional patriotism.[23]

The political and intellectual spirit of those times in Germany, in the words of Peter Gay, "*elevated apathy into a superior form of existence and invidiously compared the trader's mentality of the British and French politicians with the spirituality of the educated German.*"[24] Nevertheless, Cassirer focused attention on the Enlightenment as a *European* movement and, inspired by it, on the natural law tradition of "inalienable human rights."[25] However, the 'academic intellectual' of the Weimar Republic, to which Cassirer addressed his message, was not prepared or even able to understand Cassirer.[26] His position of liberal humanism was a creed that now was bitterly contested. Cassirer was aware of the arduous task before him, and while in Germany, he fought the losing battle with seriousness and courage up until the critical year of 1933.[27] Fritz Ringer would later identify the audience to which Cassirer addressed his message as the amorphous elite group of 'German Mandarins,' *i.e.*, the conservative group that had entrenched itself in German academic life.[28] In the next section we focus more specifically on the Weimar Republic and its Constitution in its politico-historical context, so as to put Cassirer's efforts in advocating the values of the Weimar Constitution in its context.

I. 2. What was the Politico-Historical Context of the Weimar Constitution?

Weimar was characterized by its idealistic beginnings and marked a fresh start for German democracy. The democracy of Germany, secretary of state Eduard David declared in the National Assembly of June 22, 1919, in the light of the new

---

22 Zimmerman, 1998, pp. 395–396; cf. Apelt, 1946, especially p. 366 and pp. 417 ff.

23 Paetzold, 1995, p. 112.

24 See: Gay, 1970, p. 72; cf. Krois, 1987, p. 164.

25 Ibid., 1987, p. 26.

26 Cf. Paetzold, 1995, p. 112.

27 Liebeschutz, 1956, p. 231.

28 See: Ringer, 1969; cf. Strenski, 1984, p. 367.

constitution would be the most democratic in the world. Its founders put forward the Weimar Constitution as a fundamental and permanent parting with history. For this, Article 178 of the Weimar Constitution annulled the Constitution of 1871. "*To form the German people to a self-determining nation*," declared David's predecessor Hugo Preuß, "*to establish for the first time in German history the proposition, that: The sovereignty of state lies with the people – that is the central idea of the German national constitution of Weimar.*"[29]

Nevertheless, the Weimar Constitution was not merely the fulfillment of liberal ideals, but was also the product of the lost war: President Wilson had already made clear in October 1918, that the U.S. would only accept as partner in negotiations a government that, compared to the former rulers of Germany, *i.e.*, the German Empire, had an improved constitutional attitude.[30] Moreover, in the eyes of the Allies the fall of the Emperor, who was also King of Prussia, would at the same time bring an end to the Prussian hegemony over the other federal states together with its dominant anti-social and anti-liberal policy; a view with which Hugo Preuß concurred. This explains why the Weimar Constitution did not start with announcing a a list of civil and human rights, but after characterizing the German Empire as a federal republic, began with the renewed relationships of Reich (Empire) and German States.[31] In the ensuing articles, the Constitution established the legislative competence in the federal government, as well as the principle of preemption, *i.e.*, that federal law is superior to state law.

In the second part, the material part next to the organizational, formal part, the Constitution incorporated the fundamental rights and duties of the German citizen. They consisted of the right to equality before the law, the right to personal freedom, the freedom of religion, the right to education and the freedom of establishing schools, the guarantee of societal institutes, such as property, marriage and so forth; and new fundamental social rights.[32] Furthermore, the Constitution broadened the right to vote, that was already extended to the general populace by Bismarck in

29 Cited by: Schulze, 1982, p. 86.
30 Schulze, 1982, p. 86.
31 Ibid., 1982, pp. 90–91.
32 Apelt, 1946, pp. 291–366.

1866, now to include female citizens and persons older than 21 years (the previous age limit to vote was 25).

In addition, the Constitution introduced party democracy: the electorate had to choose not for persons but for parties that could function as filters or as a first instance of synthesis of various interests; also, it divided Germany in 35 electoral districts each with its own representatives. Moreover, the Constitution provided that the populace would directly elect the president, as in the United States. The direct popular election of the president was inspired by the American model and its presidential experience, whereas the delegates to the constitutional convention rejected the French model of the parliamentary election of the president, which the French had adopted in the light of thier unfortunate experience with the popular election of Louis Bonapartes as president in December 1848. The drafters of the Weimar Constitution, however, did not take fully into consideration the negative consequences such a popular system could have, next to the preventive influence the mediation of rationally calculating politicians could exert.[33] The choice for the direct election of the president was the expression of pure democratic idealism, which was tellingly illustrated by Max Weber's remark that the right to directly elect the president constituted "*the Magna Carta of democracy*."[34] However, its method of electing the president had significant, if not fatal, consequence for Weimar. The Constitution attributed the president the task of representing the country in foreign affairs, of summoning the Prime Minister as the leader of the government, and of leadership over the army. The Constitution also granted the president the right to disband the parliament and subsequently appeal anew to the people and its authorization. Finally, there was Article 48 of the Constitution that granted incidental dictatorial powers to the president.

Although these powers were sufficient to address the problems the rule of law faced in Weimar, in the absence of an

---

[33] Goethe (the symbol of Weimar) mistrusted rule by popular appeal, and in his view of the state proposed an appointed president, see: Faust, Part II, Act V, Palace Scene, Midnight Scene; referred to by: Cahn, E.N., *Goethe's View of law – With a Gloss Out of Plato*, Columbia Law Review, Volume 49, No. 7 (Nov., 1949), pp. 904–920; here: p. 909.

[34] See: Eyck, 1957, p. 101.

established democratic culture, their abuse was not properly foreseen. Weimar's problems were not solely economic.[35] Political factions in the Left, but later also from the Right, radicalized very early, due to the historical inadequacy of legitimate channels of political expression. Whereas for the Communists Weimar was a bourgeois capitalist regime that stood in the path of progress, for the right-wing extremists Weimar symbolized the so-called "stab in the back" allegation of First World War and its aftermath. As a result, "*violence in the streets became frequent as the various paramilitary groups*" preferred to attack their "*enemies physically rather than through the ballot box.*"[36]

Examples are numerous: machine-gun fire in the streets of Berlin in 1919; uprisings in central Germany and the Ruhr area; and coups d'état from the left as well as from the right of the political spectrum. From 1923 onwards the Weimar Republic in fact lived in an uninterrupted state of emergency (whether or not it was formally declared).[37] Paradigmatic is the foundation of the National Assembly, which eventually met in the little central German town of Weimar (the city to give the Republic its name) and not in Berlin, because the prevailing mood in Berlin just made it too dangerous to house the Assembly.[38] The choice for Weimar, furthermore, also had high symbolic value. In contrast to the social and political upheaval in Berlin, Weimar as the city of Goethe placed the reconstruction of Germany under the protection of the spirit that once from there had illuminated and astonished the world: the spirit of humanity and freedom and the friendly competition among nations.[39]

However, in this period of constant turmoil, the government would not merely seek support from strictly democratic principles, but foremost found its strength in Article 48 of the Constitution and hence the President. It stipulated that in time of crisis, when the State failed to fulfill its constitutional and

---

35 Murphy, 1977, p. 21. The main economic problems were caused not only by the reparatory damages to be paid to the allied powers, but were also due to the inflation and the economic crises of the depression that struck Germany even harder.

36 Ibid., 1977, p. 21.

37 Schulze, 1982, p. 99.

38 Hiden, 1996, p. 4.

39 Eyck, 1957, p. 91.

statutory obligations, the President could suspend fundamental rights and govern by decree without consultation of or prior approval by parliament.[40] In the end, because of the endless stream of "emergencies" and the failure of parliamentary government and judiciary to respond adequately if at all, the President invoked Article 48 250 times in 14 years.[41] Finally, in January 1933 when the decree was issued in conjunction with Article 53 of the Constitution (that provided that the President could appoint the Chancellor), and President Hindenburg appointed Hitler, who in the elections of November 1932 had captured a third of the popular vote, with the task to form 'a government of national union'; it "(...) *marked the death of Weimar and the birth of a monstrosity, the Third Reich.*"[42]

The Third Reich, although inimical to democracy and the rule of law, never was interested in doffing the cloth of legality. Not only would the appearance of legality be a pragmatic means to appeal to the obedience of German citizens, it would also prove fruitful in the systematic execution of their sinister policies. Although no rationality was strong enough to logically disprove the racial myth the Third Reich introduced, legality would still provide a rationalization of its activities, hence of Nazi policies. Even the Nazi leader had a need to rationalize and systemize his plans, and accordingly law still had a role to play, albeit a subordinate one. Scholars disagree whether the Nazi takeover of power was a legal one or not. One thing is clear, though, if we assume that the Weimar Constitution still survived, its function and nature had become radically altered. However, the instrumental role allotted to the Constitution did not come about in a single day, rather it occurred gradually, and was also (unintentionally) prepared by legal practice.

When the question was put forward in 1922 in Berlin before the 'Society of German Constitutional Scholars' as to whether judicial or constitutional review was permissible, a vast majority declared it would not be in accordance with the old constitutional tradition. A few years later the minority had become the majority, meanwhile applauding the course taken by

---

[40] Murphy, 1977, p. 22.
[41] Ibid., 1977, p. 22.
[42] Ibid., 1977, p. 22; cf. Evans, 2003.

the *Reichsgericht* (the highest court of the German Empire), which fervently reviewed legislation as to its constitutionality. In this period, the new generation of scholars began to introduce new interpretations and concepts, thereby parting from the bygone tradition, in order to create an up-to-date and coherent view of constitutionalism for themselves. However, this new movement had an important flaw, in that it was inherently influenced by a political trend or attitude that was to be traced back to a turnaround in the frame of mind of the greater part of the citizenry. This frame of mind would permit challenges to fundamental rights, but resisted the Weimar Constitution and its system of parliamentary democracy.[43]

Clearly, judicial review in these circumstances was in the wrong hands, *i.e.*, the national conservative body of judges lenient toward nationalistic popular attitudes.[44] These judges were the products of the imperial age, and as the shock of revolution had fuelled the fears of "left-wing" rule, they regarded themselves as a bastion against socialism.[45] Right from the start, they had lobbied for judicial review, because they considered it as an appropriate instrument to judicial control of laws passed by parliament. Prior to 1914, there was no possibility for judicial review by the judiciary in the German Empire, *i.e.*, no entitlement of the courts of law to examine the material legality of laws and ordinances. However, under the guise of a violation of *boni mores* and equity, and later that of the infringement of basic rights, by claiming that these were "sacred to the German people,"[46] judicial review could be invoked against the democratically elected, hence sovereign parliament. It became the general tendency to first measure the "justice" of legislation by the higher standards of the Constitution, instead of adopting a presumption of constitutionality.[47] They were thereby defending

---

43 Apelt, 1946, pp. 417–418.

44 Ibid., 1946, p. 419.

45 Stolleis, 2003, pp. 271–272; cf. Ormond, 1994.

46 See: Ernst Cassirer, *Vom Wesen und Werden des Naturrechts*, Zeitschrift für Rechtsphilosophie in Lehre und Praxis, Volume 6, No. 1, 1932, pp. 1–27; here: p. 21.

47 For the presumption of constitutionality in American constitutionalism, see: McConnell, 1997, pp. 172–173, and pp. 185–189. The principle was first stated by Chief Justice Marshall in: *Fletcher v. Peck*, 10 U.S. (6 Cranch) 87,

the status quo and limiting the influence of the nation state in the sight of basic rights. "*It was no accident that the conservative and anti-positivist jurists in particular – Heinrich Triepel, Rudolf Smend, Gerhard Leibholz, Hans-Carl Nipperdey, Carl Schmitt, Erich Kaufmann – were so committed to basic rights.*"[48]

The judiciary treated the traditional, basic (non-positive) rights, particularly the rights of property and equality, as bastions against the absolute power of parliament. Parliamentary legislation, that after the First World War saw a large quantitative increase, driven by a need to overcome social and economic crises, could not be trusted *prima facie*, but had to be filtered or interpreted according to the system of values set above the law. The result was a regenerated interest in natural law and an activation of the new basic rights of the Constitution. These basic rights, thus, came to the fore not only as exponents of a liberal and individualistic, reactionary movement and for the overpowering of certain collective forces. Moreover, these basic rights were used as a conservative defense of the social status quo, and as such, they were implemented against the desires of a mass society that were oriented toward an egalitarian division of resources.[49]

The basic rights served as political weapons against parliament and government (in the name of freedom) simply as an obstruction to the democratic system.[50] This was done by construing barriers to the advancement of the principles of civil and inalienable human rights, either by regarding some of these as un-German or otherwise fundamentally flawed and its suspension (constitutionally) permissible. Most importantly, the judiciary, and the establishment it represented, were biased against any form of socialism, and in some instances endorsed the explicitly anti-communist, nationalistic stance of the Nazis. Thereby the establishment interrupted the fragile political balance, if any still existed in Weimar, and put the Nazi movement in a less disadvantaged position vis-à-vis the radical

---

128 (1810), and other subsequent examples abound, including *Washington v. Glucksberg*, 117 S.Ct. 2258, 2281 (1997).

48 Stolleis, M., 2003, pp. 266–280; here pp. 272–274; cf. Hannover, 1966.

49 Stolleis, 1999, p. 111.

50 Redlich, 2002.

socialists.[51] Nazism was regarded as a lesser evil. In addition, little was done to end the flirtation of young army officers with Nazism, despite several sentences.[52] Paradigmatically, when in 1924 Hitler and his terrorist gang started a revolt in a Munich beer hall – the so-called "beer hall putsch" – by declaring that he was ousting the Bavarian state government, the federal government in Berlin, and the President of the Republic, he was all but effectively rebutted. When tried for high treason Hitler received the minimum sentence of five years imprisonment, with the possibility of parole after six months. Not only was Hitler actually released after the six months, but he was also exempted from the deportation usually required for aliens convicted of a felony. The court stated that the defendants had been "*guided in their actions by pure patriotism and the noblest of selfless intentions*."[53] And, in the case of Hitler, who was an Austrian national, the Court rendered judgment "*that in keeping with the spirit of the law and with its declared purpose, the law can have no application in the case of one whose thoughts and feelings are as German as* Hitler's."[54] What was missing in Weimar was a normative framework to condemn and mark as anti-democratic, hence as illegitimate, the Nazi movement that more and more captured the imagination of the populace.

To state, however, that the democratic crisis in the Weimar Republic had to have ended the Weimar Constitution, is a proposition contested by arguments that originate both from will and from reason. That is to say, as will and reason are thought of as the twin sources of a legitimate legal order,[55] the Weimar Constitution continued to exist in the minds of men, not being imaginary nor in force in its entirety, but, as I hold furthermore: symbolically. That is to say, Weimar and its struggle

---

[51] See especially in this respect the study of Gumbel, E.J., *Jahre Mord*, Neues Vaterland, Berlin, 1921, and Gumbel, E.J., *View Jahre politischer Mord*, Neue Gesellschaft, Berlin-Fichtenau, 1922; both referred to by: Paulson, 2006, p. 36.

[52] After the 1923 Beer Hall Putsch the Nazi Party was declared illegal, but the Nazis founded substitute parties to continue the national socialist movement.

[53] Cited and referred to by: Paulson, 2006, pp. 34–35.

[54] Ibid., 2006, p. 35.

[55] Kahn, 1999, especially Chapter 2.

for the ideals it represented are a continuing point of reference in contemporary debate on the foundations of law and society.

In addition, it was the aim of the Nazi regime to come to power by legal means. The Nazis aimed at winning a majority in an election, so that they could exclaim "Now we are strictly legal."[56] Moreover, the *Reichsgericht* constitutionally reviewed the acts of the Nazi regime and subsequently did not sanction them.[57] In other words, the Nazi regime never abolished the Weimar Constitution, because they never expressly and legally cancelled it. The Weimar Constitution rather died a silent death by the actual events of 1933, termed by Nazi jurists as "*die legale Revolution*" (the legal revolution).[58] In effect, as the Nazi police state found its legal basis for the ensuing 12 years in the February 1933 emergency degree suspending constitutional rights sanctioned by the "strength" of Article 48(2) of the Constitution, one could hold, Weimar came to its end through "legal euthanasia."

Furthermore, it is a proposition that is not valid (when extrapolated) on a universal level. The American constitutional experience in this respect makes clear that crises of State need not necessarily result in a crisis of the law framing and founding it, or for the political elite to question the legitimacy of constitutional government.[59] Chief Justice Marshall delivered his famous opinion of *Marbury v. Madison*, for example, at a time of intense party political strife, but in that period of crisis, it was the democratic resolution that upheld.[60] The following excerpt from the midst of a crisis of state, spoken by Thomas Jefferson the day before the elections of 1801, illustrates this perfectly:

---

56 See: Evans, 2003, p. 249.

57 Schulze, 1982, pp. 104–105. We cannot elaborate here on the role of the *Reichsgericht* during the Nazi-era.

58 See: Caenegem, 1996, pp. 271–278, especially p. 277.

59 See: Jacobsen, A.J., Schlink, B., *Constitutional Crisis. The German and the American Experience*, in: Jacobsen, 2000, here: pp. 1–3, for the universal significance of Weimar.

60 See: Cahn, E.N., *An American Contribution*, in: Ibid. (ed.), *Supreme Court and Supreme Law*, Greenwood Press, Publishers, Westport, Connecticut, 1968, p. 24.

If they [the incumbents, *i.e.*, the Federalists] *had been permitted to pass a law putting the government into the hands of an officer, they would certainly have prevented an election. But we thought it best to declare openly and firmly, one and all, that the day such an act passed, the Middle States would arm, and that no such usurpation, even for a single day, should be submitted to. This first shook them; and they were completely alarmed at the resource for which we declared, to wit, a convention to reorganize the government, and to amend it. The very word convention gives them the horrors, as in the present democratic spirit of America, they fear they should lose some of the favorite morsels of the Constitution.*[61]

As indicated above, it was this very resolution that was missing in Weimar.[62] While it is possible to discern some democratic thinkers in Weimar, in general one cannot find a democratic tradition or thought. What one could find were remnants of a tradition of thought characterized by monarchist constitutionalism.[63] This tradition, holding the army and the judiciary in a strong grip, marked itself by a nostalgia for the past (monarchy) and a deep hostility toward the Weimar polity and liberal parties supporting it.[64] Next to the orthodox majority of monarchists that sympathized with the Nationalists, there was only a small minority of dedicated republicans that associated themselves with democratic thought or the Democrats.[65] Moreover, those thinkers and officials who could adapt to democracy did so for very different reasons. The great German historian Meinecke, called himself along those who agreed with him, *Vernunftrepublikaner*, republicans through reason, distinguishable from republicans at heart. Only the

---

61 *Letter to James Monroe, February 15, 1801* in 10 Bergh 201; see also: *Letter to James Madison, February 18, 1801* in 10 Bergh 202. Cited in: Cahn, E.N., *An American Contribution*, in: Cahn, 1967, p. 24.

62 For the weight of the army in the political process of Weimar, see: Evans, 2003, pp. 248 ff.

63 See: Gusy, C., *Einleitung: Demokratisches Denken in der Weimarer Republik – Enstehungsbedingungen und Vorfragen*, in Gusy, 1994, pp. 11–22.

64 Ringer, 1969, p. 201.

65 Ibid., 1969, pp. 201–202.

maintenance of public peace and the absence of an alternative road to stability made them assent to the new regime.[66]

Taken as a whole, Weimar and its judiciary were dominated by an attitude of leniency toward nationalistic popular attitudes, which dramatically culminated in putting the government into the hands of a dictator, *i.e.*, anti-democratic thought that had equal claim to the support of the populace.[67] As a result, politicians could not rely on an independent judicial branch, because the judiciary itself first had to be democratized.[68]

In this respect, as Fritz Ringer explains, the anti-modernity of the intelligentsia was shadowed by the anti-modernity of the "volk."[69] The "German Mandarins" as Ringers calls the elite governing class, unwittingly prepared the ground for the anti-intellectualism that finally overwhelmed them. The mandarins abandoned their intellectual responsibility to countenance the anti-democratic trends in Germany. Especially, they ignored the frustration of the youth and failed to consider the particular susceptibility of the youth for the National Socialist propaganda. At the least, they could have provided for greater access to academic education, hence for the cultivation of the youth of the lower strata of German society.[70] As a result, they could do nothing but watch when 1.6 million of the 2.5 million young people who entered the German political system as new voters between 1928 and 1930 voted for Hitler's party.[71] In 1928, when Cassirer set out to defend the Weimar Constitution he displayed what may be called political courage, but he could reach only a

---

66 Ibid., 1969, p. 203.

67 Cf. Sontheimer, 1962; cf. Scheuerman, 1996, pp. 5 ff. See also: Sienem, D., *Die >>Vertrauenskrise der Justiz<< in der Weimarer Republik*, in: Föllmer, 2005, pp. 139–163; here: p. 150.

68 Ibid., 2005, p. 156.

69 Ringer, 1969, p. 252.

70 Ibid., 1969, pp. 436–448.

71 Ibid., 1969, p. 521. Remarkably most of the Nazi-voters were not the unemployed – they voted mainly Communist – but that part of the working-class that the traditional left-wing parties failed to reach, viz. non-unionized, rural laborers, civil cervants wary of their social-economic status, and the self-employed (including small farmers). Most of all the Nazi party was a catch-all party of social protest. See: Evans, 2003, p. 264.

small minority of students who wished to be linked with the theme of democracy.[72]

I. 3. What was Cassirer's Constitutional Engagement?

In August 1928 at the tenth anniversary of the Weimar Republic, Ernst Cassirer defended the Weimar Constitution in his speech entitled *Die Idee der republikanischen Verfassung* (The Idea of the Republican Constitution).[73] In 1930, as rector of Hamburg University, despite strong protest from within the university, he set himself to commemorate the Constitution in an effort to search for a common notion of the State and its tasks.[74] Finally, in 1932 Cassirer underlined the merits of the natural law tradition for the constitutional state, as not being merely historical, before the Hamburg Society of Lawyers.[75] How did Cassirer set out to defend the Weimar Constitution? Moreover, what did his (constitutional) engagement amount to and where did it stem from?

Cassirer addressed his *Die Idee der republikanischen Verfassung* explicitly to the "*völkisch*" and anti-democratic movements of his time that saw in democracy a Western misconception alien to the German nation.[76] In the following years

---

72 See: Liebeschütz, 1973, pp. 3–25; here: p. 18.

73 See: Ernst Cassirer, *Die Idee der republikanischen Verfassung*, Rede zur Verfassungsfeier am 11. August 1928, Friederichsen, De Gruyter & Co. M.B.H., Hamburg, 1929.

74 See: Ernst Cassirer, *Wandlungen der Staatsgesinnung und der Staatstheorie in der deutschen Geistesgeschichte*, in: *Enge Zeit. Spuren Vertriebener und Verfolgter der Hamburger Universität im Auditorium Maximum der Universität, Von-Melle-Park 23. Februar – 4. April 1991*, Hg. von Angela Bottin unter der Mitarbeit von Rainer Nicolaysen, Hamburg, 1991; cf. Jasper, 1963, pp. 229–239: The idea and a legislative proposal, for a Constitution Day in Weimar never came from the ground; cf. Waßner, R., *Zur Philosophie des Staates. Zwei Reden Ernst Cassirers aus seiner Hamburger* Zeit, in: Carstens, 1998, pp. 219–233; here: 221–222.

75 See: Ernst Cassirer, *Vom Wesen und Werden des Naturrechts*, Zeitschrift für Rechtsphilosophie in Lehre und Praxis, Volume 6, No. 1, 1932, pp. 1–27.

76 See: Recki, B., *Die Kultur der Humanität. Ernst Cassirer als Philosoph und Bürger*, Rede aus Anlaß der Benennung des Hörsaals A im Hauptgebäude der Universität Hamburg in Ernst Cassirer–Hörsaal am 11. Mai 1999, in: Pressestelle der Universität Hamburg, *Zum Gedenken an Ernst Cassirer (1874–1945). Ansprachen auf der Akademischen Gedenkfeier am 11. Mai 1999*, Dölling und Galitz Verlag, Hamburg, 1999, pp. 16–33; here: 28.

Cassirer, on several other occasions, expressed his engagement for the Weimar Republic as a constitutional state. For this, he explored the history of ideas in order to give a genealogical account of constitutionalism, a theme, which he had already developed in his *Freiheit und Form*[77] (Freedom and Form) in 1916. In the age of Renaissance Cassirer found a binding factor of the peoples of Europe, who were headed towards a common purpose of liberal education and personal formation. In this respect, he spoke against a contemporary intellectual tendency to speak of a distinctly national – and even ethnic – path (Sonderweg) within German scholarship and culture.[78] He reached the conclusion that German philosophers, most notably Leibniz and Wolff with their ideas of freedom and equality, had authoritatively influenced the liberation movements in America and France. Subsequently, Cassirer saw Kant engaged philosophically in these revolutions, while unfolding his influential political theory. Inspired by Kant, Cassirer offers a normative framework for the State in which his conception of "inalienable human rights" is guaranteed. By reconstructing his genealogy of constitutionalism and his conception of "inalienable human rights" within the constitutionally bound state, we make clear in this section what it is that Cassirer conceived of value to defend.

Cassirer's genealogy of constitutionalism emphasizes the (original) German contribution to constitutionalism, but it was not concerned with the question of *priority*.[79] Cassirer recognized that "*the champions of the French Revolution*" and the Founding Fathers in Philadelphia were convinced that their fundamental principles were in a sense as old as the world and that knowledge of the "*indefeasible rights of man was regarded as a "common notion," as something "that has been always, been everywhere, and been by all believed.*"[80] According to Cassirer,

---

[77] See: Ernst Cassirer, *Freiheit und Form. Studien zur deutschen Geistesgeschichte*, Bruno Cassirer, Berlin, 1916.

[78] See: Hackeschmidt, 2004, p. 63.

[79] See: Ernst Cassirer, *Philosophy and Politics (1944)*, in: Ibid., *Symbol, Myth, and Culture. Essays and Lectures of Ernst Cassirer 1935–1945*, edited by D.P. Verene, Yale University Press, New Haven and London, 1979, pp. 219–232; here: p. 222.

[80] Ibid., 1979, p. 222.

the principles expressed in the American and French declarations won the hearts of the entire civilized world.

For Cassirer the Enlightenment, apart from its negative effects when it inspired the overthrow of established orders, primarily entailed a positive movement: "*Also in her boldest Revolutions it wants to be nothing more than a Restitution; a* "restitutio in integrum," *by which reason and humanity will be reinstalled in their ancient rights.*"[81] Cassirer identified this "restitution" with the historical process and period wherein the theory of natural law had had to fight a two front battle. On the one hand, it concerned the detachment of law from theological dogmatism, as initiated by Hugo Grotius (1583–1645), the Cambridge Platonists (1633–1688), and carried on further by Gottfried Wilhelm Leibniz (1648–1716) and Samuel von Pufendorf (1632–1716).[82] On the other hand, it dealt with the determination, with the marking out, and as such with the protection of the pure realm of law against the realm of state power or absolutism as embodied by Hobbes' Leviathan.[83] As we make clear below, it is from the common struggle to overcome the restraints or domination of these two realms, that law can assert its claims independently from religion and the State, because it receives its binding or compulsive character from its persuasive power; that the conditions are created for law as symbolic form.

Cassirer does not locate the original source of the American and (hence) French declarations of fundamental rights

---

81 See: Ernst Cassirer, *Die Philosophie der Aufklärung*, J.C.B. Mohr Verlag (Paul Siebeck), Tübingen, 1932, Chapter 6, p. 314; or ibid., *The Philosophy of the Enlightenment*, tr. F.C.A. Koelln and J.P. Pettigrove, Princeton University Press, NJ, 1951 (1932), p. 234.

82 See respectively Grotius' famous statement in Prolegomena 11 of his *De jure belli ac pacis libri tres* (1625); Ibid., *The Law of War and Peace*, tr. F.W. Kelsey, Bobbs-Merrill, Indianapolis, 1925. For Pufendorf's separation of natural law and moral theology, see: Luig, 1994. "*The same struggle, which Grotius carries on in The Netherlands against Calvinistic dogma and against the principle of state absolutism, is resumed later in England by the Cambridge School and fought out under similar methodological and historical conditions.*" See: Ernst Cassirer, *The Philosophy of the Enlightenment*, tr. F.C.A. Koelln and J.P. Pettigrove, Princeton University Press, NJ, 1951 (1932), p. 239n.

83 Ernst Cassirer, *Vom Wesen und Werden des Naturrechts*, Zeitschrift fur Rechtsphilosophie in Lehre und Praxis, Volume 6, 1932, pp. 6–18. We elaborate on the contribution of the Cambridge Platonists in Chapter 3.

for the individual in Locke, because for Locke the formulation of natural rights is still dependent on the question of the existence of a Deity. [84] For Cassirer it is Leibniz, who for the first time in history advocated the universal human rights of the individual and made this claim of natural law independent from any exterior authority, whether human or divine.[85] In his treatment of the institution of slavery, Leibniz comes to the conclusion that in opposition to the property right of the master over (the body of) his slave there is the antagonistic overriding weight of "(...) *le droit des âmes raisonnables qui sont naturellement et inaliénablement libres.*"[86]

Next, Leibniz' pupil Christian Wolff (1679–1754) set out to give a complete systematic account of the idea of the original and inalienable human rights (*jus connatum*), that follow immediately from the nature of man, as opposed to rights acquired later in life (*jus contracta*).[87] This systematic textbook account by Wolff of the theory of inalienable human rights, in addition to the influence of Locke, later, had decisive impact on Sir William Blackstone's (1723–1780) famous *Commentaries on the laws of England*.[88] And with Blackstone the idea of the inalienable human rights of the individual reached beyond the sphere of the purely theoretical into that of practical politics, when the constitutions of the American states, most notably that of Virginia in June 1776, took the *Commentaries* as their example.

The practical reality of the idea of the republican constitution, though, did not confine itself to America. From America

---

84 Cf. Ernst Cassirer, *The Philosophy of the Enlightenment*, tr. F.C.A. Koelln and J.P. Pettigrove, Princeton University Press, NJ, 1951 (1932), pp. 102 ff., and 107–08; cf. Wisner, 1997, pp. 157–158; cf. Ernst Cassirer, *The Philosophy of the Enlightenment*, tr. F.C.A. Koelln and J.P. Pettigrove, Princeton University Press, NJ, 1951 (1932), pp. 244 ff.

85 See: Ernst Cassirer, *Die Idee der republikanischen Verfassung*, Rede zur Verfassungsfeier am 11. August 1928, Friederichsen, De Gruyter & Co. M.B.H., Hamburg, 1929, p. 13; cf. Ernst Cassirer, *Leibniz' System in seinen wissenschaftlichen Grundlagen*, Gesammelte Werke, Band 1, Felix Meiner Verlag, Hamburg, 1998 (1902), pp. 404–405 (450–452).

86 Ibid., 1998 (1902), p. 410 (457).

87 See: Ernst Cassirer, *Die Idee der republikanischen Verfassung*, Rede zur Verfassungsfeier am 11. August 1928, Friederichsen, De Gruyter & Co. M.B.H., Hamburg, 1929, pp. 15–16.

88 Ibid., 1929, pp. 16–17.

the spark sprung to France, culminating in the declaration of 1789. According to Cassirer, no other question stirred the eighteenth century so deeply and passionately as the question concerning the eternal, immutable, and inalienable rights of man. For Kant, for example, all philosophy is inextricably allied with that basic question, because he finds therein the closing and the true completion of his philosophical thought and inquiry. "*Only through regard for this goal,* [*i.e.*, human rights] (...) *can the scholastic conception of philosophy pass over into a conception of philosophy as related to the world.*"[89] It was the *a priori* of law prepared by Grotius and the Cambridge Platonists,[90] according to Cassirer, that found widespread reception in the Enlightenment of the eighteenth century through its demand for universally valid and unalterable legal norms. Even Montesquieu, who began as an empirical scientist, did not content himself with the empirically known laws of the political world, but attempted to trace these laws back to a definite few of principles, that is to say, "the spirit of the laws" as the systematic interdependence among the various normative legal forms.

Inspired by the basic conception that "*A given heterogeneity must never prevent us from seeking the hidden uniformity; the accidental must never prevent us regarding the necessary and block our access to a knowledge of the necessary order of things,*" Montesquieu declares that justice is a certain

---

[89] See: Ernst Cassirer, *The Concept of Philosophy as a Philosophical Problem (1935)*, in: Ibid., *Symbol, Myth, and Culture. Essays and Lectures of Ernst Cassirer 1935–1945*, edited by D.P. Verene, Yale University Press, New Haven and London, 1979, pp. 49–63; here: p. 58.

[90] For the relationship between the Cambridge Platonists and the Dutch Arminians, of which Grotius was a main representative, see: Colie, 1957, p. 144: "*Arminianism was in the beginning the result of the common-sense, humanistic attitude toward religion, metaphysics, physics, and human society, attractive to men of good will in England as in Holland: it gave authority to Mede, Whichote, More, Cudworth and the fellows; it took much in turn from their philosophic idealism ... the Arminian and Platonist traditions became inextricably mixed.*" For the relation between Grotius and Herbert von Cherburys, see also: Ernst Cassirer, *Vom Wesen und Werden des Naturrechts*, Zeitschrift für Rechtsphilosophie in Lehre und Praxis, Volume 6, No. 1, 1932, pp. 1–27; here p. 11.

and unalterable relation.[91] It does not matter whether this relation is conceived by God or by an angel or by man, for Montesquieu's contention is of similar purport to that of Grotius and the Cambridge Platonists; it is impossible that God should offend against the known eternal norms of justice. "*Therefore, even if no God existed, we should have to love justice, and do everything in our power to be like a being of whom we have so sublime an idea, and who, if He existed, would necessarily be just.*" [92] Moreover, Montesquieu contends, "*Once free from the yoke of religion, we should still be subject to the rule of justice.*"[93]

In a similar vein, as Cassirer remarks, both Voltaire and Diderot, who are otherwise strongly motivated by philosophical empiricism, in the practical sphere give prevalence to ethical rationalism and maintain an enthusiasm "*for the original competence and the fundamental force of moral reason.*"[94] Although Voltaire agrees with Locke that there are no innate ideas, *i.e.*, that there is no proposition of morality innate in the soul of man, nevertheless, Voltaire proposes that the absence of such a universal moral principle can only be temporal, because "*The discovery of this principle is confined to a certain time and a certain stage of development.*"[95] Is it possible, Voltaire asks rhetorically, that nature should have everywhere aimed at "*unity, order, and complete regularity*"[96] through natural laws, and have missed only in the case of "*its highest creation, man (...) only to abandon the moral world completely to chance and whim?*"[97] By taking Newton as his example it was evident for Voltaire that just as in the physical world with its natural laws,

---

91 See: Ernst Cassirer, *The Philosophy of the Enlightenment*, tr. F.C.A. Koelln and J.P. Pettigrove, Princeton University Press, NJ, 1951 (1932), pp. 242–243.

92 Idem, 1951 (1932), p. 243, referring to Montesquieu, *Lettres Persanes, Lettre LXXXII.*

93 Ibid., 1951 (1932), p. 243, referring to Montesquieu, *Lettres Persanes, Lettre LXXXII.* The Cambridge Platonists had a much more optimistic view of religion than the French philosophers of the Enlightenment. See: Chapter 3.

94 Ibid., 1951 (1932), p. 244.

95 Ibid., 1951 (1932), p. 244.

96 Ibid., 1951 (1932), p. 245.

97 Ibid., 1951 (1932), p. 245.

there is also a fundamental law of morality that prevails in all the nations we know.

Diderot, in this respect, pointed in a new direction with his belief in the immutable moral nature of man and in the firm principle of justice arising from this nature. Diderot looked for an organic unity, because no moral system, if it wants to be viable, can be in contradiction with nature. His pragmatism concluded with the superiority of natural law and natural morality above theological ethics, based on the principle of effectiveness. Theological ethics and religion, according to Diderot, have always had a disastrous influence: "*They cut all natural bonds between man and man; they sow dissension and hatred among the closest friends and among blood relations; they debase natural duties by subordinating them to another order of purely chimerical duty.*"[98] The standard set forth by Diderot for the whole *Encyclopedia*, was further pursued by D'Alembert, who insisted that morality consists in the consciousness of our duty to human kind. Philosophical ethics for D'Alembert could have no other goal than to assign to the individual his place in human society, "*and to teach him to employ his powers for the welfare of society and for the common happiness of all.*" [99]

French philosophy of the eighteenth century, according to Cassirer, by no means discovered the idea of inalienable rights. For Cassirer this goes back to the beginnings of modern natural law, to Grotius, receives further elaboration and sophistication with the Cambridge Platonists, and undergoes further systematic justification and elucidation in the philosophy of law of German idealism, especially in the works of Leibniz and Wolff.[100] Nevertheless, French philosophy of the eighteenth century laid the foundation upon which the doctrine of human and civil rights was built. Moreover, eighteenth century French philosophy was the first to make a moral gospel of the idea of human rights and "*to embrace it passionately and proclaim it enthusiastically.*"[101] Through this enthusiasm French philosophy introduced the

---

98 Ibid., 1951 (1932), pp. 245–246.

99 Ibid., 1951 (1932), p. 246.

100 See: Chapter 1.

101 See: Ernst Cassirer, *The Philosophy of the Enlightenment*, tr. F.C.A. Koelln and J.P. Pettigrove, Princeton University Press, NJ, 1951 (1932), pp. 248–250.

doctrine of inalienable human rights into real political life and "*gave it the impetus and explosive power which it revealed in the day of the French Revolution.*"[102] Voltaire gave expression to this enthusiasm in his equation of the concept of freedom with the concept of human rights: "*In fact, what does it mean to be free? It means to know the rights of man, for to know them is to defend them.*"[103]

Immanuel Kant was a fervent admirer of the French Revolution, and although the French Revolution had proceeded in the opposite direction than had been intended, nevertheless he went out to declare that: "*In spite all of this, such a revolution finds, in the minds of all spectators, a sympathy very near to enthusiasm. Such a phenomenon can never be forgotten; because it proves that in human nature there exists an inclination and disposition to the better which no politician could ever have been able to predict by summing up the course of former events.*"[104] However, European history proved Kant's prophecy wrong. In the aftermath of the Reign of Terror and the Napoleonic wars, the Romantic writers of Europe, with only a few exceptions, not only neglected the principles of the Enlightenment and the idea of human rights in particular, but they also openly defied and attacked them. Moreover, nineteenth century philosophical and political thought was more interested in formulating elaborate systems – be it the Hegelian state or the Benthamian general welfare – without considering the individual as its ultimate point of focus. The displacement of the individual from the center of philosophical and political thought, disassociated the intellectual era more and more from the idea of human rights, and would reach its zenith in the twentieth century with the rise of the totalitarian state.

In his work "*Zum ewigen Frieden*" (Perpetual Peace, 1795), Kant proposed that every constitution should be republican in kind. It should be based on the principle of legislation that guaranteed the implementation of only those laws that could have sprung from the united will of all subjects, and wherein every member is not merely a subject, but also a citizen,

---

[102] Ibid., 1951 (1932), p. 250.

[103] Ibid., 1951 (1932), p. 251.

[104] Kant, I., *Der Streit der Fakultäten* (1798), Section II. W*orks.* Edited by E. Cassirer, Volume VII, 391 f.

i.e., he or she must be viewed as being able to agree with the general will.[105] Kant was the staunchest defender of the worth of individual autonomy, and he demanded that every legislator should take the autonomous nature of the individual as its starting point. Accordingly, the social contract as a pure idea entails the ethical imperative, according to Cassirer, that *it is the responsibility of every legislator that it demands from the totality of the people nothing else than that this totality, out of ethical claims and maxims, could demand from itself.*[106]

It was therefore unacceptable for Cassirer to hold as Hegel did, that "*the state was not only the consummation of history, but also of the moral order, the very incarnation of right and justice.*"[107] Hegel, according to Cassirer, did not intend to give a justification of the Prussian absolutist state; however, along with the culmination of the idea of freedom in the idea of the state he ignored the task or ethical responsibility of the individual.[108] What Cassirer proposed was a *Verfassungspatriotismus* (constitutional patriotism)[109] as opposed to the dominant popular "*völkisch*" patriotism of his time.[110] What it amounts to is "(...)

---

105 See: Ernst Cassirer, *Die Idee der republikanischen Verfassung*, Rede zur Verfassungsfeier am 11. August 1928, Friederichsen, De Gruyter & Co. M.B.H., Hamburg, 1929, p. 23. See also: Mertens, Th., *Am Ausgang des Neukantianismus: Cassirer und Heidegger in Davos 1929*, in: Alexy, R., Meyer, L.H., Paulson, S.L., Sprenger, G. (Hrsg.), *Neukantianismus und Rechtsphilosophie*, Nomos Verlaggesellschaft, Baden-Baden, 2002, p. 538.

106 See: Lüthje, Jürgen, *Verneigung vor Ernst Cassirer, Rede aus Anlaß der Benennung des Hörsaals A im Haubtgebäude der Universität Hamburg in Ernst Cassirer–Hörsaal am 11. Mai 1999;* in: Hamann, F., Lipert, J. (Red.), *Zum Gedenken an Ernst Cassirer (1874–1945), Ansprachen auf der Akademischen Gedenkfeier am 11. mai 1999*, Hamburger Universitätsreden Neue Folge I, Herausgegeben von der Pressestelle der Universität Hamburg, Dölling und Galitz Verlag, Hamburg, 1999, pp. 10–15.

107 Ernst Cassirer, *Force and Freedom: Remarks on the English Edition of Jacob Burckhardt's "Reflections on History"*, The American Scholar, Volume 13, No.1, 1943-44, p. 413.

108 Ernst Cassirer, *Freiheit und Form. Studien zur deutschen Geistesgeschichte*, Gesammelte Werke Band 7, Felix Meiner Verlag, Hamburg, 1998 (1916), pp. 384–385 (570–573).

109 Paetzold, 1995, Chapter 7;, here: p. 119.

110 See: Ernst Cassirer, *Wandlungen der Staatsgesinnung und der Staatstheorie in der deutschen Geistesgeschichte* (1930), in: *Enge Zeit. Spuren Vertriebener und Verfolgter der Hamburger Universität im Auditorium Maximum der Universität, Von-Melle-Park 23. Februar – 4. April 1991*, Hg.

that we in the middle of battle, in the emergency and confusion of strife do not forget the common endpoint (...) *Such an active cooperation, common labor and sympathy: this only also is the claim the constitution of the German state demands from us.* (...) *From such a will it* [the German people] *has found courage and force* (...) *to legislate.*"[111]

According to Cassirer, it is not characteristic of the constitutional state that it can produce *new* laws; rather the State and the citizens that constitute it have to recognize the given legislative content in its ascertained generality, that is to say, to grasp it reflectively. This duty to reflect on the laws of the constitutional state is not an exclusive task of the democratically elected legislator; it includes, in addition to the universities Cassirer addresses, every citizen, just as Kant envisioned in his republican ideal. For Cassirer, in fine, constitutionalism is *a process of progressive reflectivity on legislation.*[112] The primary characteristic of Cassirer's ideal constitution, as an exemplar of the republican constitution, consequently, is its respect and protection of those fundamental rights and basic values that enable the individual citizen to contribute in his moral and reflective capacity to the progress of the constitutional republic.

The self-preservation of the state, according to Cassirer, cannot be secured by its material prosperity, nor can it be guaranteed by the maintenance of certain constitutional laws. Written constitutions or legal charters have no real binding force, according to Cassirer, if they are not the expression of a constitution that is written in the citizens' minds. Without the moral support of the people the very strength of a state becomes its inherent danger.[113] The philosophy of symbolic forms in this regard is concerned with the cultivation of our critical faculties, and, ultimately, with the foundation of individual moral judgment.

---

von Angela Bottin unter der Mitarbeit von Rainer Nicolaysen, Universität Hamburg, Hamburg, 1991, pp. 168–169.

111 Ibid., 1991 (1930), pp. 168–169.

112 Ibid., 1991 (1930), p. 169. I am indebted to the discussion of this subject by Birgit Recki at the meeting of the International Ernst Cassirer Society in February 2003 in Berlin.

II. CONCLUSION

In conclusion, by defending the Weimar Constitution and instill-ling constitutional patriotism Cassirer attempted to create greater unity and, in a time of confusion, to give some moorings and a point of orientation for the German people. For that, he invited them firstly to reflect on the polity and the position they themselves take therein, instead of letting themselves being dragged away by the events of the day. Weimar has made clear to democratic polities that what makes the rule of law and the judiciary what they are, is in a great part determined by the kind of society in which they operate.[114] The dramatic history of Weimar most of all showed why judges should be formed as ethical personalities if they want to fulfill their functions as the watchmen of the rule of law.[115] Citizens of democracies and their officials should be conscious of the fact that in the forming of their judgments they have a degree of freedom, which, when they not themselves come up with a morally justified opinion, *i.e.*, with reference to the fundamental principles of the rule of law; will be influenced by other forces and processes.[116]

By taking the Weimar Constitution as their starting point Cassirer contends that individuals can make a difference in their polity, and that the republican form of government and democracy are as common to the Germans as to other nations. Moreover, German culture played an important role in the development of republicanism and democracy. For that purpose he explains how German philosophers such as Leibniz and Wolff inspired European, and consequently American constitutionalism, and, after the French Revolution, received a republican formulation by Kant. The idea of human rights plays an important role for Cassirer and it leads him to reject Hegel's view of the State, which was the dominant intellectual doctrine of the nineteenth century. Cassirer

---

114 I would like to thank the historian Moshe Zimmermann (Tel Aviv) for comments on this point.

115 Cf. Smith, 1998.

116 See: Coskun, D., *De ethiek van de rechter, Ernst Cassirer, de politiek en de rechterlijke macht in Weimar* ("The ethics of the judge. Ernst Cassirer, politics, and the judiciary in Weimar"), Trema, tijdschrift voor de rechterlijke macht (Trema, journal for the judiciary), March 2005, pp. 108–112; here p. 112.

also denounces other doctrines of the nineteenth century, which do not consider the individual as their ultimate point of focus. As the ensuing chapters elaborate, it is essential for a culture to have individuals with faith in their abilities to form their own future. However, freedom is not automatic, according to Cassirer, but has to be taken up as an ongoing task. Therewith, we already anticipate another theme that we take up in the ensuing chapters, *i.e.*, the idea that fatalism is evidently incompatible with democratic thought, and therefore democracies cannot avoid critically engaging and confronting mythical thought. Human freedom at the same time marked the principal theme of the Davos debate in 1929 between Cassirer and Heidegger, to which we turn in the next chapter.

CHAPTER 2

CASSIRER AND HEIDEGGER. AN INTERMEZZO ON MAGIC MOUNTAIN (1929)[1]

I. INTRODUCTION

In the period that Ernst Cassirer defended the Weimar Republic and the idea of human rights as embodied in the Weimar Constitution, he took a stance against the philosopher Martin Heidegger in Davos, Switzerland, during the Second Davos University Courses (hereinafterr: Davos). The debate between Cassirer and Heidegger has become a landmark in the history of twentieth century philosophy. However, it is generally viewed more as an instance of dismemberment of Cassirer's philosophy (and humanism at large) than an instance that has contributed to the attainment of Cassirer's humanistic aims. In this chapter we give a reassessment of the Davos debate by explicating the differences between the philosophical standpoints of Cassirer and Heidegger that not only precluded a real dialogue or debate between them, but that also explicate their respective practical philosophical and political philosophical outlooks. Moreover, from a jurisprudential perspective, it provided for an instance where Cassirer made clear his position in the practical sphere and hence, for us, an instance to elaborate on the philosophical sources of his view of law and society.

This chapter is organized as follows: in the immediate next paragraph, we give a short description of the institutional setting for the Davos debate. In Section I.1, we answer the question as to what was the Cassirer–Heidegger debate from a philosophical perspective. While in Section I.2, we describe the Cassirer–Heidegger debate from a jurisprudential perspective.

---

1 This chapter has resulted in the following publication: Coskun, D., *Cassirer in Davos. An Intermezzo on Magic Mountain (1929)*, Law & Critique, Volume 17, Issue 1, 2006, pp. 1–26.

In the conclusion, we assess the results of this chapter, and introduce the subject of the next chapter: Cassirer's continued appreciation of individual moral judgment when in exile.

The setting to Davis started with the plan of the Hungarian lung-doctor Professor Kollarits to found a University of Davos in the high Alps of Switzerland by an appeal to the League of Nations. Although that plan was never fully pursued, the idea of neutral Switzerland as a place for the reconciliation and unity of peoples, in particular the French and the German, persisted. Annual courses in Davos seemed a very good start and would not only benefit the lungs of the participants, but also overcome various other obstacles. Beginning in 1928, it provided many students and professors with an occasion to meet peers from abroad and from other disciplines. It was an early form of what we now call an international symposium and it took place in Grand Hotel Belvedere, Davos-Platz, which exists to this day. The main purpose of the annual courses was political, *i.e.*, to promote the "*understanding and cooperation between nations*," which was an echo of the persistent traumas of the First World War and the desperate need for ways of preventing any similar tragedy.[2] However, only afterwards did the participants and observers understand the political relevance of the discussions and disputations of these events.[3] Although the organizers planned for the Davos courses to take place annually, there were only four of them and they ended in 1931.

I. 1. What was the Cassirer–Heidegger Debate?

The Second Davos University Courses had as general topic "man and generation," and lasted from Sunday, March 17, to Saturday, April 6, 1929.[4] The Cassirer–Heidegger debate constituted the conclusion of the courses on philosophy, and the public anticipated it as the main event of the courses during 1929. It is difficult to maintain and to prove that the specific

---

2 Gründer, K., *Cassirer und Heidegger in Davos 1929*, in: Braun, 1988, pp. 290–292; cf. Waite, 1998, p. 610.

3 Cf. Röd, W., *Transzendentalphilosophie oder Ontologie? Überlegungen zu Grundfragen der Davoser Disputation*, in: Kaegi, 2002, pp. 2 ff.

4 Cf. Ernst Cassirer, *The Philosophy of Symbolic Forms*, Volume 4, *The Metaphysics of Symbolic Forms*, Krois, J.M. and Verene, D.P. (eds.), tr. Krois, J.M., Yale University Press, New Haven and London, 1996, xi.

debate in Davos between Cassirer and Heidegger was a big success philosophically or that it actually took place in philosophical terms.[5] Moreover, it would be to highlight a single occurrence and detach it from its context, *i.e.*, the discussion between Cassirer and Heidegger lasted throughout a couple of decades, whether this was explicit, as in the case of Davos, or implicit in their (future) works. Nevertheless, putting Cassirer and Heidegger to the fore in an imaginary debate as oppositional forces is not only a good way of explicating the differences between these two philosophers, but also it provides us with the opportunity to explore the contexts that sustain the deep philosophical discords between them. With this we explore the meaning structures that continue to nurture and influence current philosophical political and legal debates.[6]

However, notwithstanding the above, the debate proved a big success, in that it attracted great public interest. The *Davoser Revue* printed summaries of the presentations and with respect to the Cassirer–Heidegger debate it reported that the public consisted of about 200 students and 30 professors. The amount of attention specifically given to the Cassirer–Heidegger debate in other journals and autobiographies makes clear again its centrality during the Second University Courses. The Davos debate had, in a sense, symbolic value that already affected the participants, such as Kurt Riezler, who, as an eyewitness, compared the debate between Heidegger and Cassirer with the debate between Naphta and Settembrini in Thomas Mann's *Zauberberg*.[7] The imaginary meeting between Settembrini and Naphta in the contemporaneously published book of Mann led to a fierce debate. Therein, on the one hand, Settembrini regards himself as a child of the Enlightenment and as a tolerant humanist with great faith

5 Cf. Krois, J.M., *Warum fand keine Davoser Disputation zwischen Cassirer und Heidegger statt? [Why didn't the Davos debate between Cassirer and Heidegger take place?]*, in: Kaegi, 2002, pp. 234–246.

6 Cf. Ward, 1997.

7 Riezler, K., *Davoser Hochschulkurse 1929*, Neue Zürcher Zeitung, Samstag 30. März 1929, Morgenausgabe, Nr. 609; Thomas Mann's novel "The Magic Mountain" established Davos in world literature. Mann's visit to Davos was occasioned by the illness of his wife Katya, who suffered from lung catarrh. She spent six months in Davos sanatorium. The idea for the basic plot of the novel most likely came from a severe cold which Thomas Mann caught during his stay in Davos. See: <http://www.davos.ch/pdf/news_davos13en. pdf>.

in the power of arguments to reconcile oppositions. Naphta, on the other hand, speaks of irrationalism and becomes fascinated by the attractiveness of death and violence.[8]

Moreover, on the one hand, scholars remark that in its own way, within the context of contemporary or existential thought, the Davos debate reproduced the earlier dispute between Friedrich A. Lange and his successor in Marburg Hermann Cohen, who respectively interpreted Kant psychologically and idealistically. On the other hand, they draw the parallel between the Davos debate and the debate between Luther, for whom salvation came to the faithful entirely from the free grace of God, and Erasmus, who also gave credence to human responsibility and moral integrity in the matter of salvation.[9] These parallels are striking in that the Davos debate entailed a "battle" that was engaged in two fronts, the practical as well as the theoretical. Some scholars hold that the Davos debate did not primarily deal with issues of methodology and phenomenology, but with normative and ethical issues. Cassirer's and Heidegger's views and interpretations of Kant became the vehicle of their differences in political (philosophical) and ethical standpoint.[10] This argument is supported by the statement in the biography of Frau Cassirer, who accompanied Cassirer during Davos, that they were aware of rumors of Heidegger's anti-Semitism.[11] Contrary to what these rumors could suggest, though, Heidegger treated Ernst and Toni Cassirer respectfully.[12]

Nevertheless, it cannot be denied, that the stage (to the Davos debate) was set under the spell of a fascism that in fact amounted to anti-Semitism. A prelude to this was played out in

---

8 See: Mertens, 2000, p. 13.

9 See: Krois, 1983, pp. 153–154; Cohen, 2002; see also: the introduction to Levinas, E., *Humanism of the Other Person*, tr. N. Poller, Illinois University Press, Chicago, 2003.

10 See: Ernst Cassirer, *Symbol, Myth, and Culture, Essays and Lectures of Ernst Cassirer 1935–1945*, edited by Verene, D.P., Yale University Press, New Haven, 1979, Introduction, p. 39. Cf. Eekert, G. van, 'Synthesis Speciosa' en de taak van de filosofie. Cassirer en Heidegger voor het tribunaal van de Kritik der reinen Vernunft, in Raymaekers, 1993, pp. 230–234; and Schulz, 1997, pp. 290–312.

11 Toni Cassirer, 1981, p. 182.

12 For a different account see: Pos, H.J., *Recollections of Ernst Cassirer*, in: Schilpp, 1973 (1949), p. 69, according to whom Heidegger publicly refused to give a hand to Cassirer who had extended his.

1916, when Bruno Bauch wrote a reader's letter to the popular or "*völkisch*" journal *Der Panther*, that Hermann Cohen as a Jew could not understand the German philosopher Kant. In his letter, Bauch advocated a demotic interpretation of philosophy and wrote that Jews were "guests" in the German "mansion." Subsequently, Bauch published an article in Kant-Studien titled *Der Begriff der Nation* (The Concept of Nation), wherein he further elaborated his demotic interpretation of philosophy. What Bauch questioned was whether Cohen could be German as a Jew and as such capable of scientific analysis. Cassirer decided to respond to this article in Kant-Studien, but his response remained unpublished, because Bauch decided to step down as editor of the journal and the situation eased. While Bauch maintained that he owed no apology, after 1933 his career advanced under the Nazi's and he was chairman of the German philosophical association until his death in 1942.[13]

The issue returned, though, on February 25, 1929 – about three weeks before Davos – when an article appeared in the academically well-established *Frankfurter Zeitung* that reported similar assertions. The Viennese professor of philosophy, Othmar Spann, had spoken before a full audience in the University of Munich on "The contemporary crisis of culture," and had attacked neo-Kantianism and its representatives, *i.e.*, Hermann Cohen and Ernst Cassirer, as "foreigners" who wrongly interpreted the German philosopher Kant. It was a pity that the German nation had to be reminded of its own Kantian philosophy by foreigners, such as Cohen and Cassirer. The audience applauded the speech, and Hitler, who was also present, thanked Spann with a handshake and a deep bow. Next to the *Frankfurter Zeitung*, the speech of Spann was printed in a dozen other journals and periodicals. Although the accusations against a "Jewish neo-Kantianism" were not without precedent, such a public attack just before Davos had a decisive impact on the atmosphere on the event – it confirmed the growing interconnectedness of the critique of neo-Kantianism with anti-Semitism and made it a theme again.[14]

---

[13] Krois, J.M., *Warum fand keine Davoser Disputation zwischen Cassirer und Heidegger statt?*, in: Kaegi, 2002, pp. 234–246; here: p. 238.

[14] Ibid., 2002, p. 242. See: Haag, 1973, pp. 93–126, esp. pp. 104–105, for a detailed account of Spann and his views of Cassirer and Cohen.

The Davos debate has had a lasting influence in philosophical thought. Heavily discussed in the literature, commentators agree that in the light of the years that followed, *i.e.*, the rise of National Socialism, the Davos debate formed a landmark in the history of philosophy. Moreover, Michael Friedman in his book *A Parting of the Ways* holds that Davos was decisive for the analytic/continental divide in philosophy.[15] Both Heidegger, emerging leader of the continental tradition, and Carnap, emerging leader of the analytic tradition, sought to define themselves against the then dominant tradition of neo-Kantianism.[16] By contrast, Cassirer, who was commonly regarded as the last of the neo-Kantians, left the European Continent in 1933, never to return. Nor did neo-Kantianism come back in its original force. Ernst Cassirer's death on April 13, 1945, not only meant that he was not to see the end of the war, but also that he could not actually participate in the reconstruction of philosophical thought in Germany, something what could be and was done by philosophers such as Karl Löwith, Theodor W. Adorno, or Max Horkheimer. In addition, it meant that philosophical discussion after the war was almost completely influenced on the one side by the existentialistic phenomenology as proclaimed by Heidegger, and on the other side by the social philosophy of the "Frankfurter Schule" that was inspired by Marxism.[17] In the absence of Cassirer, Heidegger became the sole "great" philosopher of the European Continent. As a result, a gulf was created between the two intellectual traditions of analytic and continental philosophy, which rendered impossible any communication, hence disagreement between them.

Davos was neither their first, nor their last meeting. While Cassirer, in the wake of Davos, had decided to read some of Heidegger's works, Heidegger, a year before, had critically reviewed the second volume of Cassirer's philosophy of symbolic forms on mythological thought, and fundamentally questioned whether Kant's Critique of Pure Reason could be understood as a theory of the natural sciences or even could be extended to encompass a philosophy of culture as well. Cassirer's third

---

15 Friedman, 2000; cf. Friedman, 2002, pp. 263–271.

16 Neo-Kantianism was the predominant strain of thought in the philosophy of the nineteenth and early twentieth century; cf. Köhnke, 1991.

17 Frede, 1997, VIII.

volume on the symbolic form of science appeared later in 1929, and contained footnote references to several insights of Heidegger in *Being and Time*. Furthermore, in a footnote to paragraph eleven of his "*Sein und Zeit*," Heidegger mentions that he had a talk with Cassirer when he had to deliver a speech at the local Kant Society of Hamburg. They agreed, then, on the necessity of an existential analysis.[18] After Davos, Heidegger invited Cassirer to Freiburg to hold a lecture on Rousseau; Cassirer praised Heidegger's hospitality.

In Davos, both Heidegger and Cassirer gave four lectures as part of their regular courses.[19] Whereas Heidegger lectured on "Kant's Critique of Pure Reason and the task of the foundation of metaphysics," Cassirer discussed three problems of philosophical anthropology – space, language, and death – ideal subjects for taking issue with Heidegger's ontology and existential analytic. Furthermore, Cassirer gave a special lecture on "spirit" and "life" in the philosophy of Scheler, which appeared later in *Die Neue Rundschau*.[20] Although Cassirer was unwell and therefore somewhat distracted and ill-tempered, nevertheless both philosophers exhibited a remarkable attunement to each other. This was possible because Heidegger even went so far as to visit Cassirer and read to him his lectures, as if preparing him for battle.

In his lectures, Heidegger made clear, that the problem of ontology portrayed itself in nucleus form in the *Critique of Reason*, that the finitude of human knowledge was decisive in this respect, and that the basis for the possibility of the being of ontological knowledge displayed itself in the schematism chapter. A full elaboration of his view he presented later in 1929, in his book "*Kant und das Problem der Metaphysik*."[21] Therein, Heidegger presented a fundamental criticism of the neo-Kantian philosophy presented by the Marburg school. Furthermore, in the same year, upon assuming the Freiburg Chair of Philosophy,

---

18 See: Corver, 1984, p. 105.

19 See: Gründer, K., *Cassirer und Heidegger in Davos 1929*, in: Braun, 1988, p. 293.

20 Ernst Cassirer, *'Geist' und 'Leben' in der Philosophie der Gegenwart*, Die Neue Rundschau, Volume 41, 1930, pp. 244–264; an English translation appeared in Schilpp, 1973 (1949).

21 Heidegger, M., *Kant und das Problem der Metaphysik*, Friedrich Cohen, Bonn, 1929.

Heidegger had curiously pronounced his hostility toward Cohen and the neo-Kantian theory of logic, which, next to his own mentor and predecessor Husserl, extended even toward Cohen's most creative student, Cassirer, by claiming that "*philosophy can never be measured by the standards of science.*"[22] According to Cassirer, though, neo-Kantianism had become the scapegoat of the "new philosophy." As a result, Cassirer set out to confront Heidegger on his level of sophistication.

Cassirer, in his first lecture on space, made clear in line with Uexküll that man lives in a different kind of space or realm than the animal. As explicated in his *Essay on man*, man lives in two realms: the first, termed by Cassirer as the *vitale Lebensraum*, a space of action and reaction, man shares with the animals, the second, the symbolic realm, is characteristic and accessibly only to man, because of his ability to distance himself from the given of the here and now and think of it in terms of objects.[23] Heidegger's analysis of space, according to Cassirer, is restricted to the first realm, the realm of actions, *i.e.*, it is more an examination of the animal world than the human world. Heidegger regards the second realm, what he terms as *Vorhandenheit* (the present-at/to-hand), as a deterioration or downfall (Abfall). "*Everything "general," all giving in to the general is for Heidegger a "fall" – a disregarding of "authentic"* Dasein *– a giving in to the inauthenticity of the "they."*[24] By merely living in what "they" say or do, according to Heidegger, man avoids his personal finitude, and as a result avoids himself.[25] For Cassirer, though, "*The "unpersonal" does not consist merely in the pale, diluted social form of the average, the everydayness of*

---

22 Gordon, 1999, pp. 47–48; cf. Krois, J.M., *Warum fand keine Davoser Disputation zwischen Cassirer und Heidegger statt?*, in: Kaegi, 2002, pp. 234–246.

23 Paetzold, 1996, p. 89.

24 Ernst Cassirer, *Mind and Life. Heidegger*, Philosophy and Rhetoric, Volume 16, 1983, p. 160; a hitherto unpublished critique of Heidegger by Cassirer; see also: Ernst Cassirer, *The Philosophy of Symbolic Forms*, Volume 4, *The Metaphysics of Symbolic Forms*, Krois, J.M. and Verene, D.P. (eds.), tr. Krois, J.M., Yale University Press, New Haven and London, 1996.

25 See: Heidegger, M., *Being and Time*, tr. J. Macquarrie and E. Robinson, Basil Blackwell, Oxford, 1962, paragraph 51, pp. 296–299; cited by: Krois, 1983, p. 156.

the "they," but in the form of trans*-personal meaning. For this transpersonal Heidegger's philosophy has no access.*"[26]

How is it possible, Cassirer asks, that we understand another and that we can relate to another as part of a common human world, for example through language. Accordingly, in his second lecture on language, Cassirer made clear that Heidegger's analysis of "the mere man" (*bloßen* Man) who has "relapsed" in talking (*Gerede verfallenden*), describes the situation of an aphasic, who is bound to and limited by his situation or world of locomotive actions and cannot force it open, as with healthy people, through the power of language to conceptualize a world. Without the power of a symbolic system, especially that of language, our grasping of the world, to *come to terms* with it, is futile. Language in the symbolic sense of the term enables us to create our own world, but also to relate to another human being through our ability of symbolic interchange and perspectival flexibility. Moreover, through language in the symbolic sphere we are able to direct our actions into the future, *i.e.*, we create perspective for our future course of actions.

Finally, in his third lecture Cassirer made clear that categories such as existential finitude, death, and fear belong to the competence of religion. Fear is a product of religious commitment, which classical philosophy tries to overcome. Plato in his *Phaedon* maintains that philosophy is to teach people to come to terms with death and that death understood is not something terrifying. In an unpublished critique of Heidegger, Cassirer makes clear that Heidegger starts from a viewpoint derived from the philosophy of religion, as expressed by Luther and Kierkegaard. It is Heidegger's desire to "turn man around" and to direct him to face the "*severity of his destiny,*" whereas giving in to the world of the "general" is a mere looking away from oneself, a kind of "*fall from grace.*"[27] In this regard, Cassirer describes Heidegger's analysis as "pragmatic" and later even as a usurpation of Kant's philosophy.[28] Heidegger, for his part did not

---

[26] Ernst Cassirer, *Mind and Life. Heidegger*, Philosophy and Rhetoric, Volume 16, 1983, p. 161; cf. Hackenesch, 2001, pp. 114–115.

[27] Krois, 1983, p. 161.

[28] See: Ernst Cassirer, *Kant and the Problem of Metaphysics: Remarks on Heidegger's Interpretation of Kant*, in: Gram, 1967, p. 149; cf. Gründer, K.,

contradict this assertion, he rather agreed with Cassirer, that he did not have the intention to give an interpretation of Kant's philosophy loyal to Kant.

This was not the case with Cassirer. In 1929, Cassirer, in addition to his renowned philosophical position, was a recognized Kant scholar. As mentioned before, Cassirer studied philosophy in Marburg under the great Kant scholar Hermann Cohen (1842–1918). In addition, he served as the general editor of a definitive eleven-volume edition of the complete works of Kant, and individually edited or co-edited four of the eleven volumes of the complete work. Furthermore, in 1918, he published a complete intellectual biography of Kant, entitled *Kants Leben und Lehre* (Kant's Life and Thought).[29] Heidegger had had great and rapid success with his *Being and Time* in 1927, and by the time of Davos apparently had finished the manuscript of his book about Kant, but had a less impressive record on the subject.

The starting point of the Davos debate[30] was Heidegger's question as to whether Kant's Critique of Pure Reason concerned the "laying of the groundwork" of the theory of knowledge of the mathematical physical sciences, as neo-Kantians claim, or rather "laying of the groundwork" of metaphysics, as Heidegger himself claims. Neo-Kantianism, according to Heidegger, in its investigations had focused too much on the natural sciences. According to Heidegger, in an attempt to strike the "old strain of thought" in philosophy at its core, Kant's central problem was not that of scientific knowledge, but rather the problem of the metaphysical comprehension of being. Heidegger's interpretation of Kant

---

Cassirer und Heidegger in Davos 1929, in: Braun, 1988, pp. 293–297; cf. Krois, 1992, p. 451.

29 Ernst Cassirer, *Kant's Life and Thought* (*Kants Leben und Lehre*), tr. J. Haden, Yale University Press, New Haven and London, 1981 (1918).

30 The debate can be reconstructed from several documents and microfilms, among them a basic account of the debate in the *Davoser Revue* (April 15, 1929) and the *Protocol* of the debate by J. Ritter and O.F. Bollnow; see: Schneeberger, G., *Ergaenzungen zu einer Heidegger-Bibliographie,* AG, Bern, 1960, pp. 17–27; ibid., *Nachlese zu Heidegger: Dokumente zu einem Leben und Denken,* AG, Bern, 1962, pp. 1–9; Heidegger, M., *Kant und das Problem der Metaphysik,* Appendix, Klostermann, Frankfurt am Main, 1974; for a translation along with some introductory remarks, see: Hamburg, 1964, pp. 208–222. Furthermore, the debate survives in the form of minutes taken by students.

dictated that Kant had destroyed the beginnings, base, and even the approach of reason, but that Kant (along with Cassirer as a paradigm case for neo-Kantianism) "shrinks back" or even "draws back in terror" before the radical consequences of such a conclusion.[31]

According to Heidegger, Kant explicated this "shrinking back" by his amendments to the second edition of the Critique of Pure Reason. In the so-called A-version of 1781, "time" had a fundamentally more essential meaning than the B-version of 1787. Particularly in the A-version in the schematism chapter, according to Heidegger, Kant was the first, since the pre-Socratic philosophers, to think what had remained unthought-of for 2000 years, namely that temporality is the fundamental ontological concept of human existence. When faced by the destruction of the complete Western structure of the pre-eminence of logos and ratio Kant had driven back the meaning and relevance of time in favor of the reconstruction of reason. As outlined in his *Kant and the Problem of Metaphysics*, and supported by the results of *Being and Time*, Heidegger maintained that Kant had most of all laid a groundwork for a metaphysics of being. His ontology referred to a "common root" between the otherwise entirely independent passive or receptive faculty of sensibility and the active or intellectual faculty of understanding. Heidegger discovered this root in the transcendental imagination, whose ultimate basis is what he called 'temporality', which is for him the most important ontological category in the existential analytic of being.[32]

In this view, Kant had merely postponed the parting and destruction of the Western pre-eminence of reason, because Heidegger's *Being and Time* had just done this in full force. *Being and Time* was not an existential anthropology, but an analysis of "being" as it is based on "time." That analysis made clear the temporality of reason, hence its finitude. Contrary to what neo-Kantians claim, according to Heidegger, human knowledge is finite.[33] As a result, human intellect is necessarily dependent on sensible intuition. Therefore, Heidegger's philoso-

[31] Waite, 1998, p. 616.
[32] See: Friedman, 2002, p. 264.
[33] Mertens, 2000, p. 12.

phical effort was devoted to the reversal of Kant's "Copernican revolution," a return to the A-version away from the B-version of the Critique of Reason, and involved the radical conclusion from which Kant and neo-Kantians had shrunk from. In the aftermath of Davos, two years later, Cassirer summed up in a critical review of Heidegger's "*Kant und das Problem der Metaphysik*" ("Kant and the Problem of Metaphysics") his main objections against Heidegger's analysis of Marburg neo-Kantianism and against Heidegger's interpretation of Kant.[34]

In this respect, Cassirer, through his philosophy of symbolic forms, had attempted to extend Kant's "Copernican revolution" to all the other ways human beings have a world of their own, and had moved beyond the sphere of the problem of knowledge.[35] Contrary to Heidegger's allusion, Cassirer had several years since extended his investigations beyond the "mere" scientific worldview and scientific concepts. This extension included a transformation of transcendental philosophy by subsuming the problem of knowledge and that of truth under the general problem of meaning. With his philosophy of symbolic forms, Cassirer had developed an original philosophical position.[36] Moreover, on several occasions, Cassirer had tried to make clear that his position could not simply be subsumed into neo-Kantianism. In his essay *Was ist Subjektivismus?* (What is Subjectivism?) Cassirer remarks, "*Many doctrines, which are attributed in personal literature to neo-Kantianism, are not only strange to me, but are diametrically opposed to my own views.*"[37] In addition, Cassirer distinguished the *problem* of knowledge from the *theory* of knowledge. The problem of knowledge is as old as philosophy itself and something unavoidable, while the theory of knowledge represents a certain approach to a problem, *i.e.*, from

---

[34] Ernst Cassirer, Kant und das Problem der Metaphysik. Bemerkungen zu Martin Heideggers Kantinterpretation, Kant-Studien, Volume 36, 1931, pp. 1–26; translated as Ernst Cassirer, *Kant and the Problem of Metaphysics: Remarks on Heidegger's Interpretation of Kant*, in: Gram, M.S. (ed. and tr.), *Kant: Disputed Questions*, Quadrangle Books, Chicago, 1967, pp. 131–157.

[35] Krois, 1992, p. 437–453.

[36] Verene, 1969, pp. 33–46. For a further elaboration of Cassirer's relation to and subsequent disassociation from neo-Kantianism, see: Chapter 6.

[37] Ernst Cassirer, *Was ist Subjektivismus?*, Theoria, Volume 5, 1939, pp. 111–140; here: p. 114.

the perspective of a theory of scientific knowledge. Heidegger also had engaged himself in the problem of knowledge, when he, in his *Being and Time*, had discarded the notion of "eternal truths."[38] The theory of knowledge had, for historical reasons, only come up in the nineteenth century, while Cassirer had extended his explorations mainly on the field of the problem of knowledge.[39] As a result, Heidegger did not have a point or at least could not succeed in trying to place Cassirer in a certain corner, *i.e.*, neo-Kantianism.

Finally, Cassirer's philosophical elaboration beyond neo-Kantianism, in particular with respect to the symbolic form of myth, was a response to the challenges to scientific "rationalism" posed by recent works within the tradition of life philosophy (*Lebensphilosophie*) by such thinkers as Dilthey, Scheler, Simmel, and in particular Heidegger.[40] Science in the philosophy of symbolic forms is only one of many symbolic forms with distinct claims of validity. Therefore, although science is a product of a progressive evolution from more primitive symbolic forms, and constitutes the most mature form of symbolic expression, Cassirer never intended to insert a hierarchy between them as to their claims of validity.

Cassirer agreed with Heidegger, in the theoretical sphere, that the "transcendental schematism of the imagination" or the "productive imagination" functioned for Kant as a medium between the two faculties of sensibility and intelligibility. However, the intermediary representation Kant searches for in his first Critique, that makes possible the application of a category to appearances or the subsuming of intuitions under pure concepts, which Kant designates as the *transcendental schema* or as the representation of a universal procedure of imagination, Cassirer ultimately grounds in the specifically human symbolic

---

[38] Heidegger, M., *Sein und Zeit*, Niemeyer, Tübingen, 1993 (1927), p. 227: "*Daß es >ewige Wahrheiten< gibt wird erst dann zureichend bewiesen sein, wenn der Nachweis gelungen ist, daß in alle Ewigkeit Dasein war und sein wird. Solange dieser Beweis aussteht, bleibt der Satz eine phantastische Behauptung, die dadurch nicht an Rechtmäßichkeit gewinnt, daß sie von Philosophen gemeinhin >geglaubt< wird.*"Referred to by: Krois, J.M., *Warum fand keine Davoser Disputation zwischen Cassirer und Heidegger statt?*,"in: Kaegi, 2002, pp. 234–246; here: p. 236, 15n.

[39] Ibid., 2002, p. 236.

[40] See: Friedman, 2002, p. 267.

function.[41] In the symbol-concept the tension between sensibility and intelligibility is dissolved for Cassirer, and equally so in relation to the duality between the receptivity of the senses and the spontaneity of the mind. For Cassirer, in the symbolic function, the senses and the spirit join in a new form of reciprocity and correlation, since the spiritual ultimately must find its concrete fulfillment in the sensory world through the representation and expression by symbols.[42] Furthermore, Cassirer in agreement with Heidegger recognized that, for Kant, all theoretical knowledge and reason are and remain in some sense temporally bound. "*Considered theoretically, reason strives to free "the concept of the understanding from the unavoidable limitations of a possible experience" and thus to extend it beyond the boundaries of the empirical. But reason in this function does not give up the relation to the empirical. (...) Here reason directs itself primarily toward the totality of experience and thus to the entirety of existence under temporal conditions.*"[43]

All this changes, though, according to Cassirer (albeit not for Heidegger), as soon as we consider reason practically. "*Schematism and the theory of the "transcendental imagination" indeed stand at the center of the Kantian* analytic, *but not in the focus of the Kantian* system. *This system is determined and completed first in the transcendental dialectic – and further in the* Critique of Practical Reason *and the* Critique of Judgment. (...) *The theme of "Kant and metaphysics," therefore, can only be treated* sub specie *the Kantian* theory of ideas, *and, in particular,* sub specie *the Kantian theory of freedom and his theory of the beautiful, not exclusively* sub specie *the chapter on schematism.*"[44] According to Cassirer, Heidegger misconstrues the place of the analytic of the first *Critique* within the wider

---

[41] Cf. Kautz, 1990, p. 22; for an elaboration on the relation between Kantian schematism and Cassirerean symbolism, see Rotenstreich, 1974, pp. 464–474.

[42] See: Ernst Cassirer, *The Philosophy of Symbolic Forms*, Volume I, *Language*, tr. R. Manheim, Yale University Press, New Haven, 1953 (1923), p. 87.

[43] See: Ernst Cassirer, *Kant and the Problem of Metaphysics : Remarks on Heidegger's Interpretation of Kant*, in: Gram, M.S. (ed. and tr.), *Kant: Disputed Questions*, Quadrangle Books, Chicago, 1967, p. 144.

[44] Ibid., 1967, p. 149.

system of all three *Critiques.* Kant did not just tack the Critique of Practical Reason onto the theoretical portion as a second component of his system; rather he had conceived his philosophy from the start as a self-contained whole, "*and ethical problems formed an essential, integrating constituent of it.*" According to Cassirer, "*We grasp the special and most profound concept of "reason" itself, as Kant understands it, only through this relation.*"[45]

For Kant, Logic and Ethics, theoretical philosophy and practical philosophy are interdependent members of an organic system and unity. "*Without reference to theoretical philosophy moral philosophy would lose its foundation, without the reference to the moral, theoretical philosophy would lose its ideal perfection and its ultimate end.*"[46] None of them can be fully conceived and fully appreciated by itself; each of them is complementary to the other and represents its systematic counterpart. Moreover, for a proper understanding of Kantian philosophy, we must not first start with the *Critique of Pure Reason* but with the *Critique of Practical Reason.* "*In the didactic and methodic order of Kant's writings the former precedes the latter, but in the real, systematic order Kant always maintains the primacy of the practical reason.*"[47]

The principle of transcendental freedom maintained and validated by Kant in the field of theoretical philosophy meant nothing short of a complete intellectual revolution.[48] In the *Critique of Pure Reason* Kant compared this revolution with the change in cosmology effected by Copernicus. "*The condition here is the same as with the first idea of Copernicus, who, having found that the explanation of the celestial motions did not progress well when he supposed the whole host of stars to turn round the spectator, tried whether it might not succeed better if*

45 Ernst Cassirer, *Kant's Life and Thought* (*Kants Leben und Lehre*), tr. J. Haden, Yale University Press, New Haven and London, 1981 (1918), p. 233.

46 See: Ernst Cassirer, *Lectures on Kant*, Ernst Cassirer Papers, Essays and Lectures, Beinecke Rare Book & Manuscripts Library, Coll. No. GEN 98, Series No. II, Box No. 43, Folder No. 859, Lectures on Kant, pp. 4–5.

47 Ernst Cassirer, *Kant,* in: Encyclopaedia of the Social Sciences, Macmillan, New York, Volume 7, 1932, p. 539.

48 Ibid., 1932, p. 539.

he made the spectator turn, and left the stars at rest."[49] Kant showed that the conditions for the possibility of experience are at the same time the conditions under which the definitive individual objects can alone be said to be for us.

The "Copernican revolution" Kant devised for the theoretical sphere, applies for the practical sphere as well, according to Cassirer. There is also a lawfulness that is rooted in the peculiar basic orientation of the willing itself, that has the power to form the necessity and the universal validity of moral worth.[50] In critical ethics, the will and its object stand in such a relationship, according to Cassirer, that the object, the particular "matter" of desire, determines the will less than will determines the object. The basic concept of Kantian ethics, that is to say, autonomy, as the convergence of theoretical and practical reason, signifies no less than that the will submits to no other rule than that which it has itself set up as a universal norm and proposed to itself.[51] The concept of freedom for Kant thus coincides with the concept of self-legislation, or autonomy.[52]

I. 2. What was the Cassirer–Heidegger Debate from a Jurisprudential Perspective?

According to Cassirer, Kant, in his practical philosophy, went beyond the sort of problems raised by Heidegger. Through his ethics, Kant establishes a breakthrough to the "*mundus intelligibilis*," and "(...) *in the ethical realm Kant suppresses schematism*," *i.e.*, in the practical sphere, the synthetic principle of causality, in virtue of which we simply "*spell out appearances in order to be able to read them as experience*," is not adequate. In Davos, Cassirer asks Heidegger how he can account for the fact that Kant's main problem – in spite of the finitude that Kant

49 Cited by Ernst Cassirer, in: *Encyclopaedia Britannica*, 14th edition, Volume 22: *Textiles to Vascular System*, London/New York, 1929 (*Transcendentalism*), pp. 405–406; here: p. 405.

50 Ernst Cassirer, *Kant's Life and Thought* (*Kants Leben und Lehre*), tr. J. Haden, Yale University Press, New Haven and London, 1981 (1918), p. 240.

51 Ibid., 1981 (1918), p. 243.

52 Ernst Cassirer, *Kant*, in: Encyclopaedia of the Social Sciences, Macmillan, New York, Volume 7, 1932, p. 539.

himself has indicated – was that of the possibility of freedom.[53] To Heidegger, though, the question of how freedom is possible was a nonsense question, "*because freedom is not just another object to be confronted by theoretical knowledge. It can be confronted only in philosophizing. All this can only mean that there is not and cannot be any liberty except in acts of liberation. The only and proper way for man to grasp freedom is this liberation of freedom of man.*"[54] More specifically, for Heidegger, the proper meaning of liberation is man to become free for the finitude of human existence and to enter into the Geworfenheit (thrownness).[55] Here philosophy only has the task of self-liberation, "*of throwing the human being back, from the indolent posture of one who merely uses the works of the spirit, onto the hardness of his fate.*"[56]

Heidegger took as the main theme in the philosophy of Kant the finitude of man. According to Heidegger, man is essentially limited in his cognition, because for him "cognition is primarily intuition," and intuition is merely receptive.[57] In effect, access to the Infinite is impossible for man, and man's orientation toward the transcendent confirms his very finitude, *i.e.*, man cannot escape his finitude.[58] Even the categorical imperative, which is the keystone to the entire Kantian ethical structure, merely exemplifies this finitude, because the concept of an imperative contains, according to Heidegger, an essential reference to a finite creature (as God cannot experience an imperative).[59]

The question then is, "*Which road to infinity is open to man? How can he share in it?*" Cassirer's answer to this question was that this is possible only through the medium of form. "*Just this is the function of that, as existence takes on form, man can experience it as an objective* Gestalt. *Only thus does he radically liberate himself.*" Infinity, according to Cassirer, is "*the totality, the perfect fulfillment of the finite itself.* (...) *In Goethe's words: "Is the infinite your aspiration? Traverse all the finite's*

53 Lynch, 1990, p. 365.
54 Hamburg, 1964, p. 217.
55 Ibid., 1964, p. 219.
56 Cited by: Friedman, 2000, p. 140.
57 Schrag, 1967, p. 89.
58 See: Pos, H.J., *Recollections of Ernst Cassirer*, in: Schilp, 1973, p. 67.
59 See: Friedman, 2000, p. 139.

configurations!"[60] The capacity of man for symbolic formation, not only constitutes a condition of the possibility of freedom, but also implies an inner freedom, energy, or spontaneity of the individual mind. Culture, for Cassirer, is the process of the progressive self-liberation of man. "Progressive" is meant not necessarily in a linear or cumulative sense; it rather implies man's continuously recurring capacity of creating culture through freedom, in the form of liberation from ignorance, oppression, fear and other distress.[61] The ultimate aim of freedom is, according to Cassirer, to rid oneself of all fear of the actual world.[62]

Freedom stands at the center of Kant's philosophy, according to Cassirer, not as a mere indeterminacy from causality of actions, but as a means to give ethical quality to our actions independent from the materiality of what we have willed. For Kant, all *Geistigkeit* ("minding") discloses itself to us in the basic form of the *pure will*.[63] According to Kant, "(...) *the same subject that is conscious of itself also as a thing in itself considers its existence* insofar as it does not stand under temporal conditions. *It considers itself only insofar as it is determinable through laws that it gives itself through reason; and in this kind of existence there is nothing that precedes its determination of will*."[64] Accordingly, Cassirer contends, that reason knows and comprehends itself only in the "*self-determination of the will*;" "*and it is this knowledge that comprises its peculiar, most profound essence*."[65]

Although Kant would agree with Heidegger up to a point, the question remained for Kant, according to Cassirer, of how a finite creature can achieve a conception of entities, which by

---

60 Hamburg, 1964, p. 218; cf. Adams, 1991, pp. 152–155.

61 Ernst Cassirer, *An Essay on Man: An Introduction to a Philosophy of Human Culture*, Yale University Press, New Haven, 1944, p. 228; cf. Recki, 2000, p. 82.

62 Hamburg, 1964, p. 218.

63 See: Ernst Cassirer, *Freiheit und Form. Studien zur deutschen Geistesgeschichte*, Gesammelte Werke Band 7, Felix Meiner Verlag, Hamburg, 1998 (1916), p. 146; cf. Lüddecke, 2003, p. 281.

64 Immanuel Kant, Kritik der praktischen Vernunft (Cassirer edition, V, 107); cited by Ernst Cassirer, *Kant and the Problem of Metaphysics: Remarks on Heidegger's Interpretation of Kant*, in: Gram, 1967, p. 146.

65 Ernst Cassirer, *Kant's Life and Thought* (*Kants Leben und Lehre*), tr. J. Haden, Yale University Press, New Haven and London, 1981 (1918), p. 247.

definition cannot be finite themselves, as represented in the *Critique of Practical reason* and the *Critique of Judgment.* For Heidegger the finitude of human life becomes a kind of curse or fate which humans cannot but accept. For Cassirer, by contrast, "*The human is a finite being, that knows its finitude – and that in this knowledge overcomes its finitude, and becomes certain of its infinitude.*"[66] As Cassirer was later to explicate in his *An Essay on Man*,[67] man is an *animal symbolicum* (a meaning bestowing animal), and through the unique symbolizing character of his consciousness, *i.e.*, through the production of cultural forms, he freely and intersubjectively produces and objectifies meaning. Therewith, he creates freedom, and therefore opens the road for infinitude and ethicality. For Cassirer, man is not merely a receptive being; rather man imbues every sense perception with an original energy or spontaneity of the mind, as exemplified in all symbolic or cultural forms. This makes man (as *animal symbolicum*) a thoroughly expressive and normative being, because through symbolic formation the "I" progressively relates to a "Thou," and creates a unique world.

Cassirer does not object to Heidegger's ennoblement of temporality, rather he criticizes Heidegger's idealization of the temporality of being in disregard of Kant's dualism.[68] This is the real and essential objection of Cassirer: "*While Heidegger tries to relate and indeed to trace back all faculties of knowledge to transcendental imagination, the only thing left to him is the one frame of reference; namely, the framework of temporal existence. The distinction between phenomenon and noumenon is effaced: for all existence belongs now to the dimension of time and thus to finitude. But this removes one of the foundation stones on which Kant's entire position rests and without which that*

---

66 Cited by: Meyer, T., *Am Abgrund wandernd, ins Unbekannte gestoßen. Das Davoser Treffen von Ernst Cassirer und Martin Heidegger hat eine bislang unbekannte Vorgeschichte in Hamburg 1923*, Frankfurter Allgemeine Zeitung, Tuesday, February 21, 2006, nr. 44, p. 45.

67 Ernst Cassirer, *An Essay on Man: An Introduction to a Philosophy of Human Culture*, Yale University Press, New Haven, 1944.

68 See: Aubenque, p., Ferry, L., Rudolph, E.,Courtine, J.-F., Capeillières, *Philosophie und Politik. Die Davoser Disputation zwischen Ernst Cassirer und Martin Heidegger in der Retrospektive,* Internationale Zeitschrift für Philosophie, Volume 1, 1992, pp. 302–303.

position must collapse. Nowhere does Kant contend for such a monism of imagination. Rather, he insists upon a decided and radical dualism, the dualism of the sensuous and intelligible world. For his problem is not the problem of being and time but rather the problem of "is" and "ought," of experience and idea."[69]

For Kant, only the unconditioned character of the moral law, the unconditioned Idea of Freedom, or the categorical imperative, could permanently lift us beyond the circle of merely phenomenal (sensuous and temporal) existence and make us reach out into the purely intelligible order.[70] The distinguishing feature of a categorical imperative from a hypothetical one is that it must not be willed or employed in order that something further, which is presupposed as the end, may be realized, but that it is an unconditional command that has no need to borrow its validity from some further end; that it possesses its own validity by presenting an ultimate, self-evident value. Because this fundamental value is not to be sought in any particular content of willing, but only in its universal lawfulness, the categorical imperative reads as follows. "*Act only according to that maxim by which you can at the same time will that it should become a universal law.*"[71] As a value, no particular determination whatsoever can be assimilated into its substance, nor a single good asserted by it be the supreme good, lest it go straight on to discover another and higher value from which the value first posited would be derived, *i.e.*, the categorical imperative be converted into an hypothetical one. The separation of the *mundus intelligibilis* from the *mundus sensibilis* means that all human existence and all human activities are to be measured by two different modes of orientation and judgment, *i.e.*, two different standards.[72] While a human act in its temporal

---

69 See: Ernst Cassirer, *Kant and the Problem of Metaphysics: Remarks on Heidegger's Interpretation of Kant*, in: Gram, M.S. (ed. and tr.), *Kant: Disputed Questions*, Quadrangle Books, Chicago, 1967, pp. 147–148.

70 Ibid., 1967, pp. 144–145.

71 Immanuel Kant, Foundation of the Metaphysics of Morals, first sect. (IV, 256) (*Ak.* IV, 399–400); cited by: Ernst Cassirer, *Kant's Life and Thought* (*Kants Leben und Lehre*), tr. J. Haden, Yale University Press, New Haven and London, 1981 (1918), p. 245.

72 See: Ernst Cassirer, *Kant and the Problem of Metaphysics: Remarks on Heidegger's Interpretation of Kant*, in: Gram, M.S. (ed. and tr.), *Kant: Disputed Questions*, Quadrangle Books, Chicago, 1967, p. 145.

figuration and its temporal passing is, on the one hand, a joint in a chain of causes and events, what we call nature; on the other hand, it also belongs to the kingdom of ends and should be related to the systematic unity of this kingdom and must be evaluated accordingly.[73]

For Cassirer, Kant's ethical system is not a mere formalism, as is often charged, and inadequate to provide a solution for concrete individual cases and choices; what it does is to provide for a new mode of understanding ethics. Kant's own counter to this objection was: "*A critic who wished to say something against that work really did better than he intended when he said that there was no new principle of morality in it but only a new formula. Who would want to introduce a new principle of morality and, as it were, be its inventor, as if the world had hitherto been ignorant of what duty is or had been thoroughly wrong about it? Those who know what a formula means to a mathematician, in determining what is to be done in solving a problem without letting him go astray, will not regard a formula which will do this for all duties as something insignificant and unnecessary.*"[74] According to Cassirer, Kant's "formalism" draws on a deeper vein of his thought, namely the universal transcendental concept of form that underlies cognition and will alike.[75] "Forms" in the theoretical sphere are definite basic types of relation, which are invariant and constitute the object by producing an objective unity with cognition.

Accordingly, in the practical sphere, the moral worth of an action cannot lie in its hoped-for effect, but only in the principle of the will irrespective of the ends which can be realized by such an action. "*In this sense – and only in this sense – it is "form"*

---

73 Ernst Cassirer, *Determinismus und Indeterminismus in der modernen Physik. Historische und systematische Studien zum Kausalproblem*, in: *Goteborgs Hogskolas Arsskrift*, Volume 42, 1936, p. 251.

74 Immanuel Kant, *Critique of Practical Reason,* preface (V, 8) (*Ak.* V, 8Fn); cited in: Ernst Cassirer, *Kant's Life and Thought* (*Kants Leben und Lehre*), tr. J. Haden, Yale University Press, New Haven and London, 1981 (1918), p. 239.

75 For Cassirer's concept of form, see the introduction by Charles Hendel to: Ernst Cassirer, *The Philosophy of Symbolic Forms*, Volume I, *Language*, tr. R. Manheim, Yale University Press, New Haven, 1953 (1923); see also: Rotenstreich, N., *Schematism and Freedom*, Revue internationale de philosophie, Volume 110, 1974, pp. 464–474.

that is the foundation of the value of good, since it renders possible and consists in, in the one case, the interconnection of empirical perceptions into a system of necessary and a priori knowledge, in the other the unification of particular ends into the unity of a single goal and an enveloping purposiveness."[76] Kant fundamentally rejects any morality based on eudemonism, and subsequently adopts an ethics freed of all empirical principles. In this respect, because his ethics is concerned only with the transcendental form of our ethical experiences, he regards it as the decisive distinction between him and the whole of previous ethics.[77]

As Cassirer comments on Kant's works, "*In the critique of reason, theoretical as well as practical, the idea of reason, the idea of a final and supreme union of knowledge and will is taken for granted. Whoever fails to acknowledge this idea thus excludes himself from the orbit of its manner of posing problems, and from its conceptions of "true" and "false," "good" and "evil," which it alone can substantiate, empowered by its method.*"[78] Ultimately, freedom and the moral, as elements of the categorical imperative, are inscrutable in Kant's view, because they permit of no further questioning as to their "why."[79] The practical unconditional necessity of the moral imperative is incomprehensible by reason, and nothing more "*can be fairly demanded of a philosophy which in its principles strives to reach the limit of human reason.*[80] For Kant, where knowledge ends, "rational moral faith" enters. However, the existence of a Supreme Being does not necessitate morality; rather morality necessitates the existence of God as a moral cause, which we must assume in order to set before ourselves a final purpose in accordance with the moral law. "*The concept of God is the*

---

76 See: Ernst Cassirer, *Kant's Life and Thought* (*Kants Leben und Lehre*), tr. J. Haden, Yale University Press, New Haven and London, 1981 (1918), p. 245.

77 Ibid., 1981 (1918), p. 237.

78 Ibid., 1981 (1918), p. 246.

79 Ibid., 1981 (1918), pp. 261–262.

80 Immanuel Kant, Foundation of the Metaphysics of Morals, third sect. (IV, 324) (*Ak.* IV, 463); cited in: Ernst Cassirer, *Kant's Life and Thought* (*Kants Leben und Lehre*), tr. J. Haden, Yale University Press, New Haven and London, 1981 (1918), p. 263.

concrete form under which we think our intelligible moral task and its progressive empirical fulfillment."[81]

For Cassirer it was Kant's great contribution to have linked freedom explicitly to our ability to create "moral archetypes" for evaluating our particular and local actions.[82] However, for Cassirer and his Marburg teacher Hermann Cohen, religion or the existence of a Supreme Being could no longer provide for the ultimate foundation of ethics. It is only through the individual taking responsibility that ethics achieves its realization. Before we elaborate further on his own conception of ethics, though, it may first be helpful to further explicate Cassirer's exposition of Kantian ethics, so as to contrast it with Heidegger's interpretation.

In Kantian ethics, according to Cassirer, man acts as an intelligent and free personality by placing himself under the law of pure reason, *i.e.*, the categorical imperative. The moral law, though, is not rooted in a feeling of respect, as Heidegger maintains. That would involve a confusion of a psychological with an ethical problem, according to Cassirer. The feeling of respect for the moral law designates merely the way in which the law is represented in the empirical, finite consciousness, *i.e.*, it concerns merely the application of the moral law. Autonomy or the self-legislation of the will in Kantian ethics rather expresses itself through the concept of duty, which constitutes the proper sphere of ethics. "*An action is said to be in accordance with duty only when every thought of advantage to be expected from it, every calculation of present or future pleasure likely to result from it, indeed every material aim of any other kind, is eliminated and only adherence to the universality of the law, which reigns in all contingent and particular impulses, remains as the sole ground of determination.*"[83]

The lawfulness of the pure will belongs to a sphere totally distinct from that of spatio-temporal phenomena. The pure will is ultimately not concerned with a world of things or a set of causally related objects, but with free personalities or a republic of self-

[81] Ibid., 1981 (1918), pp. 264–265.

[82] Cristaudo, 1991, p. 474.

[83] See: Ernst Cassirer, *Kant's Life and Thought* (*Kants Leben und Lehre*), tr. J. Haden, Yale University Press, New Haven and London, 1981 (1918), p. 244.

sufficient subjects united by purpose.[84] Rational beings are designated as "persons," because their nature indicates that they are ends in themselves, *i.e.*, things which may not be used merely as a means. Such a being, for Kant, is an object of respect. "*Thus if there is to be a supreme practical principle and a categorical imperative for the human will, it must be one that forms an objective principle of the will from the conception of that which is necessarily an end for everyone because it is an end in itself. ... The practical imperative, therefore, is the following: Act so that you treat humanity, whether in your own person or in that of another, always as an end and never as a means only.*"[85]

As Cassirer explains, while the order of means coincides with the order of natural things, the order of ends coincides with that of pure, self-determined, intelligent beings. The rational being that universally legislates by the maxims of its will so as to judge itself and its actions from this perspective, correlatively belongs to a community of rational beings in a "realm of ends."[86] As far as we know ourselves as a person, *i.e.*, conscious of the moral law, we know ourselves as belonging to the purely intelligible world, and, moreover, with a determination of the way in which we can be active as such.[87] Consequently, for Kant, the problem was of how the freedom of each individual has to limit itself in such a way that it permits and confirms the freedom of everyone else in so doing.[88] Accordingly, it is the greatest problem for the human race and the greatest concrete task placed before it to attain a society based upon the universal law, *i.e.*, to found a society not on a mere relationship of might, that of rulers and ruled, but on the principle to consider "*every*

---

84 Ibid., 1981 (1918), p. 247.

85 Immanuel Kant, Foundation of the Metaphysics of Morals, first sect. (IV, 286–287) (*Ak.* IV, 427–429); cited in: Ernst Cassirer, *Kant's Life and Thought* (*Kants Leben und Lehre*), tr. J. Haden, Yale University Press, New Haven and London, 1981 (1918), p. 248.

86 Ibid., 1981 (1918), pp. 248–249.

87 Immanuel Kant, Kritik der praktischen Vernunft (Cassirer edition, V, 107); referred to by: Ernst Cassirer, *Kant and the Problem of Metaphysics : Remarks on Heidegger's Interpretation of Kant*, in: Gram, M.S. (ed. and tr.), *Kant: Disputed Questions*, Quadrangle Books, Chicago, 1967, p. 146.

88 See: Ernst Cassirer, *Kant's Life and Thought* (*Kants Leben und Lehre*), tr. J. Haden, Yale University Press, New Haven and London, 1981 (1918), p. 373.

one of its members as an end in himself, as a free agent who participates in the constitution and the administration of the whole and who to that extends heeds the laws only because he has given them to himself."[89]

In his ethical theory, Cassirer gives a particular turn to Kantian ethics, in accordance with the Marburg teachings of Hermann Cohen. For Cassirer, the idea of autonomy includes "autotely."[90] Accordingly, by referring to Cohen, Cassirer writes: "*ethically self-dependent and worthy is only such action that is directed to the realization of a society, in which the single individual that belongs to it is "always simultaneously an end in itself, never a mere means."*[91] Freedom for Cassirer is a regulative idea. It is an unending task for the individual; in order to have it the individual must create it for himself through his own actions, *i.e.*, by working toward a society or context wherein he is foremost an end in himself. Every individual has the responsibility to create freedom for himself. "*Men act as free agents not because they possess a* liberum arbitrium indifferentiae. *It is not the absence of a motive but the character of the motives that marks a free action. In the ethical sense a man is a free agent if these motives depend upon his own judgment and conviction of what moral duty is.*"[92] "*According to Kant freedom (...) does not mean "indeterminism," it rather means a special kind of determination. It means that the law which we obey in our actions is not imposed from without but that the moral subject gives the law itself.*"[93]

Moreover, as is explicated in Part II, for the symbolic nature of man it is no longer sufficient to consider man as a mere rational being. Here, it is not primarily an ethics of symbolism Cassirer propagates, but foremost the proposition that a reasonable action be at the same time persuasive. What is impor-

---

89 Ernst Cassirer, *Kant*, in: Encyclopaedia of the Social Sciences, Macmillan, New York, Volume 7, 1932, p. 540.

90 Ernst Cassirer, *Kant*, in: Encyclopaedia of the Social Sciences, Macmillan, New York, Volume 7, 1932, p. 539.

91 See: Ernst Cassirer, *Hermann Cohen und die Erneuerung der Kantischen Philosophie*, Kantstudien, Band 17, Berlin, 1912, pp. 252–273; here: p. 269.

92 Ernst Cassirer, *The Myth of the State*, Yale University Press, New Haven, 1945, p. 361.

93 Ibid., 1945, pp. 361–362.

tant is that an individual considers an action meaningful. Through meaningful actions the "I" becomes aware of its own humanity by considering the humanity of the other, *i.e.*, when the "He" is prevented from becoming an "It," and becomes a "You," hence also an "I."[94]

II. CONCLUSION

This chapter has given a reassessment of the Davos debate between Cassirer and Heidegger. It has made clear that in contrast to Heidegger's representation and pursuance of Kantian philosophy, Cassirer's interpretation of Kantian philosophy and his indebtedness to neo-Kantianism does not preclude the road to ethics. This chapter has already alluded to the fact that Cassirer's philosophy of symbolic forms is a truly ethical theory, insofar as it can be understood as explaining the ethical structures of culture, *i.e.*, how the "I" (through myth, language, religion, science and so forth) progressively relates to a "Thou." In fine, it is obvious that what we have called here "the Davos debate" involved the clash of two different conceptions of philosophy or even eras, *i.e.*, between humanist philosophy and the existentialist, non-humanist philosophy of the new era.[95] Both traditions were aware of the presence and the appeal or force of one another. Looking back one could say that Cassirer did whatever he could to temper the growing influence that the latter, or what he termed life philosophy, gained.[96] Heidegger's insistence on the finitude of man, man's "fate" (*Schicksal*), man being "thrown" (*Geworfen*) into his "destiny" (*Geschick*), and as

---

[94] See especially: Chapter 9 for Cassirer's indebtedness to Cohen in this respect.

[95] Cohen, 2002; see also: the introduction to Levinas, E., *Humanism of the Other*, tr. N. Poller, Illinois University Press, Chicago, 2003; cf. Krois, 1983, p. 147; and Lipton, 1978, pp. 156–159.

[96] For the relationship between life philosophy and fascism, see: Neocleous, 1997, pp. 2–4; 12 ff.; see also: Lukács, G., *Die Zerstörung der Vernunft*, 3. Auflage, Berlin/Weimar, 1984. On life philosophy as a tradition of German philosophy see: Schnädelbach, 1991, p. 176; cf. Scherer, 1996, pp. 158–159, 391n. For some recent monographs on life philosophy, see also: Albert, 1995; Fellmann, 1993; Grossheim, 1991; Grossheim, 1994.

such being delivered over to the destiny of the truth of being, made Heidegger particularly appealing to the pre-pro-Nazi-public, who were already under the spell of defeat, globalizing unemployment, and accompanying experience of powerlessness.[97] Weimar has shown the world, that belief in fate is incompatible with democratic thought, that no democracy can exist between human beings, who feel unable to influence their conditions of life, and that without the sober belief in one's own modest faculty of acting independent from the determinations of fate, there cannot be a democracy.[98] Democracy therefore calls for democratic philosophers.[99]

The defeatist and pessimistic tonality of Heidegger's philosophy constitutes a persisting point of criticism of Cassirer. Heidegger is religiously inspired by Luther and Kierkegaard, but religion as well as philosophy, serve merely to substantiate Heidegger's position, which is nothing less than a secular form of eschatology.[100] It is no coincidence that Heidegger reviewed Cassirer's second volume of the philosophy of symbolic forms on myth. Through his philosophy of symbolic forms, in particular when he refers to myth, Cassirer sought to countenance the fatalistic account of life philosophy, of which Heidegger was an important representative. Heidegger persists to view man as the *terminus a quo*, but a philosophical system that puts the human being central only as *terminus a quo*, and not as *terminus a quo*

---

97 Cf. Baumgardt, 1947, pp. 223–237.

98 See: Steinvoth, U., *Demokratisches denken in der Weimarer Philosophie*, in: Gusy, 1994, pp. 96–114; here: pp. 113–114; cf. Coskun, D., *De ethiek van de rechter*, Ernst Cassirer, de politiek en de rechterlijke macht in Weimar ("*The ethics of the judge*. Ernst Cassirer, politics, and the judiciary in Weimar"), Trema, tijdschrift voor de rechterlijke macht (Trema, journal for the judiciary), March 2005, pp. 108–112.

99 As Edmond Cahn puts it, "*We shall always welcome visitors of every persuasion to our cultural salon, but such hospitality is not inconsistent with counting the democratic silver after they have departed.*" See: Cahn, E.N., *Goethe's View of law – With a Gloss out of Plato*, Columbia Law Review, Volume 49, No. 7 (Nov., 1949), pp. 904–920; here: p. 920.

100 The same has been said for National Socialism by Richard Karwehl, which, however, could be understood only in its "*opposition to the eschatology of (Marxist) socialism.*" See: Karwehl, R., *Politisches Messiastum. Zur Auseinandersetzung zwischen Kirche und Nationalsozialismus*, in: Zwischen der Zeiten, München, 1931 (9), pp. 519–543; here: p. 539; referred to by Lübbe, 2003, p. 108; 133.

and *terminus ad quem* simultaneously, cannot guarantee human dignity.[101] Moreover, humanity trapped in the history of being, freedom as a mere contingency, as Heidegger envisions, surrenders man's destiny to history and out of the rule by universal standards of truth and morality.[102] In effect, man loses his basis for self-respect.[103]

In later works, especially during his exile, Cassirer connects Heidegger's thought with the intellectual climate of National Socialism. Cassirer does not hold Heidegger's thoughts responsible for the events of the 1930s and the Second World War, but he does contend that Heidegger contributed influentially to the failure of philosophy to fulfill its primary duty.[104] According to Albert Schweitzer, philosophy has the duty to watch over and inform humanity of its cultural ideals, but "*the watchman slept, who should have kept watch over us.*" Cassirer maintains, moreover, that the watchman did not merely "sleep," but assisted, as an interested and supporting bystander, in the robbery of Western culture. Peter Gay has stated this more precisely: "*Among these prophets, Heidegger was perhaps the most unlikely candidate to influence. But his influence was far-reaching, far wider than his philosophical seminar at the University of Marburg, far wider than might seem possible in light of his inordinately obscure book,* Sein und Zeit *of 1927, far wider than Heidegger himself, with his carefully cultivated solitude and unconcealed contempt for other philosophers, appeared to wish. (...) What Heidegger did was to give philosophical seriousness, professional respectability, to the love affair with unreason and death that dominated so many Germans in this hard time.*"[105]

---

101 Cf. Orth, E.-W., *Goethe als Therapeutikum. Zu Ernst Cassirers Pathologie des Symbolischen*, in: Naumann, 2002, pp. 137–156; here: p. 143.

102 Cf. Cohen, 2002; see also: the introduction to Levinas, E., *Humanism of the Other*, tr. N. Poller, Illinois University Press, Chicago, 2003.

103 See: Ernst Cassirer, *Symbol, Myth, and Culture, Essays and Lectures of Ernst Cassirer 1935-1945*, edited by Verene, D.P., Yale University Press, New Haven, 1979, pp. 40–41.

104 See: Chapter 4.

105 Gay, 1968, pp. 81–82; cf. the introduction by Donald Philip Verene in: *Symbol, Myth, and Culture, Essays and Lectures of Ernst Cassirer 1935–1945*, edited by Verene, D.P., Yale University Press, New Haven, 1979, pp. 41–42, 52n.

Whereas Cassirer remained the advocate of law and reason in Weimar until the end, Heidegger, more than three months after the Nazis came to power, accepted rectorship of Freiburg University and openly endorsed the Nazi regime and its ideology. Heidegger's inaugural speech of 1933 was entitled *Die Selbstbehauptung der deutschen Üniversität* (The Self-assertion of the German University), but in fact it propagated the surrender of the German university to the Fuehrer, *i.e.*, to politics. Cassirer distinguished himself (again exemplarily) from Heidegger, when he as rector of Hamburg University on the celebration of Constitution Day on July 22, 1930, had cautioned his public to defend the academic character of the university from political claims and intrusions. As an interrelation, a series of political intrusions in academic life and Cassirer's anticipation of them, *i.e.*, the Nazi law that prohibited the commission of Jews in public institutions, ultimately forced Cassirer to flee Germany.

CHAPTER 3

CASSIRER IN EXILE: AN ESSAY ON THE RECOVERY OF INDIVIDUAL MORAL JUDGMENT

I. INTRODUCTION

In this chapter we follow Cassirer's life in exile, and focus on his development to a more systematically elaborate and explicit stance in matters pertaining to moral philosophy, jurisprudence, and political science. Cassirer's life in exile consisted of three periods. First, his period in England, where, from the summer of 1933 onwards, he spent 2 years teaching the history of philosophy at All Souls College at Oxford. Of particular relevance is Cassirer's meeting in Oxford with Albert Schweitzer, who made Cassirer realize the urgency or necessity for philosophy to fulfill its normative task. Second, his period in Sweden from September 1935 until May 1939 is an important period for Cassirer, because it gives him the opportunity to elaborate more specifically on his ethical and jurisprudential views. Through his philosophy of symbolic forms, Cassirer tried to answer the question, "*Are there general binding supra-individual, supra-state, supra-national ethical claims?*"[1] Cassirer's affirmative answer to this question confronts the prevalent emotive theory of the Scandinavian realist Axel Hägerström at his level of sophistication. Moreover, it provides the starting point for our specific investigation into law as a symbolic form. We will elaborate on Law as Symbolic Form and Cassirer's period in Sweden in Chapter 7, and in this chapter focus on the contribution of ancient Greek thought and the Cambridge Platonists to the development of the idea of justice as an *a priori* principle, its relation to individual moral judgment, and, as is elaborated

---

[1] Ernst Cassirer, *Symbol, Myth, and Culture, Essays and Lectures of Ernst Cassirer 1935–1945*, edited by Verene, D.P., Yale University Press, New Haven, 1979, p. 61.

below, hence to Law as Symbolic Form. Finally, his period in the United States, where he taught at Yale from 1941 to 1944, and at Columbia, beginning in the fall of 1944 until the spring of 1945.[2] In his books *An Essay on Man*[3] and *The Myth of the State*[4] Cassirer attempts to come to terms with and give a diagnosis of the crisis in Western culture. We focus on Cassirer's pathology of the totalitarian state in Chapter 4, and in this chapter elaborate on the question of how the nineteenth century contributed to the dismemberment of the individual, foremost through the suspension of individual moral judgment.

During his stay in Oxford, Cassirer came into contact with a number of academicians who were in the same predicament; academicians who made one remember the old or ideal Germany. Among them were internationally prominent representatives of the German academic life, such as Gilbert Murray, Albert Einstein, and Erwin Schrödinger. All of them, in different ways, had to cope with the situation of a sudden end to their once reciprocal relations with Germany. Cassirer expressed his feelings, first, by declaring never to write a single page again in the face of the futility of his works, and, later, by deciding to write a philosophical refutation of the National Socialist movement.[5] Of particular importance, in this regard, was Cassirer's acquaintance with Albert Schweitzer, who was not in forced exile but, through his charitable works as a doctor in the jungles of West Africa, had followed and analyzed the developments in Europe from a unique perspective. For Schweitzer as well as for Cassirer it was important to understand the destructive forces of Western culture and the task philosophy had of protecting Western civilization.

According to Schweitzer, contemporary philosophy displayed an obvious moral deficit by disregarding the normative dimension of cultural life, and in particular its relation to the individual and its moral reason. Philosophy rather has to focus on the individual and the constant social forces that work upon him, especially through such phenomena as "collective thought" and

---

2 See: Krois, 1987, pp. 28–31.

3 Ernst Cassirer, *An Essay on Man: An Introduction to a Philosophy of Human Culture*, Yale University Press, New Haven, 1944.

4 Ernst Cassirer, *The Myth of the State*, Yale University Press, New Haven, 1945.

5 Paetzold, 1995, p. 151.

nationalism, and the dangers that accompany them. Before explaining the importance of Cassirer's encounter with Schweitzer, though, the next section focuses on the contribution of the Cambridge School of Platonism to the development of the idea of justice as an *a priori* principle, and its connection to the individual moral judgment. Not only was the Platonic Renaissance in England an important source of inspiration for developments that contributed to such projects as the separation of church and state in America,[6] also it proved an important force in countenancing the Hobbesian view of the state, the Hobbesian view of law vis-à-vis the state, and his view of the state's relation to the individual.

Moreover, Cassirer's study of the meritable contribution the Cambridge Platonists made to the development of the idea of justice in opposition to theological dogmatism and state absolutism makes clear why Cassirer did not have difficulty later in his life to take a practical philosophical and jurisprudential position; in several instances throughout his oeuvre he had already prepared and anticipated this. Cambridge Platonism was particularly interested in theological questions and their religious skepticism distinguished them from the Florentine Academy. Furthermore, it was exactly what the Cambridge Platonists viewed essential in their practical philosophy, that is to say, the *a priori* character of justice, hence its conceptual connection to individual moral judgment, which marked the starting point of Cassirer's critique of the nineteenth century philosophical thought, as ignited by the ethical zeal of Schweitzer. As a result, Cassirer fundamentally agrees with Schweitzer's critique of the nineteenth century and its dismemberment of the individual, but Cassirer foremost criticizes Hegel, with his fatalistic account of culture and the pessimistic role he accords to the individual. Nevertheless, Cassirer does not completely discard nineteenth century philosophical thought, because in the works of Wilhelm von Humboldt Cassirer finds fruitful soil to set up a neo-humanist philosophy of culture, and in and through Goethe Cassirer finds the perfect poetic expression of the ideal of individuality. Finally, in twentieth century life philosophy Cassirer perceives a latent

---

6 Cf. Coskun, D., *Religious Skepticism, Cambridge Platonism, and Disestablishment,* University of Detroit Mercy law Review, Symposium Issue, Volume 83, forthcoming (2007); see also: McConnell, 2003, p. 2121 ff.; cf. Cobb, 1970 (1902), p. 156; and Meyer, 1930, pp. 5–6.

danger that represents a continuing tendency toward fatalism, as well as a susceptibility to mythical thought. With that we have already anticipated Cassirer's political pathology, which is the theme of Chapter 4.

This chapter proceeds as follows. First, in Section I.1, we address the question of what was the Cambridge School of Platonism. Furthermore, in Section I.2 we elaborate on the ancient Greek conception of justice and its culmination in Plato's works. In addition, in Section I.3 we explain the Cambridge Platonists' stance toward the idea of justice and its relation to human self-understanding. Moreover, in Section I.4 we link the insights of the Cambridge Platonists as to the *a priori* nature of justice and as it was inspired by ancient Greek thought, to Schweitzer's diagnosis of Western culture. In addition, after establishing the philosophical friendship of Cassirer and Schweitzer and their common interest in culture, in Section I.5, we explicate the particular direction Cassirer's critique of nineteenth century thought took in his neo-humanistic founding of culture. Finally, in the conclusion, we not only give an assessment of the results of this chapter, but also allude to the subject of the next chapter: Cassirer's pathology of the totalitarian state.

I. 1. What was the Cambridge School of Platonism?

It was typical of Cassirer, writes James P. Pettegrove, the translator of *The Platonic Renaissance in England*, that he chose as the subject of his first lecture at All Souls College the Greek origins of the idea of justice. "*At Oxford with characteristic patience and cheerfulness he resumed, in an alien tongue, his interrupted studies.* (...) *throughout the year, neither his personal remarks nor his lectures reflected in any way the threats and indignities that reached him daily from his homeland. On the contrary, his words and actions were full of that devotion to reasonableness and tolerance, to justice and truth, which is part of the precious heritage of the modern world from the English Platonists* (...)."[7] His ideas concerning the

[7] See: Ernst Cassirer, *The Platonic Renaissance in England* (*Die platonische Renaissance in England und die Schule von Cambridge*, B.G. Teubner, Leipzig, 1932), tr. James P. Pettegrove, University of Texas Press, Austin, 1953, translator's forward, p. v.

Greek origins of the idea of justice appeared later as *Logos, Dike, Kosmos in der Entwicklung der griechischen Philosophie* (Logos, Dike, Kosmos in the Development of Greek Philosophy),[8] and is further elaborated in the unpublished manuscript *Die Idee des Rechts und ihre Entwicklung in der modernen Philosophie* (The Idea of Law and its Development in Modern Philosophy).[9] Together with the following two sections we explicate here the connection between the idea of justice in ancient Greek culture and that of the English Platonists, *i.e.*, the *a priori* nature of justice and its relation to individual moral judgment, so as to anticipate Schweitzer's and Cassirer's lamentation of the nineteenth century from the perspective of Enlightenment-inspired thinking. We now turn to the question of what was the Cambridge School of Platonism. For that purpose we first give a depiction of Renaissance thought, as it was the precursor of the Platonic Renaissance in England.

The Renaissance represented a transition and a new equilibrium, by introducing a new dynamic that heretofore had remained merely latent and never expressed in full force and concreteness. From the beginning of the fifteenth century onward the individual asserts himself as that new force, and slowly the balance between other forces, such as society, state, religion, church, art, and science, begins to shift. Renaissance thought effectuated a new relation between the general and the individual, or the universal and the particular.[10] Before the Renaissance the human being pictured itself only as a race, people, party, corporation, family or any other form of generality.[11] What the Renaissance initiated was a revolution through its discovery of the individual as a *creative* being and by giving the creative

---

8 Ernst Cassirer, *Logos, Dike, Kosmos in der Entwicklung der griechischen Philosophie*, Göteborgs Hogskolas Arsskrift, Volume 37, 1941, pp. 1–31.

9 See: Ernst Cassirer, *Die Idee des Rechts und ihre Entwicklung in der modernen Philosophie*, Ernst Cassirer Papers, Essays and Lectures, Beinecke Rare Book & Manuscripts Library, Coll. No. GEN 98, Series No. II, Box No. 43, Folder No. 845.

10 See: Ernst Cassirer, *Some Remarks on the Question of the Originality of the Renaissance,* Journal of the History of Ideas, Volume 4, 1943, pp. 49–56; here: p. 55.

11 See: Ernst Cassirer, *Individuum und Kosmos in der Philosophie der Renaissance* (1927) 2., unveränderte Auflage, Wissenschaftliche Buchgesellschaft, 1963, p. 37.

individual an independent *locus standi* in all aspects of cultural life. The assertion of the significance of individual life would find support in ancient thought, but for that purpose it moved even beyond Greek thought, *i.e.*, qualitatively.

The Renaissance (and with it modernity) was initiated by the Platonic Academy in Florence. The goal of the Florentine Academy, as set by its founder Marsilio Ficino (1433–1499), was the philosophical proof of the fundamental truths of Christianity.[12] However, revelation by the religious thinkers of the Renaissance is no longer understood in a strictly "orthodox" narrow and dogmatic sense. Revelation admits of many interpretations, and all of them will lead therein to the same end, to the knowledge of God.[13] "*We can enjoy the divine mind,*" Ficino says, "*through various ideas, see it through various traces (vestigia), travel toward that goal by various paths. God so disposed the intellectual eyes and the tendencies of various Souls in different manners, in order that we may approach the different possessions of the manifold divine goods by different paths.*"[14] In this respect, the Florentine Academy eschews and brings to fruition ideas that were introduced by the Humanists, who had mainly taken literary and philological interest in the ancients.

According to Cassirer, it was the German philosopher Nicholas of Cusa (1401–1464) who originated the idea that the plurality of religious viewpoints and configurations need not result in mere tolerance and peaceful coexistence, but that this plurality itself signifies the power of religious belief. The latter may differ in its concrete expressions, but nevertheless maintains its basic direction.[15] Cusa writes, "(…) *because all dispositions and usages are mere sensible signs, not the signified subject to replacement and change.*" Whenever the Divine is

---

[12] See: Ernst Cassirer, *Giovanni Pico della Mirandola, A Study in the History of Renaissance Ideas*, Journal of the History of Ideas, Volume 3, 1942, pp. 319–346; here: 335.

[13] Ernst Cassirer, *Ficino's Place in Intellectual History* (Book Review), Journal of the History of Ideas, Volume 6, 1942, pp. 483–501; here: pp. 495–496.

[14] Ibid., 1942, p. 496.

[15] See: Ernst Cassirer, *Individuum und Kosmos in der Philosophie der Renaissance* (1927) 2., unveränderte Auflage, Wissenschatliche Buchgesellschaft, 1963, pp. 31–32.

worshipped, according to Cusa, there the idea of the Divine is at the same time presupposed. No single viewpoint possesses the truth, because the truth for Cusa consists only in the totality of viewpoints of the Divine. The world, for Cusa, becomes the symbol of God.[16] The Renaissance would take up this symbolic nature of religious knowledge and extend it to all aspects of culture, so as to set up a worldview independent of religious thought, but nevertheless still saturated by its symbolism.

What was a principle of negative theology for Cusa, becomes a positive principle for Giovanni Pico della Mirandola (1463–1494), author of the "*Oratio de hominis dignitate.*"[17] Pico also sees the Many as expressions, as images, as symbols of the One.[18] But Pico goes further, because for him, "*Neither word nor picture, neither rite nor any other external action can exhaust the deepest meaning of the religious.*"[19] Whatever is substantial and sacramental dissolves and becomes intimation, an image of something purely spiritual, according to Pico. It is the task of man to search for this spiritual truth for his own. What Pico defends and advocates is a new ideal of human freedom. Pico's ideal of freedom not only makes possible, but at the same time demands a new form of "individualism." The individual cannot merely accept an already assigned, *i.e.*, a fixed and determined position, rather he must seek his position independently. "*This search is not only his right, it is his duty: in his pursuit of it he must not be hindered?*"[20] In this respect, Pico not only rejects any compulsion in matters of faith, but also finds it ineffective and futile. "*For it is not in man's power to accept or reject a proposition of faith on external command.*"[21]

The human intellect attains to truth, be it philosophical or be it religious, by an active inquiry, that is to say, that human intellect itself must produce the conviction of a proposition before an individual can appropriate a proposition internally.

---

16 Ibid. (1927), 1963, p. 38.

17 See: Ernst Cassirer, *Giovanni Pico della Mirandola, A Study in the History of Renaissance Ideas*, Journal of the History of Ideas, Volume 3, 1942, pp. 319–346; here: 322.

18 Ibid., 1942, pp. 123–144; here: p. 138.

19 Ibid., 1942, p. 139.

20 Ibid., 1942, pp. 327–328.

21 Ibid., 1942, p. 328.

For that purpose, the conviction of the truth of a certain proposition must rest on determinate grounds. This explains in part the constant inner restlessness of man, for Pico, because man cannot merely passively accept his surroundings, but gives to it his own form. Especially the Arts express for Pico the paradigmatic and distinguishing factor of mankind as a whole. Man becomes the "sculptor" that brings forth and shapes his own form. In this respect Cassirer remarks, for Pico, "*Beauty becomes* (...) *the "symbol of morality": for in the capacity of man to produce from himself a world of forms, there is expressed his innate freedom.*"[22]

Accordingly, the deciding factor that confers on man his exceptional and privileged position in relation to the rest of nature is that "*he owes his moral character to himself – and he derives from himself the pattern he shall follow.*" Therefore, the likeness of man to God does not consist of an impressed upon seal on his soul, or that he is created after the image of God. The likeness and resemblance to God is rather something to be worked out, an achievement toward which to strive; "*it is* to be brought about *by man himself.*" It is exactly his ability to bring about what he has set out for himself that is the highest gift man owes to Divine grace.[23] For Pico, the dignity of man "*consists in the fact that the work of man is the expression of his own will, not the influence of the stars and the gift of higher powers.*"[24] In the quality of his creative capacities man feels himself most intimately related to God.[25] For Pico this contention is not curbed even by the doctrine of original sin, which is maintained characteristically and strictly by scholastic theology. For Pico, "*Man must be capable of sin, that he may become capable of good.*"[26] Neither sin, nor good can be the end point for man, according to Pico, because the human predicament is characterized exactly by the constant struggle of man to choose between good and evil. Pico sees the perfect expression of human nature in the fact, that "*The way to both lies ever open before him – and the decision is placed within his own power.*"

---

22 Ibid., 1942, p. 333.
23 Ibid., 1942, pp. 320–321.
24 Ibid., 1942, p. 344.
25 Ibid., 1942, p. 336.
26 Ibid., 1942, p. 329.

Man must forever confront the *problem* of good and evil, and its solution can only come from his own powers and independent judgment. Because he must constantly seek his own path, the uncertainty of making his own choices between good and evil renders him out of the realm of security that befalls upon the rest of nature. But at the same time his capacity to choose his own path, to choose his own form of life, constitutes the greatness of man, according to Pico. "*Man can arrive at the highest only if he does not restrain this power of self-moulding he feels in himself, but allows it free scope in every direction; and this mutability, taken as the power of self-formation, constitutes his greatness.*"[27] Human freedom for Pico consists in the fact that man molds his own life and that for this molding he must perform an inner struggle and in a sense "*make trial of the most varied spheres of existence.*"[28] In this respect the doctrine that the Florentine Academy most vehemently opposes is that of the "immortality of the soul" and its ascetic import.[29] Accordingly, the concern for the moral life *in this world* constitutes the pinnacle principle that is constructively pursued in all its ramifications by the Cambridge Platonists.

The main representatives of the Cambridge School of Platonism were Benjamin Whichcote (1609–1683), Henry More (1614–1687), Ralph Cudworth (1617–1688), John Smith (1618–1652), and Nathaniel Culverwel (1619–1651), and also included Joseph Glanvill (1638–1680) and John Norris (1657–1711).[30] The Cambridge School of Platonism is usually regarded as the most important representative of 'rational theology', as it developed in seventeenth century England.[31] In that interpretation of the

---

27 Ibid., 1942, p. 333.

28 Ibid., 1942, p. 332.

29 See: Ernst Cassirer, *The Platonic Renaissance in England* (*Die platonische Renaissance in England und die Schule von Cambridge*, B.G. Teubner, Leipzig, 1932), tr. James P. Pettegrove, University of Texas Press, Austin, 1953, p. 18.

30 Cragg, 1968, pp. 3–7.

31 Tulloch, J., *Rational Theology and Christian Philosophy in England in the Seventeenth Century*, in two volumes, Edinburgh and London, 1872; Volume II is entitled 'The Cambridge Platonists.' See: Ernst Cassirer, *The Platonic Renaissance in England* (*Die platonische Renaissance in England und die Schule von Cambridge*, B.G. Teubner, Leipzig, 1932), tr. James P. Pettegrove, University of Texas Press, Austin, 1953, p. 4.

Cambridge Platonists, their significance for the history of ethics usually is subsumed under the history of theology. However, according to Cassirer, that does not do justice to the real influence of the Cambridge School on later centuries, as well as the intellectual setting in which it originated.

English humanism exhibited important differences from Continental humanism, especially from the Italian model.[32] Whereas the Florentine Academy looked upon (institutionalized) religion with a cool and deliberate skepticism and pushed on to the struggle against Christian ethics and the Christian way of life, in England, humanism never directed its skepticism against religion.[33] Their skepticism rather worked for the improvement of religion by combating scholastic systems and 'barbaric' forms of theological learning as represented by the various strains of the English Puritan movement. This was already exemplified very early in Thomas More's (1478–1535) *Utopia*, which for the first time, according to Cassirer, maintained and promulgated a "religion within the bounds of reason." More's supreme legislator in *Utopia* would not make any stipulation concerning religion, because he was not sure whether God Himself does not intend manifold and diverse forms of worship, and hence give to some this and to others that form of religious interpretation. The universal grounds, the *a priori* of religion the Florentine Platonists had reconstructed, becomes "*the instrument with which the Cambridge thinkers attack the whole intellectual world, and by means of which they seek to undermine on the one hand the central position of English empiricism and on the other the views of the orthodox church system and of several religious sects.*"[34] As

---

32 Ibid., 1953 (1932), p. 11.

33 The humanism in Italy, next to the more imaginative and religious strain of Platonic humanism of the Florentine Academy, was characterized by a naturalistic, Aristotelian humanism that was widespread and rapidly gained in strength; see: Cassirer, E., Kristeller, P.A., and J.H. Randall (eds.), *The Renaissance Philosophy of Man, Petrarca, Valla, Ficino, Pico, Pomponazzi, Vives*, The University of Chicago Press, Chicago, Illinois, 3rd, 1954, p. 11. Ibid., 1954, p. 18: The secular "this-worldly" morality of the Florentine Academy can be explained primarily by their opposition against the doctrine of the immortality of the soul.

34 See: Ernst Cassirer, *The Platonic Renaissance in England* (*Die platonische Renaissance in England und die Schule von Cambridge*, B.G. Teubner,

religious moralists they hold that religious conviction should be subordinated to the law of sufficient reason, that is to say that faith can and should exist only after examination and justification by reason. While all truths of religion are attainable only with the aid of divine grace, *i.e.*, the super-rational, nevertheless, religious faith must be in accordance with such rationality so as to provide persuasive grounds for believing.[35]

The philosophy of religion of the Cambridge School should not be equated, according to Cassirer, with the theological rationalism that permeated the systems of English deism in the eighteenth century and German philosophy of the Enlightenment. Although deism is the direct result of the insistence of the Cambridge School of Platonism that faith should be in harmony with reason, rationality was not its primary concern. The Cambridge Platonists rather established a shift of emphasis in religious matters from the object to the subject, "*from sacrament and dogma to moral attitude and conviction.*"[36] Henry More's (1614–1687) '*Enchiridion ethicum*' forms the principal ethical work of the Cambridge School.

"*To estimate the fruit of virtue by that imaginary knowledge of it which is acquired by mere definition, is very much the same as if one were to estimate the nature of fire from a fire painted on the wall. ... Every vital good is perceived and judged by life and sense. ... If you have ever* been *this, you have* seen *this.*"

Goethe's saying, '*Wie einer ist, so ist sein Gott*' ('as a man is, so is his God'), is also maintained and developed in all its implications by the Cambridge School.[37] Religion itself, according to the Cambridge Platonists remains always the same. What

---

Leipzig, 1932), tr. James P. Pettegrove, University of Texas Press, Austin, 1953, pp. 23–24.

35 Ibid., 1953 (1932), pp. 38–40.

36 Ibid., 1953 (1932), p. 41.

37 'Such as Men themselves are, such will God himself seem to be' (John Smith 'Of the True Way or Method of Attaining to Divine Knowledge,' *Select Discourses*, ed. Worthington, London, 1660, p. 5); see: Ernst Cassirer, *The Platonic Renaissance in England* (*Die platonische Renaissance in England und die Schule von Cambridge*, B.G. Teubner, Leipzig, 1932), tr. James P. Pettegrove, University of Texas Press, Austin, 1953, pp. 31–32.

is subject to change is thought and speech about religion. According to Cassirer, it was already Cusa who introduced into modern philosophy that between the subject and the object of religious knowledge, between man and God, there is a correlation and reciprocity. Cusa maintains that God is for every man what he perceives God to be, and that the form of this perception depends on that of the individual.

What this insight amounts to and means, though, is already made clear, according to Cassirer, in and by early Greek philosophy, *i.e.*, that at the moment the human being achieves a new sense of self, the representation of the divine must change as well. It must likewise be refined into a purer form. And vice versa, the refined conception of the heavenly subsequently reflects itself in man's self-conception.[38] Moreover, because it functioned as the center and focus point of its society, the idea of justice in early Greek philosophy and poetry influentially shaped Greek theogony and therefore its understanding of the human predicament. We now turn to the contribution of Greek culture to the development of the idea of justice as an *a priori* principle from a theogonic perspective. Next, we consider the critical pursuance of that *a priori* principle by the Cambridge Platonists in their struggle against Puritan dogmatism and Hobbesian absolutism.

I. 2. What was the Contribution of Greek Culture?

In the history of Western civilization ancient Greek culture was the first to appreciate justice as an eternal and unchanging phenomenon. Through philosophy, according to Cassirer, Greek culture for the first time in the history of mankind managed to establish a synthesis between theoretical and practical reason, between truth and justice, between Logos and Diké, by relating them to a common root, *i.e.*, Kosmos or the cosmological order, and thereby giving them both, justice as well as truth, features common to the cosmological order.[39] For the Greeks the natural order was not created *ex nihilo*. Although Aristotelian physics

---

[38] See: Ernst Cassirer, *Logos, Dike, Kosmos in der Entwicklung der griechischen Philosophie*, Göteborgs Hogskolas Arsskrift, Volume 37, 1941, pp. 16–17.

[39] Ibid., 1941, pp. 19–20.

considers God as the "initial mover," it never questions the origins of matter. In the words of Heraclites, "*This world order, that is the same for all beings, was not created by any god or by any man, rather it was always there and it is and it will always be.*"[40] By relating justice to the cosmological order, by equating it with the thought of the unbecoming truth and the unbecoming nature, it acquired the characteristic of being unalterable: "*a postulate that seems to contradict every experience, but which "reason" again and again constructs and maintains.*"[41]

Logos and Diké do not depart from each other, because both are recognized as *kainon kai theion* (as belonging together and divine). Genuine thought (Logos) and genuine ethical mentality (Diké) belong together and can be derived from the conviction of a single and all-combining order. The common endpoint, to which ethical as well as theoretical self-determinacy lead, is general in nature and liberated from all individual delusions and wishful thinking. Accordingly, when man links and equates law with the cosmological order, *i.e.*, its common root with truth, law is liberated from particularity, coincidence, and arbitrariness. With that link, it becomes possible, for example, for Sophocles, through the words and actions of Antigone, to invoke the power and validity of the "unwritten laws" against the arbitrariness of positive provisions. The contention that laws are not mere arbitrary, theoretical constructs, but permeate the whole Greek polis, is best explicated by Heraclites' statement that "*the people must fight for their laws as for their walls.*"[42] Its laws constitute the soul of the polis, the invisible fortress of the polis, next to the visible polis defended by its stone walls.[43]

In addition, the ancient Greeks were the first to interpret the relationship between law and freedom as one of correlativity and compatibility. By defending their laws, their symbolic walls, the ancient Greeks were aware that they defended their freedom. Law becomes the true expression of freedom and the true

---

40 Ibid., 1941, p. 20.

41 Ibid., 1941, p. 21.

42 Jaeger, 1943, p. 110.

43 Ibid., 1943, p. 110; cf. Coskun, D., *Constitutioneel Patriottisme voor Europa. Wat Ernst Cassirer verdedigde voor Weimar*, in: E.J. Kaars Sijpesteijn (ed.), *Grenzen aan Europa. Het Volk en Europa*, Vereniging voor Democratisch Europa, Amsterdam, 2004, pp. 83–93.

distinction between Greeks and barbarians. Law had become for the ancient Greeks a modus of self-assertion. For the Greek citizen subordination to or domination by the demand of a single man did not exist. In Jason's quarrel with Medea, in Euripides' Medea, the first thing Jason mentions that Medea owes to him is the fact that Medea dwells in Greece, instead of her "*barbarian land, and hast learned what justice means and how to live by law, not by the dictates of brute force.*"[44] According to Cassirer, "*The meaning and content of such words we experience now perhaps even more intensely and profoundly than any time before. Today we know also, that it is not mere scholarly interest that we invest in Greek philosophy and Greek education. We do not merely take a retrospective view, but what motivates us is the care for our intellectual future. We know that this future is most severely endangered, when we cannot manage to make that bond between truth and justice, between Logos and Diké, again in the same way as the Greeks linked them for the first time in human history.*"[45] Obviously, Cassirer refers here to the collapse of the Weimar Republic and the sudden rise to power (politically as well as culturally) of the Nazi regime.

This theme recurs in Cassirer's writings during his stay in England, Sweden and the United States. Later, he even gives a philosophical refutation of Nazi ideology.[46] What we explicate in this section therefore is the contribution of Greek culture to the idea of justice as an *a priori* principle. The *a priori* nature of justice, and its necessary link to individual moral judgment, to which Cassirer emphatically refers in the citation above, subsequently was pursued as no other by the Cambridge Platonists, through which they not only refuted the Puritan legalistic view of law, but also the authoritarian demands of the Hobbesian Leviathan. We now turn to the Greek inception of the idea of justice as an eternal order that stands above, and even regulates the divine world.

---

44 Euripides, *Medea*, V. 536 ff., cited by: Ernst Cassirer, *Logos, Dike, Kosmos in der Entwicklung der griechischen Philosophie*, Göteborgs Hogskolas Arsskrift, Volume 37, 1941, p. 22.

45 See: Ernst Cassirer, *Logos, Dike, Kosmos in der Entwicklung der griechischen Philosophie*, Göteborgs Hogskolas Arsskrift, Volume 37, 1941, p. 23.

46 See: Chapter 4.

Contrary to what one may expect, though, the thought that there is an unchanging and eternal law, even before any written or posited law, was not the product of philosophical thought, nor was it introduced by ancient Greek mythology and religion; rather it was created and embraced by Greek drama. Henceforth the idea of justice as an eternal and unchanging order would represent one of the greatest themes in the history of mankind, when it would receive its stamp from the tragedies of Aeschylus to Sophocles and from Sophocles to Euripides.

The Greek tragedies, though, do not immediately denote the eternal order of justice with the names of its highest deity, *i.e.*, Zeus. The divine order is not yet permeated with the ideal of justice that will characterize it altogether when Greek drama imprints its stamp on it. First with Aeschylus this name of the highest deity begins to explicitly adopt a different meaning as against the convictions of ancient Greek popular religion, which we still encounter in the Homeric poems. Homer explicates an anthropocentric tendency in Greek culture by placing man (the hero) and his fate in the foreground. However, Homer still offers a conventional "objectivity" and a distanced perspective in his epos.[47]

First with Hesiod the poet expresses a commitment for justice and introduces the idea of Justice as a central theme in his poetry.[48] In Hesiod's poetry Diké becomes an independent divinity who sits next to her father Zeus and complains whenever men do wicked things. As a result, action follows directly as a reaction to any distortion of justice upon the earth, because the gods are now the guardians of justice while their rule ultimately entails the victory of justice over injustice.[49] Although he borrows from Homer the content of his ideal of justice, Hesiod replaces the "distanced" perspective of the epos by the poet's passionate defense of the unavoidable demise of injustice and the inevitable victory of justice.

Subsequently, with Solon, Hesiod's idea of justice is pursued to its logical conclusion. Again and again, Solon emphasizes the power of Diké and that ultimately human hubris will

---

47 Jaeger, 1943, pp. 51–53.
48 Ibid., 1943, p. 62.
49 Ibid., 1943, p. 69.

not remain unpunished.[50] With Solon it also becomes clear, though, that man can have a share in his own destiny, that is to say, man can avoid divine wrath by taking his responsibilities seriously. Furthermore, no longer does Solon consider divine sanctions in terms of famine and pestilence, as Hesiod presumed. In Solon's works every transgression of justice rather results in the immanent rupture of the social organism as the necessary balancing out of human hubris transgressing the boundaries of justice. Solon's turn to immanency in the idea of justice for the first time acknowledges that the violation of justice procures the disruption of the life of the community.[51] A man may consider himself to have escaped the sanctions of Diké, but nothing precludes Diké from getting justice after all from his next of kin, especially from his children; a recurring element in Attic tragedy. What Solon demonstrates, analogous to the Milesian natural philosophers, is the existence of an immanent order in human life, a rule of law in the social order.

With the development of Attic tragedy in Greek drama a new turning point in Greek history occurs. While the epos viewed everything from the historical perspective to give a theogonical account of history in the form of an explanation of the source and the becoming of the gods, Greek drama explicitly maintains a different interest. In drama everything has to be revived into the present world. Due to this form of the narrative, myth – the source from which Greek drama draws its inspiration – becomes part of the world of actions. The mythical world, that is, the world of the gods, acquires a new dimension and enters into a different relationship with man. The elemental and highest aim of the tragic poets is the representation of divine life and suffering in its deepest sense. The Prometheus of Aeschylus is the first and insurmountable example of how the conflict between man and the gods diminishes nothing as to the ideality of the conflict we are allowed to follow so closely.

The central theme of the drama of Prometheus is not primarily his theft of fire; rather it is his leniency or intention to regard man worthy of freedom, *i.e.*, as morally and intellectually

---

50 Ibid., 1943, pp. 140–141.
51 Ibid., 1943, p. 141.

mature.[52] Prometheus' is a conscious act, not one of stupidity or blindness. Therefore, Zeus is not in the position to completely eradicate this consciousness in Prometheus. To the contrary, in the end, at the zenith of Aeschylus' drama, in Agamemnon, even Zeus himself has to give way internally and changes before our own eyes. Zeus is no longer the harsh tyrant acquiring power through force and trickery, as in Prometheus, but has become the guardian and protector of justice. The executors of his decrees are no longer Kratos and Bia, force and violence, but Diké and Aidos, justice and piety.

The choir in Agamemnon now praises Zeus as a strong and stern, but at the same time as a just and gracious ruler. [53] The Zeus of Aeschylus is no longer the distanced natural god on Mount Olympus, but becomes the defender and administrator of the eternal order of justice. With the changed perception of the divine world effectuated by Greek drama, man's understanding of himself had to change as well. The response of the choir in Agamemnon to Clytemnestra's claim, that not she but the damning ghosts of the house have murdered Agamemnon, already forms an indication for this change: it is she alone, who has committed the act and it is she who has to be held responsible.[54]

Subsequently, it is from the unwritten laws of the eternal order of justice that Sophocles' Antigone derives the moral force to decry the orders of Kreon. That is a new belief, that is, the belief in a law that does not stem from the arbitrariness of a human authority, but that has its seat with the gods, but which also has not been created by them, because the eternal order of justice (as part of the cosmos) confronts them with an independent power. Diké or justice has never been created by the gods and is their equal in status and class. Indeed the eternal order of justice even goes beyond the gods in force and

---

[52] See: Ernst Cassirer, *Logos, Dike, Kosmos in der Entwicklung der griechischen Philosophie*, Göteborgs Hogskolas Arsskrift, Volume 37, 1941, pp. 14–15.

[53] Ibid., 1941, p. 16.

[54] See: Ernst Cassirer, *Logos, Dike, Kosmos in der Entwicklung der griechischen Philosophie*, Göteborgs Hogskolas Arsskrift, Volume 37, 1941, p. 18.

ancienty.[55] There is something special about the ancient laws (agropoi nomoi). Whereas we can relate a genealogy of the gods, the eternal and unchanging laws that Sophocles introduces in his tragedies do not allow questioning of their genesis and origin. "*Not now and yesterday they have their being – But everlastingly, and none can tell the hour that saw their birth.*"[56] We cannot ask for its beginning and wherefrom, and, accordingly, it is not merely accidental that the eternal order of justice receives its force exactly from its arcane nature.[57]

Notwithstanding, with Euripides we see another development, because Euripides does not refrain from that originary question. For Euripides mythico-religious representations no longer entail an objective force that immediately compels, because he is now thoroughly inspired by Greek philosophy. Euripides rather approaches justice with a deliberate criticism that gradually adopts the form of skepticism.[58] If justice is an eternal phenomenon that exists independent from the gods and regulates their world as well as the world of finite creatures, we should figure out what is the nature of justice, just as we figure out what is the essence of the natural order.

In Plato's works we are provided with two answers to that question, *i.e.*, that given by the Sophists, and that given by Socrates. For the Sophists we need not look afar, because justice for the Sophists is but an implement of power and the vested interests of the powerful. Justice is a conventional matter and does not distinguish itself or rises above that what we find in laws and decrees of the sovereign, *i.e.*, the state. For Socrates that cannot be the answer as to the true nature of law and

---

55 See: Ernst Cassirer, *Die Idee des Rechts und ihre Entwicklung in der modernen Philosophie*, Ernst Cassirer Papers, Essays and Lectures, Beinecke Rare Book & Manuscripts Library, Coll. No. GEN 98, Series No. II, Box No. 43, Folder No. 845, pp. 10–13.

56 Cited by: Ernst Cassirer, *Die Idee des Rechts und ihre Entwicklung in der modernen Philosophie*, Ernst Cassirer Papers, Essays and Lectures, Beinecke Rare Book & Manuscripts Library, Coll. No. GEN 98, Series No. II, Box No. 43, Folder No. 845, p. 15.

57 See also: Chapter 7.

58 See: Ernst Cassirer, *Die Idee des Rechts und ihre Entwicklung in der modernen Philosophie*, Ernst Cassirer Papers, Essays and Lectures, Beinecke Rare Book & Manuscripts Library, Coll. No. GEN 98, Series No. II, Box No. 43, Folder No. 845, pp. 15–17.

justice. It cannot be a mere technicality, a rhetorical device with which to produce any wished for conviction with its hearers or with the judge. What Socrates proposes is that it is better to undergo injustice than to act unjustly, because what is the advantage, asks Socrates, of winning the world when one's soul is damaged thereby? As Socrates states in the Gorgias, "*In my opinion the wrongdoer or the unjust is wretched anyhow; more wretched, however, if he does not pay the penalty and gets no punishment for his wrongdoing, but less wretched if he pays the penalty and meets with requital from god and men.*"[59] All injustice corrupts the soul, for Socrates, and the healing of the soul can only come from punishment.

What distinguishes Socrates from his contemporaries is best expressed by the accusation of his adversaries, that he introduces "new gods." Moreover, what he could not accomplish when alive, he establishes with his death. Socrates dies because he resists the state, because he defies its laws (Nomoi), because against them he holds and venerates "new gods." But his decline simultaneously entails the rise of a new power that transcends the domain of the state and that of "positive law." What law and what justice is, does not coincide with the sum total of the positive provisions of law. Viewed in the light of the "Being" of law, its concept, its inner truth, these positive provisions of law can go completely up to nothing – they can prove themselves as the expression of the highest injustice. Rather, justice has an independent "Being," and it must be cleansed of the merely perceptual and opiniative; it must be thought of in its being as something eternal and unchanging. Justice asserts itself against the mere lawful, as the epitome of custom, usage and tradition, and even makes demands on the laws of the state from its tribunal to either affirm or to reject them. Socrates' theory of the "just in itself" leads to a theoretical and ethical revolution, that foremost attempts to effect an inner change in the individual. Whereas Socrates is accused of introducing "new gods," what he in fact proposes is a new attitude toward the gods, wherein

---

[59] See: Ernst Cassirer, *Die Idee des Rechts und ihre Entwicklung in der modernen Philosophie*, Ernst Cassirer Papers, Essays and Lectures, Beinecke Rare Book & Manuscripts Library, Coll. No. GEN 98, Series No. II, Box No. 43, Folder No. 845, pp. 41–44.

individual conscience is empowered to choose its own course and follow its own judgment.

In this regard, Plato's image of the transmigration of the soul in Chapter 10 of his *Republic* explicitly hints at the ethical turn initiated by Socrates that dispenses with the mythical account of human self-understanding. Lachesis, the maiden daughter of Necessity, explains, "*Souls that live for a day, now is the beginning of another cycle of mortal generation where birth is the beacon of death. No divinity shall cast lots for you, but you shall choose your own deity. Let him to whom falls the first lot first select a life to which he shall cleave of necessity. But virtue has no master over her, and each shall have more or less of her as he honors her or does her despite. The blame is his who chooses: God is blameless.*"[60] Not the demon is to save the soul, but the soul is to save the demon (within him). From the mythical point of view the demonic stands for all that is beyond that which man can know and will.

In this respect, in Plato's works, what was in mythical thought previously accorded to the damning influence of the demons, now is accepted as guilt or responsibility by the individual as an ethical personality.[61] Consequently, happiness or *eudemonia* in Plato's works is not a predicament that passes to somebody exteriorly, as something that just happens to the soul, but it is an inner attitude of the soul that is self-imposed; the '*Deisidemonia*' has evolved into '*Eudemonia*'.[62] The synthesis that early Greek philosophy established had far reaching consequences for the idea of justice, while it continued to be considered as the quintessence and the summation of all virtues.[63] The eternal order of justice that regulates the divine world has now become accessible to the individual, and through his own judgment the individual can choose to live the good or moral life. We now turn to the pursuance of this ideal by the Cambridge

---

60 Plato, *The Republic, Books VI–X*, The Loeb Classical Library No. 276, ed. J. Henderson, tr. P. Shorey, Harvard University Press, Cambridge, Massachusetts, 2000 (1935), pp. 505–507, 617E-D.

61 See: Ernst Cassirer, *Logos, Dike, Kosmos in der Entwicklung der griechischen Philosophie*, Göteborgs Hogskolas Arsskrift, Volume 37, 1941, p. 18.

62 Ibid., 1941, p. 18.

63 Ibid., 1941, p. 19.

Platonists, in their efforts to combat the absolutisms of Hobbes and the English Puritans.

I. 3. What was the Contribution of the Cambridge School of Platonism?

In a time that bore the mark of religious civil war and upheaval, Thomas Hobbes was the foremost exponent of the view that a strong state was the solution for the reconstruction and maintenance of order. For the sake of order Hobbes was prepared, nay he was necessitated to maintain the view that an absolute, unfettered monarch should be installed. The powers of this sovereign monarch could not be limited to the regulation of the mere outward actions of the subjects, but could even encompass the proper direction the consciousness of its subjects could take. For the purpose of his theory of the state, analogous to the empiricist Bacon's elaborations in the sciences, Hobbes gave a strictly atomistic theory of the state and of society. According to Hobbes, if one is to understand the state, one must first resolve it into its basic elements and then reconstruct it from them. The aggregate of individual wills of the people, more specifically their summation in a contract would subsequently form the foundation of the state. Furthermore, if the state was not again to dissolve into its single parts, some provision had to be made so that this contract, once entered into, became inviolable. The contract of Hobbes, although itself a product of human choice and arbitrariness had therefore to bring an end to individual likes and dislikes; it had to be permanent and unalterable by the act of submission to the rule of the inescapable coercion of an absolute authority. All political and social existence once conceded by the people in the contract could subsequently be traced back to and should be based on the juridical right of coercion.

However, this could not be the starting or the end point for the Cambridge Platonists. For them the state could have no other foundation than in an ethical *a priori*. A contract is tenable and meaningful only after an original agreement in the form of a rational and moral conviction that precedes any written law.[64]

---

64 See: Ernst Cassirer, *The Platonic Renaissance in England* (*Die platonische Renaissance in England und die Schule von Cambridge*, B.G. Teubner,

The law of nature in this regard, which must be understood for the Cambridge Platonists as both a moral and a religious law, is the guarantor of the positive law of the state. It spiritually supports the positive law, because no accumulation or concentration of external coercive incentives in one person could be in a position to ensure the stability of the state, according to the Cambridge Platonists.[65]

To overcome the original heterogeneity of wills and to make a real unity out of an aggregate of individual wills, which no mere external power can possibly overcome completely, the Cambridge School alluded to the Stoic conception of natural law. In addition, they placed the logical *a priori* on the same level with the ethical *a priori*, and both were perceived from a common viewpoint and derived from the same source. These *a priori* ideas were not innate ideas as Locke understood them, but a product of an action or freedom of the intellect.[66] What this insight of the Cambridge School amounts to is an anticipation of Kant's Copernican Revolution and the significance of transcendental freedom, according to Cassirer. "*It* [the Cambridge School] *continually points out that it is the strangest perversion of the simple phenomenological state of things to make perceptions the presupposition of the ego, rather than the ego the presupposition of perceptions. Before the ego there are no perceptions as such, as the elements out of which the ego is composed. Perceptions exist only for and by virtue of the ego.*"[67] The Cambridge Platonists regarded the unity of the ego as the ultimate constitutive condition for all sensible or reflective consciousness. Consequently, a legal order that ignores that its subjects are capable of forming rational and moral convictions for themselves and in so doing support the constitution of the land, rests its basis for power on feeble foundations.

The Cambridge School had to wage battle anew with the same adversary, but now in a different guise, *i.e.*, Puritanism, as that type of piety and religious metaphysics which came into ascendancy in seventeenth century England, and finally into

Leipzig, 1932), tr. James P. Pettegrove, University of Texas Press, Austin, 1953, pp. 54–55.

65 Ibid., 1953 (1932), pp. 55–56.

66 Ibid., 1953 (1932), pp. 56–64.

67 Ibid., 1953 (1932), p. 64.

almost unlimited authority during the English Republican Era of Oliver Cromwell. Both empiricism and Puritanism sprang forth from the same strictly practical spirit that was characteristic of seventeenth century England, as they both claimed total dominion over things as well as men. The Cambridge School sought to repudiate both of them from the standpoint of a firm and clear intellectual and moral position. Empiricism and Puritanism approach the practical world or the world of actions in different ways, but once they reach their objects they hold on to it with a "death-grip," as Cassirer puts it. "*In empiricism the tendency prevails to subject nature to the will of man and to establish on earth the regnum hominis. In Puritanism* (...) *the significance of all activity is seen exclusively in the fulfillment of the divine commandments and in the magnification and dissemination of the glory of God. But the evaluation of practical activity remains the same under both assumptions.*"[68] While the empiricism of Bacon enlists experience (as accumulated throughout history) against mere logic and dialectic, Puritanism resists presumptions of logical reason and of philosophical speculation in favor of faith.[69]

It may be true, according to Cassirer, "*that English Puritanism has been the real champion and protector of religious individualism and that, through the energy with which it took up and defended the cause of religious freedom, it also prepared the grounds for the idea of democracy in modern times.*"[70] However, the indirect historical effect which English Puritanism has exercised in this regard stands in stark contrast with its own substance and nature. English Puritanism did not recognize or reserve a place for religious freedom; it was quite inimical to the conception of religious freedom of conscience; "*they* [the leaders of the puritan movement, *i.e.*, Eliot and Pym] *demand again and again the most severe persecution and the most merciless destruction of all dissidents.*"[71]

---

68 Ibid., 1953 (1932), pp. 69–70.

69 Ibid., 1953 (1932), p. 72.

70 Ibid., 1953 (1932), pp. 74–75.

71 Max Kraus, *Scholastik, Puritanismus und Kapitalismus*, especially pp. 19 ff.; referred to by: Ernst Cassirer, *The Platonic Renaissance in England* (*Die platonische Renaissance in England und die Schule von Cambridge,*

The dogma of predestination forms the core element of the Calvinistic Puritan creed, on the basis of which "*some men and angels are predestinated unto everlasting life, and others foreordained to everlasting death.*"[72] This Calvinistic creed implies, according to Cassirer, that there can be no questioning of the foundation or justification of God's decisions concerning the human predicament, because it would be tantamount to a frivolous exaggeration, an elevation of human reason above God.[73] Calvin's theology conceives the relation between God and man not from the perspective of love, but from that of a rigorous justice. "*God confronts man primarily as a judge; he stands before him in all the sublimity and awe of the judiciary office. For His word is unalterable, His decision incontestable. God's decision is not bound by reasons; for every reason would be a barrier, annulling His absolute sovereignty.*"[74] This Biblical portrayal of God emphasizes God as the creator not only of justice but also that of the cosmos, which explains for the dramatic difference between the ancient Greek and the Biblical account of jurisprudence, *i.e.*, conception of natural law.[75] Because the God of the Bible is Himself the source of justice and law, an unjust divine pronouncement, for Biblical jurisprudence, is a contradiction in terms. The emphasis on divine justice by Puritanism had the practical effect that the puritan faith found itself increasingly forced over to the realm of mere legality. All of this would not remain without consequences for man's self-conception, were not the Cambridge Platonists to intervene.

B.G. Teubner, Leipzig, 1932), tr. James P. Pettegrove, University of Texas Press, Austin, 1953, p. 74.

72 Statutes of the Westminster Synod of 1543, Chapter III, article 9, No. 3; cited by: Ernst Cassirer, *The Platonic Renaissance in England* (*Die platonische Renaissance in England und die Schule von Cambridge*, B.G. Teubner, Leipzig, 1932), tr. James P. Pettegrove, University of Texas Press, Austin, 1953, p. 75.

73 See: Ernst Cassirer, *Die Philosophie der Aufklärung*, J.C.B. Mohr Verlag (Paul Siebeck), Tübingen, 1932, Chapter 6, pp. 320 ff.

74 See: Ernst Cassirer, *The Platonic Renaissance in England* (*Die platonische Renaissance in England und die Schule von Cambridge*, B.G. Teubner, Leipzig, 1932), tr. James P. Pettegrove, University of Texas Press, Austin, 1953, p. 75.

75 Cf. Lytton, 2002–2003, pp. 40–41.

In the hands of the Puritans, the relationship between God and man was gradually turning from a purely religious into a juridical one. For that, increasingly the puritans attempted to understand this relationship through legal analogies and in terms of legal categories. They readily translated promises in the Scriptures into covenants or legal pacts with God, while elevating formal legality to the primary criterion and symbol of conduct to please God. According to Cassirer, "*The whole puritan movement is penetrated with and governed by this spirit of 'self-righteous and sober legality'.*"[76] Here again, unexpectedly, Hobbes (the empiricist) and the Puritans meet together in concord. In many respects Hobbes is the antipode of Puritanism – in his relinquishment of all ties the state has with religious institutions, in his elevation of the state to absolute authority over religion and religious sentiment, and by considering the positive law of the state as the sole legitimate source of religion (sic). However, in his basic assumption of an absolute will, as embodied by Leviathan, dictating unrestrained submission to an individual will, he reaches the same goal and conclusion as the Puritans, but only from a different perspective.[77] Just as criticism at God's decisions is for Puritanism a return to heathendom – "*an appeal to that* recta ratio *which the heathen philosophers dreamed of, but which is nowhere to be found*" [78] – for Hobbes, any finding of fault by an individual with the content of the law, the decree of his 'mortal God' in the form of the state, is tantamount to rebellion. The law of the land, for Hobbes, defines and constitutes at the same time the (limits of the) conscience of the citizen; it is a medium through which the absolute Being absorbs man's intellect and will alike. The law even exclusively establishes religion, lest it be, for Hobbes, indistinguishable from mere superstition.

---

76 See: Ernst Cassirer, *The Platonic Renaissance in England* (*Die platonische Renaissance in England und die Schule von Cambridge*, B.G. Teubner, Leipzig, 1932), tr. James P. Pettegrove, University of Texas Press, Austin, 1953, p. 77: "*We are bankrupt debtors, God is a sure Creditor, Christ sets all on his score. We are ignorant Clients, God is a skilful Judge, Christ is our Advocate to plead our cause for us.*" From a sermon by Thomas Adams (1629).

77 Ibid., 1953 (1932), pp. 77–78.

78 Ibid., 1953 (1932), p. 78.

The Cambridge School passionately protested to such a subordination of ethical reason to an external law, whether in the form of an empirical law of the state or in the form of the transcendent law of God. Cudworth, in his work *The true intellectual System of the Universe*, emphasized that moral duty could not arise from the mere expression of the will of the divine lawgiver, but only from His right and authority to command. The foundation of this authority, lest it be looked upon as ridiculous or absurd, must be based upon natural justice and equity. The binding of God's will to fixed and eternal norms, though, is not a limitation to divine power. Rather it is the expression of the expectation (or reasonable insight) that God is obedient only to the dictates of His own nature.[79]

The Cambridge Platonists insist on and defend the self-sufficiency of moral reason in religious matters: "*As, for instance, if God makes a promise, He must perform it; if He makes a creature intelligent and voluntary, He must use him as such. ... This stands to reason, and has the support of Scripture. ... There is that in God that is more beautiful than power, than will and Sovereignty, viz. His righteousness, His goodwill, His justice, wisdom and the like.*"[80] According to the same principle, the state has the right to exercise authority over the individual insofar as it respects the unity and moral integrity of the ego, *i.e.*, insofar as it views the individual as an autonomous moral person, which alone stands at the foundation of state and society. Although the Cambridge Platonists did not envision a moral order that precedes or exists independently from divine provenance, nevertheless, they presumed the necessity of such an order respecting the unity of the ego as a moral person for any subsequent social order to survive, be it regulated by divine order or human command.

By emphasizing the inalienable value of reason as the last criterion of morality, by connecting Logos and Diké, the Cambridge Platonists, according to Cassirer, cleared the ground

---

[79] Ibid., 1953 (1932), p. 80.

[80] Whichcote, *Sermons*, Aberdeen, 1751, Volume II, p. 244. Cited by Ernst Cassirer, *The Platonic Renaissance in England* (*Die platonische Renaissance in England und die Schule von Cambridge*, B.G. Teubner, Leipzig, 1932), tr. James P. Pettegrove, University of Texas Press, Austin, 1953, p. 82.

for Leibniz and subsequently for Kant. They aided them in their efforts to move "*from the concept of freedom of the Reformation* [*i.e.*, Luther] *to the concept of freedom of idealism, from the principle of justification by faith to the principle of the autonomy of the will and of the practical reason.*"[81] What Cassirer makes clear by his insistence on the link between Logos and Diké, between truth and justice, and theoretical and practical reason, is that such interrelation is essential for the existence of every democratic society, *i.e.*, for a society wherein subjects are not merely subjects but also citizens. Commands therefore, whether secular or divine, cannot rest on sheer coercion, but must be accompanied by reasons, *i.e.*, they must be persuasive for the individual if it is to conceive itself as an autonomous moral person. It is essential for a democracy that its subjects perceive themselves as citizens, hence capable of influencing the particular directions their polity takes.

Without the demand of the connection of truth and justice, without the possibility of questioning after the *quid iuris*, the intellectual abyss, the subordination of a (single) person to another (single) person comes rapidly in view. In his book *The Myth of the State*, Cassirer discusses in detail how and why Nazi Germany could be driven to self-sacrifice by the Fuehrer. He explains how it was possible for the bond between truth and justice to have given away in Weimar, and, moreover, how almost the whole polity could stay passive throughout the whole façade. As an explanation, Cassirer conceived a modern crisis of culture and accorded it to modern man's lack of self-knowledge.[82] Cassirer's ethical view is clearly inspired by the work of one man, *i.e.*, Albert Schweitzer. Both Cassirer and Schweitzer lamented one thing: the diminution of the capacity of the individual to judge for himself, to critically enquire into the whence and whither of the conditions of its life, and to demand that nothing should be done in its name that could not withstand the scrutiny of its individual reason and moral convictions.

---

81 Ibid., 1953 (1932), p. 85.

82 See: Ernst Cassirer, *An Essay on Man: An Introduction to a Philosophy of Human Culture*, Yale University Press, New Haven, 1944, p. 21.

I. 4. What was the Philosophical Friendship between Schweitzer and Cassirer?

For Cassirer, Schweitzer was the first German thinker who, very early on, felt the danger of the decline and inevitable destruction of human culture that was attributable to the dramatic gap between truth and justice, *i.e.*, the dismemberment of the individual as a moral person, that enveloped itself in the period leading to and in the aftermath of the First World War. The only encounter between Cassirer and Albert Schweitzer took place in Oxford, October 18, 1934. In a letter sent to Schweitzer on January 30, 1936, Cassirer makes clear how important this single encounter was for him, because it made him aware of in what way he agreed with him in fundamental philosophical and ethical questions.[83] Schweitzer appreciated Cassirer's interest in his work in a letter sent to him on July 6, 1936, by taking notice of Cassirer's inaugural lecture at the University of Göteborg. In the letter Schweitzer announces that he is about to publish the third volume of his philosophy of civilization (*Kulturphilosophie*) later the same year.[84]

Schweitzer began as a historian of religion and as a theological critic. His first works include *The Quest of the Historical Jesus* and *St. Paul and His Interpreters*. Subsequently, he passed to music and musicology, among others giving interpretations of the work of Johann Sebastian Bach. But later on he became a missionary and a physician, most notably by founding a hospital in Lamabaréné for the inhabitants of the jungles of West

---

83 Günzler, 1995, p. 313.

84 See: Beinecke Rare Book and Manuscript Library, Ernst Cassirer Papers, Correspondence, Coll. No. GEN 98 Series No. III, Box No. 55, Folder No. 1093 (Schweitzer, Albert 1934–59, n.d.), *Brief von Schweitzer an Cassirer*, 6.7.36. Schweitzer's third volume of "*The Philosophy of Civilization*" would not appear that year, and would remain unpublished until recently. His third volume in 4 parts has appeared in German due to the efforts of the Commission for the Intellectual Work of Albert Schweitzer, of the Association Internationale de l'Hôpital Albert Schweitzer à Lambaréné et de son Œuvre (AISL). Schweitzer, A., *Die Weltanschauung der Ehrfurcht von dem Leben: Kulturphilosophie III*, part I and II, hrsg. C. Günzler und J. Zürcher, Beck, München, 1999; and; idem, *Die Weltanschauung der Ehrfurcht von dem Leben: Kulturphilosophie III*, Part III and IV, hrsg. C. Günzler und J. Zürcher, Beck, München, 2000.

Africa, then French Africa. As described in his book *On the Edge of the Primeval Forest: Experiences and Observations of a Doctor in Equatorial Africa*, during the First World War, he began to form his first ideas about the decay and the restoration of civilization.[85] Already in 1923, Schweitzer published his main philosophical works *Verfall und Wiederaufbau der Kultur* (The Decay and Restoration of Civilization) and *Kultur und Ethik* (Civilization and Ethics), which were bound together as *Kulturphilosophie* (Philosophy of Culture).[86]

Schweitzer's main concern was that civilization in the technological sense had superseded civilization in the ethical sense. According to Schweitzer, no civilization can exist without an ethical theory supporting it. The decay of civilization in the ethical sense, for Schweitzer, only foreshadowed the decay of civilization in its totality. For Schweitzer, civilization has an ethical import and should be distinguished from civilization as mere material progress. The word civilization, for Schweitzer, is best expressed by the German term "Kultur," "*viz., the development of man to a state of higher organization and a higher moral standard.*"[87] In this regard, for Schweitzer, it was the task of philosophy to show us "*that we have to struggle for the ideals on which our culture rests.*"[88] However, philosophy from the nineteenth century onwards, according to Schweitzer, had just failed to do this. Schweitzer's accusation does not direct itself specifically to a certain philosophical school or system, but has a more general and graver or serious import, so as to attack the very *character* of nineteenth century philosophic thought.

While philosophy in the eighteenth century and the early part of the nineteenth century played a leading role in the

---

85 Ernst Cassirer, *Philosophy and Politics (1944)*, in: Ibid., *Symbol, Myth, and Culture. Essays and Lectures of Ernst Cassirer 1935–1945*, edited by D.P. Verene, Yale University Press, New Haven and London, pp. 219–232; here: pp. 230–231.

86 Schweitzer, A., *The Philosophy of Civilization*, tr. C.T. Campion, University Press of Florida, Tallahassee, 1981 (1923) or Prometheus Books, Buffalo, NY, 1987 (1923).

87 Ibid., 1987 (1923), p. 23.

88 See: Ernst Cassirer, *The Concept of Philosophy as a Philosophical Problem (1935)*, in: Ibid., *Symbol, Myth, and Culture. Essays and Lectures of Ernst Cassirer 1935–1945*, edited by D.P. Verene, Yale University Press, New Haven and London, 1979, pp. 49–63; here: p. 60; cf. Ringer, 1969, pp. 87–90.

formation of public opinion, and busied itself with questions that presented themselves to mankind and with keeping the thought of civilized man actively reflecting upon them, from the second half of the nineteenth century onwards philosophy had become a stranger to the world.[89] It philosophized about everything except for civilization and passed by the problems of life that occupied most persons. Philosophy established an entirely theoretical view of the world, unaware that a theory constructed only out of history and science would accordingly be unoptimistic and unethical and "*would remain forever an "impotent theory of the universe," which could never call forth the energies needed for the establishment and maintenance of the ideals of civilization.*" According to Schweitzer, "*So little did philosophy philosophize about civilization that she did not even notice that she herself, and the age along with her, were losing more and more of it. In the hour of peril, the watchman who ought to have kept us awake was himself asleep, and the result was that we put up no fight at all on behalf of our civilization.*"[90] Modern culture had become sick with an illness that put it under the sign of collapse and made it drive "*along in a current full of formidable eddies.*"[91]

A first and alarming symptom, according to Schweitzer, was the ascendancy of that new form of thought that he described as "collective thought." Schweitzer gives the following description of "collective thought" as an obstruction to the development of higher forms of ethical thought.

"*The modern man is lost in the mass in a way which is without precedent in history, and this is perhaps the most characteristic trait in him. His diminished concern about his own nature makes him susceptible to an extent that is almost pathological, to the views which society and its organs of expression have put, ready made, into circulation. Since, over and above this, society, with its well-constructed organization, has become a power of*

---

89 See: Ernst Cassirer, *Albert Schweitzer as Critic of Nineteenth-Century Ethics*, in: Roback, A.A., *The Albert Schweitzer Jubilee Book*, Sci-Art Publishers, Cambridge, Massachusetts, 1946, pp. 241–257; here: p. 250.

90 Cited by Ernst Cassirer, *Albert Schweitzer as Critic of Nineteenth-Century Ethics*, in: Roback, A.A., *The Albert Schweitzer Jubilee Book*, Sci-Art Publishers, Cambridge, Massachusetts, 1946, pp. 241–257; here: p. 251.

91 Ibid., 1946, p. 242.

as yet unknown strength in the spiritual life, man's want of independence in the face of it has become so serious that he is almost ceasing to claim a spiritual existence of his own. He is like a rubber ball which has lost its elasticity, and preserves indefinitely every impression that is made upon it. He is under the thumb of the mass, and he draws from it the opinions on which he lives, whether the question at issue is national or political or one of his own belief or unbelief."[92]

As a result of collective thought the individual makes it a rule for himself always to take into account the views which prevail in organized society. He starts by taking it for granted that "*both for himself and his neighbors there are certain views which are determined by nationality, creed, political party, social position, and other elements in one's surroundings.*"[93] Accordingly, these views cannot be a legitimate subject of conversation, due to the respect the individual has to display for other people's convictions. But when the collective body works more strongly in the individual than the latter does upon society, the spiritual and moral worthiness of the individual is necessarily constricted and hampered. Consequently, spiritual and moral life degenerates, rendering society incapacitated in understanding and solving the problems which it has to face, and hence making catastrophe unavoidable. Schweitzer is resolute in his solution: "*Either the moral standard of personality raises the moral standard of society, so far as possible, to its own level, or it is dragged down by it.*"[94]

The same disease, according to Schweitzer, infected modern culture by another symptom, *i.e.*, "*the ever increasing spirit of nationalism.*"[95] For Schweitzer, nationalism is "*an ignoble*

---

92 Cited by Ernst Cassirer, *Philosophy and Politics (1944)*, in: Ibid., *Symbol, Myth, and Culture. Essays and Lectures of Ernst Cassirer 1935–1945*, edited by D.P. Verene, Yale University Press, New Haven and London, pp. 219–232; here: p. 232.

93 Cited by Ernst Cassirer, *Albert Schweitzer as Critic of Nineteenth-Century Ethics*, in: Roback, A.A., *The Albert Schweitzer Jubilee Book*, Sci-Art Publishers, Cambridge, Massachusetts, 1946, pp. 241–257; here: p. 243.

94 Schweitzer, 1987 (1923), p. 293.

95 Ernst Cassirer, *Albert Schweitzer as Critic of Nineteenth-Century Ethics*, in: Roback, A.A., *The Albert Schweitzer Jubilee Book*, Sci-Art Publishers, Cambridge, Massachusetts, 1946, pp. 241–257; here: p. 243.

kind of patriotism exaggerated till it has lost all its meaning, which bears the same relation to the noble and healthy kind as the fixed idea of an imbecile does to normal conviction."[96] Although all the other ideals of civilization declined, the idea of nationalism maintained itself and became the ideal which summed up what remained of all other ideals of civilization. Whereas it was before tempered by the other moral ideals, now unrestrained, nationalism "*began a career of independence*" and henceforth itself directed the course of civilization. Nationalism, in this respect, "*through abnormal nationalist conceptions and dispositions brings into active existence an elaborate system of uncivilization.*"[97] Schweitzer here refers to the unhealthy character of nationalism's "practical" politics, which gives way to popular passion in even the simplest questions. In addition, Schweitzer refers to the phenomenon that each nation claims to have a *national civilization*, which, moreover, does not remain limited to that particular nation, but feels "*called upon to impose itself upon others and make them happy! Modern nations seek markets for their civilization, as they do for their manufactures!*"[98]

Whereas in previous ages one could envision an indivisible human civilization, that ideal could no longer be maintained in the nineteenth century. The cause of the loss of the ideal of a single human civilization lay, according to Schweitzer, in the sinking of the level of civilization in the moral sense of the term. "*When the tide ebbs, shallows which separate bodies of deep water become visible; while the tide is flowing they are out of sight.*"[99] Although materially humans were closer to one another as never before, from the moral perspective nationalism had almost exhausted the capacity of its subjects to act ethically, that is to say, to progressively relate to other humans appreciative of their humanity. Mere materialism, according to Schweitzer, cannot provide a basis to sustain such relationships. Schweitzer did not expect real help to come from an improvement of social and economic conditions.

---

96 Cited by Ernst Cassirer, *Albert Schweitzer as Critic of Nineteenth-Century Ethics*, in: Roback, A.A., *The Albert Schweitzer Jubilee Book*, Sci-Art Publishers, Cambridge, Massachusetts, 1946, pp. 241–257; here: p. 243.

97 Ibid., 1946, p. 244.

98 Schweitzer, 1987 (1923), pp. 30–33.

99 Ibid., 1987 (1923), p. 34.

These are necessary but not sufficient conditions, because they only carry "*a little nearer* [to the] *solution, never to the goal.*"[100] What is required is the adoption of a new frame of mind or an inner change of character by society, *i.e.*, a new sense of reality.

A true sense of reality, according to Schweitzer, is first achieved through insights on reality inspired by ethical ideas. Without ethical standards or ideas governing our sense of reality we cannot gain control over events, and eventually are "*delivered over into bondage of them.*"[101] Consciously and deliberately Schweitzer takes up the position which the eighteenth century defended so "*stoutly.*" For him the period between the (second half of the) nineteenth century and contemporary society was an intermezzo of thought, "*an intermezzo which had extraordinarily rich and interesting motifs, but yet was all the same a fatal intermezzo.*"[102] What was lost during the second half of the nineteenth century was a philosophy that engaged itself with issues that directly concern man's moral life and that maintained an enthusiasm for civilization in the ethical sense.[103]

Without the influence exerted by the *Aufklärung* in the form of rationalism and optimism, according to Schweitzer, "*the seeds were sown for the* [First] *World War to come to pass.*"[104] Rationalism is for Schweitzer the catalyst of all true progress in the world. It demands that we base our views of the universe on thought and thought alone. However, it must be complemented by the force of an ethical optimism in respect of life. "*That theory of the universe is optimistic which gives existence the preference as against non-existence and thus affirms life as something*

[100] Ernst Cassirer, *Albert Schweitzer as Critic of Nineteenth-Century Ethics*, in: Roback, A.A., *The Albert Schweitzer Jubilee Book*, Sci-Art Publishers, Cambridge, Massachusetts, 1946, pp. 241–257; here: p. 245.

[101] Ibid., 1946, p. 245.

[102] Ibid., 1946, p. 246.

[103] Ernst Cassirer, *Philosophy and Politics (1944)*, in: Ibid., *Symbol, Myth, and Culture. Essays and Lectures of Ernst Cassirer 1935–1945*, edited by D.P. Verene, Yale University Press, New Haven and London, pp. 219–232; here: p. 232.

[104] Ernst Cassirer, *Albert Schweitzer as Critic of Nineteenth-Century Ethics*, in: Roback, A.A., *The Albert Schweitzer Jubilee Book*, Sci-Art Publishers, Cambridge, Massachusetts, 1946, pp. 241–257; here: p. 246.

possessing value in itself."[105] Only with such a theory of a universe that is both optimistic and rationalist, according to Schweitzer, can we begin to restore civilization.

According to Cassirer, Schweitzer's rationalism is not of the same kind as that of Hegel, nor is their optimism of the same purport. For Hegel, who as no other thinker in the nineteenth century had influenced the moral, political, and moral ideas, the rational is real and the real is rational. Furthermore, in his unbounded optimism, he sought to give a theodicy, by claiming that "*Our intellectual striving aims at realizing the conviction that what was* intended *by eternal wisdom is actually accomplished in the domain of existent, active Spirit, as well in that of mere Nature*."[106] Hegel's rationalism and optimism is on the historical level or domain. Reason, for Hegel, manifests itself not in the "subjective" but in the "objective mind." Accordingly, he makes a clear-cut distinction between what he calls "*Moralität*" (morality) and "*Sittlichkeit*" (ethicality). Whereas morality belongs to the sphere of the individual and has no right of its own, ethics belong to the sphere of the objective mind, which is represented and embodied in the life of the state.

Characteristically, Hegel denies that there are such things as "*the so-called inviolable and inalienable rights of the individuals*." It is beyond the reach of Hegel's thought to accord individuals any rights or claims as against the state. In his treatise on the German constitution Hegel states, "*All right originates from the state. It is the state that has to decide, not chance, not documents nor other legal titles. Since the rules of morality apply only to private life and private conduct, they are not applicable to political life, to the conduct of states*."[107] Consequently, "custom" ("*Sitte*") plays a necessary and important role in man's ethical life. As Hegel relates in his early work on the scientific modes of treating "natural right," "*The striving for a morality of one's own is futile, and by its very nature impossible of attainment; in regard to morality, the saying of the wisest of antiquity is the only true one – to be moral is to live in accordance*

---

[105] Cited by Ernst Cassirer, *Albert Schweitzer as Critic of Nineteenth-Century Ethics*, in: Roback, A.A., *The Albert Schweitzer Jubilee Book*, Sci-Art Publishers, Cambridge, Massachusetts, 1946, pp. 241–257; here: p. 248.

[106] Ibid., 1946, p. 249.

[107] Ibid., 1946, p. 253.

with the moral traditions of one's country."[108] With Hegel, according to Cassirer, historical thought reached an apotheosis and definitely took precedence over ethical thought.

Philosophy, as Hegel makes clear in the introduction to his *Philosophy of law*, comes always too late. "*Philosophy, as the thought of the world, does not appear until reality has completed its formative process and made itself ready. What is thus thought by the nation, history always shows to be necessary; only in the ripeness of reality does the ideal appear over against the actual, and builds up for itself that same world, apprehended in its substance into an intellectual kingdom. When philosophy paints its grey in grey, one form of life has become old, and by means of grey in grey, it cannot be rejuvenated but only known. The veil of Minerva takes its flight only when the shades of night are gathering.*"[109] For Schweitzer, though, philosophy only comes too late when it forfeits its mission and principal duty, *i.e.*, that it play a leading role in the reconstruction and maintenance of modern civilization, and for that purpose that it educates modern man. As opposed to Hegel's *historical* rationalism and optimism, Schweitzer's *ethical* rationalism and optimism contradicts any philosophical quietism, whether that of Hegel, who exclusively sought "*to understand, to interpret, and justify his "present world,""* or any other nineteenth century philosophic thought that attests to the power of Hegel's system.[110]

Schweitzer is concerned about the coercive means adopted by states to hinder the ethical capacities of individuals. "*During the war the control of thought was made complete. Propaganda definitely took the place of truth ... If we find among men of today too few whose human and moral sensibility is still undamaged, the chief reason is that the majority have offered up their personal morality on the altar of their country, instead of remaining at variance with the mass and acting as a force which impels the latter along the road to perfection.*"[111] Schweitzer's subsequent propagation of the belief in thought and reverence

---

[108] Cited by Ernst Cassirer, *Albert Schweitzer as Critic of Nineteenth-Century Ethics*, in: Roback, A.A., *The Albert Schweitzer Jubilee Book*, Sci-Art Publishers, Cambridge, Massachusetts, 1946, pp. 241–257; here: p. 254.

[109] Ibid., 1946, p. 256.

[110] Ibid., 1946, p. 257.

[111] Ibid., 1946, pp. 254–255.

for truth is ethically inspired. He does not follow Hegel in his proposition that the history of the world is the judgment of the world, that there is no higher Court of Appeal than the Reason of history. Following Kant, Schweitzer adheres to the principle of "the primacy of practical reason," that reason is the practical power of the individual to organize the human world. Schweitzer seeks the very center of our cultural life in the depth of individual life and individual consciousness. Philosophy, in this regard, has to trust its own power. Its principal duty is to fulfill its educational task, *i.e.*, to teach modern man "*how to develop his active faculties in order to form his individual and social life.*"[112] In relation to the predicament of modern man, Schweitzer fundamentally agrees with the philosophical thought of the eighteenth century, that the fear of public opinion has to be superseded and all ideas have to justify themselves again to his individual moral reason.

Cassirer fundamentally agrees with Schweitzer's appeal to the reconstruction of the primacy of ethical thought in culture, and the reinstatement of individual moral judgment to the center of all cultural life. However, for Cassirer, not the materialism of the nineteenth century (for example in the form of nationalism), but the idealistic systems of the nineteenth century, that were profoundly influenced by Hegel's thought, were responsible for the loss of the primacy of ethical thought: "*Ethics itself abdicated its inherent rights* (...)," because "*it submitted to the verdict of historical reality.*"[113] Cassirer's critique of nineteenth century philosophy resulted in a neo-humanistic foundation of culture and a consequent critique of twentieth century life philosophy that had the same appeal and fallacies as the nineteenth century fatalist and quietist tendencies. For Cassirer the most ardent danger posed to the ethical personalities of individuals, and their critical potential to ask

---

[112] Ernst Cassirer, *Philosophy and Politics (1944)*, in: Ibid., *Symbol, Myth, and Culture. Essays and Lectures of Ernst Cassirer 1935–1945*, edited by D.P. Verene, Yale University Press, New Haven and London, pp. 219–232; here: p. 230.

[113] See: Ernst Cassirer, *Albert Schweitzer as Critic of Nineteenth-Century Ethics*, in: Roback, A.A., *The Albert Schweitzer Jubilee Book*, Sci-Art Publishers, Cambridge, Massachusetts, 1946, pp. 241–257; here: p. 255.

about the conditions of their life and the direction it takes, was represented by fatalism.

An individual that is overwhelmed by fatalism fails to see or believe that he can make a difference, and that he can make a difference only when taking up his responsibility to use his moral reason. Through fatalism or the appeal to a common fate, out of desperation, the individual could be reduced to the masses and steered in any direction. Myths were essential for that process, and Cassirer had already anticipated that danger with his philosophy of culture. As he himself conceded it would take the catastrophic events of the Second World War before he could grasp the seriousness of the crisis, and Schweitzer made that clear to him as no other. Whereas the endeavors of the ancient Greeks, and the Cambridge Platonists were all directed to the (re)instatement of the worth of individual moral judgment as the pole star of all cultural activity, faced by the ruptures plaguing Western culture, Cassirer set out to explain the causes of those ruptures. He traced them back to the fatalistic tendencies of the idealistic systems of the nineteenth century, and he explained in what respect the strengthening of individual symbolic capacities, *i.e.*, the formative power of the individual, would provide a route for the recovery and progressive development of culture. We now turn to Cassirer's critique of those fatalistic tendencies that curbed the individual in making moral assessments, hence in his sense of individuality. In the conclusion, we explicate the way in which Cassirer's humanism offers a perspective for the individual.

I. 5. What are the Humanistic Premises of Cassirer's Philosophy of Culture?

Although "culture," as cultural life or cultural world, is an important theme in Cassirer's works, the term "culture" first appears as a title term in 1939 in Sweden, *i.e.*, after his acquaintance with Schweitzer. Both Cassirer and Schweitzer had in common that they regarded culture as an ongoing task, a process of normative meaning giving.[114] According to Cassirer, and as

---

114 Günzler, 1995, pp. 312–319; here: p. 319; cf. Orth, 1990, pp. 156 ff., for a description of Cassirer's meeting with Schweitzer, see Toni Cassirer, 1981, pp. 216–220.

elaborated below, for man as an animal symbolicum this process, hence the future or progress of a culture is guaranteed so long as human creativity and its symbolic capacities are not seriously hampered or impaired.[115] A culture is as strong as its individuals. In this respect, the philosophy of culture of Cassirer may be described as a neo-humanistic philosophy of culture. Next to Kant, it was primarily the neo-humanist statesman, philosopher, and linguist Wilhelm von Humboldt (1767–1835) Cassirer discussed in his works.[116] Just as Schweitzer, Cassirer criticized nineteenth century philosophy for its neglect of the worth of individual moral judgment. However, Cassirer made exceptions for thinkers, such as Wilhelm von Humboldt and Goethe who, against the strong tide of the time, did not attach increasing importance to the abstract and the general, but rather considered the lively circumstances of the individual as was still common in the eighteenth century. In their works they reinstated the individual at the center stage of philosophic thought and culture.

The humanism of the eighteenth century no longer restricted its investigations to the past, but directed them primarily into the future.[117] Furthermore, it did not confine itself to the ethical dimension, but held that ethical, social and political life were the product of the *humanitas* and represented its most noble fruit. For eighteenth century humanism humanity stretches itself along all that which is the expression of the formative power of

---

115 See: Ernst Cassirer, *Naturalistische und humanistische Begründung der Kulturphilosophie*, Göteborgs Kungl. Vetenskaps- och Vitterhets-Samhälles Handlingar. Femte foljden, Ser. A, Bd. 7, Nr. 3, 1939, pp. 1–28; here: p. 28; for a translation of this text see: Ernst Cassirer, *Introduction. Naturalistic and humanistic philosophies of culture*, in: ibid., *The Logic of the Humanities*, (*Zur Logik der Kulturwissenschaften. Fünf Studien*, in: Göteborgs Högskolas Arsskrift, Volume 48, Heft 1, 1942, pp. 1–139), tr. C.S. Howe, Yale University Press, New Haven, 1961, pp. 3–38.

116 Of great significance is Johan Wolfgang von Goethe (1749–1832), but Cassirer is much less explicit in his references to Goethe. Only later, in his (originally unpublished) fourth volume of his philosophy of symbolic forms Cassirer refers explicitly to Goethe, who is of great importance for Cassirer's philosophy; see especially: Chapter 5.

117 See: Ernst Cassirer, *Naturalistische und humanistische Begründung der Kulturphilosophie*, Göteborgs Kungl. Vetenskaps- och Vitterhets-Samhälles Handlingar. Femte foljden, Ser. A, Bd. 7, Nr. 3, 1939, p. 15.

the human being. The humanism of the eighteenth century was guided by the principle that it is characteristic of the human being that it does not lose itself in the multitude of external impressions, but that it learns to curb this multitude, when it imprints those impressions with a certain intellectual form that ultimately originates from the human mind, *i.e.*, from the thinking, feeling, and willing subject.[118]

According to Cassirer, this will and faculty to form stood at the basis of what Herder and Humboldt think of as the essence of language, of what Schiller thinks of as the essence of the play and of art, of what Kant thinks of as the structure of theoretical knowledge, and of what Goethe thinks of the formation of our perceptual world.[119] It is the characteristic of *humanitas* that it has the capacity to be productive, that is to say, to give expressive form to impressions. In this respect, Herder and Goethe do not follow Kant in his distinction between the *mundus intelligibilis* and the *mundus sensibilis*, *i.e.*, they do not allot *humanitas* a specific ontological status; rather they recognize in it only a certain capacity – and Cassirer concurs with the latter position. What is important is the capacity of the individual to progressively attain stages of higher objectivity through his formative powers, by focusing on and encapsulating a multitude of impressions in a certain point.[120] When comparing this neo-humanist tendency in the philosophy of culture – the humanism of Goethe, Herder, and Humboldt, that still has its foundation in the depths of individual life and consciousness – with the great idealistic systems of the nineteenth century, there appears a great gap. In the meantime, with nineteenth century idealism, the individual seems to have lost its central position and seems to have made way for the absolute and the abstract. To understand how philosophy lost sight of the individual as the

---

118 Ibid., 1939, p. 16.

119 On the relation between Cassirer's notion of "symbolic pregnance" and Goethe's theory of color or perception, see: Naumann, B., *Talking Symbols: Cassirer's Repetition of Goethe*, in: Rudolph, E. and Küppers, B.-O., *Kulturkritik nach Ernst Cassirer*, Cassirer–Forschungen; Bd. 1, Felix Meiner Verlag, Hamburg, 1995, pp. 353–372; here: pp. 368 ff.

120 See: Ernst Cassirer, *Naturalistische und humanistische Begründung der Kulturphilosophie*, Göteborgs Kungl. Vetenskaps- och Vitterhets-Samhälles Handlingar. Femte foljden, Ser. A, Bd. 7, Nr. 3, 1939, p. 17.

focus point of culture, Cassirer explores the challenges posed to what he calls the neo-humanist account of the philosophy of culture.

A first challenge to culture (and the individual as its focus point) thus understood came from Romanticism, according to Cassirer. The philosophy of culture of the romantic era related all conscious phenomena to what is called the "*Volksgeist*" or the national spirit. Culture, for Romanticism, is not an autonomous phenomenon, nor does it originate in an original spontaneity of the individual. Rather, it is a gradual becoming and growing from the national spirit that can only be lived through, that is to say, experienced as, faith. Accordingly, for Savigny for example, law rests on custom, on tradition and popular belief, and can only grow from such an internal and calmly progressing accumulation.[121] Cassirer distinguishes between three types of fatalism or historical determinism that flow from this romantic impetus. Next to a physical and psychological fatalism, Cassirer distinguishes a metaphysical fatalism.[122]

In physical fatalism the individual is impaired in its spontaneity and its life is (pre-)determined by natural laws, *viz.* the physical complexity of affairs, the kind of land, the climate, the laws of heredity and the laws that regulate social heritage. In the theory developed by Auguste Comte, though, individual activity does not recede completely, because the individual has yet to adapt himself to his environment and in this way modifies his environment to himself within fixed limits or what Comte calls "*fatalité modifiable.*"[123] Positivism in the Comtean train does not refrain completely from individual life. On the contrary, the French positivist Hippolite Taine proposes that "*Rien n'existe que par l'individu; c'est l'individu lui-même qu'il faut connaître.*"[124] Basically, he declares, there is no myth or language. All there is are people who need words and images and who create concepts. History, for Taine, cannot be treated but through considering active, physical and visible men, *i.e.*, men "*in their working conditions, behind their desks, on the fields, with their sun, their soil, their houses, their children,*

[121] Ibid., 1939, pp. 5–6.
[122] Ibid., 1939, pp. 12–14.
[123] Ibid., 1939, pp. 12–13.
[124] Ibid., 1939, p. 20.

their meals (...)."[125] He wants to avoid giving an historical account simply through mass movements; rather he wants to give access to historical eras by considering the life of the individual and by representing the individual in its full and concrete definiteness.

However, the individual of Taine does not appear as the "monadic" being with formative power that the eighteenth century humanists envisioned. Rather, once we have discovered the physico-psychological matter and hence the driving force of man, we can discern man in his entirety, with all his ideas and ideals. Accordingly, in this respect man is nothing but an animal of a higher rank. For Taine, man is an animal that produces poems and philosophical systems with the same necessity as silkworms produce their cocoons or bees their honey-cells. Inspired by the same idea he proposes in the preface to "*Les Origins de la France contemporaine*" that as a historian he should be allowed to proceed as a natural scientist and without any hidden motive to describe the political history of France as one would describe the metamorphosis of an insect.[126] In this respect, the individual cannot affect any diversion from this history, nor can it set its own course.

The second form of fatalism Cassirer calls psychological fatalism as it was represented by Spengler at the first half of the twentieth century. That what positivism holds for the individual, *i.e.*, that it is governed by certain external (natural) laws, Spengler simply applies to cultures in general. Moreover, for Spengler, physical factors do not determine a culture, rather they are the expression of a certain spirituality. The inception of a culture is effectuated through a mythical act. However, the mythical act that stands at the foundation of a culture does not admit of being asked from where it comes or why it has occurred, but can only be accepted as an irreducible fact. In Spengler's mystical fatalism, as a result, the individual is determined in his being and doing by an inexorable necessity that does not even give room to the modifiable fate of the naturalistic positivism of Comte.

[125] Ibid., 1939, p. 21.
[126] Ibid., 1939, p. 24.

Furthermore, for Spengler, culture cannot be the proper object of science in whatever form, because the true logical instrument of culture can only be poetry. As a result, Spengler decides to compose the epos of the history of the world and the tragedy of the decline of the West.[127] In Spengler's account of culture the individual cannot but surrender himself captive to its destiny and can only gaze at its own nothingness in respect to its fate. Nor can a single person do anything to avert the rise and decline of individual cultures, which are simply twists of fate.[128] All cultures have their own course of life, and it would be an error to assume that a certain individual can make a difference in respect to its historic development. If not one certain individual stands up to fulfill its historical task, surely it is only a matter of course that another eventually will effectuate the destined course of a culture. As such, the psychological fatalism of Spengler has a common ground with a third form of fatalism.

Contrary to what one may expect *prima facie*, a third form of fatalism, according to Cassirer, is represented by Hegel in the form of a metaphysical fatalism. Although Hegel's philosophy wants to be a philosophy of freedom, nevertheless, it directs its acts of liberation not at the finite subject, but only and exclusively at the infinite, absolute subject. The former is nothing but a pawn through which "world spirit" materializes its course. Individual subjects in Hegel's metaphysical system are merely instruments of a higher power that guides them according to its objectives and subordinates them to its orders. Here also, the individual may assume that it is acting on its own accord and responsibility, but this independence of action and thought is merely illusory.[129] The dialectical meaning of Hegel's concept of the development of culture is very clear about the fact that all development is aimed at a single and highest goal, that everything is directed to the realization of the "absolute idea."[130]

---

[127] Cf. Spengler, O.A.G., *Der Untergang des Abendlandes: Umrisse einer Morpholohie der Weltgeschichte*, Beck, München, 1918–1922.

[128] See: Ernst Cassirer, *Naturalistische und humanistische Begründung der Kulturphilosophie*, Göteborgs Kungl. Vetenskaps- och Vitterhets-Samhälles Handlingar. Femte foljden, Ser. A, Bd. 7, Nr. 3, 1939, pp. 1–28; here: pp. 13–14.

[129] Ibid., 1939, p. 14.

[130] Ibid., 1939, p. 24.

Reason for Hegel is substance and infinite power, that is to say reason is "*not so faint to merely make it to an ideal, to make it to ought.*"[131] Rather, for Hegel, the rational is real and the real is rational. The original spontaneity of the individual cannot have, for Hegel, a constructive role in culture, nor can it give rise to the formation of culture.

Facing these challenges to the neo-humanist account of the philosophy of culture, Cassirer asks, "*Is there against this threefold bondage, as it is presented to us here by physics, by psychology, and by metaphysics, some leeway, and in what way can we gain leverage to regain an independent meaning and an independent worth for the individual being and individual activity?*"[132] Against the substantive conception of reason with which Hegel's system is governed and permeated, Cassirer proposes a functional conception of reason. For Cassirer reason is never a mere present or an *actual*, but a constant and ever *actualizing*, "*not a* given *but a* task."[133] According to Cassirer, we must seek reason in the continual self-renewing work of spirit that finds its expression in the "*weight of our will and our personality.*"[134]

The thinker Cassirer singles out for this purpose, *i.e.*, to countenance or to find some intellectual counterweight against fatalism in all its forms, is Wilhelm von Humboldt. For Cassirer, Humboldt provides a bridge to close the gap nineteenth century philosophic thought had created with respect to the "worth" and "place" of the individual in culture. Humboldt's work, according to Cassirer, stands in contrast to the metaphysical systems of German nineteenth century idealism. For Humboldt, every universal in the field of culture cannot be viewed but through the acts of individuals, because only through them can it find its actualization and its true realization. [135] As Humboldt stated at

---

131 Ibid., 1939, p. 28.

132 Ibid., 1939, p. 14.

133 See: Ernst Cassirer, *The Concept of Philosophy as a Philosophical Problem (1935)*, in: Ibid., *Symbol, Myth, and Culture. Essays and Lectures of Ernst Cassirer 1935–1945*, edited by D.P. Verene, Yale University Press, New Haven and London, 1979, pp. 49–63; here: p. 62.

134 Ibid., 1979 (1935), p. 62.

135 See: Ernst Cassirer, *Naturalistische und humanistische Begründung der Kulturphilosophie*, Göteborgs Kungl. Vetenskaps- och Vitterhets-Samhälles

the end of his life, "*Also in world occurrences and in the results states achieve, the actual most important thing always remains that which concerns the doing, the minding* (Geist) *and the experience of individuals. Man is presently everywhere the centre point, and every man stands in the end alone, so that only that which goes on in and from himself, has relevance for him.*"[136] While the universal has no significance but through the particular, accordingly the individual attains to its true meaning first when placed in its context, *i.e.*, humanity.

Accordingly, for Humboldt, the clearest evidence that "*man does not possess an intrinsically separate individuality, that "I" and "you" are not merely complementary concepts, but that if we could go back to the point of separation, they would prove to be truly identical,*" comes from language.[137] Language, for Humboldt, is rooted in the ultimate depths of humanity and leads us right back to it. It is not simply an act (*ergon*), a passively perceived, finished and lifeless product, but it is an activity (*energeia*), a production stemming from an inner energy, creativity, or spontaneity of the individual mind; it is characterized by what Cassirer calls "symbolic formation."[138] For Humboldt, language displays a certain basic tendency toward unity and totality, *i.e.*, "*a notion or inner conviction that humankind despite all diversification and variety is still in its core and in its ultimate goal indivisible and one.*"[139]

Handlingar. Femte foljden, Ser. A, Bd. 7, Nr. 3, 1939, pp. 1–28; here: pp. 18–19.

[136] See: Ernst Cassirer, *Freiheit und Form. Studien zur deutschen Geistesgeschichte*, Gesammelte Werke Band 7, Felix Meiner Verlag, Hamburg, 1998 (1916), p. 354 (526).

[137] See: Ernst Cassirer, *Critical Idealism as a Philosophy of Culture (1936)*, in: ibid., *Symbol, Myth, and Culture. Essays and Lectures of Ernst Cassirer 1935–1945*, edited by D.P. Verene, Yale University Press, New Haven and London, 1979, pp. 64–91; here: p. 73.

[138] See: Ernst Cassirer, *The Concept of Philosophy as a Philosophical Problem (1935)*, in: Ibid., *Symbol, Myth, and Culture. Essays and Lectures of Ernst Cassirer 1935–1945*, edited by D.P. Verene, Yale University Press, New Haven and London, 1979, pp. 49–63; here: p. 56.

[139] See: Ernst Cassirer, *Naturalistische und humanistische Begründung der Kulturphilosophie*, Göteborgs Kungl. Vetenskaps- och Vitterhets-Samhälles Handlingar. Femte foljden, Ser. A, Bd. 7, Nr. 3, 1939, pp. 1–28; here: p. 19.

Individuality may divide everything into pieces, but this division, for Humboldt, in a curious way establishes a feeling of unity and offers the possibility of at least representing this unity as an idea, *i.e.*, of attesting to it symbolically. Man is characterized by his wish to progressively transcend above the divisive limitations of his individuality, and to lift his individuality into a higher sphere by – as is explained more to the full below – reaching out and relating to the other. Von Humboldt writes in his treatise "On the task of the historian", "*Greece framed ... an idea of national individuality that had never existed previously or afterwards, and since the secret of all existence* (Dasein) *lies in individuality, likewise lies in that degree* [of individuality] *the freedom and peculiarity of the interaction of all world historical advancement of mankind.*"[140] In Humboldt, according to Cassirer, the principle of individuality had found its purest and deepest reception. Moreover, for Cassirer, the principle of individuality found its poetic expression as no other in the works and life of Goethe.[141] In the works of Goethe, Cassirer sees the consummation of what it means to strive toward "one's own independent views in science, in art, in life."[142] Such an active involvement, according to Cassirer, is mostly the works of great, truly productive individuals – and, in this respect, Goethe is exemplary for that as well.

Cassirer's cultural theory does not commit itself to making prophecies about the future of culture, because it does not deal with mere physical being and occurrences, but deals with human actions. Human action becomes self-conscious only in its own fruition and in the light of the presented possibilities.[143] The future of a culture therefore does not admit itself

---

140 Ibid., 1939, p. 20; for a different view on Greek nationalism, see: Jaeger, 1945, pp. 288–289.

141 See: Ernst Cassirer, *Goethe und die geschichtliche Welt. Drei Aufsätze*, Verlag Bruno Cassirer, Berlin, 1932, pp. 19 ff.; cf. Naumann, B., *Umschreibungen des Symbolischen. Ernst Cassirers Goethe*, in: Naumann, 2002, pp. 1–23; here: pp. 14–15. For an exquisite treatment of Goethe's development from lawyer to philosophical poet, see: Edmond Cahn, *Goethe's View of law – With a Gloss out of Plato*, Columbia Law Review, Volume 49, No. 7 (Nov., 1949), pp. 904–920.

142 Cited by: Naumann, B., *Talking Symbols: Cassirer's Repetition of Goethe*, in: Rudolph, E. and Küppers, B.-O., *Kulturkritik nach Ernst Cassirer*, Cassirer–Forschungen; Bd. 1, Felix Meiner Verlag, Hamburg, 1995, pp. 353–372; here: pp. 353–354.

to be foretold. The only thing Cassirer maintains is, that "*culture will be and make progress, insofar as the formative powers, that ultimately must be put about by ourselves, do not break down or slacken.* This *prediction we can sure enough make and it is for ourselves, for our own action and for our own judgments the single most important. Because it does not guarantee us beforehand the unconditional achievability of the objective goal; but it teaches us as against this goal our own, subjective responsibility.*"[144] It is Cassirer's main ethical position that culture does not as so much promise happiness to mankind, as it promises that every human person is equally worthy of happiness. The aim of culture is not so much as to realize happiness on Earth, as it is to achieve freedom, autonomy in the true sense of the term. That means not the technological mastery of man over nature, but rather more the moral mastery over himself. It is Cassirer's aim to empower and strengthen personal individuality that can and must assert itself meaningfully through various symbolic forms. The assertion of individuality can only be in the form of a self-liberation, because "*everything that liberates our mind, without giving mastery over ourselves, is corruptive.*"[145]

II. CONCLUSION

In this chapter we have explicated Cassirer's view of the importance of individual moral judgment, its origins in ancient Greek thought, and the pursuance of that ideal, as it was expressed paradigmatically by Socrates, and explored in full depth and width with Renaissance thought, by the Cambridge

---

143 Cf. Orth, E.-W., *Goethe als Therapeutikum. Zu Ernst Cassirers Pathologie des Symbolischen,* in: Naumann, 2002, pp. 137–156; here: p. 150.

144 Ibid., 2002, pp. 151–152.

145 Goethe, *Maximen und Reflexionen,* cited by: Ibid., 2002, p. 153; cf. Ernst Cassirer, *Goethes Idee der Bildung und Erziehung* (Pädagogisches Zentralblatt 12 (1932), pp. 340–358), Gesammelte Werke, Band 18, *Aufsätzeund kleine Schriften 1932–1935,* Meiner Verlag, Hamburg, 2004, pp. 127–147; here: p. 147.

Platonists. Cassirer was impressed by the ethical zeal of Albert Schweitzer. After his encounter with Schweitzer, Cassirer more explicit than ever addressed practical problems in the field of moral philosophy, jurisprudence, and political science. However, Cassirer already prepared for this practical turn in his intellectual life. Through his study of the Cambridge Platonists he underscored the relevance of the connection between individual reason and its notion of justice as an *a priori* principle for the viability of any culture. That is an insight that has already been discovered by and put at the center of intellectual life of ancient Greek culture. As it did in Greek culture, that insight would change the face of Western culture as well, *i.e.*, in respect of our understanding of the individual, the state, and the Divine. Cassirer basically agrees with Schweitzer's diagnosis of Western civilization, but gives a particular cultural turn to it. Not the materialism of the nineteenth century, but the fatalistic tendencies of its idealistic systems were the prime cause of the crisis in Western culture. Fatalism accords no active role for the individual in culture, and, at its extremes, attempts to negate individuality altogether.

A culture dominated by fatalism does not provide for a fruitful soil for its own development and thriving. Moreover, an individual that is discredited as to its capability of questioning the world as to its *quid iuris*, *i.e.*, curbed in (the formation of) its individual moral judgment or reasoning; is at the same time discouraged to contribute to the flourishing of culture in general, and the maintenance of democracy in particular. That *democracy is the reign by persuasion rather than the reign by force*, and that democracies find their power in persuasion rather than derive their persuasiveness from force, is an insight that has repeatedly been asserted throughout the history of human civilization. Moreover, its importance has found its most tragic assertion with the rise of totalitarianism. The next chapter explains in what sense totalitarianism is intrinsically tied to mythical thought or mentality. Although myth forms the matrix of all cultural life, and the individual cannot completely discard or ignore it, especially during times of crises, nevertheless, the road to freedom is not foreclosed, because the individual has available a variety of symbolic forms with which to pave the road to freedom. As Goethe puts it, *"Is the infinite your aspiration? Traverse all the finite's configurations!"*

CHAPTER 4

THE POLITICS OF MYTH. CASSIRER'S PATHOLOGY OF THE TOTALITARIAN STATE[1]

I. INTRODUCTION

Cassirer was compelled to flee from the Nazis a second time, when Sweden was threatened by invasion, and he managed to take the last civilian transport ship from Europe to America. His forced exile across the Atlantic made clear to him that it was a different world he lived in now. He was no longer in the German Empire, where his opinion did not matter or was not appreciated, because he was a Jewish scholar, nor had he to defend the last shreds of hope he had for the Weimar Republic and its constitutional and democratic structure. In the relatively secure environment of the U.S.A., watching Germany fatally succumb to a disastrous fate, he had no alternative but express himself on what seemed to be a radically altered world. In the meantime, students, friends and colleagues of Cassirer were asking him whether he could explain the crisis that held Europe and the world in its grip; "why this war, why this barbarism?"[2] They looked upon him as a man with great wisdom and knowledge, unequalled in his time. As a result, Cassirer wrote his intellecttual testament in the field of political science, *i.e.*, "The Myth of the State." This chapter focuses on Cassirer's perspective on the political in more detail, by explicating its structures and its relation to his all-encompassing theoretical view, *i.e.*, the philosophy of symbolic forms.

It is important to note that Cassirer had already devoted considerable energy to countenance the very forces that had

---

1 This chapter has resulted in the following publication: Coskun, D., *The Politics of Myth. Ernst Cassirer's Pathology of the Totalitarian State*, Perspectives on Political Science, Volume 36, No. 4, Winter 2006.

2 See: Vergely, 1998, pp. 7 ff.

made possible, if not prepared for, the rise of Nazi ideology through his study of the role and function of myth in modern human culture. His appeal to reason and moral progress in culture was of no avail, though, for a public already under the spell of a pre-Nazi ideology. Myth for Cassirer represented a process, or state of mind that involved pessimism and fatalism, in which there is no space for individual initiative, responsibility, or moral judgment, but only deference to something more encompassing, such as the cosmos, nature, or for that matter, the State, in which all individuality, hence individual responsibility, dissolves. As is explicated below, myth is a remarkable phenomenon, because in the process of feeling one with something more encompassing the individual first gains a sense of himself, *i.e.*, as part of a greater unity. However, in the mythical phase any sense of individuality is still something suspect and something that must be suppressed. Whereas through myth we achieve a first sense of self, it also becomes an impediment for achieving individuality and developing our personality. Only in later phases, such as the religious and the ethical – symbolic forms, as Cassirer calls them – individuality becomes something to which one ought to strive. Not only was Cassirer unique in making myth a serious focus of philosophical investigation, he also was unique in explicating that the mythical aspects of culture can never be completely overcome, and, especially at times of crises, can dominate our social and political lives as well. Myth in the political domain makes us think in terms of collectivities instead of individual human persons, and in terms of good and evil instead of human dignity. Culture or civilization is never a mere given, according to Cassirer, but always a process or task that we must set for ourselves.

While we have given a brief description of what myth stands for in the theory of Cassirer, in the following, we elaborate further on Cassirer's conception of the mythical relative to his political pathology. Myth is a symbolic form for Cassirer, that is to say, it is a particular mode through which we have a view of the world and relate to one another. Symbolic forms are processes by which we create a world of our own through a web of meanings, and engage in relations with others and create communities through our human capability of what we call "symbolic interchange" and "perspectival flexibility." While we can relate to one another through myth, language, religion, law, politics, and science, simultaneously and adjacently, *i.e.*, without apparent conflict between them, the symbolic forms do not come out of a void. According to Cassirer, the various symbolic forms develop out of a common matrix, *i.e.*, that of myth. Myth is the very first attempt of the human being to come to terms with the world symbolically. We cannot discuss here what constitutes a symbolic form as a symbolic form – something we elaborate on in Chapter 5 – but when important to understand Cassirer's political science we will elucidate matters summarily.

In his *Essay on Man*, Cassirer maintains that Western culture is in a crisis. In his *The Myth of the State*, moreover, written shortly after the Essay on Man, Cassirer reflects his view on the political by explicating the connection between the Western cultural crisis and contemporary political developments. His insights prove fruitful in explaining, not that the politics of myth in the form of National Socialism was the result of a failure of Western rationality or reason, as Horkheimer and Adorno contended, but rather that it was the result of the failure of culture. This is not to contend that Western culture was or is bound to fail, but rather that every culture especially at the political level, finds itself on "*volcanic soil*," as Cassirer put it. By claiming that the politics of myth together with its atrocities was not the failure of rationality, but that of culture, Cassirer distinguishes himself from political theorists such as Horkheimer and Adorno. Essential for the modern failure of culture, according to Cassirer, was the interplay between myth and technology in the political domain. It proved an explosive mix in the hands of what he called the politicians of myth.

This chapter explores more fully Cassirer's diagnosis of the cultural crisis, and the consequent impact and relationship of the cultural crisis with the political. This chapter proceeds as follows: In Section I.1, we explain in what sense Cassirer's philosophy was responsive to so-called life philosophy, which more and more characterized (post-) *fin-du-siècle* philosophy on the European Continent. Furthermore, in Section I.2, we explain the cultural crisis according to Cassirer and its causes. In addition, in Section I.3, we elaborate on how the technological age contributed influentially to the cultural crisis by establishing its hegemony over the whole of cultural life in disregard of its moral dimension.

Moreover, in Section I.4, we explicate how the totalitarian state sustained the cultural crisis by creating myths of the state through political craftsmanship or technology. Subsequently, in Section I.5, we explicate Cassirer's insight of how the cultural crisis provided a matrix for the thriving of the totalitarian state. Finally, in the conclusion, we not only give an assessment of Cassirer's pathology of the totalitarian state, but also point out that understanding and coming to terms with myth is essential for any democracy. In the conclusion to Part I, we give an assessment of the results of this Part, and allude to the subject of the next Part: Law as Symbolic Form.

I. 1. What was Cassirer's Critique of Life Philosophy?

Cassirer's philosophy of symbolic forms is a reaction to life philosophy and the latter's insistence on the immediacy of experiencing life. At various occasions he referred to the commonalities between life philosophy on the one hand and myth on the other. Cassirer's engagement with the philosophical study of myth was a method for him to analyze life philosophy and to understand its strengths and weaknesses. Indeed, when looking back one could say that Cassirer did whatever he could to temper the growing influence that life philosophy claimed on the intellectual life of the era.[3] For Cassirer, the leading contemporary figure of life philosophy was Martin Heidegger, with whom he was not only a colleague in Marburg, but who also stood in a decades long debate, for example as exemplified at Davos in 1929. Already at Davos, Cassirer pointed to Heidegger's insistence on the finitude of man, man's "fate" (*Schicksal*), man being "thrown" (*Geworfen*) into his "destiny" (*Geschick*), and as such being delivered over to the destiny of the truth of being, which made Heidegger particularly appealing to the pre-pro-Nazi public, who were already under the spell of defeat, globalizing unemployment, and accompanying experience of powerlessness. The defeatist and pessimistic tonality of Heidegger's philosophy constitutes a persisting point of criticism of Cassirer, and although Heidegger is religiously inspired, Cassirer sees in it nothing less than a secular form of eschatology.

---

[3] Schnädelbach, 1991, p. 176; cf. 1996, pp. 158–159, 391n.

Therefore, at the start of the twentieth century the sky was all but clear for the proper reinstatement of the individual to its central place in culture. Fatalistic, hence individuality-defying tendencies were still prevalent and even growing in strength to seriously undermine any democratic project in Germany. As a result, Cassirer had to clear his ground, so to speak, by taking a stance with, and countenancing, the fatalistic tendencies in the Weimar culture, and Western culture in general. The philosophical currents that found inspiration in these tendencies Cassirer subsumed under the term *Lebensphilosophie* or "life philosophy." For Cassirer life philosophy stood for those trends in culture, which center on the premise that the "*the truth of life seems to be given only in its pure* immediacy (…)."[4] The term "life philosophy" has a history that reaches at least back to German Romanticism, wherein "life" is an apposite concept to define the struggle against the rationalism of the enlightenment, and, which is identified with it, the mechanical naturalism in the conception of nature. The students and editors of the philosopher Wilhelm Dilthey first used the term *Lebensphilosophie* to describe and entitle the master's later works,[5] and it would reach its consummation in the works of Cassirer's early mentor, Georg Simmel. Cassirer agrees with Dilthey that life philosophy originates with Goethe,[6] but, for Cassirer Goethe does not represent a diametrically opposite thinker to the rationalism as represented by Kant. Both Kant and Goethe, for Cassirer, were interested in the representational view of nature.[7] In the twentieth century, life philosophy acquired a more inclusive and encompassing

---

4 See: Ernst Cassirer, *The Philosophy of Symbolic Forms*, Volume I, *Language*, tr. R. Manheim, Yale University Press, New Haven, 1953 (1923), p. 111; cf. Möckel, 1998, pp. 355–386.

5 Ringer, 1969, p. 336.

6 Krois, 1987, p. 63; cf. Dilthey, W., *Selected Works*, Volume 5, *Poetry and Experience*, R. Makreel and F. Rodi (eds.), Princeton University Press, Princeton, NJ, 1985, pp. 19–22.

7 Naumann, B., *Talking Symbols: Cassirer's Repetition of Goethe*, in: Rudolph, E. and Küppers, B.-O., *Kulturkritik nach Ernst Cassirer*, Cassirer–Forschungen; Bd. 1, Felix Meiner Verlag, Hamburg, 1995, pp. 353–372; here: pp. 369–370. Cf. Goethe's famous remark: "*The ultimate would be to understand that everything which is factual is already theory.*" See also: Naumann, B., *Umschreibungen des Symbolischen. Ernst Cassirers Goethe*, in: Naumann, 2002, pp. 1–23; here: pp. 8 ff.

meaning. When Heinrich Rickert wrote a critique of life philosophy in 1920, he explained the subject matter as a "*broad and fashionable*" movement.[8] It included, next to Dilthey and Simmel, diverse names as Klages, Hartmann, Bergson, Scheler, and Eucken. Moreover, Cassirer associates life philosophy with the line of post-idealistic philosophy that runs through Schopenhauer, Nietzsche, Kierkegaard, and Heidegger.[9]

To illustrate, Schopenhauer takes the view of the "intellect" as the complete slave of the will. However, this servitude has its limits and conditions, because the intellect as the will's creation can break free from the chains of the will, by recognizing the latter as "blind will" and, in so doing, effect its negation. With Nietzsche, though, the all-powerful "Will to Power" does not permit any independence of the intellect anymore. What remains, after Nietzsche, is the complete devaluation and rejection of *Geist.*[10] Ludwig Klages, in his three volumes on "*Geist as the enemy of the soul,*" would carry this doctrine to its extreme, when he portrayed all conceptual knowledge and "Geist" as hindrances or "enemies" of life.

Furthermore, life philosophy encapsulates those thinkers that construe life as the ultimate criterion of truth and morals, thereby providing points of departure favorable to the programs of Social Darwinism (Spengler) and that of the moralists of the will to power (Nietzsche, Bergson).[11] In effect, life philosophy established a departure in philosophy with respect to its established values and interests, from the belief in reason, from the natural sciences, and from the nineteenth century aspiration of social and technical advancement, to wholeness, to forgotten and suppressed irrational feeling, and to the tragic and the fateful.[12] As a reaction to rationalist and positivist philosophy, respecttively

---

8 See: Rickert, H., *Die Philosophie des Lebens. Darstellung und Kritik der philosophischen Modeströmung unserer Zeit*, 2. Auflage, Mohr, Tübingen, 1922.

9 See: Ernst Cassirer, *The Philosophy of Symbolic Forms*, Volume 4, *The Metaphysics of Symbolic Forms*, Including the text of Cassirer's manuscript on Basis Phenomena, Krois, J.M. and Verene, D.P. (eds.), tr. by Krois, J.M., Yale University Press, New Haven and London, 1996, p. XI.

10 Ibid., 1996, p. 27.

11 Ringer, 1969, p. 338.

12 Möckel, 1998, pp. 355–386; here: p. 357.

the culture of reason or Enlightenment, it expressed the new "life feeling" (*Lebensgefühl*), accompanied by a considerable amount of crisis-consciousness, critique of culture, passimism, and nihilism.[13] All life philosophers had in common that in their works they laid emphasis on the doctrine that life in its immediacy is man's primary reality.

However, broad as the concept of life philosophy may be, for Cassirer it signified more than merely a name for a popular or fashionable trend in philosophy. Cassirer's approach to life philosophy distinguishes itself from the critique of life philosophy of what Fritz Ringer called the German Mandarins or intellectual elite. His account or critique of life philosophy stops short of depicting it as, or reducing it to, a sheer irrationalism, although some forms of life philosophy were clearly anti-rationalist in their purport.[14] As a matter of fact, Cassirer expressly addressed his intellectual message to those Mandarins who were attracted to life philosophy because of their disdain of contemporary "inhuman" or "alienating" culture, in an attempt to put them on a more constructive track. As Ivan Strenski puts it, "*Cassirer opposed the Mandarins, yet represented the best of them.*"[15]

In *The Metaphysics of Symbolic Forms*, Cassirer compares life philosophy with "negative theology." "*Just as all "negative theology" in its dispensing with the* logos *is itself an act, a deed of* logos, *so too is the return to the pure immediacy of life only possible by a particular act of "seeing," of the "intuition" of life.*" For Cassirer, this intuition too is a way of giving form to our world.[16] "*There is no seeing that is merely receptivity, that does not include a formative function. Even myth (…) is still a kind of configuration of reality. As the expressivity of the world, it necessarily involves its metamorphosis, its transformation into an image.*"[17] By renouncing the achievements of the intellect, by regarding it as nothing more than a degeneration of pure,

---

13 Ibid., 1998, pp. 358–359.

14 Ringer, 1969, p. 339 ff.; cf. Scherer, 1996, pp. 158–159.

15 Strenski, 1984, p. 368.

16 See: Ernst Cassirer, *The Philosophy of Symbolic Forms*, Volume 4, *The Metaphysics of Symbolic Forms*, Including the text of Cassirer's manuscript on Basis Phenomena, Krois, J.M. and Verene, D.P. (eds.), tr. by Krois, J.M., Yale University Press, New Haven and London, 1996, pp. 13 ff.

17 Ibid., 1996, p. 30.

immediately lived life, life philosophy engages itself in a form of negation. This negation is, according to Cassirer, nevertheless inherently an act of self-assertion, because the mere act of negation presumes criteria, value perspectives from which the negated object is negated, and through which those criteria and values find their affirmation. "*Even if the entire sphere of the intellect were conceived of as something negative, even if all its activities were denied and rejected, the mere assigning of this negative meaning is itself a new act that holds us firmly in the sphere of Geist that we had hoped to flee.*"[18]

Next to its constructive contribution to idealist philosophy as a philosophy of culture, Cassirer's attempt to formulate a philosophy of symbolic forms is thus written as a critique of life philosophy. Accordingly, the philosophy of symbolic forms explains why all human knowledge, be it in the form of language, myth, religion, or science, unavoidably is of a mediated form. Through his philosophy of symbolic forms Cassirer cast new light upon "*a last fundamental antithesis, with which modern philosophy has struggled since its beginnings and which it has formulated with increasing sharpness,*" *i.e.*, the antithesis of life and spirit.[19] In other instances too, Cassirer attempted on the theoretical level to repudiate the claims of life philosophy.[20] What distinguishes Cassirer from all other philosophers of his era is his elaboration with mythical thought as an independent symbolic form. Moreover, Cassirer's engagement with myth as a

---

18 Ibid., 1996, p. 33.

19 See: Ernst Cassirer, *The Philosophy of Symbolic Forms*, Volume I, *Language*, tr. R. Manheim, Yale University Press, New Haven, 1953, p. 111.

20 In the following instances Cassirer elaborates on life philosophy: Ernst Cassirer, *Henri Bergsons Ethik und Religionsphilosophie*, in: Der Morgen, Berlin, 1933, Volume 9, Nr. 1, pp. 20–29, and Nr. 2, pp. 138–51; *"Spirit" and "Life" in contemporary philosophy*, in: Schilp, 1973, pp. 857–88n; *The "Tragedy of Culture,"* in: *The Logic of the Humanities*, (*Zur Logik der Kulturwissenschaften. Fünf Studien*, in: Göteborgs Högskolas Arsskrift, Volume 48, Heft 1, 1942, pp. 1–139), tr. C.S. Howe, Yale University Press, New Haven, 1961, pp. 182–217; also important is the publication of a fourth volume that deals with "contemporary philosophy" as Cassirer calls it and that Cassirer announced in earlier writings, but remained for a great part a manuscript until recently: Ernst Cassirer, *The Philosophy of Symbolic Forms*, Volume IV, *The Metaphysics of Symbolic Forms*, tr. J.M. Krois, Yale University Press, New Haven/London, 1996. See: Scherer, 1996, p. 161, 394n.

symbolic form quite appropriately results in a criticism which life philosophy has to face from the perspective of Cassirer. Its encouragement of modern man to disregard the value of rational symbolic worlds marks life philosophy as a destructive force in culture for Cassirer, because it provides incentives for mythical thought to find renewed strength. The consequent re-emergence of mythico-magical expectations, commitments and relationships created a situation wherein individuals could be susceptible to the artificial myths created by an inhumane politics, and hence could attain a lethal impact.[21]

In his critical assessment of life philosophy in *The Myth of the State* Cassirer refers specifically to Spengler – with his gloomy forecast of the decline of the West – and to Heidegger – with his view of man being thrown into or abandoned in the world (*Geworfenheit*). He holds that life philosophy, as represented by Spengler and Heidegger, enfeebled and slowly undermined the forces that could have resisted the modern political myths. Such philosophy, according to Cassirer, "[has] *given up all hopes of an active share in the construction and reconstruction of man's cultural life. Such philosophy renounces its own fundamental and ethical ideas. It can be used then as a pliable instrument in the hands of the political leaders.*"[22] In this way, according to Cassirer, life philosophy (paradigmatically in the persons of Spengler and Heidegger) was not merely symptomatic of, but sustained the cultural crisis and made way for the emergence of what may be called *the politics of myth*. We now turn to an assessment of the cultural crisis perceived by Cassirer.

I. 2. What was the Cultural Crisis Perceived by Cassirer?

Although Cassirer's philosophical sources of inspiration are multifarious,[23] some sources of inspiration have had a peculiarly strong impact, for example, when Cassirer encountered Albert

---

21 Möckel, 1998, pp. 377–378; cf. Marcuse, 1964, pp. 189 ff.

22 Ernst Cassirer, *The Myth of the State*, Yale University Press, New Haven, 1946, p. 293; cf. Strenski, 1984, p. 374.

23 This ranged from thinkers as Cusanus, Vico, Leibniz, Kant, Goethe, Humboldt, Hegel, Simmel, Cohen, and Natorp, to (contemporary) thinkers, such as Husserl, Heidegger, and Schweitzer; cf. Gadol, 1974, pp. 207–225; Verene, 1969, pp. 33–46.

Schweitzer and developed a philosophical friendship with him. After his encounter with Schweitzer, Cassirer made his normative stance in philosophy much more explicit, for example by producing works in the field of jurisprudence, philosophical anthropology, and political science. After Schweitzer's accusation or judgment on philosophy that it had failed in its function as watchman of civilization, Cassirer could not simply give an English translation of his "Philosophy of Symbolic Forms," he wrote *An Essay on Man*, a refined edition and contemporary reformulation of his all-encompassing theoretical view. This work is important in understanding Cassirer's philosophy of symbolic forms and underlines the moral import of his oeuvre. It maintains that Western culture is in a crisis and gives an analysis of the crisis, by relating it back to a lack of self-knowledge in the Socratic sense of the term, and accordingly, to the individual incapable of making moral judgments and taking responsibility for its own actions.

In his *Essay on Man*, Cassirer states that Western culture finds itself in a cultural crisis, a crisis that is due to man's lack of self-knowledge. The question of what man is, according to Cassirer, was never so intensely discussed and asked as in the twentieth century. For example, whereas Nietzsche proclaims the will to power as essential, and Freud comes to the fore with the sexual instinct, Marx glorifies the economic instinct of man. Each and every vision of man is subsequently used as a point of departure to deal with empirical facts, without reflection on the presumption one takes with respect to the particular view on the nature of man. As a result man lost his intellectual center-point, *i.e.*, witnessed a true intellectual anarchy. Cassirer makes clear in his Essay on Man, that the problem of the nature of man cannot be solved by any substantial view of man, rather man, as elaborated below, is to be approached from a functional perspective. Man is an *animal symbolicum*, *i.e.*, man cannot but symbolize; where one finds man, necessarily one finds culture in one form or the other.

The concept of the symbol with Cassirer is indeed very broad; it entails every action through which we render something conceptual into something concrete, when we represent something universal in something particular. Symbols are distinct from mere signs, because whereas the latter are merely a physical matter, the former are active in transferring something conceptual, *i.e.*, meaning. Through symbols we transfer and thereby create meaning. Our symbols are handed over to us, or rather we create them by the various symbolic forms, such as language, myth, and science, and a variety of others. Culture is created by man whenever he gives an enduring form to his surroundings, whenever he objectifies into meaning the various impressions of his life in works. These works are meant to last (in the sphere of meaning) and not whither away as the day turns. We cannot know a man, according to Cassirer, by what he *is*, rather, we can know him only by his actions, *i.e.*, by his *works*. This is at the same time the core of Cassirer's philosophy of symbolic forms. It explains how through various symbolic forms we progressively relate to one another. Through his actions or works the "I" progressively relates to a "Thou," which makes the human being as an *animal symbolicum* a thoroughly expressive and normative being. By relating to another person say by works or actions in language, religion, law, or the state, the "I" is confirmed in his individuality as a symbolic being. Works or actions therefore never stand by themselves, because they are always directed to another person whether in the present or in the future.

While that was his view on the nature of man, in what has been called his intellectual testament, *The Myth of the State*, Cassirer connected the crisis of culture to the contemporary political arena. Cassirer in no way denied, that the most pressing cause for the emergence of totalitarian systems, wherein the return to myth by modern culture could take place, should be attributed to the economical and social crises of the Interbellum. These crises, though, did not entail for Cassirer a sufficient reason for such a development.[24] As all cultures, European culture has experienced a number of deep crises, but the contemporary tendency to relinquish established cultural standards and to replace these with primitive magico-mythical modes of expression and methods of problem solving could not be attributed to any crisis or conflict in particular. The problem of culture in the twentieth century, for Cassirer, was that it faced a structural

---

24 Cf. Evans, 2003, p. 264. For a different assessment, see: Mommsen, 1996 (1989).

problem or crisis, as a result of which it could not take up against the latent destructive forces that reside within every culture.

This structural problem of Western culture was for Cassirer what he called, in *An Essay on Man*, the problem of man's lack of self-knowledge; the "*know thy self,*" which Socrates had advocated from the beginnings of Western culture.[25] As a result of this crisis, Cassirer subsequently contended in *The Myth of the State*, the state could resort to a dangerous alternative, *i.e.*, to the employment of mythico-magical solutions for practical political problems. While knowing one's self requires self-reflection and active use of reason, *i.e.*, a sense of individuality and responsibility by the individual; in mythical thought all self-reflection, reasoning, and responsibility are deferred to the collective.[26] As no other century before, the twentieth century witnessed the implementation of mythical forces through the use of communication technology, by which the individual was reduced to the "masses" and hence could be directed in any way. Culture, not rationality had failed in the eyes of Cassirer, especially in cherishing the individuality of persons and hence their creative potential. A culture is as strong as its individuals, and by giving in to myth the individual was left vulnerable and unprotected. Therewith, Cassirer's critique differs importantly from that of Horkheimer and Adorno.[27]

For Adorno and Horkheimer, the Enlightenment idea of the autonomy of reason exhibited a latent nihilism, that is to say, it contained the nucleus for its own destruction. According to Horkheimer and Adorno, the rationality of Enlightenment thought procured an irresponsible technical domination of life that necessarily had to end in myth. Enlightenment according to Horkheimer and Adorno dialectically reverts to myth. Cassirer does not deny the presence of destructive forces in modern culture that cannot possibly be erased completely or definitely.[28] He refuses to believe that the destruction of human civilization is inevitable; rather he states that this destruction only becomes inevitable when man gives up hope that he can create culture out

---

[25] Stark, 1997, p. 662.

[26] Cf. Vergely, 1998, pp. 7–9.

[27] See: Horkheimer, 1972 (1944); cf. Paetzold, 1994, pp. 112, 122 ff.; Paetzold, 1993, p. 127; and Mosse, 1985, pp. 53–54.

[28] Cf. Krois, 1997, pp. 273–289; here: p. 282.

of freedom, that he can make a qualitative contribution or difference. The latent destructive forces that Adorno and Horkheimer hint at find their express concretization for Cassirer in mythological thought but, by contrast for him, that is not the end result of Enlightenment thought. On the contrary, myth stands in opposition to rationality; and only through the active cultivation of the various intellectual forms are we in a position, according to Cassirer, to subdue and to tame mythical thought. For Cassirer, instrumental, *i.e.*, sheer technical, thought does not exhaust Enlightenment thought, rather the latter stands for a vast array of intellectual, ethical, and aesthetic forces that represent the formative power of the individual or its spontaneity of the mind.[29] Only when these binding intellectual, ethical, and aesthetic forces loose momentum, mythical thought "*starts to rise anew and to pervade the whole of man's cultural and social life.*"[30] Cassirer's *The Myth of the State* has in common, though, with the analysis of Horkheimer and Adorno, that it tries to understand and give an assessment of fascism, especially in the form of National Socialism.[31]

Cassirer's assessment of this fascism operates through the perspective of his philosophy of symbolic forms. The analysis he gave of the pathology of the symbolic consciousness, he now applies to social and political life.[32] In his philosophy of symbolic forms Cassirer found support for his theory of the symbolic in psychopathological studies conducted by Gestalt-psychologists on patients with disorders in their symbolic capacities. These included patients with apraxia, agnosia, and aphasia. What these patients have in common, according to Cassirer, is that they have lost the capacity to react with flexibility and creativity to certain practical problems of life.[33] Their actions are in one or

---

29 Cf. Krois, 1979, pp. 199–217; here: p. 214.

30 See: Ernst Cassirer, *The Myth of the State*, Yale university Press, New Haven, 1946, p. 298.

31 Ibid., 1993, p. 105; as such Cassirer's work stands in a tradition of other works in the same sense: Plessner (*Die verspätete Nation*, 1935), Bloch (*Erbschaft diese Zeit*, 1935) Lukács (*Die Zerstörung der Vernunft*, 1954), and Arendt (*Origins of totalitarianism*, 1951).

32 See: Ernst Cassirer, *The Philosophy of Symbolic Forms*, Volume 3, *Science*, tr. R. Manheim, Yale University Press, New Haven, 1957 (1929), pp. 205–277; cf. Paetzold, 1993, p. 106; see also: Chapter 5.

33 Paetzold, 1993, pp. 105–106.

more ways hampered by the fact that they do not possess a variety of perspectives or ways of giving meaning to certain situations. When confronted with certain problems that require taking into consideration different views with one particular object or problem, they are "stuck," *i.e.*, unable to imagine or consider alternative points of view or alternative solutions. Cassirer gives the example of a patient who is given a plate of yoghurt with a spoon, but subsequently is unable to use the spoon to assist in repairing a gadget because spoons are things with which one eats food, and not to repair things.

Being flexible and dynamic is essential for a culture to survive and to deal with problems or conflicts internally or externally that present themselves to it. "*No advance in human history that was of any great importance,*" writes John Dewey, "*was ever made by taking steps along old lines.* (...) *Taking steps along old lines aids in perfecting principles and methods that are already established, but they never initiate the great steps in human progress. These always come by finding a new method of attack upon the problem.* (...) *I submit to any engineer that no significant step forward in mechanical improvement has ever occurred excepting by finding a new method of approach to get around the obstacles which had piled up and blocked old methods. And the same is true of all social progress.*"[34] Accordingly, Cassirer holds that culture finds itself by necessity involved in conflicts of opposing forces, between forces of conservatism and innovation, between the individual and the society. However, these oppositions within culture are not mutually exclusive, rather they are interdependent.[35] The hypothetical and sometimes unavoidable contrariety of the various ways we have a world of our own, for example through language, myth, religion, science, law, or politics need not result in a stalemate.

For Cassirer, these opposing forces, notwithstanding their potential conflict, stand in a functional unity and harmony; as he

---

34 Dewey, J., *Characters and Events: Popular Essays in Social n Political Philosophy*, edited by J. Ratner, Volume 2, Henry Hold & Co., New York, 1929, pp. 662–663; cited by: McClain, E.F., *A law from the burning bush. The moral foundations of the legal philosophy of Edmond Cahn*, Thesis (M.A.)-Southern Illinois University, Department of Philosophy, Carbondale, Illinois, 1963, p. 32; cf. Koestler, 1966.

35 Cf. Krois, 1987, p. 173.

says at the end of his *Essay on Man*, "*Human culture taken as a whole may be described as the process of man's progressive self-liberation*."[36] In this respect, "progressive" entails for Cassirer man's continuously recurring capacity of creating culture through freedom.[37] Moreover, for Cassirer, the progressive character of the development of culture can take a linear or cumulative form only when the symbolic capacities of man, hence his individuality, are not seriously impaired or imperiled.[38] In his *The Myth of the State*, Cassirer maintains that the state had turned the interdependence of the various cultural or symbolic forms into one of a permanent dependence through the technical generation and exaltation of myth. In the hands of the Nazi state, myth became the dominant mode through which the individual could frame his view of the world or could relate to others.

Alternate ways of having a world or relating to one another, for example through religion or ethics, if not suspect became irrelevant and had to be first subjected to the scrutiny of the Nazi myth of the race. While all the other cultural forms, each of them with their own peculiar forms of objectivity and cultivation, and all of them counterbalancing each other and competing for the composition of the worldview of the individual, were subjected to the power of myth artificially construed and maintained by the state, a retreat into barbarism and cultural despair became inevitable, according to Cassirer. While myth is indispensable for a culture, however, if it is unrestrained by other cultural forces it may pose a significant danger. Just as a culture that is completely dominated by religion can suffocate an individual, and seriously restrict his creativity and individuality, equally (and, as is shown below, especially) in the case of myth monolithically determining culture, it would prove lethal. Only a plurality of worldviews can guarantee the thriving of a culture.

---

36 Ernst Cassirer, *An Essay on Man: An Introduction to a Philosophy of Human Culture*, Yale University Press, New Haven, 1944, p. 228.

37 See: Chapter 2.3; cf. Ernst Cassirer, *An Essay on Man: An Introduction to a Philosophy of Human Culture*, Yale University Press, New Haven, 1944, p. 228; Recki, 2000, p. 82.

38 See: Chapter 3.5; cf. Ernst Cassirer, *Naturalistische und humanistische Begründung der Kulturphilosophie*, Göteborgs Kungl. Vetenskaps- och Vitterhets-Samhälles Handlingar. Femte foljden, Ser. A, Bd. 7, Nr. 3, 1939, pp. 1–28; here: p. 28.

In no previous age had the danger of mythical thought, so fiercely battled by philosophy at various instances in its history and by the philosophy of the Enlightenment in particular, become visible and actual to such an extent. The reason for this, according to Cassirer, is that the invention of the technique of myth or the artificial manufacturing of myth was something reserved for our technological age. This is not merely to be understood that only in the twentieth century did it become technologically possible to have such a technique of myth-making, for example through modern communication technology and mass media. More than that, for Cassirer technology is the most powerful force in twentieth-century culture[39] and it stands at the basis of the cultural crisis that created the economy for the re-emergence of the power of myth. In this he agrees with the diagnosis of Western culture by Albert Schweitzer, but he pursues Schweitzer's analysis even further.[40] Cassirer suggests that philosophers such as Heidegger and Spengler aided on the theoretical level – by their abandonment and discouragement of faith in the formative power of the individual and its sense of responsibility – the artificial disturbance of the cultural process by the state in practice.[41] Furthermore, for Cassirer, the philosopher has a clear task of enlightened intervention here. To defeat an enemy, Cassirer contends, it is necessary to know it and to face it. Therefore, we have to have a clear definition of what myth is, and understand in what way historically philosophy has always engaged in battle with and has been victorious over myth. Moreover, Cassirer maintains, we have to consider the particular way in which myth has found its contemporary modus operandi, *i.e.*, political craftsmanship or technology.[42]

According to Cassirer, the technological age had itself contributed importantly to the cultural crisis, and it was only with the discovery of modern technology by fascist politicians that the whole system crumbled as a house of cards. In the meantime, though, the people were brought to a state in which it could be receptive to manipulation in the first place. In this section we have elaborated on the crisis in culture Cassirer perceived and

---

39 Krois, 1987, p. 198.
40 Schweitzer, 1987 (1923).
41 See: Chapter 5; cf. Vergely, 1998, pp. 80–82.
42 Paetzold, 1994, p. 113.

have related it to rise of the technological era. However, it is not merely the materialism that is responsible, because that is not a sufficient reason for Cassirer. The crisis in culture is related to a lack of self-knowledge with the individual, hence the basis for its sense of moral reason and responsibility. In this respect, Cassirer also distinguishes himself from other analysts of the collapse of the Enlightenment project during the first half of the twentieth century. For Cassirer it was not the failure of reason, but the failure of culture in the maintenance of our critical moral faculties that was determinative. The next section deals with the question of the way in which the technological age contributed to the crisis in Western culture so as to make it receptive to the manipulation of the totalitarian state through the use of mythological thought. Section I.3 elaborates on the question of what are the characteristics of the myth of the state, while the fourth section deals with the question of what is the politics of myth. The conclusion sums up the most relevant insights of this chapter, while providing useful insights to gain greater understanding of our current global political and cultural predicament.

I. 3. How did the Technological Age Contribute to the Cultural Crisis?

In the twentieth century, according to Cassirer, technology, as no other symbolic form or modus of how to understand and deal with the world, has tried to dominate the other symbolic forms, by imposing its norms on all the other aspects of cultural life.[43] It does not content itself by establishing itself as an independent and autonomous form, but it tries to dominate and transform the modus of human experience in its totality; social life, space and time are all reduced to its own modalities.[44] Whereas Cassirer understands that technology can be a form of self-liberation of man, he also recognizes that it can be a phenomenon of alienation. Cassirer agrees on many points in this question with his former mentor Georg Simmel.[45] As for Simmel for Cassirer too

---

[43] See: Ernst Cassirer, *Symbol, Technik, Sprache: Aufsätze aus den Jahren 1927–1933*, E.W. Orth and J.M. Krois (eds.), Felix Meiner Verlag, 1985, p. 78; cf. Krois, 1987, p. 198.

[44] Paetzold, 1993, pp. 105–106.

[45] Skidelsky, 2003, pp. 365–381.

the methods of mass production constantly create new products that increase the level of consumption, while these new products do not actually fulfill needs, but rather create them. Moreover, for Cassirer, in the face of the ever-increasing desire for material goods, the horizon of the individual will shrinks ever back. "*Every satisfied need only serves to bring forth more needs in an increased measure – and for the one who is caught in this vicious circle there is no escape. Even more unrelenting than the treadmill of work, man is confined in the machinery of what is made and produced by the technical culture in which he finds himself and in which, in a never ending frenzy, he is thrown from desire to gratification and from gratification to desire.*"[46] Cassirer, here, anticipates the critique of Herbert Marcuse,[47] but this line of argument goes even back to Simmel's theory of subjectivity.

In the naturalistic subjectivism of Simmel, the subject is the primary reality, whereas the object is its "alienation" or "reification." The epitomization of this alienation or dehumanization he found in money, as the objectification of subjective values.[48] This objectification, though, of viewing persons and things in terms of their monetary value, strips for Simmel every subject of its specific qualities and reduces it to a single dimension.[49] What is central for Simmel (in his later works) is the non-exchangeability of life. Indeed, he chooses for a life without money, because that is a spontaneous, unmediated, and non-objectified existence.[50] Simmel's use of the term alienation accords with the description of the alienation of labor given by Marx. However, Simmel explicitly takes a naturalistic and vitalistic standpoint, *i.e.*, he does not take the subject as a supreme rational principle in the sense of Hegel. His basic outlook is rather one of *fin-du-siècle* fatalism: "*he shares Weber's gloomy vision of an "iron cage" of objective forces progressively crushing the individual*

---

46 See: Ernst Cassirer, *Symbol, Technik, Sprache: Aufsätze aus den Jahren 1927–1933*, E.W. Orth and J.M. Krois (eds.), Felix Meiner Verlag, 1985, pp. 87–88; translation by: Krois, 1987, pp. 200–201; cf. Marcuse, 1964.

47 See: Marcuse, 1967.

48 Simmel, 1990 (1900), p. 107.

49 Skidelsky, 2003, pp. 365–381; here: p. 371.

50 See: Morris-Reich, A., 2002, pp. 131 and 135.

personality."[51] For Simmel, culture takes a course that is beyond the influence of individuals, and becomes that which individuals cannot claim to be truly their own, or with which they can identify themselves.

Cassirer could not agree with this tragic outline of Simmel's view of culture, any more than he could with other representatives of life philosophy that absolutize the conflict between life and culture. For Cassirer the tragedy of culture becomes a drama, but the dramatization of culture requires an active involvement of individuals. Culture for Cassirer is not alienation, but Socratic self-knowledge.[52] His reaction to the point of the alienation of man from his nature may seem to be stoical, when he insists that: "*there is no remedy against this reversal of the natural order. Man cannot escape from his own achievement. He cannot but adapt to the condition of his own life.*"[53] But it is also an expression of his optimism of the will as well as the intellect, which was more an exception than the rule, especially during and after the Interbellum.[54] Next to a refusal to give in to a fatalism that had lethally threatened the very foundation of the liberal democracy of Weimar and that represented for him the retrogression from philosophy to mythology,[55] in line with the optimism of Schweitzer, Cassirer's optimism expresses an ethical optimism.[56]

Cassirer believes that the alienation posed by modern technological society can be resisted and overcome; hence its destructive potential for the progressive development of culture can be avoided. Just as "progressive" does not entail for Cassirer a linear, inevitably positive or cumulative development, nor is cultural decay for Cassirer an inevitable outcome.[57] Technology

---

[51] Skidelsky, 2003, 372.

[52] See: Bayer, T.I., *Book Review, Ernst Cassirer,* The Logic of the Cultural Sciences: Five studies, tr. by S.G., Lofts, Yale University Press, New Haven, 2000, Journal of the History of Philosophy, Volume 39, 2001, pp. 451–543; here. P. 542; cf. Bayer, T.I., *Socratic Self-Knowledge and the Philosophy of Symbolic Forms,* <http://www.pdcnet.org/bayer.pdf>(last visited: March 8, 2006).

[53] See: Ernst Cassirer, *An Essay on Man: An Introduction to a Philosophy of Human Culture,* Yale University Press, New Haven, 1944, p. 25.

[54] Skidelsky, 2003, p. 380.

[55] Ibid., 2003, pp. 380–381.

[56] Schweitzer, 1987 (1923).

[57] Skidelsky, 2003, p. 380.

provided for a great leap for mankind; it facilitated the shift from a culture that found its power in wishful thinking to that which finds its power in its own will. Through implements and tools man first managed to cut himself loose from his immediate environment. Before the tool age, according to Cassirer, man had to grasp everything in his environment with his limbs, with his corporal organs, *i.e.*, physically, to achieve his goals. Man was in the position to grasp everything, but he could not yet fully display the faculty of understanding, of grasping things conceptually.

First, with the use of tools, man distances himself from the immediate reality and learns how to play with his environment; he learns the rules of mediated life. Liberating or distancing oneself from the immediacy of life opens up possibilities of a kind unattainable to any other species; it creates the possibility of having a view of the future. It raises the human being from the dependence on its immediately given sense perceptions and impulses or instincts to forms of action that are directed to goals presently absent in space or remote in time.[58] With that the human being reaches a new form of consciousness. "*The human being stands now at that great turning point in his destiny and self-knowledge, which the Greek myth of* Prometheus *relates. The fear of demons and gods finds itself confronted by titanic pride and consciousness of freedom. (...) The wonderland and dreamland, wherein which magic had encapsulated man, is dethroned; he sees himself deferred to a new reality which receives him in all its seriousness and with all its severity, with a necessity against which all his wishes are smashed.*"[59]

At the stage wherein he gains the awareness that he cannot direct the world merely through his wishes, the human being rather learns more and more to rule the world through his will by the extension of technology or tools. He cannot move the world directly through his inner subjectivity,but, mediated by tools, he learns to achieve his ambitions. He leaves the stage of immediacy and learns to play with the world through various technological media. In that way technological activity is for man at the same time an act of self-acknowledgment and a medium to

---

[58] See: Ernst Cassirer, *Symbol, Technik, Sprache: Aufsätze aus den Jahren 1927–1933*, E.W. Orth and J.M. Krois (eds.), Felix Meiner Verlag, 1985, pp. 61–62.

[59] Ibid., 1985, pp. 66–67.

obtain self-knowledge, as he becomes aware of his own limits and conditions through (and to the extent of) using tools. On the other hand, Cassirer remarks, with this step, with this new technological awareness of the self, "*with this first enjoyment from the fruit of the tree of knowledge,* [man] *has cast himself forever out of the paradise of the pure organic being and life.*"[60]

The new sphere within which man finds himself is ruled by its own rules and principles, which Cassirer calls along with Marx, the law of the "emancipation from organic boundaries."[61] As opposed to Cassirer (and Simmel), though, Marx conceived of this emancipation in a naturalist way. For Marx, there is a final stage of technology where productivity far exceeds the limits inherent in manual labor. By contrast, Cassirer conceives of a qualitative and more radical change, instead of a merely quantitative one.[62] As opposed to primitive tool-use and manual labor, the instruments of completely developed technology, according to Cassirer, have freed man from the model that nature presents to them and man has, in a certain sense, left it, *i.e.*, nature, behind. Technology, in the dominant position it finds itself in modern culture, does not concern itself anymore directly with nature. Rather it becomes something that operates only by its own rules and goals set for itself. More and more, technology shifts its focus from nature to culture, and aims at securing a place for itself in the cultural domain. Moreover, it does not stop short in radically changing its own configurations and nature, but attempts to shape the totality of man's cultural life to its own modalities. Technology becomes another cultural dimension through which we view the world and relate to one another, but also with its own claims of validity and ambitions.

Man may attempt to return its tools back to the natural order by imbuing them with life and organic spirit, what Cassirer calls the feeling of solidarity with one's craft, as when the craftsman recognizes the material in front of him as his own work,

---

60 Ibid., 1985, p. 73.

61 Cassirer borrows this designation from Marx's analysis of "Machinery and Modern Industry", see: Krois, 1987, p. 201.

62 Ibid., 1987, p. 201.

his personal activity.[63] However, the more the law of the "emancipation from organic boundaries," as Cassirer understands it, progresses, the more this unity between worker and work vanishes. It is replaced by another kind of unity or solidarity, *i.e.*, solidarity of labor, wherein ultimately all work for the one and the one for all.[64] But this is for Cassirer more a community of fate (*Schicksalsgemeinschaft*) in the sense of "serving some purpose," than, what he terms, a community of will (*Willensgemeinschaft*), wherein the common purpose has an ethical form. Technology can be made instrumental, according to Cassirer, for humanity; it could be inspired by a truly ethical will and raised to ethical consciousness. In its contemporary form or stage, though, technology did not fulfill that function; it did not stand in service of the promotion of ethical standards; rather it tried and succeeded in absolutizing its own norms and settled, so to speak, its hegemony over man's cultural life as a whole. Subsequently and combined with myth, technologically applied and maintained by the state, a dark cloud made this hegemony gloomier than anyone could have imagined. Technology not only stood at the basis of the cultural crisis that made the individual receptive for manipulation by the totalitarian state, it also provided for the tools to achieve the same.

At its base, as Albert Schweitzer had explicated and so thoroughly diagnosed, stood the loss of the feeling of the self as a moral person.[65] Schweitzer also suggested a solution for the crisis: "*Either the moral standard of personality raises the moral standard of society, so far as possible, to its own level, or it is dragged down by it.*"[66] In what is to come hereinafter, Schweitzer's admonition is strikingly accurate in that the totalitarian state aimed exactly at dragging down the individual to a level that would render it more manageable. Moreover, Cassirer through his philosophy of symbolic forms had exactly formulated a philosophy that would explain how it was possible for the individual to attain its individuality. Cassirer's philosophy of symbolic forms explains

---

63 See: Ernst Cassirer, *Symbol, Technik, Sprache: Aufsätze aus den Jahren 1927–1933*, E.W. Orth and J.M. Krois (eds.), Felix Meiner Verlag, 1985, pp. 74–76.

64 Ibid., 1985, p. 88.

65 Cf. Schweitzer, 1987 (1923).

66 Ibid., 1987 (1923), p. 293.

how the human being creates a world for himself by relating to other persons through the various symbolic forms. By relating to other persons through language, myth, religion and so forth the individual attests to its own individuality, and evinces itself of it all the more when it adopts a variety of perspectives or symbolic forms, but also from increasing levels of objectivity starting from the depths of myth and ranging into the heights of science.

I. 4. What are the Characteristics of the Myth of the State?

Myth is a symbolic form for Cassirer. Myth is a relatively stable mode of understanding the world for the human being by making possible for it to relate to others, and in so doing, to create a "common world."[67] Hence, it entails a certain formation of our experiences of the world as we express them to others.[68] As such it is the expression of the spontaneity of our mind, as Kant put it, through which a manifold of experiences is poured into a unity and that reality is given a certain shape or form.[69] However, because myth is by itself capable of making sense of the world, it cannot be completely reduced to other facts or principles, be it psychological or be it logical, other than those one finds in and through myth itself.[70] Through myth those facts first make sense. Myth, therefore, does not merely refer to a primitive or pre-logical state of mind; rather it has its own definite logical structure.[71] "*Even the uncivilized man cannot live in the world without a constant effort to understand that world.*" Myth in this context expresses the "*classifying instinct*" of man; "*the desire of human nature to come to terms with reality, to live in an ordered universe, and to overcome the chaotic state in which things and thoughts have not yet assumed a definitive shape and structure.*"[72]

Myth, according to Cassirer, can best be understood through its relation with language, for, although they differ in

---

67 Paetzold, 1994, p. 113.

68 Paetzold, 1993, p. 57; cf. Krois, pp. 199–217; here 202 ff.

69 Paetzold, 1994, p. 7.

70 See: Ernst Cassirer, *The Myth of the State*, Yale University Press, New Haven, 1946, p. 13.

71 Ibid., 1946, pp. 13–14.

72 Ibid., 1946, p. 15.

their structure – language shows always a logical character, whereas myth seems to defy logic – nevertheless they have a common root.[73] This root can be found, according to Cassirer, in "*a very general and very early experience of mankind, an experience of a social rather than of a physical nature.*"[74] Language and myth are the earliest attempts of man as a symbolic being to give form to the immediate impulses or sense-impressions that spring up from life. Whereas myth is the first symbolic expression of the strong emotional aspects of life that hold mythical man in a tight grip, language is the first attempt of man to give form to, or, as Cassirer says, to put an intellectual stamp on sense impressions. Their commonality lies not only in an undifferentiated common root in life, but also in their function as a particular modus of expression or their formative power to create meaning. First through this function we have differentiations in life that are of distinctive significance.

Myth starts with the awareness of the universality and fundamental identity shared by all of life. "*It is a deep and ardent desire of the individual to identify itself with the life of the community and with the life of nature. (...) Here individuals are melted into one shape – into an undistinguishable whole.*"[75] The cohesive powers that bind the individual in mythical thought to its community or to nature cannot be ascribed to any causal bond, rather more to an emotional bond. "*What matters here are not the empirical relations between causes and effects, but the intensity and depth with which human relations are felt.*"[76] The same applies to man's relation with nature; in mythical thought man belongs to one great system of life that is in constant flux. There is for myth no sharp distinction between animate and inanimate life. The latter is not perceived as a physical thing governed by physical laws, but, as in animate life, it is necessarily part of a cycle of regeneration and constant renewal. "*The life and death of nature is part and parcel of the*

---

[73] Ibid., 1946, p. 18.

[74] See: Ernst Cassirer, *An Essay on Man: An Introduction to a Philosophy of Human Culture*, Yale University Press, New Haven, 1944, p. 110.

[75] See: Ernst Cassirer, *The Myth of the State*, Yale University Press, New Haven, 1946, p. 37–38.

[76] Ibid., 1946, p. 38.

great drama of man's death and resurrection. (...) *Even nature is in need of constant regeneration – it must die in order to live.*"[77]

In this way, it expresses a fundamental solidarity between all of life and accommodates the deep desire of the individual to be freed from all fetters of its individuality, "*to immerse itself in the stream of universal life, to lose its identity, to be absorbed in the whole of nature* (...)."[78] Furthermore, myth tries to relate everything to this common denominator. It purports to give an explanation of everything by explicating its origin. It directs itself, therefore, to a physiognomy, to the physical formation of things, be it material or be it spiritual – although it never poses a sharp distinction between these two.[79] However, its primary power does not reside primarily in its all-encompassing explanatory and absorptive drive; it is not solely involved in (albeit logic defying) intellectual processes. Myth not only sprouts forth from deep human emotions, but also forms the *expression* of these emotions. As such it involves a radical change of man's emotional life. "*The expression of a feeling is not the feeling itself – it is emotion turned into an image.* (...) *What hitherto was dimly and vaguely felt assumes a definite shape; what was a passive state becomes an active process.*"[80] Through this active, expressive process the emotions become much more specified, as they refer to special classes of *objects*.

Myth is the first symbolic reaction of man in the world. It is the first attempt of man to objectify his emotional world, *i.e.*, the world of feelings.[81] In myth man "*raises the question of what these things "mean," he inquires into the why and whither, he tries to understand where they have come from and to which end they go.* (...) *As soon as man begins to wonder about his acts, he has entered upon a new way which will in the end lead him far from his unconscious and instinctive life.* (...) *In language, myth, art, religion our emotions are not simply turned into mere acts; they are turned into "works.""*[82] As symbolic expressions the

---

[77] Ibid., 1946, pp. 39–40.

[78] Ibid., 1946, p. 41.

[79] Cf. Paetzold, 1994, pp. 7–8.

[80] See: Ernst Cassirer, *The Myth of the State*, Yale University Press, New Haven, 1946, p. 43.

[81] Ibid., 1946, p. 45.

[82] Ibid., 1946, p. 46.

works of myth persist and maintain themselves beyond the duration (in time and space) of the physical signs through which they were expressed. While these latter lose momentum and ultimately perish, myth as a symbolic expression may become a "*momentum aere perennius.*"[83] In myth man does not primarily seek to give an exact representation or produce a copy of his feelings, rather it is for him a way first to organize them, to transform them into images understandable for the human mind.[84]

However, it must be borne in mind, that myth is not the objectification of man's individual experience; in mythical thought there is not yet discernable a concept of the individual that can understand itself separated from social or natural life. Myth is still and foremost an objectification of man's social experience.[85] For mythical thought there is as yet no true self, there is not a soul existing independent from the body, rather it is nothing other than life that is necessarily attached to the body.[86] Soul for mythical thought, in its earlier configurations, is taken as part of nature; "*it is an outward, alien force that is manifested in him as a demonic power, to which he succumbs unless he can ward it off by magical means.*"[87]

Only with Socrates' concept of *eudaemonia*, according to Cassirer, does the individual cease to experience its soul merely as a natural potency, and apprehends itself as an ethical subject. From that ethical moment on, when the Socratic theme of ethical responsibility is introduced through dialogic enquiry, man is "*free from the unknown, from the fear of demons, because he no longer feels that his self, his innermost being, is dominated by a dark mythical power but knows himself capable of molding this self from clear insight, through a principle of knowledge and will.*"[88] However, it is still a long way from the moment that, not the demon choosing man, but man choosing his own demon.

---

83 Ibid., 1946, p. 47: Cassirer here alludes to Horace's depiction of his poems.

84 Ibid., 1946, pp. 47–49.

85 Ibid., 1946, p. 47.

86 See: Ernst Cassirer, *The Philosophy of Symbolic Forms*, Volume II, *Myth*, tr. R. Manheim, Yale University Press, New Haven, 1955 (1925), pp. 158–159.

87 Ibid., 1955 (1925), p. 168.

88 Ibid., 1955 (1925), p. 172.

In the earliest stages of mythical thought the feeling of *self* cannot be separated from a definite mythical–religious feeling of *community*. "*The I feels and knows itself only insofar as it considers itself as a member of a community, insofar as it sees itself grouped with others into the unity of a family, a tribe, a social organism.*"[89] Myth therewith becomes one of the most important *factors*, according to Cassirer, of the feeling of community and social life. It is one of those media of consciousness through which the "I" can create a bond with a "Thou," and through which the individual creates and relates itself to the community.[90] For myth, though, this must be understood in a rather static way, especially in primitive societies ruled and governed by taboos and rites.[91] The taboos of mythical society are directed to outward actions only and define that what is to be avoided at any cost.[92] Rites prescribe what should be done at any cost if a certain action, for example a hunt or a prayer for rain, is to succeed. In such a society the tasks or performances of the individual are firmly and in detail prescribed through rites and taboos by penalty of failure of a whole societal undertaking. The subjective intentions of the individual, though, are not significant, nor can they be distinguished from those of the community.

Stronger even, any sign of individuality is suppressed and exorcised – for that is a sign of being possessed by an evil demon. "*Man feels a deep mistrust in himself and his individual abilities.* (...) *What gives to the magician, to the wizard and sorcerer his real force is that he does not act as an individual, but that in him the power of the whole tribe is condensed and concentrated.*"[93] For mythological thought, only the collective body has responsibility or "moral personality," individuality still remains something suspect and something that must be suppressed. Although first experienced through it (as something to be suppressed or feared),

89 Ibid., 1955 (1925), p. 175.
90 Ibid., 1955 (1925), p. 177.
91 See: Ernst Cassirer, *The Myth of the State*, Yale University Press, New Haven, 1946, p. 285.
92 Paetzold, 1983, p. 240.
93 See: Ernst Cassirer, *The Technique of our Modern Political Myths*, in: ibid., *Symbol, Myth, and Culture. Essays and Lectures of Ernst Cassirer 1935–1945*, edited by D.P. Verene, Yale University Press, New Haven and London, 1979, pp. 242–267; here: p. 250.

myth is still an impediment for the development and maintenance of the sense of self or individuality.[94] The individual must constantly struggle against mythical forces and constraints to attain to its individuality. That is Cassirer's fundamental message.

It is therefore not surprising that the politics of myth found, in myth, a perfect medium for its sinister purposes. Moreover, the recourse to myth was instigated in and reserved for a time when the whole German social and economic system was threatened with a complete collapse. The diplomatic transactions, the legislative measures, and the economic policies by the leaders of the Weimar Republic seemed all to have been in vain. This was just the moment for myth to come in and wherein it could perform its function, when the National Socialist state introduced its myths in the political field through technological means, while the technological age had plummeted culture into a crisis. We now turn to an assessment of the politics of myth.

I. 5. What is the Politics of Myth?

In primitive societies, according to Cassirer, in all those cases that can be dealt with by his technical skills, man does not resort to the power of magic rites and formulae; there remains therefore always a sphere unaffected by magic or mythology, *i.e.*, a secular sphere. As Malinowski puts it, "*When the native has to produce an implement, he does not refer to magic. He is strictly empirical, that is, scientific, in the choice of his material, in the manner in which he strikes, cuts and polishes the blade* (...) *There is no exaggeration in saying that in all matters where knowledge is sufficient the native relies on it exclusively.* (...) *There is a body of rules, handed from one generation to another, which refer to the manner in which people live in their little shelters, make their fire by friction, collect their food and cook it, make love to each other and quarrel.* (...) *That this secular tradition is plastic, selective, intelligent, and also well-founded, can be seen from the fact that the native always adopts any new*

---

[94] See: Ernst Cassirer, *The Myth of the State*, Yale University Press, New Haven, 1946, pp. 284–285.

and suitable material."[95] Only when man is confronted with a problem or task that seems by far to exceed his natural powers or that is dangerous and its issues uncertain, does myth become a viable option. Myth though does not become an effective means to solve his problems. Through myth man makes sense of his world, and explains not how he himself can change his world, but rather the gods and demons that he or the shaman invokes in the name of the community through exactly prescribed rituals. Conscious of his limitations man resorts to myth as a final solution, as a method to control the forces that tease his life by accepting them as his fate, and only by doing so does he believe himself to have any influence upon them and consequently be in a position to ameliorate his predicament.[96]

The role of magic and mythology is not exclusively reserved for primitive societies, according to Cassirer, but applies equally well to highly advanced stages of political life. "*In desperate situations man will always have recourse to desperate means – and our present day political myths have been such desperate means. If reason has failed us, there remains always the* ultima ratio, *the power of the miraculous and mysterious.*"[97] What we call quiet and peaceful times, periods of relative stability and security, are those times when the binding forces of man's social and intellectual life are able to subdue the (demonic) mythical powers that accompany a culture. Myth, for Cassirer, is the very first intellectual expression of life. Life, for Cassirer, is the powerful source that nurtures all cultural activity, *i.e.*, it is a basic phenomenon (*Urphänomän*), in the sense of Goethe, for all symbolic forms.[98] It is characteristic of myth, according to Cassirer, that it is "*an instrument of the great process of spiritual differentiation through which basic determinant forms of social and individual consciousness arise from the chaos of the first*

---

[95] See: Malinowski, B., *The Foundations of Faith and Morals*, Oxford University Press, London, 1936, pp. 32 ff.; cited by Ernst Cassirer, *The Myth of the State*, Yale University Press, New Haven, 1946, p. 278.

[96] Ibid., 1946, pp. 277–278.

[97] Ibid., 1946, p. 279.

[98] Möckel, 1998, pp. 355–386; cf. Krois, J.M., *Urworte: Cassirer als Goethe-Interpret*, in: Rudolph, 1995, pp. 297–324; here: pp. 311–313; see also: Chapter 5.

indeterminant life feeling."[99] Myth is the first symbolic response to this life feeling, and as such, it expresses or conveys material that is still, so to speak, hot from the oven, *i.e.*, that still has some indeterminacy, immediacy, or unrefractedness. Myth finds itself at the lowest level of perceptual and imaginative sophistication; it is closest to the raw material that life presents to us.[100] Although the image-world of myth consists of symbols, it is still highly dramatized. When other mediating forms of culture spring up and take over the mediating function that myth had engaged itself in, then, tentatively with respect to life, man is more and more in a position to resolve the immediacy with which life presents itself into more manageable "degrees" or proportions. It is one of the central points of Cassirer's The Myth of the State, that because of myth – which is always latently if not actively present – we should be conscious in our social and political life of the fact that we always find ourselves on "volcanic soil."[101] As a result, "*We must always be prepared for violent concussions that may shake our cultural world and our social order to its very foundations.*"[102]

In times of crises, what appears predominantly is the call for leadership. Myths, according to Cassirer, are in this respect the personifications of collective wishes. When a collective desire has reached an overwhelming strength and the usual, secular means seem to have failed, the desire is not only deeply felt, but also personified. "*The intensity of the collective wish is embodied in the leader. The former social bonds – law, justice, and constitutions – are declared to be without any value. What alone remains is the mystical power and authority of the leader and the leader's will is supreme law.*"[103] A people that are strongly and intensely determined by a collective wish, can easily be persuaded that they need only a strong leader or the right man to achieve it. The modern politician engaged in the politics of myth – what we henceforward call the politician of myth –

---

99 See: Ernst Cassirer, *The Philosophy of Symbolic Forms*, Volume II, *Myth*, tr. R. Manheim, Yale University Press, New Haven, 1955 (1925), p. 178.

100 See: Luft, 1984, pp. 3–13; here: p. 9.

101 See: Ernst Cassirer, *The Myth of the State*, Yale University Press, New Haven, 1946, p. 280; cf. Margreiter, 1997, pp. 252–258.

102 See: Ernst Cassirer, *The Myth of the State*, Yale University Press, New Haven, 1946, p. 297.

103 Ibid., 1946, p. 280.

though, finds himself in a paradoxical situation, according to Cassirer. Although civilized man is subject to the most violent passions, and these can ultimately culminate in his yielding to the most irrational impulses, he seems never capable of entirely forgetting or denying the demands of rationality. He is always in need of "reasons," of a "theory" to justify his creeds. Therefore, the politician of myth has to act both as *homo magus* and as *homo faber* to effect or fulfill the collective wish. He becomes the priest of a new, entirely irrational and mysterious religion, the man who can avert all the evils and fulfill the collective wish, but when he sets out to defend and propagate this new religion, *i.e.*, the collective wish, he has to proceed very methodologically. He proceeds as in mystical rites, but now with technical precision and sophistication. "*Nothing is left to chance; every step is well prepared and premeditated. It is this strange combination that is one of the most striking features of our political myths.*"[104]

The National Socialist state employed three predominant myths, viz. the myth of hero-worship, the myth of the race, and the myth of the state. We cannot pursue here how Cassirer gives an historical account of the emergence and reintroduction of the myth of hero-worship by Carlyle, the myth of the race by Gobineau, or Hegel's myth of the state. All of these myths were central to the ideology of National Socialism or fascism in general, however, what is more fundamental is the way in which political myths could be construed by the state so as to take away from man what is most precious to him, his autonomy or moral personality. In his *The Myth of the State*, Cassirer seems to suggest that four conditions had to be satisfied for the rise and the establishment of the hegemony of fascism and its necessary corollary, the totalitarian state.[105]

First, man had to be put in a state of fatalism, so that he could see no way of freeing himself from social and economic malaise through ordinary means. His state of hopelessness and desperation would result in the creation of a collective wish that would subsequently be embodied by a strong and magical leader. Therewith, the foundation was laid for the myth of hero-worship.

---

[104] Ibid., 1946, pp. 281–282.
[105] Krois, 1987, pp. 193–195; cf. Paetzold, 1993, pp. 120–122.

Second, the state had to proclaim a single, simple, supreme value, around which the members of society could find "true" unity, and which would not permit another value next to it.[106] This supreme value could be a race, a nation, or an ethnically defined community. Most of all, it had to be a value that stressed the emotional bond between the individual and the community, and that could not be repudiated through rational, and discursive arguments.[107] Any questioning of the supreme value of such a community would have to invoke strong and ambivalent feelings. This value in fact did not work as a value at all, that is, as an ideal standard guiding human action. By transforming the normal sense that value has, by assuming that what ought to be is to be measured by what is, and not vice versa, the supreme value attains a cloak of invulnerability.

For the National Socialists, race, paradigmatically a phenomenon interrelated with physiognomy and emotionality, was declared the supreme value. At the core of the myth of the race lies the assumption that one is noble or virtuous not on account of what one does but, because of what race or bloodline one belongs to, and every action of man is evaluated according to the latter. Its message was very simple and reassuring, for the image or form it apprehends is absolute and admits of no change or exceptions through individual action alone. Any criticism of initially held beliefs is ruled out, because criticism is *ex ante* regarded as a form of conspiracy, of betraying the spirit of one's belief that is by definition the supreme point of view.[108] What Cassirer explicated and warned against was the incomprehensibility of the myth of the race through logical means alone and the absolutizing effect it had on the imaginations of men as a supreme value.

Third, the ethically binding or cultivating forces of other cultural forms, that suggested other perspectives on life, that reminded one of the facts that one is foremost a reflective being, not free of responsibilities, but free because of taking responsibility for one's own actions; had to be made ineffective. This was accomplished through the absolutizing effect of myths. The

---

[106] Krois, 1987, p. 193.
[107] Paetzold, 1993, p. 121.
[108] Krois, 1987, p. 194.

instant power of myth paralyzed the flexibility of the human faculty to find solutions for a problem through a variety of other symbolic schemes.[109] The impairment of man's symbolic capacities first affected man's linguistic functions. *Sapere aude*, was the maxim of Kant, to free oneself from self-incurred tutelage. It is perhaps noteworthy that the politics of myth directed its attack against the autonomy of man through a change in the structure of language. For Cassirer too, language had a liberating effect, that when we feel anger or fear and express these feelings, we not only seem to experience a kind of discharge of emotions, but, moreover, that we therewith are removed from the mere emotional. As a result of this distancing, we raise ourselves to a higher level of objectivity to one degree or another.

Not all language, though, can perform this function. Cassirer distinguishes between language on the merely expressive or emotional level (1), representative or semantic language (2), and symbolic language, *i.e.*, language on the level of pure meaning (3). Only gradually does man seem to be able to raise himself from lower to higher forms of language, that is to say, language that brings with it higher forms of objectivity in signification or meaning giving. One of the most important ways of giving or expressing meaning is, of course, through language. Through language we learn to direct our actions, find a way of controlling our emotions, and convey our intentions and thoughts. This cannot be though merely through language on the emotional level, for example through sorrow or yelling in anger, despite the possibilities of emotional discharge. First when man has distanced himself from these immediate emotions, and has tried to represent them or mediate them through some modus of meaning giving, he can achieve some form of objectivity or determinacy. Still later, man may be in the position to take a more objective view of an event. In that instance, he finds himself in the sphere of the symbolic or pure meaning, whereby meaning exists separated from all original sense impressions that accompanied an event.

It is difficult to determine whether the National Socialists were aware of these different functions and degrees of objectivity in language. What their attack on, or transformation of, the

---

[109] Paetzold, 1993, p. 109.

structure of language consisted of, though, was the introduction of new words and the revision of old words that together established the replacement of "ordinary," semantic or propositional language by emotional or magical language. Changes or innovations that on the first sight may seem trivial had strong implications for the insider of Nazi Germany. Such were the words "*Siegfriede*" and "*Siegerfriede,*" the first representing peace after a successful outcome of the war for the Germans, the latter in the case of allied victory. A simple change of a syllable in a word was often good enough for the stirring up of violent political passions.[110] Paechter, Hellman, Paechter, and Paetel (1944), provided more examples of this sort in their book "*Nazi-Deutsch. A Glossary of Contemporary German Usage.*"[111] More and more the emotional aspects of language were appealed to and generated to the disadvantage of the objectifying, hence liberating function of language.

The fourth step consisted in the introduction of new rites. "*Nothing is more likely to lull to sleep,*" writes Cassirer, "*all our active forces, our power of judgment and critical discernment, and to take away our feeling of personality and individual responsibility than the steady, uniform, and monotonous performance of the same rites.*[112] The result is often the preclusion of questioning one's own environment and an attitude of acquiescence. No other practice seems to bind the individual stronger to the community than rites performed by all. Of course, it explains the rites of initiation to certain societies, of becoming a member, of being accepted, of having undergone the same fate. But the rites introduced by the politics of myth went much further and encompassed the life of the individual in its totality, just as in the rituals of primitive tribes. "*Every class, every sex, and every age has a rite of its own. No one could walk in the street, nobody could greet his neighbor or friend without performing a political ritual. And just as in primitive societies the*

---

[110] See: Ernst Cassirer, *The Myth of the State*, Yale University Press, New Haven, 1946, p. 284.

[111] Ibid., 1946, p. 283; cf. Klemperer, V., *The Language of the Third Reich. LTI – Lingua Tertii Imperii. A Philologist's Notebook*, tr. M. Brady, Athlone Press, London and New Brunswick, NJ, 2000 (1946).

[112] See: Ernst Cassirer, *The Myth of the State*, Yale University Press, New Haven, 1946, pp. 284–285.

neglect of one of the prescribed rites has meant misery and death. Even in young children this is not regarded as a mere sin of omission. It becomes a crime against the majesty of the leader and the totalitarian state."[113]

Moreover, the rites of the politics of myth did not confine themselves to material results, to the regulation of the outward actions of individuals. They directed themselves to the character and consciousness of men, in order to change them from within. What the politics of myth could not achieve through deliberative means, through persuasion, it managed to do through manipulative rites. These rites gave men a certain sense of belonging; at least they felt, talked, and acted in the same way. But they were unaware of or became indifferent to the fact, that step by step, by each subjugation of their own faiths to the community and by each hail to the magical leader, they in fact gave away their own sense of moral personality. They no longer thought for themselves, rather the group or the magical leader did that for them. "*The political myths acted in the same way as a serpent that tries to paralyze its victims before attacking them. Men fell victims to them without any serious resistance. They were vanquished and subdued before they had realized what had actually happened.*"[114] The politicians of myth knew quite well that the masses could not be directed at will by sheer physical force; they knew they had to be subdued through the force of imagination.

II. CONCLUSION

Through the propagation of mythological thought by technological means the politicians of myth took away the essential element of human freedom and replaced it by illusions, empty promises, and options of escape from individual responsibility.[115] No longer did the individual fill up his sense of the future through self-chosen motives; this future was embodied and

---

113 Ibid., 1946, p. 284.

114 Ibid., 1946, p. 286.

115 Ibid., 1946, pp. 287–288; for more aggressive methods used for the same purpose, see: Meerloo, 1968; and Meerloo, 1956.

defined by the magical leader, who, so to speak, assumes the role of a public fortune-teller. "*Prophecy is an essential element in the new technique of rulership. The most improbable or even impossible promises are made; the millennium is predicted over and over again.*"[116] The question of what ought to be done, is replaced by what "must" be done from the point of view of historical necessity. This prophetic conception of history enjoyed, according to Cassirer, academic respectability and wide acceptance under the educated public even before its endorsement by the Third Reich. Spengler, with his *Untergang des Abendlandes*, and Heidegger with his conception of man's "thrownness" into the world, both proclaim, according to Cassirer, the need to submit to "fate."[117] They do not teach, says Cassirer, the individual to develop the active use of his faculties, to form his own individual and social life; they rather discourage the individual from creating freedom for himself.

Freedom, according to Cassirer, does not consist in a liberum arbitrium indifferentiae. "*It is not the absence of a motive but the character of the motive that marks a free action. In the ethical sense a man is a free agent if these motives depend upon his own judgment and own conviction of what moral duty is.*"[118] Along with Kant, Cassirer argues that ethical freedom is not a datum, rather it is a task or ethical imperative; in order to have it, man must create it. If man were merely to follow his natural instincts he would choose for dependence, rather than strive for freedom. "*Obviously it is much easier to depend upon others than to think, to judge, and to decide for oneself.*"[119] Therefore man experiences ethical freedom often as a burden, and, according to Cassirer, when man finds himself under extreme difficult circumstances, he tries to cast off this burden.

This is when the totalitarian state and the political myths step in, according to Cassirer. On the one hand, they provide an escape for the "burdened" individual: because myths are impene-

---

116 See: Ernst Cassirer, *The Myth of the State*, Yale University Press, New Haven, 1946, p. 289.

117 See: Krois, 1987, p. 195; cf. Coskun, D., *Cassirer in Davos. An Intermezzo on Magic Mountain*, Law & Critique, Volume 17, Issue 1, 2006, pp. 1–26.

118 See: Ernst Cassirer, *The Myth of the State*, Yale University Press, New Haven, 1946, p. 287.

119 Ibid., 1946, p. 288.

trable through logic alone – they cannot be combated through syllogisms – and as such, they provide a license against any logical force or constraint.[120] On the other hand, they simultaneously deprive men of their individual sense of responsibility. Through his exposition of mythical thought, Cassirer sought to warn of the kind of continuous threat myth poses to the fragile structure of rationality that stands at the basis of every liberal democratic culture.[121] It seems almost obvious, that a person who cannot give meaning to his own actions or life, but acts or lives in this or that way merely through what another deems significant, cannot act autonomously, except as may be the case (hypothetically) by the first act of relinquishing his judgment to the other.[122] Moreover, Cassirer's work explains why the politics of myth easily assumes inhumane characteristics, because the politics of myth feels and finds itself unbound by the ethical constraints of reason, *i.e.*, human rights.

Cassirer distinguishes himself from other political philosophers through his engagement with the study of myth. As a political philosopher he has made clear that myth may pose a danger to democracy. Although first through myth we gain awareness of a sense of self and that of a community, it also has its drawbacks. Myth is inimical to individuality and disapproves of individual initiative and responsibility. Myth is a process through which the individual relates to others and its community by accepting a common fate. However, although it may pose a danger to democracy, myth cannot and may not be eradicated, because it is important for the formation of society and culture. If we want to speak of a democratic culture, then we have a different task to fulfill. It is the task of democracy to turn the energies of myth to its own use by cultivating it with the help of other symbolic forms, such as language, religion, science, but also law and political science.[123] The key to the success of

---

[120] See: Ettelt, 1972, p. 59.

[121] Strenski, 1984, p. 370.

[122] For independent meaning giving as a central concept in liberal theory, see: Ackerman, 1980, especially p. 231.

[123] For an elaboration of politics as a symbolic form, see: Kahn, P.W., *The Question of Sovereignty*, Stanford Journal of International Law, Volume 40, Issue 2, 2004, pp. 259–282; cf. Verene, D.P., *Cassirer's Political Philosophy*, in: Rudolph, 1999, pp. 19–42.

democracy vis-à-vis fascism and communism was the particular, penultimate role the individual plays in its politics. They all start from the individual (or its "fallen" nature), but only democracy takes the individual not merely as its starting point, but also as its aim.

The critical engagement by a democracy with (its founding) myths, for example that of democracy itself or the rule of law, not only involves coming to terms with its own specific cultural identity, but also prevents them from becoming mere dogma. Democracies need to be particularly wary of becoming complacent, as if democratic values are eternal and always at hand. Myth in the twentieth century has made possible the worst crime imaginable by man, *i.e.*, genocide. Because it thinks in terms of collectivities instead of individual human persons, and in terms of good and evil instead of human dignity, mythic mentality inspires the demonization and dehumanization of the other, *i.e.*, persons that do not share a common (communal) fate. Understanding myth and coming to terms with it, therefore, is important for any democratic project.

CONCLUSION TO PART I

Part I has given an account of Cassirer as a practical philosopher and has shown that he was not a mere theoretical philosopher, disengaged from the world to build up a theoretical world.[1] As a result, the reading of Cassirer as a mere theoretical philosopher, an idea found among many of his critics and still prevalent in the popular imagination of those who are not fully acquainted with his works, must be dispensed with. In the Cassirer literature, a product of the recent Cassirer Renaissance, which finds its main impetus in the insight that Cassirer was not merely a neo-Kantian philosopher, several attempts have been made to support the thesis that Cassirer's was not a mere theoretical philosopher. The first position is defended by Birgit Recki. Recki maintains that there is an implicit or latent moral tonality throughout the works of Cassirer and that the reason why he has not written an ethics or a moral philosophy of his own is his high regard for Kantian moral philosophy, which was more or less conclusive for Cassirer.[2] We have to respectfully disagree with this position. Cassirer intended to go beyond Kant with his ethics. Indeed, Cassirer agrees with Kant that the ultimate question of ethics is the question of "What is man?," but he disagrees with Kant that man is a mere rational being and that ethicality is only reserved for rational creatures. For Cassirer the human is foremost an *animal symbolicum*, a symbolic being, and his symbolic nature makes the human a thoroughly expressive and normative being as he continuously tries to relate to other human beings to set up his own world. Kant's ethics were not conclusive for Cassirer, and only so insofar as he agrees with Kant that ethics is ultimately concerned with the question of "What is man?"[3]

---

1 For examples of this reading of Cassirer see among others: Gay, P., *The Social History of Ideas: Ernst Cassirer and After*, in: Wolff, K.H. and Moore, B., jr., *The Critical Spirit, essays in honor of Herbert Marcuse*, Beacon Press, Boston, 1967, pp. 106–120; Strauss, L., *Cassirer, Ernst, "The Myth of the State" (Book Review)*, Social Research, Volume 14, 1946, p. 125.

2 Her views on Cassirer's moral philosophical dimension can be found in: Recki, 2004.

3 For the philosophy of symbolic forms as but an essay in the systematic answer to the question of "What is man?", see: Orth, E.-W., *Goethe als*

A second position is represented by Oswald Schwemmer. Schwemmer also conceives of a moral tendency in Cassirer's works by observing that the philosophy of symbolic forms represents the constant process of cultivation man is engaged in, which by necessity entails a form of moralization or moral progress.[4] Although we agree with Schwemmer as to the moral dimension of the various symbolic forms, we also have to note that Schwemmer claims too little and too much at the same time. Schwemmer does not contend that every symbolic form is in the position of providing ethical tools for human beings, rather he understands Cassirer's project in its entirety as describing the road to cultivation for the human being, from its mythic beginnings to its scientific horizon. In this respect he claims too little, because every symbolic form is in the position of cultivating the human with its own claims of validity and objectivity; if by cultivation Schwemmer refers to the process by which the human being escapes the chaos of mere subjective impressions and achieves an objectively constructed, hence principled world. Schwemmer claims too much when he gives too much weight to Cassirer's entire project as involving cultivation, not only because some symbolic forms such as ethics, religion, and science are far more effective in achieving cultivation than others, *i.e.*, myth in particular, but also because Cassirer is not merely concerned with moral progress. His cultural theory not only explains how cultures progressively achieve higher forms of objectivity (cultivation), but also how cultures are in danger of degeneration or decay by the continuing presence of mythical thought.

A third position is taken by John Michael Krois. Krois has given a more elaborate explanation and systematical treatment of Cassirer's practical philosophy.[5] He concludes that Cassirer is appreciative of the natural law tradition and its tradition of

---

Therapeutikum. Zu Ernst Cassirers Pathologie des Symbolischen, in: Naumann, 2002, pp. 137–156; here: p. 143.

4 See: Schwemmer, O., *"Moralisierung" durch "Kultivierung"? Über den Zusammenhang zwischen wissenschaftlichen Verstehen und moralischer Kultur*, Jahrbuch für Wissenschaft und Ethik, Volume 2, 1997, pp. 55–73; ibid., *Ernst Cassirer. Ein Philosoph der europäischen Moderne*, Akademie Verlag, Berlin, 1997, especially the chapter on ethics.

5 Krois, 1987, especially the chapter on morality and law; cf. also Krois, 1979, pp. 199–217.

human rights and that Cassirer has given a new interpretation of natural law through his philosophy of symbolic forms. In practical philosophy, according to Krois, Cassirer perceived the natural law tradition as the final stage of morality, the so-called sphere of pure meaning, now in the practical field. Our main objection to the latter approach does not stem from a predisposition against the natural law tradition. Indeed, for Cassirer the natural law tradition is important, and, as is shown below, he accords a role to it in his philosophy of law that is beyond the mere historical significance of natural law theory. My point is that it was not natural law but the concept of individual human rights, detached from its origins in natural law, and, moreover, distinct from (historic) natural rights, which Cassirer sought to vindicate with his philosophy of symbolic forms. This detachment from natural law is not a trivial matter, because Cassirer sought to give the concept of human rights a more firm foundation, *i.e.*, a philosophical anthropological justification supported by the latest scientific data. The *animal symbolicum* is a thoroughly expressive and normative being. Every action and step that it takes is unavoidably mediated and accompanied by meaning and ultimately involves a personality giving or searching for this meaning. No higher goal seems worthy of respect in the form of a human right than the freedom to develop one's personality for the purpose of the fundamentally human activity to have a meaningful life. As is shown in Part II, the symbolic nature of the human being entails certain limits upon every state action.

Part I has tried to elucidate that Cassirer's works, at least from *Freiheit und Form* (1916) onwards, were ethically motivated.[6] Part II will explicate that Cassirer's philosophy of symbolic forms lays the foundation for a normative theory of man. Cassirer opposes the notion that man is guided by *the will to power* in a Nietzschean sense. Against Nietzsche and other nihilistic trends in philosophy and political life, Cassirer proposes that man is foremost driven by *the will to formation.* Following *Freiheit und Form* (1916), *Kants Leben und Lehre* (1921), *Naturalistische und humanistische Begründung der Kultur* (1939), Cassirer makes clear in *An Essay on Man* (1944), that: "*Human culture taken as a whole may be described as the*

---

6 Cf. Sandkühler, 2003, p. 276.

process of man's progressive self-liberation."[7] This freedom for Cassirer is autonomy, man's moral mastery over himself. As to his public engagement, Part I has revealed Cassirer as a republican and a defender of the Weimar Constitution and its values, as represented by the natural law tradition of human rights. In Davos, Cassirer gives a philosophical defense of humanism by extolling human freedom against the eschatology of Heidegger. His consideration of the importance of individual moral judgment for the maintenance of any social and legal order, paradigmatically that of a democracy, makes him agree fundamentally with Albert Schweitzer. Finally, in exile, he turns his philosophical weapons against any apotheosis of the state, including that of Hegel, and in particular against fascism, through his critique of modern political myths.

It is neither a socio-economic superstructure as in Marx, nor an absolute reason in the sense of Hegel, nor a Romantic spirit of the people, but man's capacity to symbol, his constant struggle with life to create a meaningful world through symbolic forms that determines human life and culture. When Weimar began to show signs of disintegration, Cassirer did not principally stress the need for economic reform, because he knew that it was not a mere question of material crisis that plagued Weimar. He saw in the Weimar Constitution a document with symbolic significance that could inspire and guide the minds of people in a direction that found its inspiration in Enlightenment ideals and that of German idealism. His defense of the Weimar Constitution in the form of a constitutional patriotism was an exceptional act of civic courage, but also very ingenuous and insightful in this respect. The Weimar Constitution could exert a symbolic power that would give the people an incentive to contribute to the maintenance of the Weimar polity. It could infuse, so to speak, the masses that were struck by fatalism with an enthusiasm and hope for a common future.

Part II gives a full account of the philosophy of symbolic forms. Furthermore, it attempts to grasp or understand *law* as a symbolic form. It is a conceptual analysis of the law, but necessarily entails a normative framework too. To understand this

---

7 Ernst Cassirer, *An Essay on Man: An Introduction to a Philosophy of Human Culture*, Yale University Press, New Haven, 1944, p. 228.

framework, to grasp the preconditions of Law as Symbolic Form, in this Part, an anticipation of law's genetic development was indispensable. When we turn from the object of our study to its subject, it becomes obvious, that an individual that has no sense of self as a moral person or is hampered therein cannot be an active bearer of rights. Conversely, the maintenance of a democratic polity is dependent upon the capacity of its subjects to hold it accountable, *i.e.*, to make reflective, moral judgments. It is essential for morality as well as law that its subjects have developed and maintain an individual sense of self as moral persons. Accordingly, the totalitarian state that had reduced the individual to the masses, need not concern itself with (human) rights. Nor were its subjects inclined to rise up and demand that the state address and treat them as morally and intellectually autonomous persons. As a result, the totalitarian state did not and needed not to feel itself obliged to be accountable to the law of the people. *Democracy is the reign by persuasion rather than the reign by force.* It is no coincidence that foremost democracies have managed to establish the rule of law and that they are particularly inclined to respect human rights. *Law is the reign of persuasion rather than the reign of force.* That insight was not only anticipated by German idealism, but also by the Cambridge Platonists and the ancient Greeks in their insistence on the connection between justice and truth, *i.e.*, individual moral judgment. Because Cassirer emphatically brought this insight to our attention (again), we now consider his main theoretical work, *i.e.*, the philosophy of symbolic forms, so as to understand and spell out its relevance for jurisprudence.

PART II: LAW AS SYMBOLIC FORM

INTRODUCTION

In this part we focus on Cassirer's philosophy of symbolic forms and apply it to the domain of law. In Chapter 5 we give a systematic elaboration and assessment of the philosophy of symbolic forms. Chapter 5 proposes that Cassirer's philosophy of symbolic forms was an ethical project, because it explains how the individual human being, through the various symbolic forms, progressively relates to others. Symbolic forms are media through which we relate to others, and, hence, to the world.[1] Symbolic forms define the personal outlook, hence the identity of the individual. It is insightful to pursue the interplay between the various symbolic forms, also because that interplay denotes the hermeneutical dimension of Cassirer's cultural theory. As a result, we explicate the ideal of tolerance as a hermeneutical imperative for Cassirer, and assert individual freedom as a culture imperative.

Therewith we come to a point in which it becomes clear that the neo-Kantian approach to Cassirer's philosophy, *i.e.*, as though Cassirer was a mere neo-Kantian philosopher pure and simple, no longer suffices. It remains necessary, though, to explicate Cassirer's indebtedness to neo-Kantianism and his subsequent move above and beyond neo-Kantianism, because it explains why and how Cassirer developed his philosophy of symbolic forms. Therefore, in Chapter 6, we give a philosophical positioning of Cassirer vis-à-vis neo-Kantianism, and, as a result, give a contextual assessment of Cassirer's philosophy of symbolic forms.

Moreover, in Chapter 7 we apply Cassirer's philosophy of symbolic forms to law. We explain why and how law is a symbolic form with independent claims of validity and a unique perspective of the world. Law too finds its matrix in myth, and only gradually, primarily with the help of the symbolic form of

[1] Cf. Balkin, 1998, p. 102, especially footnotes 2 and 3.

language, does it manage to overcome the mythic sphere. Law, in the symbolic sphere, becomes a referential system that sustains itself by the mutual recognition and reference of its key concepts. As a result, it provides a framework wherein human rights make sense, which, in their turn, progressively spur the legal system to achieve higher degrees of universality, hence objectivity. Futher-more, by its interrelatedness to other cultural forms and by its relation vis-à-vis and contribution to culture taken as a whole, law sustains its own objective grounding. Law progessively contributes to culture by its particular mode of objectification in the sphere of actions.

In Chapter 8, we explore the social contract theory of Cassirer. It becomes obvious, though, why Cassirer's conception of the social contract becomes central to any understanding of law. The concept of the promise stands at the foundation of every act of law. In this respect, Cassirer understands the social contract not as a static given, but as an ongoing process constituted by the promissory function of the human, that is symbolic in nature. Next to a genealogical account of social contract theory, we therefore pursue the specifically symbolic nature of the act of promising from a genetic perspective, and explain why the act of promising is reserved for the specifically human sphere of the symbolic. Moreover, we explain how and why the right to contract is related to human dignity.

In addition, in Chapter 9, we address Cassirer's position relative to neo-Kantian jurisprudence. Chapter 9 highlights important aspects or elements in neo-Kantian jurisprudence common to most, if not all, of its representatives. In Chapter 9, we make clear that a jurisprudence inspired by Cassirer's philosophy of symbolic forms is something distinctly *Cassirerean*. Nevertheless, his indebtedness neo-Kantian jurisprudence, as is the case with neo-Kantianism in general, remains obvious. But while investigating the commonalities with neo-Kantian jurisprudence, due regard is given to the distinguishing elements of Cassirer's legal theory. As a result, the conclusion of Chapter 9 gives an assessment of Cassirer's jurisprudence and its relation to the neo-Kantian approach to jurisprudence. Finally, in the conclusion to this part, we present the results of our research, and also evaluate the results of our contextual assessment of Cassirer's philosophy and legal theory.

CHAPTER 5

THE PHILOSOPHY OF SYMBOLIC FORMS

I. INTRODUCTION

In this chapter we give a detailed analysis of the philosophy of symbolic forms and answer the question of what is the philosophy of symbolic forms. Throughout previous chapters we have already alluded to and mentioned symbolic forms, and tentatively have offered descriptions and explanations of what symbolic forms amount to. We are compelled therefore not only to give a positive account of symbolic forms by discussing its various ramifications and configurations, but also to give a more limitative account of symbolic forms by marking out the limitations to and the conceptual boundaries of what constitute symbolic forms as symbolic forms. However, it is important to note, that Cassirer gave no elaborate and definitive formulation of a symbolic form that enables us to assess as by a syllogism whether a certain phenomenon or process can be considered a symbolic form, nor can we attempt such a thing here. Cassirer's philosophy of symbolic forms is an open-ended project, not a doctrinal system. Hence a rigid conceptual account, although conceptually more strict and simple, would not do justice to Cassirer's project. Moreover, his philosophy of symbolic forms is often misunderstood and, more importantly, underestimated as to its ethical import. We cannot aspire to take up and vindicate that proposition in this single chapter, but venture to contend that, once put in its context, *i.e.*, neo-Kantianism,[1] so as to explicate his indebtedness to and subsequent disassociation from neo-Kantianism, and read in conjunction with our subsequent chapters relative to the jurisprudential dimension of Cassirer's works, it is plausible to maintain that the philosophy of symbolic forms is an ethical project.

In this chapter we set out to explicate Cassirer's project of the philosophy of symbolic forms. This chapter proceeds as follows. First, in Section I.1, we answer the question of what

---

1 See: Chapters 6 and 9.

were the objectives of Cassirer with his philosophy of symbolic forms. Next, in Section I.2, we elucidate the characteristics of a symbolic form, by elaborating on Cassirer's provisional definition of "symbolic form" given in a debate with the Swedish philosopher Marc-Wogau, explicate the triadic, logical structure of symbolic forms – respectively the expressive, the representative, and the significative phase – and, finally, by investigating the conceptual demarcations of what can constitute a symbolic form. Furthermore, in Section I.3, we elaborate on the dynamism or interplay that stands at the core of any culture and cultural form, *i.e.*, the interplay between myth and language. In addition, in Section I.4, we work toward the thesis that through the interplay between the various symbolic forms, Cassirer introduced a new concept of truth in culture, hence a hermeneutics of culture, as well as explicate Cassirer's hermeneutical imperative of tolerance. Moreover, in Section I.5, we explicate the ethical dimension of Cassirer's philosophy. More particularly, in Section I.5, we vindicate the position that Cassirer's philosophy of symbolic forms is an ethical theory. Ethicality for Cassirer entails *the active process through which the "I" progressively relates to a "Thou."* We reach to the conclusion that individual freedom (to thought, exercise, and expression) constititutes a cultural imperative. Finally, in the conclusion, we not only give an assessment of the results of this chapter, but also allude to the subject of the next chapter: Cassirer's move above and beyond neo-Kantianism.

I. 1. What are the Objectives of the Philosophy of Symbolic Forms?

The philosophy of symbolic forms was a response to the critique and concerns of life philosophy – that more and more dominated the intellectual life in the first half of the twentieth century – through its consideration and serious study of mythical thought. However, especially through Cassirer's insistence on the mediated nature of human life, the philosophy of symbolic forms was primarily antithetical to life philosophy and sought to complement it at a fundamental level so as to put it on a more constructive tack. Life philosophy, according to Cassirer, did little in contributing to the solution of the crisis of culture and even dwelled upon it. The crisis in culture for Cassirer consisted in the fact that modern man displays a lack of self-knowledge, while he is at the same time bombarded with numerous conceptions of self-understanding that attemptted to explicate his true and essential being. For example, whereas Nietzsche proclaimed the will to power as essential, and Freud came to the fore with the sexual instinct, Marx glorified the economic instinct of man. What was established by intellectual culture was an anarchy wherein every thinker gave his or her own view as to human nature and culture, without the individual person being provided a guiding principle.[2] As a result of this intellectual anarchy and due to the disorientation the individual experienced, human freedom came into danger.

Cassirer's solution to this crisis is not to provide another substantial definition of human nature, but to provide a strictly functional definition of the human being. A human being cannot be defined by what he is; rather we can know a human person only through his works and deeds. At the same time, a human being cannot gain self-knowledge by mere introspection and reflection on his "true being"; rather the human being can attain to self-knowledge only by relating to another human being through his works. Culture is the result of the progressive endeavors of mankind to give its works an enduring form. A philosophy of culture in the form of a philosophy of symbolic forms provides for a common center through which the human being can place his works in a meaningful perspective so as to explicate and lay out before him the various ways he can attain to self-knowledge by relating himself to other human beings. Cassirer equates culture with the history of man's self-knowledge, and describes it as a history or process of man's progressive self-liberation, from fear, ignorance, and injustice. The guiding thread throughout his exposition of this specifically human development is represented by the concept of the symbol.

Furthermore, as a post-Darwinian philosopher, albeit not in complete concord with Darwinianism, and certainly challenged by it, Cassirer was in search for the characteristically human sphere of life, *i.e.*, the symbolic sphere.[3] Man is not merely an

---

2 Schrems, 1967, p. 180.

3 Cf. the Cassirer chapter in: Randall, 1977.

animal rationale, as stated by Aristotle, but he is primarily symbolic in nature, *i.e.*, an *animal symbolicum*, as Cassirer introduced.[4] At first for human kind there is only myth, *i.e.*, merely sense perception and emotion, albeit in an articulated and expressive form. Only gradually, with the symbolic forms of language and technique (the use of artificial tools), man manages to overcome and direct the immediate given of the here and now, and create for himself an objective world in the typically human sphere of the symbolic. The symbolic sphere is not merely bound by the actual and the given of the here and now, but transcends these by including the future and the possible. Subsequently, this uniquely human access to and continued progress toward the symbolic eventually creates the conditions for the possibility of phenomena such as ethics and law. The philosophy of symbolic forms is concerned with the explication of how the human being is characterized by its mediated relation toward the world. It suggests that the supposed immediate experience of life as proposed paradigmatically by life philosophy is merely illusory, and that the anti-rationalist and anti-scientific critique of life philosophy is not an insurmountable hurdle. Life philosophy, once cleansed of its naïve conceptions, can be complementary to critical idealism.

In addition to a fundamental critique of life philosophy, and a philosophical anthropological project, the philosophy of symbolic forms was foremost a continuation of the tradition of critical idealism.[5] Cassirer did not intend to establish a new branch of philosophy nor did he intend to provide a conclusion to or consummation of all previous philosophy. Cassirer's philosophy of symbolic forms rather has the modest intention to provide a mere prolegomenon to a future philosophy of culture and for that purpose offers only a new perspective on philosophy. In this respect, Cassirer's philosophy of symbolic forms attempts to effectuate a transformation of Kant's Critique of Reason into a Critique of Culture. Whereas Kant directed his critique toward scientific concepts, Cassirer includes all forms of intellectual

---

4 See: Ernst Cassirer, *An Essay on Man: An Introduction to a Philosophy of Human Culture*, Yale University Press, New Haven, 1944, pp. 25–26.

5 Cf. Eekert, G. van, Ernst Cassirer. Philosophie der symbolischen Formen, Hermeneutische vernieuwing als voortzetting van de kritisch-idealistische traditie, in: Boey, 1997, pp. 125–144.

expression, through which the creative individual interprets and relates to the world.[6] Its objectives therefore differed and moved beyond those of critical idealism.

Kant had brought the "Copernican Revolution" to theoretical philosophy. It entailed the radical modification of the relation between cognition and its object, that we must first ascertain the fundamental form of judgment by an analysis of reason, and thus that we must begin with the law of cognition, rather than with the determination the objects exert upon our intuitions. It was Cassirer's aim to carry over Kant's "Copernican Revolution" to all the other phenomena of culture. Kant himself already recognized that mathematics and physics do not exhaust all reality, "*because they are far from encompassing all the workings of the human spirit.*"[7] With the philosophy of symbolic forms, the critique of reason therefore becomes the critique of culture. "*It seeks to understand and to show how every element of culture, insofar as it is more than an isolated element, insofar as it is grounded in a universal principle of form, presupposes an original act of the human spirit.*"[8] The project of the philosophy of symbolic forms directs all the various products of culture toward the common goal of transforming the passive world of mere *impressions*, "*in which the spirit seems at first imprisoned, into a world that is pure* expression *of the human spirit.*"[9] Only when philosophy through the philosophy of symbolic forms extends its analysis to all the products of culture, and does not limit itself to the analysis of *pure cognition*, can it wholly discredit the naïve–realistic view of the world, according to Cassirer.

Therefore, in the "philosophy of symbolic forms" Cassirer applied his findings on the structure of mathematical and scientific thought, as he presented it in his book *Substanzbegriff und Funktionsbegriff* (Berlin, 1910) and magnificently elaborated in his treatment of the problem of knowledge (*Das Erkenntnisproblem in der Philosophie und Wissenschaft der Neueren Zeit*, 4 Volumes, 1906–1957), to the cultural sciences. However, it

---

6 Inspired by Von Humboldt, Hertz, and Goethe, the notion of symbolic form is an original creation of Cassirer. See: Krois, 1987, p. 50.

7 See: Ernst Cassirer, *The Philosophy of Symbolic Forms*, Volume I, *Language*, tr. R. Manheim, Yale University Press, New Haven, 1953 (1923), p. 79.

8 Ibid., 1953 (1923), p. 80.

9 Ibid., 1953 (1923), p. 81.

became clear to him that general epistemology, with its traditional forms and limitations could not provide an adequate methodological basis for the cultural sciences. For this, epistemology should broaden its investigations to all the various fundamental modes of man's "understanding" of the world, "*and apprehend each one of them as sharply as possible in its specific direction and characteristic spiritual form.*"[10] Through his philosophy of symbolic forms Cassirer offers a general theory of cultural forms, and shows that different configurations of subjectivity are determined by a specific spiritual perspective. Each symbolic form fulfills its own function in the growth of the human spirit and each symbolic form is subject to a particular law. It is the task of philosophy, and this is what the philosophy of symbolic forms amounts to for philosophy, to take into consideration the various symbolic forms by which man creates and holds an objective world.

Moreover, philosophy in this regard, has a unifying function as to the various symbolic forms. The philosophy of symbolic forms attempts to bring a solution to the unavoidable conflicts of culture and the antinomies within the concept of culture. "*In the course of its development every basic cultural form tends to represent itself not as a part but as the whole, laying claim to an absolute and not merely relative validity, not contending itself with its special sphere, but seeking to imprint its own characteristic stamp on the whole realm of being and on the whole life of the spirit.*"[11] The philosophy of symbolic forms attempts to overcome the spiritual conflicts that result from the demonstration of the specific power of each cultural form in battle with the other. For that purpose it searches for a standpoint that is situated above the specific cultural forms and yet does not relate them to any external, "transcendent" being or principle. The philosophy of symbolic forms recognizes the *autonomy* of all cultural forms by taking into consideration "*nothing other than the purely immanent relation of all these forms to another.*"[12] This relationship is explicated below as embodied by the concept of the symbol.

---

10 See: Ernst Cassirer, *The Philosophy of Symbolic Forms*, Volume I, *Language*, tr. R. Manheim, Yale University Press, New Haven, 1953 (1923), p. 69.

11 Ibid., 1953 (1923), p. 81.

12 Ibid., 1953 (1923), p. 82.

Finally, Cassirer's philosophy of symbolic forms was concerned with the attainment of a specifically semiotic objective. Taking Humboldt's extension of Kant's Critique of Reason into the field of linguistic concepts as his example, Cassirer explains how every cultural form, analogous to that of language, displays an original formative power of its own. Taking the efforts of von Humboldt as his starting point, Cassirer maintains that language is not a mere formal system of rules, but a living, formative force; in other words, not a mere *ergon*, but an *energeia*. Language is an active process through which we understand and relate ourselves to the world, and stands at the basis of the development of all other symbolic forms.[13] Whenever a certain ontological meaning is expressed by language, this is always inflected by the medium in which it is presented, and hence receives a particularly linguistic dimension.[14] Therewith, the philosophy of symbolic forms is an early conception of philosophy that has now come to be known as the linguistic or Semiotic turn in philosophy but, at the same time, it establishes an expansion of it in all cultural fields.[15]

Every symbolic form is understood by Cassirer to be constituted by its symbolics and semiotics, and is evaluated as to its level of expressive sophistication – *i.e.*, as being expressive, representative, or significative in import – and as to its interrelatedness with other symbolic forms. The philosophy of symbolic forms is a theory of semiotics only to a certain extent, though. On the one hand, the symbolic form of language is prototypical for all the other symbolic forms; on the other hand, the philosophy of symbolic forms transcends the purely linguistic domain for example into the logical–mathematical domain, paradigmatically in the symbolic functions of mathematics. Of all the symbolic forms, however, language is most paradigmatic in that it stands in interaction with all other symbolic forms. That is not the case with myth, for example, which cannot be interconnected in the same way as language with regard to science. The symbolic form of science also plays a special and central role, because through science the human being reaches the highest realm of the symbolic or that of pure meaning; and

---

13 Krois, 1987, p. 51.
14 Moynahan, 2003, p. 68.
15 Krois, 1992, p. 440.

all development seems to be directed toward it. Nevertheless, with the latter Cassirer did not intend to insert a hierarchy between the symbolic forms, but only to express a tendency of the human spirit to progressively search for higher forms of objectivity in its relation to the world. To complement, science, on the other hand, does not stand completely on its own, because it can shed its lights only when it receives an impetus from other intellectual processes, such as myth, language, religion, and so forth. All symbolic forms are therefore characterized by a relationship of interdependency, and make complete sense only in this relationship, rather than through a hierarchy.

I. 2. What are the Characteristics of Symbolic Forms?

Cassirer mentions as symbolic forms or forms of objectivity: Myth, Language, Religion, Science, Art, Technology, Economy, State, Ethics, and Law,[16] but they are not limited to the forms enumerated here.[17] Every symbolic form is a closed world of images and signs, that operates through symbols, but one must not ask about the role the symbol plays therein, but rather investigate in what way this world (be it in language, myth, or science) in its totality bears the character of symbolic formation.[18] Every type of symbolic form stands for a different kind of objectification and cannot be understood save "*in terms of its own canon of intelligibility*."[19] In other words, each symbolic form is autonomous, has its own "inner form,"[20] and is not reducible to any other symbolic form completely.

In the philosophy of symbolic forms, each particular form takes its meaning solely from the systematic place in which it stands. The content and significance of each form is charac-

---

16 Scherer, 1996, p. 55.

17 For example, as to my knowledge, no one has yet discussed and elaborated whether sexuality or erotics constitutes a symbolic form, because it has all the pretensions and features that it does, from the physical deed, the erotic appeals, to the symbolic acts of (pure) love.

18 See: Ernst Cassirer, *Der Begriff der symbolischen Form im Aufbau der Geisteswissenschaften*, Vorträge der Bibliothek Warburg, 1921/1922, 6, pp. 174–175.

19 Gadol, 1974, p. 224.

20 See: Ernst Cassirer, *The Philosophy of Symbolic Forms*, Volume I, *Language*, tr. R. Manheim, Yale University Press, New Haven, 1953 (1923), p. 81.

terized by "*the richness and specific quality of the relations and concatenations in which it stands with other spiritual energies and ultimately with totality.*"[21] For this, according to Cassirer, we have to discover a factor, which recurs in each basic cultural form but in no two of them takes exactly the same shape, *i.e.*, without losing the incomparable particularity of any of them. The question is whether there exists a medium, through which all the configurations effected in the separate branches of cultural life must pass, "*but which nevertheless retains its particular nature, its specific character.*"[22]

Cassirer finds this medium in the concept of the 'symbol' taken in its broadest meaning, *i.e.*, as the expression of something intellectual through sensory signs and images.[23] Through the concept of the symbol, Cassirer finds "*an all-embracing medium in which the most diverse cultural forms meet,*" and for which the idealistic opposition between the *mundus sensibilis* and the *mundus intelligibilis* is no longer irreconcilable and exclusive.[24] The symbol is characterized by a new form of reciprocity and correlation, *i.e.*, a new cooperation between the senses and the spirit. The cooperation consists in the fact that "*The content of the spirit is disclosed only in its manifestations; the ideal form is known only by and in the aggregate of the sensible signs which it uses for its expression.*"[25] As a result, for Cassirer, "[t]*he conceptual definition of a content* (...) *goes hand in hand with its stabilization in some characteristic sign.*"[26] Accordingly, Cassirer describes the meaning of experience as a progressive *process* of determination.[27] In the symbolic sphere, what we call the intellectual or the spiritual ultimately has to

---

21 Ibid., 1953 (1923), p. 82.

22 Ibid., 1953 (1923), p. 84.

23 See: Ernst Cassirer, *Der Begriff der symbolischen Form im Aufbau der Geisteswissenschaften*, Vorträge der Bibliothek Warburg, 1921/1922, 6, p. 174.

24 See: Ernst Cassirer, *The Philosophy of Symbolic Forms*, Volume I, *Language*, tr. R. Manheim, Yale University Press, New Haven, 1953 (1923), pp. 86–87.

25 Ibid., 1953 (1923), p. 86.

26 Ibid., 1953 (1923), p. 86.

27 See: Ernst Cassirer, *The Philosophy of Symbolic Forms*, Volume III, *Science*, tr. R. Manheim, Yale University Press, New Haven, 1957 (1929), pp. 421–422.

find its fulfillment in something sensory; it appears only by and in a sensory sign.[28]

For Cassirer the opposition between the objective and the subjective is not so much the *solution*, as it is the perfect *expression* of the problem of cognition. According to Cassirer, sensibility consists not merely of passivity and receptivity, but also has an active element of formation. Out of the chaos of immediate sense impressions man creates order or some kind of permanence, paradigmatically by using linguistic signs, such as names. Through language, the content of what was first perceived to be chaos receives a certain intellectual mark. As a result, the content of sense impressions rises above the mere sensual level: because it has acquired an intellectual articulation the sensory qualities no longer regulate it absolutely. Symbolic forms create systems of sensuous symbols, which display a function or mode of objectification. It is characteristic of symbols that they transgress individual consciousness and claim universal validity by confronting the subjective with the universal. In the sciences, the symbol embodies the "*fundamental principle of cognition that the universal can be perceived only in the particular, while the particular can be thought only in reference to the universal.*"

For Cassirer, this function of the symbol is not limited to the sciences but runs through all the other cultural forms as well.[29] Therefore, all symbolic forms contain and display a specific kind of symbolic formation, whereby the symbol represents the relationship between the idea and the sign, the universal and the particular. However, Cassirer is not interested in a substantial definition of the 'symbol' or what the symbol signifies in this or that specific discipline. He rather asks in what respect a certain discipline, such as language, myth, or science carries with it the general function of symbolic formation: "*all truly strict and exact thought is sustained by the* symbolics *and* semiotics *on which it is based.*"[30] Symbolic forms are, therefore, functional systems.

---

28 See: Ernst Cassirer, *Zur Logik des Symbolbegriffs*, in: Ibid., *Wesen und Wirkung des* Symbolbegriffs, Wissenschafliche Buchgesellschaft, Darmstadt, 1959 (urspr. Teubner, Leipzich, 1925), p. 210.

29 Ibid., 1953 (1923), p. 86.

30 Ibid., 1953 (1923), p. 86; cf. Ernst Cassirer, *Der Begriff der symbolischen Form im Aufbau der Geisteswissenschaften*, Vorträge der Bibliothek Warburg, 1921/1922, 6, p. 174.

According to Cassirer, "*in all symbolic forms that basic phenomenon is expressed in that our consciousness does not suffice itself only to receive the impresssion of the exterior, but that it accompanies and permeates every impression with a free act of expression. A world of self-created signs and images confronts what we call the objective world of objects and challenges it with independent substance and original force.*"[31] They are symbol or meaning "machines" we have developed for our use whenever we interpret or relate ourselves to the outer world. Symbolic forms are mediators between the subjective and the objective, between the "I," the "You," and the "world."[32] "*All symbolic forms,*" writes Cassirer, "*operate between ourselves and the objects; but by that they do not denote merely the negative distance, in which the object places itself before us, but they create the only possible, sufficient mediation and medium by which any intelligible being becomes tangible and understandable to us.*"[33] We explore that more specifically in the following paragraphs.

In his Substanzbegriff und Funktionsbegriff, Cassirer proposed that concepts should no longer be viewed from the perspective of the naïve or copy theory of knowledge, but by the functional theory of knowledge. According to Cassirer, the naïve copy theory of knowledge was discredited in the history of philosophy and had to make way for the functional theory of knowledge. The latter theory of knowledge or of conceptualization was in its core a new theory of representation. According to the functional theory of knowledge, representation is never a mere copying, but always a representing of a particular content in and through a whole (or larger) system of relations. In the end, there is no present, no immediate given, without representation. All knowledge first is given to us mediated by the various symbolic forms. "*The fundamental concepts of each science, the instruments with which it propounds its questions and formulates its*

---

31 Ibid., 1921/1922, 6, pp. 175–176.

32 See: Ernst Cassirer, *The Philosophy of Symbolic Forms*, Volume I, *Language*, tr. R. Manheim, Yale University Press, New Haven, 1953 (1923), pp. 91–93.

33 See: Ernst Cassirer, *Der Begriff der symbolischen Form im Aufbau der Geisteswissenschaften*, Vorträge der Bibliothek Warburg, 1921/1922, 6, p. 176.

solutions, are regarded no longer as passive images of something given but as symbols created by the intellect itself."[34]

In this regard, Cassirer is importantly inspired by the mathematical physicist Heinrich Hertz, who was among the first to formulate this new ideal of knowledge. He observed that in the attempts of the natural sciences to foresee future experience, the scientists make use of "inner fictions or symbols" of outward objects, "*and these symbols are so constituted that the necessary logical consequences of the images are always images of the necessary natural consequences of the imaged objects.* (...) *The images of which we are speaking are our ideas of things; they have with things the one essential agreement which lies in the fulfillment of the stated requirement, but further agreement with things is not necessary to their purpose.*"[35] In place of the requirement of a similarity of content between the image of the object and the object itself, the natural sciences now introduce a highly complex logical relation. The natural sciences now describe an object only within the essential categories of natural science, and therewith have come to renounce the claim of an "immediate" grasp and communication of reality. Accordingly, scientific concepts are never mere designations for the given and present, rather they point the way to new, hitherto unexplored fields. Therewith, they prepare the way for "*a process of interpolation and extrapolation.*"[36] In fine, concepts must no longer be taken in their substantial, but in their functional sense, *i.e.*, "*not primarily as an expression of a simple existence or occurrence, but as an expression of a determinate order, a specific mode of contemplation.*"[37] They are not responsive to reality, but confront reality with a particular question and direction of thought.

Cassirer maintains that the concept can be understood only by investigating the structure of conceptualization itself and

---

34 See: Ernst Cassirer, *The Philosophy of Symbolic Forms*, Volume I, *Language*, tr. R. Manheim, Yale University Press, New Haven, 1953 (1923), p. 75.

35 Ibid., 1953 (1923), 75.

36 See: Ernst Cassirer, *The Philosophy of Symbolic Forms*, Volume III, *Science*, tr. R. Manheim, Yale University Press, New Haven, 1957 (1929), pp. 440–441; e.g. as in the consecutive chemical formulas of ClOH, ClO3H, ClO4H → ClO2H.

37 Ibid., 1957 (1929), pp. 429–430.

the possibility of such a structure.[38] This structure cannot be derived back to a single material principle, which holds good for all concepts. Rather, what comprises the ultimate foundation of a concept and accounts for its fundamental character is its meaning. With his account of the functional theory of knowledge, Cassirer makes clear, that an object of knowledge can be described only when mediated by a particular logical and conceptual structure, *i.e.*, by symbols articulated through symbolic forms. Accordingly, Cassirer concludes, "*a variety of media will correspond to various structures of the object, to various meanings for "objective" relations.*"[39] To put it otherwise, the form (or "meaning machine") with which an object is articulated determines its fundamental meaning.[40]

As referred to above, for Cassirer, next to cognition, the life of the human spirit as a whole also knows a variety of other modes or forms of "objectification," by means of which it raises a particular to the level of the universally valid. Although these forms of objectification achieve universal validity by methods entirely different from the logical concepts and the laws of logic, nevertheless, each one of them has in common with cognition, that "*it does not merely copy but rather embodies an original, formative power. It does not express passively the mere fact that something is present but contains an independent energy of the human spirit through which the simple presence of the phenomenon assumes a definite "meaning," a particular ideational content.*"[41] Furthermore, the answer to the question of how a certain phenomenon assumes a certain "meaning" or how it is possible that something assumes "meaning," Cassirer finds in the concept of "symbolic pregnance."

---

38 Cf. Ernst Cassirer, *Zur Logik des Symbolbegriffs*, in: Ibid., *Wesen und Wirkung des Symbolbegriffs*, Wissenschafliche Buchgesellschaft, Darmstadt, 1959 (Teubner, Leipzich, 1925), p. 203.

39 See: Ernst Cassirer, *The Philosophy of Symbolic Forms*, Volume I, *Language*, tr. R. Manheim, Yale University Press, New Haven, 1953 (1923), p. 76.

40 See: Ernst Cassirer, *The Philosophy of Symbolic Forms*, Volume III, *Science*, tr. R. Manheim, Yale University Press, New Haven, 1957 (1929), p. 435; cf. Moynahan, 2003, p. 68.

41 See: Ernst Cassirer, *The Philosophy of Symbolic Forms*, Volume I, *Language*, tr. R. Manheim, Yale University Press, New Haven, 1953 (1923), p. 78.

By symbolic pregnance, Cassirer understands, "*the way in which a perception as a 'sensory' experience contains at the same time a certain non-intuitive 'meaning' which it immediately and concretely represents.*"[42] "*The simplest and in a sense the most original and primitive type of this relation* [*i.e.*, symbolic pregnance] *is found*," says Cassirer, "*wherever a sensory experience of some sort confronts us possessing a certain content of meaning such that a kind of expressive value adheres to it with which it seems to be saturated.*" In this regard, the sensory content does not stand before us like a "mute picture on a tablet," "*but rather immediately manifests an inner life as something that appears through its objective nature.*"[43] Symbolic pregnance is the condition for the possibility of all of giving meaning (through signs).[44]

Through the concept of symbolic pregnance, it becomes understandable what Cassirer means by symbolic form. A symbolic form is a certain way to interpret signs and images,[45] an intermediate process through which we first gain access to reality,[46] and through which we relate ourselves to the outer world. Cassirer gives the following definition of a symbolic form, which can be dissected in four components: it comprises of "*every energy of the mind* [Energie des Geistes]" [1], through which "*a mental content of meaning* [geistiger Bedeutungsgehalt] [2] *is connected to a concrete, sensory sign* [konkretes sinnliches Zeichen] [3] *and made to adhere internally to it.* [4]"[47] By "energy of the mind" – the first component of the definition – Cassirer refers to the original, formative power "*through which the simple*

---

42 See: Ernst Cassirer, *The Philosophy of Symbolic Forms*, Volume III, *Science*, tr. R. Manheim, Yale University Press, New Haven, 1957 (1929), p. 202.

43 Ernst Cassirer, *The Problem of the Symbol and Its Place in the System of Philosophy* (1927), tr. Krois, J.M., *Man and World*, Volume 11, 1978, pp. 411–428.

44 For Cassirer's indebtedness to the Gestalt psychologist Kurt Goldstein, in particular relative to his (central) concept of "symbolic pregnance", see: Krois, 1992, pp. 448–452. Cassirer gives a metaphysical foundation for his theory of meaning in the Goethean basis phenomenon.

45 Ibid., 1992, p. 449.

46 Cf. Lindahl, 1998, p. 19.

47 See: Ernst Cassirer, *Der Begriff der symbolischen Form im Aufbau der Geisteswissenschaften*, Vorträge der Bibliothek Warburg, 1921/1922, 6, p. 175; translation by: Krois, 1987, p. 50.

presence of a phenomenon assumes a definite 'meaning'", *i.e.*, the process through which there is such a thing as symbolic pregnance.[48] Hence "energy of the mind" comprises every act of interpretation, be it in finding meaning in what others do or say, or be it in conveying meaning to others by what we ourselves do or say.[49] "Energy of the mind," in an obvious way, also refers to Wilhelm von Humboldt's distinction between language as *ergon* and language as *energeia*. As mentioned before, taking Humboldt's extension of Kant's Critique of Reason into the field of linguistic concepts as his starting point, Cassirer explains how every cultural form, analogous to that of language, displays an original formative power of its own. To illustrate, just as in myth every overwhelming arousal of the senses is interpreted as the expression of a demonic or divine power, *i.e.*, assumes a mythic meaning through mythical formation, language too is not merely a given thing, but displays a formative power through its articulation of verbal meanings or symbols, as a result of which every linguistically accompanied act automatically receives a semantic dimension.

We cannot pursue here fully the question of the meaning of meaning,[50] so as to answer what Cassirer means by "*a mental content of meaning* [geistiger Bedeutungsgehalt]" – the second component of the definition – which is too comprehensive a question for our present purposes, but we do intend to make clear in what way Cassirer's perception of the sign is already saturated by meaning. Because in Cassirer's view of it, "*a concrete, sensory sign* [konkretes sinnliches Zeichen]" – the third component of the definition – is already connected to "*a mental content of meaning* [geistiger Bedeutungsgehalt]," as they both share a common root in the symbol. Symbols, for Cassirer, cannot be conceived without the giving of signs, yet they are distinct from signs, as symbols constitute what he understands

---

48 See: Ernst Cassirer, *The Philosophy of Symbolic Forms*, Volume I, *Language*, tr. R. Manheim, Yale University Press, New Haven, 1953 (1923), p. 78.

49 See: Krois, J.M., *Cassirer. Symbolic Forms and History*, Yale University Press, New Haven and London, 1987, p. 51.

50 Cf. Ogden, 2001 (1923), to which Cassirer refers in his *An Essay on Man* as the ultimate question he likewise wishes to address. See also: Richards, 2001 (1936).

under the mental content of meaning. Whereas the sign fades away when the physiognomic characteristics that make up a sign lose their force to appeal to the senses, symbols maintain their force in the sphere of meaning, irrespective of the diminishing quality of the sensory material that accompanied them. However, the sign for the philosophy of symbolic forms is never a mere cloak, an accidental and outward garment for thought, because when thought uses a sign it represents a basic tendency and form of thought. The sign "*serves not merely to communicate a complete and given thought-content, but is an instrument, by means of which this content develops and fully defines itself.*"[51] This becomes more obvious when we discuss the fourth component of the symbolic form, to which we turn now.

The sensory material, the material of perception, *i.e.*, the sign, is not a real being that can be isolated and put to the fore in this isolation as a pure given, as a psychological datum. We apprehend the symbolic sign as an inward energy, which assumes objective form in the outward world. In other words, when we strive to (intersubjectively) objectify our subjective intentions through symbolic formations of various kinds, we do not merely make meaning, but also give it a place in our own perception and consciousness. Once conferred, we ourselves as the originators of meaning eventually cannot circumvent them. The meanings we have produced (in conjunction with other members of an interpretive or symbolic community) become part of that (particular) objective world, and we subsequently have to deal with them as any other outward reality; in other words, we are "*made to adhere internally to it*" – the fourth component of the definition – or rather bring ourselves to adhere to them when acting accordingly (as we are also free to negate them).[52] With that we have explained the four components of Cassirer's definition of symbolic form.

It is characteristic of the symbol – as the expression of a universal in some concrete, sensory sign – that in it expression,

---

[51] See: Ernst Cassirer, *The Philosophy of Symbolic Forms*, Volume III, *Science*, tr. R. Manheim, Yale University Press, New Haven, 1957 (1929), pp. 410 ff.

[52] The negation of a meaning, *i.e.* the rejection to adhere internally to it, is still a negative affirmation, so that we cannot completely avoid or neglect it. I cannot dwell here upon the pathology.

representation, and signification converge with one another. However, not all symbolic forms are equally well equipped to grapple with pure meaning or even display representational features. Cassirer distinguishes three various dimensions in symbolic formation, *i.e.*, the expressive or mythic, the mimetic or representational, and the significative dimension or the sphere of pure meaning. When Cassirer takes up Kant's insight that objects are not "given" to consciousness in a rigid and finished state, but are first constituted by a synthetic unity of the consciousness, and broadens its range of applicability to any (cultural) cosmos that was formed out of a chaos of impressions; he does not contend that every phase of human consciousness is on a par as to its level of symbolization or objectification. Mythic mentality has objective claims of validity, and comprises of an independent cosmos or a characteristic and typical worldview, but its claims only apply in the mythic realm. For Cassirer myth also involves a process of objectification, that is to say, of transforming mere impressions into formed representations. However, as is explicated below, the transformation myth achieves in our perceptual or sensual world does not reach a representative or significative dimension, because that is reserved for the symbolic forms of language, religion, science, and so forth. If we want to understand myth, though, we cannot do that by contrasting it with the claims of science. To understand myth, we have to consider it only in its own terms, and for that we have to reach back to strata even preceding theoretical object-consciousness. As Cassirer writes, "(...) *before man thinks in terms of logical concepts, he holds his experiences by means of clear, separate mythical images.*"[53] However, not only does Cassirer explore the typical formation of objectifications in the depths of mythical thought,[54] he also contends that myth in this respect is the matrix of all cultural life.

First with the help of language man manages to overcome the mere expressive phase of human life, when through language certain demons or gods are no longer directly presented in their full force and awe, but a certain distance is created with respect to

---

53 See: Ernst Cassirer, *Language and Myth*, tr. S.K. Langer, Dover Publications Inc., New York, 1946, p. 37.

54 See: Ernst Cassirer, *The Philosophy of Symbolic Forms*, Volume II, *Myth*, tr. R. Manheim, Yale University Press, New Haven, 1955 (1925), p. 29.

that constructed reality. The representative function of symbolic forms is reserved for symbolic forms other than myth. In Judaic religion, paradigmatically, the mere expressive form of life is superseded and even discredited by that of the representative and the significative forms. The Divine can no longer be presented in all its actuality by mere words or images. "*Thou shalt not make unto thee a graven image*," is the most compelling formulation of how religion dispenses totally with mythical elements, which reside merely within the expressive sphere, that is to say the sphere that ascribes to expression an immediacy of being. With the representative function, as is elaborated below,[55] words as phonetic phenomena are differenttiated from their meanings, although still dependent upon physiognomic features. Only in the symbolic sphere or that of the pure meaning, the dependency on a continuing or recurrent flow of physical features ends, and do we grasp and hold on to meaning even when the concrete sensory sign with which it was originally conveyed fades away.

From a practical point of view, the philosophy of symbolic forms is essentially a cultural theory of how human beings find, give, and pass meaning (from one generation to another).[56] Through the various symbolic forms we make sense of our world; we give it meaning and make it understandable for ourselves as well as for others. But are these ways of creating meaning indefinite and inexhaustible? To a certain extent the answer is yes, and to a certain extent the answer is no. The array of symbolic forms is malleable, yet not in constant flux, shifting steadily, yet not indeterminate.[57] Although symbolism is infinite in its comprehension of the world, symbolic forms are limited to those processes that entail a particular way of giving meaning. For Cassirer, each symbolic form is potentially all encompassing, in that it can incorporate in the meaning–structure that it offers and articulates any possible object. Through each symbolic form we can have a whole and self-contained world. The number of

---

55 See also: Chapter 8.

56 See: Krois, 1987, p. 44; cf. Balkin, 1998.

57 The internet era provides a good example of how the combined intellectual efforts of man can open a whole new world, and can create a whole new space called cyberspace. It is too early, though, and it would move beyond the scope of this study to assess the semiotic and symbolic structures of cyberspace, with is own sets of signs, images, and symbols.

symbolic forms is therefore limited by the criterion of universal applicability, *i.e.*, its all-comprehensive nature.[58] In a way, every act of the human intellect is symbolic insofar as it makes representations of certain processes or laws, or when it puts a certain occurrence in a certain perspective or functionality. That is important for, but not definitive of a symbolic form. A symbolic form encapsulates and fully contextualizes a certain experience and as a result gives it a characteristic meaning that is contestable only on its own terms. It is a process that involves the phenomenon of symbolic pregnance, because through every symbolic form we give shape to our perceptions by already directing them into a certain direction. Progressively, according to Cassirer, we reach higher forms of objectivity, *i.e.*, purer forms of meaning, that is, only when the human being can freely develop and realize his symbolic functions.[59]

In this regard, the all-comprehensive characteristic of the various symbolic forms can also obstruct the development toward increasingly higher forms of objectivity. Whereas each symbolic form is a self-sufficient medium for understanding and making understandable the world, it can also assume a dominant or hegemonic position with respect to the complete intellectual horizon of the individual. In pejorative terms, these are aberrations or reductions of the multi-dimensionality of human life. When myth holds the life of man in its grip, in an absolute and dominant way, we may call it archaism, primitivism, or barbarism. In the case of religion, we encounter the same totalizing effect upon human life in the form of fundamentalism (as distinct from Puritanism). Law, too can degenerate in a mere formalism or a total juridification of human life. It is up to philosophy to explicate their interconnectedness, and the delicate balance between them that stands at the core of human freedom.

In the next sections, we begin to discuss the development of mythical thought and the results it achieves through the interplay with the force of language. Next, as a result of the interplay between the various (other) symbolic forms we explicate the hermeneutical dimension of Cassirer's philosophy of culture.

---

58 Krois, 1987, p. 51.

59 See also: Chapter 4.

Finally, in Section I.5, we introduce the ethical import of Cassirer's philosophy.

I. 3. What is the Significance of the Interplay between Myth and Language?

Myth is a symbolic form, according to Cassirer, because it is characterized by what Cassirer calls "the will to formation," that progressively propels the individual to form order out of chaos, to produce works and actions that have meaning. What distinguishes a human being from an animal is that the human has created a distance between the sensory-world and himself. As we have seen before,[60] through tool-use man is in the position to play with reality, and to understand himself not merely as a being that merely passively accepts and adapts to his environment, but moreover as an actor that shapes his reality. Through distancing himself from it man is in the position to better grapple with the world and to envision the sphere of the possible, *i.e.*, what could happen (the future) and what could have happened (history). Man's actions become self-conscious in light of the future and of the past, *i.e.*, the possible. Moreover, they can assume meaning over time when given an enduring form (through the various symbolic forms) in works.

Myth is the very first example of how man's making sense of his world can gain an enduring form, by creating an order, framework, or community of meanings that shapes and, so to speak, determines the direction of the perceptions of its participants. Through myth man gives shape, order, and meaning foremost to his emotional world. In myth, whatever expression or outward sign man perceives is interpreted as a sign of anger or good will, as an act of hostility or of friendliness. However, it is not an objective description or explanation of the world around him, in the conventional sense of the term, but rather a dramatization of it. Nevertheless, through this dramatization the mere mass or chaos of sense impressions receives an intellectual expression, and assumes a certain, preliminary, form.

In myth there is yet no distinction between the human world and nature; all are related back to a single unity of life, to

---

60 See: Chapter 4.

an emotional bond that permeates everything. This all pervading bond is perceived as a "supernatural power," what we may call a mythical "field of force," for example as embodied in the Melanesian concept of mana. For the Melanesians mana is a positive concept of "power" that can be vested now in this and now in that place, object, or being.[61] It is a power that can take any shape or form, and it is venerated for its "holiness," as well as feared for the dangers it contains. Mana, perceived as a form of divine potency, stands opposite to a negative concept of "power," *i.e.*, "taboo." The interaction between mana and taboo is important, because through the employment of the "Taboo–Mana Formula" mythological thought produces an organization of reality, by establishing a demarcation of the sphere of the holy and that of the profane.[62] However, at this stage there are not yet concrete, determinable deities or demons that represent in a concentrated form the potency that is felt all around by myth, be it in animate or inanimate objects. At this stage, that which besets a man with sudden terror or wonder still has an entirely impersonal or "anonymous" character.

Under the influence of language, though, the phenomenon of "polynomy" sets in, a significant development in the progress of human consciousness. In this regard, the emotional world of man first finds its expression in an objectifying sense, as distinct from mere emotional discharge, through what Usener has called "momentary gods."[63] The momentary gods are divinities that originate from spontaneous feelings, they come and go, appear and dissolve like the subjective emotions from which they arise. "*Whatever comes to us suddenly like a sending from heaven, whatever rejoices or grieves or oppresses us, seems to the religious consciousness like a divine being.*"[64] However, when man's intellectual and cultural development makes progress, his relation to the outer world more and more assumes an active attitude. Accordingly, with the determinative force of language,

---

61 See: Codrington, *The Melanesians: Studies in their Anthropology and Folk-Lore*, 1981, referred to by: Ernst Cassirer, *Language and Myth*, tr. S.K. Langer, Dover Publications Inc., New York, 1946, p. 62.

62 Cf. Eliade, 1959; and Otto, 1950.

63 See: Ernst Cassirer, *The Myth of the State*, Yale University Press, New Haven, 1946, p. 18.

64 Ibid., 1946, p. 18.

different and recurring emotional or sensory experiences and situations are allotted a characteristic deity of their own.

Man reaches a next stage, when the deities he addresses no longer express a certain nature, but accompany and express a certain activity. These "special" or "functional gods," as Usener has called them, guide the practical performances of man. And moreover, "(...) *none of these undertakings can be successful unless its appropriate god has been invoked in prescribed fashion and by his correct name.*"[65] It is no longer what stirs the emotions of people that are ranked among the deities, but that which is conceived as necessarily accompanying a certain department of human activity and that to which the successful completion or the failure of the activity is ascribed to. Each special god is invested with a special name that characterizes the particular activity that has given rise to it in the first place. Accordingly, the many divine names and divinities correspond to the variety of separate activities man performs in his daily life.

It takes a further step to unite these many divine names and fuse them in *one* proper name, so as to connote the conception of a *personality.*[66] The personal god, as Usener has called him, "*is now capable of acting and suffering like a human creature; he engages in all sorts of actions, and instead of being wholly consummated in one function he is related to it as an independent subject.*"[67] Henceforth, through the primordial linguistic concepts of momentary, functional, and personal gods mythological thought creates from the world of sense impressions a characteristic and independent mental or image world dominated by gods and demons.[68] However, this mental world does not appear to man as something subjective, as something created by himself, rather it confronts him as "*something existent and significant in its own right, as an objective reality.*"[69] Myth, as mentioned before, is the very first expression of man's will to formation.

The will to formation reaches yet to higher stages, again primarily through the medium of the symbolic form of language.

---

65 Ibid., 1946, p. 20.
66 Ibid., 1946, pp. 20–21.
67 Ibid., 1946, p. 21.
68 Ibid., 1946, p. 28.
69 Ibid., 1946, p. 36.

Linguistic concepts gain their form through the simple relations of "similarity" and "dissimilarity," of "nearness" and "farness." With their articulation of phenomena a general change of attitude sets in, because they bring about an inner transformation of the perceptual world. The mere flow of sense impressions is articulated in a characteristic way and condensed in definite centers, to which the manifold is referred to and around which it is grouped. They set the stage for symbolic thought that no longer depends merely on sense impressions but contains meaning independent from them.

Language has become foremost a symbolic system. Accordingly, a person gone blind does not need an actual image or a sense impression of a certain phenomenon itself, for example of a grey cloud or the smell of impending rain, to grasp it conceptually, because he or she can visualize bad weather independent of sense impressions and relate it to a certain context and understand its meaning, when (only) once referred to in linguistic concepts or signs.[70] Moreover, non-human, sentient beings are in constant need of and are dependent upon the quality of their sense impressions to relate or adapt themselves to their changing environment. Symbolic beings have distanced themselves qualitatively from the rest of nature. Through symbolic representation they can achieve the same more effectively, and even with sensuously poorer and hence less concrete material. Language has had to go through various phases before it could fulfill the significative or symbolic function it now displays in human life.[71] In this respect, language in the significative sense becomes instrumental for the abridgment of mythical thought.

In mythical life, language primarily has an expressive function. The demonic or divine images it produces through its primordial concepts do not represent a certain spirituality or a divinity, rather those images are imbued by, embody, or present the divinity in all its actuality. The presence of a demon is invoked by the proper expression of its name. To put it otherwise, through the proper invocation of its name mythical thought already perceives the presence of a divinity in full force and awe. There is yet no distinction between the name of an object and the

[70] Cf. Keller, 1954 (1902); and Lash, 1980.
[71] See also: Chapters 7 and 8.

meaning it represents. Mythical thought identifies the word with the object itself. In mythical thought, there is originally no division between the real and the ideal, between the sphere of "existence" and that of "meaning," but there is rather a continuous flux between the two spheres, both in man's thought and belief, and in his actions.[72] In mythological thought the "word" itself assumes a certain power or substance. The word is hypostatized and venerated for its own sake, because through it something spiritual, a demon or divinity, is made present. In a paradoxical sense, the existence of the deity is made dependent on the proper invocation of its name.

Also, in man's subjective life, the word or the name assumes substantive characteristics. In mythic thinking, a person's ego, his very self and personality, is indissolubly linked with his name.[73] "*Among the Algonquins, a man who bears the same name as some given person is regarded as the latter's other self, his alter ego. If, in accordance with a prevalent custom, a child is given the name of his grandfather, this expresses the belief that the grandfather is resurrected, reincarnated in the boy.*"[74] However, mythic personality, which results from the fetishization of the name, is never something fixed and unchanging; rather, every *phase* of man's life entails a change of personality, which is inaugurated by a new name. A new name, in mythic thought, involves a new self. By assuming a new name a person can escape the wrath of demonic powers or even the responsibility for his actions performed under a previous name. As asserted before,[75] in mythic thought there is yet no real sense of an individual self, or an "I." The individual first attains a sense of self, when it has learned to make use of higher forms of language, through which it can relate itself to others, and in these interrelations discovers its individuality. "*For it is language that makes his existence in a* community *possible; and only in society, in relation to a "Thee," can his subjectivity assert*

---

[72] Cf. Ernst Cassirer, *The Philosophy of Symbolic Forms*, Volume II, *Myth*, tr. R. Manheim, Yale University Press, New Haven, 1955 (1925), p. 36 ff.

[73] Ernst Cassirer, *Language and Myth*, tr. S.K. Langer, Dover Publications Inc., New York, 1946, pp. 49–50.

[74] Ibid., 1946, p. 51.

[75] See: Chapter 4.

itself as a "Me."[76] Discursive thought is possible only when the physico-magical power comprised in the "word" is superseded in significance by the meaning of the *sentence*. In this regard, for Cassirer, the search for truth should be supplanted by something more encompassing, *i.e.*, the search for meaning.

I. 4. What is the Hermeneutical Dimension of Cassirer's Philosophy of Culture?

Language plays its characteristic role in human culture first when it discovers the power of the sentence. In the sentence, the power of the word is made relative and contextualized, because the word is no longer simply expressive, but assumes representational and significative characteristics. However, Cassirer maintains, "[the] *very hypostatization of the Word is of crucial importance in the development of human mentality. For it is the first form in which the spiritual power inherent in language can be apprehended at all; the Word has to be conceived in the mythic mode, as a substantive being and power, before it can be comprehended as an ideal instrument, an organon of the mind, and as a fundamental function in the construction and development of spiritual reality.*"[77] Gradually language attains a mimetical or analogical and ultimately a significative function. For Cassirer, this is to be understood both in an evolutionary as in a developmental or pedagogical sense. Neither animals, nor humans in their early childhood can reach beyond the mere expressive phase. First, when language manages to detach itself from the immediate given of the here and now, and represents the given by asserting or conveying its meaning – and it can do that only through sentences – does it open a whole new and unique world for man. As such, language forms the most important or the most frequented symbolic form in human life. Language stands at the basis of a characteristically human life. Although instrumental for it, language, of course, does not exhaust human life in all its ramifications, nor can it completely satisfy (in its discursive use) man's progressive search for higher forms of intersubjectivity and

[76] Ernst Cassirer, *Language and Myth*, tr. S.K. Langer, Dover Publications Inc., New York, 1946, p. 61.

[77] Ibid., 1946, p. 62.

objectivity. Man reaches these "higher" forms among others in religion, art, and science. However, although distinct from and sometimes even standing in an antagonistic relation to them, for example in the case of science, these forms still receive their original impulse from myth. Myth, for Cassirer, provides for the first treatment of the "raw material" of life, and makes it fit for further processing through the various symbolic forms. As such, all the symbolic forms stand in a relation to myth, or at least have to deal with the fact that our experiences or the interpretation of them still bear, in one form or the other, a mythical mark.

Linguistic concepts have in common with mythological concepts or images that they comprise of an intellectual articulation of sense impressions and experiences. Therefore, for language, there are no clear, separate images that are given to the human mind *ab initio* as copies or representations of a definite world of facts. Moreover, linguistic concepts do not simply compare experiences and select certain common characteristics between them; rather they lead to a concentration or distillation of these experiences into a common center point. This concentration and distillation, therefore, is not a process detached from the sensory or emotional world of man. "[T]*he manner of this concentration always depends upon the direction of the subject's interest, and is determined not so much by the content of the experience as by the teleological perspective from which it is viewed. Whatever appears important for our wishing and willing, our hope and anxiety, for acting and doing: that and only that receives the stamp of verbal "meaning."*[78] Before sense impressions are solidified through the denotation of words, they need to be "noticed" first. This "noticing" only takes place for those impressions that are somehow related to our focus point of willing and doing, that prove to be essential for our lives and activities. In this respect, humans do not differ from animals, in that, what appears as "there" (in an objective sense), is somehow related to sense impressions or impulses, such as the nutritional and sexual impulses, or the quest for knowledge, notwithstanding giving a specifically human example.

However, for the animal, as soon as the impulse fades away, as soon as the desire is fulfilled, that which appeared as

---

78 Ibid., 1946, p. 37.

present for the animal, that which appeared as having assumed the form of a certain order of perceptions, immediately loses its significance. The animal always lives in the narrow confines of its actual drives and excitations, and is unable to retain or form an image of these impulses detached from their actual presence. The formation and fixation of images, by which the past is retained and the future is anticipated schematically, is only possible through symbolic expression. Through symbols the distinctions in meaning are not merely *made*, but *fixed* in consciousness. It is this function of the symbol that Cassirer refers to with the last part of his definition of symbolic form, "*made to adhere internally to it.*" Accordingly, verbal meaning once bestowed by the human mind through words, for example, does not fade away again, because through their fixation in consciousness they contribute to the maintenance of, and are incorporated into, a worldview. Symbolic forms are the various ways symbols receive their articulation and relational ordering or integration into a distinct worldview.

None of the symbolic forms in themselves, though, not even language, can do full justice to the human spirit or can totally exhaust it. The significance of a symbolic form, furthermore, is foremost dependent, not on its degree of pervasiveness in human life, but on the richness of its relations vis-à-vis other symbolic forms. Language, for Cassirer, is the most fundamental factor in human life, not only because the symbolic products of language, *i.e.*, verbal meanings or symbols, have become indispensable to it, but also because without language various phenomena such as religion, law, or science, however distinct from it, could not have reached or maintained their position as a symbolic form. On the other hand, language assumes a higher degree of significance only insofar as it provides richer forms of relationships than other symbolic forms.

Understanding the world, for Cassirer, is only possible through meaning, produced through the various symbolic forms, and when given enduring form in works or actions. We understand the world when we are actively involved in its creation or realization by acts of interpretation. Accordingly, in addition to offering a genetic account of it, the philosophy of symbolic forms provides for a hermeneutics of culture. In this regard, the individual reaches or advances toward attaining truth in the world more accurately, the more the totality of the symbolic forms directs the individual into the same direction of meaning. If we say that each symbolic form is a spotlight, then the convergence of several symbolic forms on a certain point of a once-dark stage will make this point brighter than before, *i.e.*, brings it nearer to what we perceive to be real or true. Conversely, the less symbolic forms there are to "highlight" a certain cultural phenomenon or when the symbolic forms obstruct each other's "radiation" of meaning, the less truth-value we can attach to such a cultural phenomenon. Truth of a certain event, for Cassirer, is attainable only through the convergence and the totality of meanings we can produce with respect to that event. As a result, a diversity of viewpoints or the toleration thereof, for Cassirer, is not a mere moral virtue, but becomes a hermeneutical imperative.[79] Also, this makes clear the extent to which Cassirer places the concept of meaning at the center of his whole theory. Consequently, with his theory of symbolism or meaning, Cassirer also offers a new theory of subjectivity or how the individual attains to its sense of self or individuality by progressively relating itself to others; what may be called his ethical theory. From his hermeneutical imperative of tolerance, we now turn to the ethical import of Cassirer's philosophy of symbolic forms.

I. 5. What is the Ethical Dimension of Cassirer's Metaphysics of Culture?

Philosophy starts with a question, and once the act of questioning has established itself nothing is able to resist it. Indeed, its unlimited character becomes its basic trait. "*The outset of "reflection" has (...) begun – and it stops now at nothing, at no "last things." It subjects everything to its corrosive "criticism." Philosophy, at least, was henceforth addicted to this criticism and it cannot protect itself from it without forfeiting its own nature.*"[80] The unlimited questionability of reality, though, can be expressed symbolically, according to Cassirer, in what he

---

[79] See: Krois, J.M., *Die Goethischen Elemente in Cassirers Philosophie*, in: Naumann, 2002, pp. 157–172; here: p. 164.

[80] Cited by: Naumann, B., 1999, 579.

calls, with Goethe, basis phenomena.[81] Therewith, especially in the posthumously published fourth volume of the philosophy of symbolic forms, Cassirer has given an ultimate, metaphysical foundation for his cultural theory.[82] Cassirer's metaphysics does not seek to offer an ontological explanation, rather it attempts to rest his theory (of symbolism) on basis phenomena – "Basisphänomene" or "Urphänomene" as Goethe called them – that allow of no further reduction or explanation, and can be explained only through each other, and merely symbolically.[83] However, the notion of the basis phenomenon is not so much an end solution for his cultural theory as it is the ultimate expression of the problem, *i.e.*, the problem of man's progressive search for the ultimate foundation upon which various and distinct phenomena rest. Basis phenomena not only explain the futility of searching for what lies behind, for the world behind the "looking glass" in respect of certain phenomena, but at the same time they also express the human desire to question after the why and whereto of phenomena; and, in those instances, basis phenomena, as explained below, are indispensable.

Basically, it comes down to the insight that, if we want to put forward the question of what is the ultimate foundation of a certain phenomenon, we must presume a basis phenomenon.[84] However, while we can put forward foundational questions because of basis phenomena, we cannot further pursue after the foundation of the basis phenomena themselves. "*Here we stand at a point*," writes Cassirer in respect of the basis phenomenon of

---

81 Next to Cassirer's explicit adaptation of Goethe's *Basis* – or *Urphänomen*, he was also thinking of Carnap's notion of *Basis* as expressed in *Der logische Aufbau der Welt* (1928); see: Ernst Cassirer, *The Philosophy of Symbolic Forms*, Volume 4, *The Metaphysics of Symbolic Forms*, J.M. Krois and D.P. Verene (eds.), tr. J.M. Krois, Yale University Press, New Haven and London, 1996, xix.

82 See Ernst Cassirer, *The Philosophy of Symbolic Forms*, Volume 4, *The Metaphysics of Symbolic Forms*, J.M. Krois and D.P. Verene (eds.), tr. J.M. Krois, Yale University Press, New Haven and London, 1996.

83 See: Ernst Cassirer, *Goethe und die geschichtliche Welt. Drei Aufsätze*, Verlag Bruno Cassirer, Berlin, 1932, p. 117. Cf. Naumann, B., *Umschreibungen des Symbolischen. Ernst Cassirers Goethe*, in: Naumann, 2002, pp. 1–23; here: pp. 19 ff.

84 See: Ernst Cassirer, *Goethe und die geschichtliche Welt. Drei Aufsätze*, Verlag Bruno Cassirer, Berlin, 1932, p. 19.

life, "*where every question about a further ulterior goal, every question about the "Why" and "Whereto" must stop.*"[85] For example, but also paradigmatically, we cannot think about life without already taking it as the starting point of our reflections. More specifically, we cannot question about "life" and its various manifestations we wish to question also, without already presupposing it as a basis phenomenon. Life first loses its character as a united and encompassing whole when we project our inquiries into it, but also because we put to the fore such unity in the first place through a basis phenomenon we call "life." "*The mind cannot think as united, what sensibility has provided it in separate parts, and so remains the opposition between the conceived and the ideally constructed, evermore unexhausted.*"[86]

The basis phenomenon, as Goethe himself already related, cannot be exhausted via discursive means; we can approach it only by expressing it symbolically.[87] But even so, it basically remains a marginal concept and fundamentally distinguishes itself from the Platonic Idea. The Platonic Idea was such that a Noumenon may not be a Phenomenon, but nevertheless it remains something comprehensible. The Goethean basis phenolmenon, by contrast, remains the incomprehensible moment of any lively phenomenology.[88] Kant progressively indicates the incomeprehensibility of that which is the world beyond our experiences. But Goethe is much more concerned with the unexplored that is beyond the already explored, that we can merely admire "calmly" as an ultimate, unpronounceable, and in which our wisdom finds its end.[89] Goethe attempts to show in his science that while we may not fully comprehend the organic beyond our perception, we may still investigate the structure of the ultimate boundaries of our perceptual world. As must become obvious, these structures

---

85 Ibid., 1932, p. 17.

86 Goethe, *Bedenken und Ergebung,* Naturw. Schr. XI, 57. Cited by: Ernst Cassirer, *Goethe und die geschichtliche Welt. Drei Aufsätze*, Verlag Bruno Cassirer, Berlin, 1932, pp. 119–120.

87 See: Stephenson, R. H., *"Ein künstlicher Vortrag": Die symbolische Form von Goethes naturwissenschaftlichen Schriften*, in: Naumann, 2002, pp. 25–42; here: pp. 27–29.

88 Cf. Rudolph, E., *Logos oder Symbol? Cassirer über Goethes Platonismus*, in: Naumann, 2002, pp. 97–112; here: pp. 111–112.

89 Simmel, G., *Kant und Goethe*, p. 457; referred to by: Naumann, p. 82.

are symbolic in nature, in that basis phenomena always represent totality in a particular, and vice versa.

Basis phenomena are the point of departure for our view of the world and crystallize themselves first in concrete acts and works. They are a necessity of thought, a necessary thought of unity, as a result of which we can think analytically and synthetically; "*to renew one has to destroy.*" Basis phenomena make clear that we cannot transcend, move beyond the symbolic, which is always constituted by the interaction of the sensible and the intelligible. We can describe basis phenomena not as something that "is," that is present in the sense of an absolute being, nor can we derive their "being" syllogistically from an already established absolute reality. In this sense, Goethe does not propose a new theory of Gestalt; rather what he proposes is what he has coined "morphology." Goethe proposes a change from form [*Gestalt*] to formation [*Bildung*], from the *forma formata* to the *forma formans.* We may describe, *i.e.*, perceptually detect regularity in the transformations of various forms in plant life for example, but what we cannot perceive is the generative *power* by which the regularity in forms is achieved.[90] That making power always remains a potentiality. "*The visible image is not static, nor sensibly moving, but displays by its very configuration a* felt potency to be otherwise."[91] Goethe's morphology investigates the transition of one form to another form, but to grasp such morphology we must presuppose a unity that generates multiple potentials. A particular form is first brought to our attention when put in this general unitary context, as a form that is preceded by previous forms but that at the same time is giving way to another form. An individual form cannot be separated from it before and after, and is at the same time a disclosure of another sort of form, *i.e.*, it represents something more than itself.

Moreover, this is not a mere static 'theme' preserved in all variations; rather "*What we become aware of in experience, are generally only single cases, that with some study can be brought under general empirical categories. These again subordinate into*

---

[90] See: Brady, *Form and Cause in Goethe's Morphology*, in: Amrine, 1987, pp. 257–300; here: pp. 274–280.

[91] Ibid., 1987, p. 286.

scientific categories that further forebode upon that through which indispensable conditions of appearances become known to us. Therefrom everything assembles itself bit by bit according to higher rules and laws that do not present themselves in words and hypotheses, but in perceptival phenomena. We call them basis phenomena, because nothing lies above them but, in contrast, they are fully qualified, that one may gradually, as one previously ascended, descend to the most common cases of daily experience."[92] Basis phenomena are the concrete instruments of the ways or modi through which we mediate ourselves with reality; they are the windows for our knowledge of reality, that through which we open up reality for ourselves at the most basic, fundamental, and at the same time necessary and essential level.

Such is the presumption that what we observe is not only given to me but also to others. For something to be given it means, that it is given to a subject, to a "me" or "others." As a result, the "I"-factor – a basis phenomenon Cassirer adopts – cannot be described pure physicalistically, but can only be defined as a general point of departure.[93] In respect of basis phenomena Goethe says, "*we should leave them in their harmony and incomprehensibility.*" The original unity of basis phenomena may appear to come always with a broken unity, because they are subjected to the scrutiny of the questioning nature of man, but that is because the cognitive function of questioning, according to Cassirer, also belongs to those original and essential functions of the mind, that we may call basis phenomena.

For the purposes of the metaphysical foundation of his philosophy of culture, Cassirer distinguishes between three basis phenomena, *i.e.*, the "I," the "You," and the "work" phenomenon. The three basis phenomena represent three different spheres of life, *i.e.*, the "I," the "You," and the "It"-sphere. These basis phenomena respectively correspond to what we call feeling, willing, and thinking. By feeling Cassirer means expression, or the way in which the pure "inwardness" of the subject testifies to its own

---

92 Goethe, *Farbenlehre*, cited by: Witte, *Urphaenomen,* 1998, p. 1081.

93 See Ernst Cassirer, *The Philosophy of Symbolic Forms*, Volume 4, *The Metaphysics of Symbolic Forms*, J.M. Krois and D.P. Verene (eds.), tr. J.M. Krois, Yale University Press, New Haven and London, 1996, p. 100 ff.

monadic being and life. By willing Cassirer has in mind the acting self that is trying to influence the other by the evocation of sensory "signs" of some kind. Finally, by thinking Cassirer refers to the function of the human mind to make representations, that is to say, the "positing" of something objective by relating our perception to an object.[94]

Cassirer recognizes that humans cannot be atomistic beings or monads, nor are they thrown into the world as into an abyss, in a Heideggerian sense.[95] Rather they are "cushioned" or socialized into a community of meanings, which makes it possible that the "I" understands the "you."[96] Moreover, for Cassirer, the "I" only comes into existence first through these (socializing) symbolic forms.[97] The philosophy of symbolic forms is in this sense an account of the genealogy of the "I,"[98] of the "I" progressively understanding the world and himself through his own actions and works.[99] As a meaning – bestowing being the "I" enters into a relationship with the other through his works.[100] By reaching out and making himself known to the other through

---

94 Scherer, 1996, pp. 152–153.

95 See: Chapter 2.

96 I cannot elaborate here on the relation between Taylor's notion of dialogical identity to that of Cassirer's. Taylor draws on Mikhail Bakhtin's ideas. For Cassirer as a source of inspiration to Bakhtin, see: Brandis, 2002, pp. 521–537.

97 Cf. Habermas, J., *Struggles for Recognition in the Democratic Constitutional State*, in: Taylor, 1994, pp. 107–148; here: p. 126.

98 I am indebted for this insight to John Michael Krois (Berlin). See also: Breckon, 1971, pp. 278–291.

99 See: Ernst Cassirer, *The Philosophy of Symbolic Forms*, Volume II, *Myth*, tr. R. Manheim, Yale University Press, New Haven, 1955 (1925), pp. 155 ff.

100 For Cassirer the concept of "work" is not merely a utilitarian, political, or any other form of a substantial concept, but a functional concept, which is constituted through (social) meanings and finds its true meaning only by the position it holds in its context as a whole vis-à-vis other concepts. Therefore, for Cassirer too, there is no "norm-free" system of economic or other social processes. See, on this point: Honneth, A., *Redistribution or Recognition: A Response to Nancy Fraser*, in: Fraser, 2003, pp. 110–197; here: 138–142. These are rather constituted and permeated by (social) meanings or symbols (through the various symbolic forms). See also: Schwemmer, O., *Der Werkbegriff in der Methaphysik der symbolische Formen. Zu Cassirers Konzeption eines vierten Bandes der Philosophie der symbolische Formen*, Internationale Zeitschrift für Philosophie, 1997, pp. 226–249.

meaningful actions, by being active and reactive to the other as a meaningful being, the "I" testifies to its own existence. While others can know us only in our work, as what we do and make, as what we say and write, or what we buy and sell, we can know ourselves only in our regard of the other as a meaningful being.[101] Cassirer's philosophy of culture is not a theory of human creativity or productivity; rather it is a theory of the human communicative life. The concept of work Cassirer introduces is not the endpoint of his theory, because ultimately it is a "Thou," or the other subject, that receives and transforms the work in the medium in which it was formulated originally. The work is rather an intermediary between "I" and "You," and not before the adversary becomes an "I" as well, does the reciprocal process come to a conclusion.[102]

Culture is created out of the various ways individuals give meaning to their lives through their works, *i.e.*, by giving this meaning an enduring form. Therefore, culture may be defined as a dynamic network of meaningful actions. According to Cassirer, the structure of the effects of our works in history "exists" and is understandable for us only by virtue of its manifestation in enduring creations. However, Cassirer does not merely refer here to the sheer physical "existence" of these creations or works of man, for example the canvas on which the painting appears, the wood or marble of a sculpture, as is the case in the "plastic articles." For Cassirer, they can also be quite "immaterial," as in the case of the law of the state. What is essential for Cassirer is that they have somehow "become flesh", for example as the law and the state can both be viewed as "incarnated," customary ethics. What is important is that the fleeting, temporary, transitory must somehow be held fast, that it must become "objective spirit" in the sense of Hegel. According to Cassirer, "*This occurs only when it becomes condensed and expressed in a*

---

[101] See Ernst Cassirer, *The Philosophy of Symbolic Forms*, Volume 4, *The Metaphysics of Symbolic Forms*, J.M. Krois and D.P. Verene (eds.), tr. J.M. Krois, Yale University Press, New Haven and London, 1996, pp. 128–130.

[102] Cf. Peters, G., *Prometheus und die "Tragödie der Kultur". Goethe – Simmel – Cassirer*, in: Naumann, 2002, pp. 113–136; here: pp. 132–133.

system of works – the works of politics (constitutions, law books), works of art, literature, philosophy, and science."[103]

Cassirer refers here to "works" that do not exclusively belong to the world of willing, or are completely exhausted by that sphere. Of course, no work of man can be realized without passing through the sphere of willing, through the actions of man. Nevertheless, for Cassirer, "*There are "works" whose content, whose meaning, whose "sense" does not consist exclusively in their bringing about a specific "effect," their making any physical or psychical changes in things, or their intervening in the physical or psychical causal order.*"[104] Besides the "technical" usefulness and the effects they have on the "souls" of men, these works, display a particular content of their own, an enduring "being." With this "being," Cassirer means the basic determining factor in the make-up of a "work" that prevents it from being dragged into the turmoil of momentary physical and psychical activity, and that grants it the character of outliving the ever-changing circumstances of daily human life.[105] What Cassirer alludes to is the Socratic notion of "*the determination of the will through its own pure form.*"[106] With his ethics of the work, Cassirer notes, Socrates achieved a turning point in human consciousness.

Socrates, according to Cassirer, did not call for "self-knowledge" in the sense of some pure, monadic, looking inward, in the sense of an intuitive introspection of the "I" as a pure act of *cogito*. Rather, it means something completely new and unique for him. Socrates' call to self-knowledge requires knowing your work to know "yourself" in your work; by knowing what you do, you can do what you know. "*Give shape to what you do; give it form by starting from mere instinct, from tradition, from convention, from routine, from "experience" and "habituation" in order to arrive at "self-conscious" action – a work in which you recognize yourself as the sole creator and actor.*"[107] Socrates, according to Cassirer,

---

103 See Ernst Cassirer, *The Philosophy of Symbolic Forms*, Volume 4, *The Metaphysics of Symbolic Forms*, J.M. Krois and D.P. Verene (eds.), tr. J.M. Krois, Yale University Press, New Haven and London, 1996, p. 159.

104 Ibid., 1996, p. 183.

105 Ibid., 1996, p. 183.

106 Ibid., 1996, p. 189.

107 Ibid., 1996, pp. 185–186.

sought with his philosophy to encourage people to "*Submit to the imperative of the work.*" In our doing and acting, we should not merely ask about its mere "influence," its direct effects or utility in daily life, but about the "work" in its "being" or pure form, *i.e.*, that what remains of it when the physical effects of it fade away. For Socrates, only the pure form endures.

This was also the goal that Plato set for himself as a politician: "*To put productive activity under the guidance and protection of pure form and law of pure form.*"[108] Politics, for Plato, had to be delivered from the sphere of power and productive activity. Plato aimed at taking politics up into the sphere of knowledge, of "contemplation." Therefore, he proposed that the "philosophers," the masters at seeing the Ideas and contemplation, should govern the state – "*not the mere "practicians," the active individuals striving for power.*" For Plato, the "imperative of the pure form" had to permeate and determine the actions of the individual as well as of the people in general. Accordingly, "just law" can arise only from the standard of pure form; as with truth it is comparable to and ascertainable by "geometrical equality," because it belongs to the realm of pure form.[109]

Culture, Cassirer makes clear, bears witness to social action; it can be understood only as a social phenomenon. Accordingly, culture cannot be regarded as the creation of single individuals, *i.e.*, because individuals wanted them to be so according to a plan, by tracing them back to single acts of the will. Nor can it be explained by tracing "works" back to "gifts from above," as when in myth whole cultures or even tools are brought by saviors (for example the fire brought by Prometheus), or are implanted in man by divine revelation. The general answer of the Enlightenment, of classical "Rationalism" has been to give an immanent explanation of works, and to limit the explanation to the human domain. All works of culture, according to Enlightenment thought, can be traced to the acts of single persons, to individuals, which join together in their production. "*This is how contract theories arise, which are applied in different ways to the origin of language, society, law, and the state.*"[110]

---

[108] Ibid., 1996, p. 188.
[109] Ibid., 1996, p. 188.
[110] Ibid., 1996, p. 160; see also: Chapter 8.

According to Cassirer, though, the weakness of such an approach is obvious: "*such "works" cannot be grasped in this way as the sum of individual acts. They are not based upon reaching agreements, stipulations, contracts, and so forth.*"[111]

In this regard, with Romanticism, for example as found in organological theories, but also, albeit in a fundamentally different way, with Hegel, we find that they both reject in principle the Enlightenment solution. Both Romanticism and Hegel attempt to find firmer footing for their theories by moving the basis of their solutions into the superempirical and supersensual. Romanticism goes directly back to myth by conceiving a world of spirits. The works of culture (for example poetry, art, law, the state, customary morality, and so forth) belong to and stem from the "spirit of the people." "*At work here are "underworld" forces and out of their volcanic activity the mountain of human "works" rises up.*"[112] As against this "underworld" Hegel conceives of an "overworld," "*of the "Idea" as that agency whose self-development hammers out these works with an immanent, dialectical necessity.*"[113]

However, according to Cassirer, both Romanticism and Hegel are subject to the same objection by referring to some unknown X as their final "underpinning." "*They* (...) *commit the same fundamental mistake of metaphysical substantialization and hypostatization.*"[114] According to Cassirer, it is not from an "overworld" (Hegel), not from an "underworld" (Romanticism), nor do we need to trace works, directly to creative personalities, in order to give a reading of them and "understand" them. Rather, it must be preceded by another, more general understanding, *i.e.*, that of giving meaning. In this regard, the philosophy of symbolic forms explores and establishes a unity between the universal and original forms of giving meaning.

Culture, for Cassirer, is dynamic in the sense that rather than equating culture to the totality of works produced by man, Cassirer lays stress on the process through which we, intellect-

---

111 See Ernst Cassirer, *The Philosophy of Symbolic Forms*, Volume 4, *The Metaphysics of Symbolic Forms*, J.M. Krois and D.P. Verene (eds.), tr. J.M. Krois, Yale University Press, New Haven and London, 1996, p. 160.

112 Ibid., 1996, p. 160.

113 Ibid., 1996, p. 160.

114 Ibid., 1996, p. 161.

tually, have these works in the first place. Moreover, these works are, for Cassirer, no guarantee that there will be such thing as culture in the future. For Cassirer, it is never certain whether a culture will prosper or whether it will decay. It is paramount, though, that the capacity of man to create culture out of freedom, that is to say, his symbolic functions that determine his personal outlook, are not seriously imperiled or impaired.[115] It is fundamental for the viability of any culture that every person has a right to the free development of his or her personality, and to create a meaningful life. Freedom is not a fact or a given, for Cassirer, but arises and develops first in the interplay between the various symbolic forms. What Cassirer insists upon is that equilibrium be maintained between the various symbolic forms, because the one always tries to dominate the other symbolic forms, and in so doing can obstruct the progressive development of culture. Nevertheless, the various symbolic forms, be it the state, language, religion, or law, find themselves in a relationship of interdependence and in a functional unity. They can all serve the freedom of the individual human being, which is, for Cassirer, not merely an *animal rationale*, but rather an *animal symbolicum*.[116]

The human being as an *animal symbolicum* is a thoroughly normative and expressive being. In human life, we are not merely passively addressed or do we merely perceive the life of the other in a diluted form; rather we engage actively with other humans in a reciprocal relation by entering into a debate with them. In personal relations we achieve reciprocal forms of recognition, in the form of "giving and taking" through ethical claims and enunciations. In the discourse between the "I" and the "other" we achieve "*a pure reciprocity, a pure reversible relationship, where the recognition is mutual.*"[117] Through mutual recognition we lay the basic form for an ethical community or society. Such an ethical life is possible only on the symbolic level,

---

115 See also: Chapter 4.

116 See: Ernst Cassirer, *An Essay on Man: An Introduction to a Philosophy of Human Culture*, Yale University Press, New Haven, 1944, p. 26.

117 See: Ernst Cassirer, *Geschichte. Mythos. Mit Beilagen: Biologie, Ethik, Form Kategorienlehre, Kunst, Organologie, Sinn, Sprache, Zeit*, Nachgelassene Manuskripte und Texte, Band 3, Herausgegeben von K.C. Köhnke, H. Kopp-Oberstebrink und R. Kramme, Felix Meiner Verlag, Hamburg, 2003, pp. 198–199.

that is to say, by accepting or recognizing the other as a symbolic being capable of meaningful reciprocity.[118] That is at the same time a most fundamental expression of human equality and dignity that is *inalienable*.[119] By accepting the other into discourse we already presume the equality of that person on the symbolic level, *i.e.*, as capable of grasping and conveying meaning through symbolic forms. The philosophy of symbolic forms underlines the ethical nature of the human being, because through the various symbolic forms the individual human being progressively relates to others, and only in that relating attests to its individual humanity. Indeed, the symbolic nature of a human being stands at the core of human dignity.

However, that we use symbols also makes us vulnerable to different dangers. As in the myth of king Midas everything he touches turns into gold, when the human being "grasps" reality he finds himself enmeshed in meanings or symbols. Consequently, we have so enveloped ourselves in symbols and symbolic meanings that they have become part and parcel of the very structure of our intellect and feeling, *i.e.*, our personality. Because of this, as Susanne K. Langer has explained, failure or destruction of life symbols important to any person "*is always felt as the most intolerable injury one man, or group of men, can do to another. Freedom of conscience is the basis of all personal freedom. To constrain a man against his principles* (…) *is to endanger his attitude toward the world, his personal strength and single-mindedness* (…) *the very expression of an alien mythology, incompatible with one's own vision of "fact" or "truth," works to the corruption of that vision.* (…) *Common insult is a blow at one's ego; but constraint of conscience strikes at one's ego and super-ego, one's whole world, humanity, and purpose.*"[120]

---

118 See: Coskun, D., *Der* linguistic turn *in der Theorie des Gesellschaftsvertrags. Ernst Cassirer und die Bedingungen der Möglichkeit des Versprechens*, in; Schneider, M. (Hrsg.), *Die Ordnung des Versprechens. Naturrecht – Institution – Sprechakt*, Wilhelm Fink Verlag, Paderborn, 2005, pp. 257–274.

119 Cf. Leibniz' treatment of the institution of slavery, who concludes that next to the property right of the master over (the body of) his slave there is the antagonistic overriding weight of "(…) *le droit des âmes raisonnables qui sont naturellement et inaliénablement libres*." See: Ernst Cassirer, *Leibniz' System in seinen wissenschaftlichen Grundlagen*, Gesammelte Werke, Band 1, Felix Meiner Verlag, Hamburg, 1998 (1902), p. 410 (457).

120 Langer, 1960 (1942), pp. 290–291.

The human being is characterized by the will to formation and, accordingly, displays the desire to express himself through symbolic forms. On the other hand, it is impugning to its sense of self when the human being is confronted by the demand to adhere to the symbols of others, or with the demand to stick indefinitely to one's own symbols.[121] Symbols may assume different meanings across time, they may go and come back, but what endures is the capacity of the human being to symbolization. As the meanings of its symbols shift, the identity or the personal outlook of the individual changes along with them, and *vice versa*. Not only does the individual have the freedom to produce his own symbols, but also the freedom to interpret these symbols or to give meaning to them in its own way. Whereas the former, the freedom to produce symbols, is something the individual performs naturally – that is to say, so long as he displays the capacity for symbolization – and is very difficult, if not impossible, for anyone to frustrate; the latter, interpreting and giving meaning to and with symbols, whether consciously or unconsciously, may come to be outside the command of the individual. Symbols may assume public meaning, and once this meaning is established it can entrench itself in public consciousness. It is by critical investigation and the openness of a society to the public contestation of its values that such rigidification can be prevented and the progressive development of a culture can have its way. Individual freedom (of thought, exercise, and expression) therefore is not a mere moral virtue, but becomes a cultural imperative.[122]

II. CONCLUSION

In this chapter we have given a systematic elaboration of Cassirer's philosophy of symbolic forms. Step by step we have elucidated the various components of Cassirer's definition of symbolic form. Furthermore, we have indicated and explained

---

[121] Cf. Povinelli, 2002, pp. 7 ff.

[122] Cf. Cassirer's hermeneutical imperative, as elaborated by: Krois, J.M., *Die Goethischen Elemente in Cassirers Philosophie*, in: Naumann, 2002, pp. 157–172. See also: Chapter 5.4.

the triadic, logical structure of symbolic forms. In addition, we have discussed the conceptual demarcations of what can constitute a symbolic form. Moreover, we have explicated the hermeneutical dimension of Cassirer's cultural theory, because every symbolic form provides a unique perspective from which to view, interpret, and evaluate the world. For that purpose we have considered the interplay between the various symbolic forms, and articulated Cassirer's hermeneutical imperative of tolerance.

In particular we have considered the interplay of myth and language, so as to explicate not only the matrix of culture, but also the process of how the human being manages to abridge mythological thought. The maxim "*Thou shalt not make unto thee a graven image*," announces a new era in human life, because through it the mere expressive qualities of spirituality is superseded by the symbolic or meaning perspective. Religion although interrelated with myth, becomes an independent symbolic form, because it is more and more directed toward the ethical. And, if ethics stands for the discipline through which we ascertain the rules or principles for how one *ought* to act, then Cassirer's philosophy of symbolic forms considers the conditions for the possibility of all ethics. Because through the philosophy of symbolic forms Cassirer explicates the various ways through which the "I" progressively relates to a "Thou." That explains our position that Cassirer's philosophy of symbolic forms is an ethical project, the foundation for which he provides in his metaphysics through basis phenomena in the sense of Goethe. Moreover, we have explained the significance of symbolization for the maintenance and progress of culture. As a result, we have asserted that individual freedom of thought, exercise, and expression constitutes a cultural imperative.

Herewith we have come to a point of no return in relation to previous interpretations of Cassirer's cultural project, which pertains to the question of his relationship to neo-Kantian philosophy. As is shown below, with his metaphysics of basis phenomena and his ethical theory Cassirer distinguishes himself from neo-Kantianism – or moves above and beyond neo-Kantianism as we call it – to which relationship we now turn in the next chapter.

CHAPTER 6

CASSIRER'S POSITION IN RELATION TO NEO-KANTIANISM?

I. INTRODUCTION

In this chapter we maintain and demonstrate that Cassirer with his philosophy of symbolic forms is liberated from, and rises above and beyond neo-Kantianism, especially as it was formulated by the Marburg School. We focus specifically on the Marburg School and only mention the tenets of the South-West or Baden School of neo-Kantianism in passing. Cassirer's relation to the Baden School is relevant, but Cassirer was primarily influenced by and followed the Marburg School, albeit in new and various ways.

This chapter is constructed as follows. First, in Section I.1, we elaborate on neo-Kantianism in general by answering the question of what was neo-Kantianism. Then, in Section I.2, we focus more specifically on the Marburg School, and answer the question of what was the contribution of the Marburg School to the critical pursuance and reformulation of Kant's philosophy in the twentieth century. In addition, in Section I.3, we consider criticism raised against Marburg neo-Kantianism and give an assessment of that critique, especially as it was voiced by life philosophy. In Section I.4, we answer the question as to the achievements of Cassirer above and beyond neo-Kantianism. Finally, in the conclusion, we not only give an assessment of the results of this chapter, but also refer to the subject of the next chapter: Law as Symbolic Form.

I. 1. What was Neo-Kantianism?

Neo-Kantianism was a philosophical movement that commenced in Germany in the 1860s. What bound the individual thinkers of this philosophical movement together were not so much their interpretations of Kant, which varied extensively, but rather their methodological approach or principle. All were concerned with the Kantian project of pursuing philosophy as a science and the condition for such a philosophy as science. Kant expressed this fundamental principle in the preface to the "Critique of Pure Reason" and in the "Prolegomena," so as to lead philosophy "*into the safe road of a science.*"[1] In the twentieth century, most prominent in neo-Kantianism were two philosophical schools, known as the Marburg School of neo-Kantianism and the South-West or Baden School of neo-Kantianism.[2] Whereas the first concentrated on the logical foundations of scientific knowledge through the Kantian *a priori* or transcendental method, the second found in Kant's critique a proper method to deal with the value and meaning structures of cultural phenomena.[3]

The Baden or South-West School of neo-Kantianism was established by Wilhelm Windelband (1848–1915) and Heinrich Rickert (1863–1936), but later also comprised exponents such as Hugo Münsterberg (1863–1916), Max Weber (1864–1921), Jonas Cohn (1869–1947), Emil Lask (1875–1915), Bruno Bauch (1877–1942), and Gustav Radbruch (1878–1949).[4] In reaction to purely positivistic and epistemological strands in neo-Kantianism during the nineteenth century, as exemplified foremost by Alois Riehl (1844–1924), the Baden School, which was in this respect profoundly inspired by the Kant works of Kuno Fischer (1824–1907),

---

1 Cf. Immanuel Kant, Kritik der reinen Vernunft, hrsg. v. Albert Görland (Werke, in Gemeinschaft mit Hermann Cohen u.a. hrsg. v. Ernst Cassirer, Bd. III), Berlin, 1913, S. 13, 15 f. 19, 22, 25 u. 29 (B VII, XI, XIV, XIX, XXIII, XXX u. XXXVI): "sicheren Gang einer Wissenschaft"; referred to by Ernst Cassirer, *Neo-Kantianism*, The Encyclopedia Britannica. A New Survey of Universal Knowledge, Volume 16, 14th edition, London/New York, 1929, pp. 215–216, in: Ernst Cassirer, *Gesammelte Werke. Hamburger Ausgabe*, Volume 16, *Aufsätze und kleine Schriften. 1927–1931*, hrg. B. Recki, Meiner Verlag, Hamburg, 2003, pp. 308–315; here: p. 308 (215).

2 Handbooks on neo-Kantianism enumerate more than seven different neo-Kantian schools. See: Kersting, W., *Neukantianistische Rechtsbegründung. Rechtsbegriff und richtiges Recht bei Cohen, Stammler und Kelsen*, in: Alexy, 2002, pp. 23–68; here: p. 23.

3 Ibid., 2002, pp. 23–24.

4 Holzhey, 2004, pp. 104–122; cf. Cassirer's publications in the journal of the Baden School, "Logos, Internationale Zeitschrift für Philosophie der Kultur": Ernst Cassirer, *Hölderlin und der deutsche Idealismus,* Logos, Internationale Zeitschrift für Philosophie der Kultur, Band 7, 1917/18, pp. 262–282; idem, *Hölderlin und der deutsche Idealismus II,* Logos, Internationale Zeitschrift für Philosophie der Kultur, Band 8, 1918/19, pp. 262–282.

formulated a philosophy of culture that essentially entailed a theory of values or a science of norms ("*Normalbewußtsein*").[5]

The philosophy of culture of Windelband and Rickert attempted to establish a connection between the realm of "reality" and the realm of values.[6] The sharp line first drawn by Wilhelm Dilthey (1833–1912) between the natural ("nomothetic") sciences and (the "ideographic") science in the form of history, is now carried to its fulfillment by Windelband and Rickert, in particular in relation to the realm of values. "*It is only the concept of value that makes history possible as a science: for only through the values attached to culture can we obtain a definite principle of selection within the infinite manifold of the historical facts, and thus establish the conception of an historical individuality which is capable of description.*"[7] Culture for the Baden School was a completely different realm from that of the natural sciences. The former constituted a realm of values or an idiographic realm, while the latter represented a realm of pure laws or a nomothetic realm.

The Marburg School was less concerned with the distinction between the natural sciences and cultural sciences, and indeed sought to explain the latter from insights gained from the former. The transcendental method, the central concept of the Marburg School, was implemented not only for the scientific constitution of society, but also served to provide for a foundation of the cultural sciences. The Marburg School was founded by Hermann Cohen (1854–1924) and Paul Natorp (1854–1924), and included, next to Ernst Cassirer, representatives as Wilhelm Hermann (1846–1922), Rudolph Stammler (1856–1938), Martin Rade (1857–1940), Karl Vorländer (1860–1928), Albert Görland (1869–1952), Nicolai Hartmann (1882–1950), Heinz Heimsoeth (1886–1975), and Franz Staudinger (1849–1921).[8] In the following paragraphs we focus more specifically on the Marburg School

---

5 Ernst Cassirer, *Neo-Kantianism*, The Encyclopedia Britannica. A New Survey of Universal Knowledge, Volume 16, 14th edition, London/New York, 1929, pp 215–216, in: Ernst Cassirer, *Gesammelte Werke. Hamburger Ausgabe*, Volume 16, *Aufsätze und kleine Schriften. 1927–1931*, hrg. B. Recki, Meiner Verlag, Hamburg, 2003, pp. 308–315; here: pp. 314–315 (216).

6 Ibid., *Neo-Kantianism*, 2003 (1929), Volume 16, p. 315 (216).

7 Ibid., *Neo-Kantianism*, 2003 (1929), Volume 16, p. 315 (216).

8 Holzhey, 2004, pp. 78–83.

and its philosophical standpoints, so as to position Cassirer's philosophy.

Although neo-Kantianism more or less disappeared from philosophical discourse after the Second World War, it would continue to have a significant influence on the intellectual era in the second half of the twentieth century. While epoch-making in philosophy itself, neo-Kantianism became a matrix of ideas and provided for a methodology that could easily be adopted by other disciplines, whether in the sciences or in the humanities. Effectively, neo-Kantianism would encompass an incredible array of scholarship, including aesthetics, law, religion, and ethics; it was also closely affiliated with and the source of inspiration of various other schools. Neo-Kantianism was an important factor for the formation of the ideology of German social democracy as expressed in words and deeds by Bernstein, Vörlander, and Eisner. Hermann Cohen was one of the principal architects of the so-called movement of "ethical socialism" that deeply affected the German socialist party,[9] and inspired the emergence of a socialism (in Europe and elsewhere) that in principle was not communistic in outlook, but operated within the frameworks of a capitalistic society.[10] Moreover, it inspired the reformulation of law that would lead to Hans Kelsen's pure theory of law,[11] it stood as the basis of the philosophy of law of Rudolf Stammler,[12] and contributed to the functionalist turn of jurisprudence by Siegfried Marck.[13] Furthermore, neo-Kantianism provided for the institutional setting and philosophical context for the development of modern existentialism[14] and ontological philosophy by Heidegger,[15] Hartmann,[16] and Rosenzweig.[17] In addition, it proved important for the development of modern history and critical theory as

---

9 Moynahan, 2003, pp. 38–39.
10 Cf. Holzhey, 1991.
11 See: Kelsen, 1967, p. 204; cf. Kelsen (1911) 1923; and Kelsen, 1922.
12 Cf. Müller, 1994.
13 Cf. Marck, 1925; see: Chapter 7.
14 Gordon, 1999, pp. 30–53.
15 See: Chapter 2; see also: Orth, 1992.
16 See: Hartmann, N., *Kleinere Schriften*, Volume 3, *Vom Neukantianismus zur Ontologie,* edited by Frida Hartmann, De Gruyter, Berlin, 1958.
17 Adriaanse, 1993, pp. 292–302.

represented by Bakhtin,[18] Blumenberg,[19] Elias,[20] Kantorowicz,[21] and Lukács.[22] Finally, it was responsible for the redevelopment of the history and philosophy of science through Koyré, Meyerson, and Wind.[23] For our present purposes, though, we restrict our investigations to the Marburg School of neo-Kantianism, in particular as it inspired the philosophy of symbolic forms of Cassirer.

I. 2. What was the Contribution of the Marburg School of Neo-Kantianism?

With the advent of the nineteenth century, the progress and achievements of the natural sciences had posed new and difficult challenges to the post-Kantians. In the light of the degree with which the post-Kantians still admired Newton's mechanics, and their high regard for Euclidean geometry, it was not surprising, therefore, that the first decisive impetus for the revival of Kant's fundamental ideas came from within the natural sciences. In his lecture "*Über das Sehen des Menschen*" ("On the Sight of the Human") (1855), Hermann von Helmholtz was one of the first to give a scientific vindication or empirical affirmation of Kant's central insights by focusing on the active character of the sense organs in the formation of our ideas; a theme already developed and prepared by the psychologist Johannes Müller (1801–1858) in 1826.[24] Kant held that the quality of the sensation was

---

18 For Cassirer as a source of inspiration to Bakhtin, see: Brandis, 2002, pp. 521–537n; Brandis, 1997, pp. 20–27; and Poole, 1998, pp. 537–578.

19 See: Blumenberg, H., *Ernst Cassirers gedenkend bei Entgegennahme des Kuno-Fischer-Preises der Universität Heidelberg 1974*, in: Blumenberg, 1981, pp. 163–172.

20 Goudsblom, 1995, pp. 121–126.

21 See: the preface to Kantorowicz, 1957.

22 See: Keil, S., *Neukantianismus in Lukács Arbeit der zwanziger Jahre*, Deutsche Zeitschrift für Philosophie, Volume 25, No. 3, 1977, pp. 322 ff.

23 Moynahan, 2003, pp. 35–75; here: p. 36; cf. Friedman, 2002; see also: Friedman, T., *Ernst Cassirer and the Philosophy of Science*, www.nd.edu/~hps/Friedman=Cassirer.doc, 2002 (last visited: September 18, 2006).

24 See: Ernst Cassirer, *Neo-Kantianism*, The Encyclopedia Britannica. A New Survey of Universal Knowledge, Volume 16, 14th edition, London/New York, 1929, pp. 215–216, in: Ernst Cassirer, *Gesammelte Werke. Hamburger Ausgabe*, Volume 16, *Aufsätze und kleine Schriften. 1927–1931*, hrg. B. Recki, Meiner Verlag, Hamburg, 2003 (1929), Volume 16, pp. 308–309 (215).

neither a form of intuition nor a category, but that it belonged "*merely to the subjective constitution of the manner of sensibility*."[25] It was the fundamental insight of Helmholtz, and his essential contribution to the ideas that were further developed by Marburg neo-Kantianism, that he considered the quality of the sensation to be essentially linked to cognition rather than merely a property of the object that imprints itself passively on the senses. Accordingly, together with time and space, Helmholtz classified sensation as a form of intuition.[26]

Philosophers such as Friedrich Albert Lange (1828–1875) and Eduard Zeller (1814–1908) adopted Helmholtz' interpret-tations and systematically incorporated his insights on human cognition throughout the Kantian system. Systematically and consistently pursued, Kant's theory of apriorism in the hands of Lange lead to the conclusion that the concept of the "thing-in-itself," an important and central concept for Kant's philosophy, could not be an absolute, but rather only a "limiting term" (*Grenzbegriff*).[27] Subsequently, Otto Liebmann (1840–1912) in his book "*Kant und die Epigonen*" (1865) maintained, that the successors to Kant had all mistaken the thing-in-itself for an absolute. Fichte, Schelling, and Hegel, but also Herbart, Fries and Schopenhauer, suffered from a common fault, according to Liebmann. "*They all assign to the concept of the "Absolute" or of the "thing-in-itself" a central place and make it a fundamental concept of metaphysics, whereas Kant's doctrine, if rightly understood and further developed, implies the very opposite, namely, that this concept is a non-concept, that all cognition moves within the realm of mere relationships, but can never grasp or positively determine an "Absolute."*"[28]

---

25 Immanuel Kant, *Critique of Pure Reason*, tr. N. Kemp Smith, The Humanities Press, New York, 1929, B44; referred to by: Fullinwider, 1990, p. 44.

26 Ibid., 1990, p. 44.

27 See: Ernst Cassirer, *Neo-Kantianism*, The Encyclopedia Britannica. A New Survey of Universal Knowledge, Volume 16, 14th edition, London/New York, 1929, pp 215–216, in: Ernst Cassirer, *Gesammelte Werke. Hamburger Ausgabe*, Volume 16, *Aufsätze und kleine Schriften. 1927–1931*, hrg. B. Recki, Meiner Verlag, Hamburg, 2003, pp. 308–315; here: p. 309 (215).

28 Ibid., *Neo-Kantianism*, 2003 (1929), Volume 16, p. 311 (215).

According to Cassirer, the post-Kantian philosophers were originally divided into two camps, respectively the camp of Fichte, Schelling, and Hegel, who offered a metaphysical interpretation of Kant's thought; and the camp of Fries and his pupils and Herbart, who saw in Kant's thought a new psychological method. Foremost, the Marburg School of Neo-Kantianism, *i.e.*, the school of Hermann Cohen and Paul Natorp, the successors to Friedrich Albert Lange, sought to overcome this dichotomy in the first upwelling of neo-Kantianism in the nineteenth century. In particular Hermann Cohen, by constructively pursuing the alternative elaborated by Lange, sought to display the inadequacy of both the metaphysical and the psychological method as represented by the respective camps.[29] Marburg neo-Kantianism held that Kant had primarily introduced nothing more than a new theory of experience. In significant respects, neo-Kantianism, as represented by Cohen, deviated from Kant's theory of knowledge. According to Cohen, a critical theory of experience could not answer ontological questions concerning the "thing-in-itself," but had to focus on the "general conditions" or "form" of experience, as represented by the so-called transcendental method.[30] He sought to present a coherent version of philosophical idealism in the sense in which it was understood by such early thinkers as Plato and Parmenides.

Moreover, the goal of the Marburg School of neo-Kantianism was to reconcile Kant's transcendental philosophy with contemporary achievements in the natural sciences.[31] The Marburg School assumed that Kant did not merely ask for the conditions for the possibility of experience as such, but, more specifically, that he critically inquired after the conditions for the possibility of scientific experience, as it lay present at that time in the form of Euclidian geometry and Newtonian mechanics. Contemporary achievements in the natural sciences, though, especially in quantum mechanics and relativity theory, proved Newton mistaken and Euclidian geometry outdated in their conceptions of (absolute) time and space; it rather vindicated

---

29 Cf. Paetzold, H., *Die Frage nach Ernst Cassirers Neukantianismus mit Blick auf Cohen und Natorp*, in: Krijnen, 1998, pp. 219–235; here: p. 223.

30 See: Ernst Cassirer, *Hermann Cohen, 1842–1918*, Social Research, Volume 10, No. 2, May 1943, pp. 219–232; here: pp. 223–224.

31 Ihmig, 1993, p. 30.

Leibniz' (non-absolute or relative) process view of time and space.[32]

Therefore, the Marburg School could no longer accept the scientific premises upon which Kant developed his philosophy of experience. Time and space could no longer be regarded as pure forms of the mind, but only as pure forms of scientific thought.[33] Accordingly, objects were never a mere given fact for the Marburg School, but always an assignment to thought, *i.e.*, yet to be constructed by thought. Objects do not constitute absolute, substantial things; rather they represent a process through which we have experience and a determinate notion of objects. The Marburg school considered the creation of the objective world as an ongoing and unending task, the solution of which could be approached only approximately. What the exponents of the Marburg School held in common was the presumption that objects do not constitute a constant factor in human experience. Only the method through which objects are construed by thought is constant and invariable.[34] Therefore, they rejected the Kantian notion of a thing-in-itself (*Ding an sich*), because for the Marburg School every object necessarily stands in relation to a method of thought.[35]

Accordingly, Cohen's so-called principle of origin, central to his philosophical system, expresses the problem that all being, objectivity, or "nature of things" ultimately originates in thought. "*A reality outside the sphere of thought and exempt from its principles and conditions is a meaningless concept.*"[36] In this respect, for Kant, sensibility was devoid of any active principle, and expressed the "receptivity" of the human mind. Understanding, by contrast, was considered by Kant as a form of spontaneity. The dichotomy between sensibility and under-

---

[32] See: Ernst Cassirer, *Leibniz und Jungius*, in: Meyer, A. (hrsg.), *Beiträge zur Jungius-Forschung*, Paul Hartung Verlag, Hamburg, 1929, pp. 21–37.

[33] Cf. Ernst Cassirer, *Substance and Function & Einstein's Theory of Relativity*, tr. W.C. Swabey and M.C. Swabey, Dover Publications, New York, 1953 (1910).

[34] Cf. Marx, W., *Cassirers Philosophie – ein Abschied von kantianisierender Letzbegründung?*, in: Braun, 1988, pp. 75–88.

[35] Ihmig, 1993, pp. 28–62; here: p. 31.

[36] See: Ernst Cassirer, *Hermann Cohen, 1842–1918*, Social Research, Volume 10, No. 2, May 1943, p. 224.

standing introduced by Kant, however, was explicitly rejected by Cohen. In effect, Cohen proposed to efface the term "receptivity" altogether. "*Neither in its sensuous experience nor in its rational activity is the human mind a* tabula rasa, *an empty tablet upon which outward things may make their impressions, it is active in all its functions, in perception as well as in conception, in feeling as well as in volition.*"[37] There is no such thing as something given that the human mind has to accept as a bare fact, according to Cohen, without the human mind already impressing its own form on it.

With Hermann Cohen neo-Kantianism reached a new apex. His three works on Kant, "*Kants Theorie der Erfahrung*" ("Kant's Theory of Experience") (1871), "*Kants Begründung der Ethik*" ("Kant's Foundation of Ethics") (1877), and "*Kants Begründung der Ästhetik*" ("Kant's Foundation of Aesthetics") (1888), proved epoch-making in that from that point forward the study of Kant shifted its primary focus to a specific central theme, *i.e.*, the transcendental method.[38] For Kant the problem of transcendentalism consisted of the question: "*how are synthetical propositions* a priori *possible, i.e., how can pure intuitions and pure concepts, which are entirely* a priori *and not derived from nor founded on experience, refer to objects of experience and claim for these objects universal and necessary validity.*"[39] The concept of transcendentalism for Kant differed from its original, scholastic meaning. For Kant "transcendental" or "transcendent" concepts no longer denote concepts that transcend the realm of finite, conditioned being making possible metaphysical and religious consciousness; rather it was closely related to his revolution of the mode of human thinking, *i.e.*, his

---

37 Ibid., 1943, p. 226.

38 See: Ernst Cassirer, *Neo-Kantianism*, The Encyclopedia Britannica. A New Survey of Universal Knowledge, Volume 16, 14th edition, London/New York, 1929, pp. 215–216, in: Ernst Cassirer, *Gesammelte Werke. Hamburger Ausgabe*, Volume 16, *Aufsätze und kleine Schriften. 1927–1931*, hrg. B. Recki, Meiner Verlag, Hamburg, 2003 (1929), Volume 16, p. 311 (215).

39 Immanuel Kant, *Kritik der reinen Vernunft*, S. 79 (B 73); referred to by: Ernst Cassirer, *Transcendentalism*, The Encyclopedia Britannica. A New Survey of Universal Knowledge, Volume 22, 14th edition, London/New York, 1929, pp. 405–406, in: Ernst Cassirer, *Gesammelte Werke. Hamburger Ausgabe*, Volume 22, *Aufsätze und kleine Schriften. 1927–1931*, hrg. B. Recki, Meiner Verlag, Hamburg, 2003, pp. 328–332; here: p. 328 (405).

Copernican revolution.[40] Kant's revolution consisted of no less a contention that our intuition does not follow the constitution of objects, but rather that the objects of our senses follow the constitution of the faculty of intuition.[41] Transcendentalism, for Kant, was not concerned with objects, but rather with our mode of knowing objects *a priori*.[42] Accordingly, his transcendental idealism was concerned foremost with the exhibition of the foundations of empirical cognition. Therefore, Kant's transcend-dental idealism does not apply to non-empirical absolute concepts, nor does it concern itself with "*merely empirical incidents*," because its "*validity is strictly universal*."[43]

Hermann Cohen, consequently, definitely rejects any psychological interpretation of Kant's transcendental method or theory of apriorism. In his "*Das Prinzip der Infinitesimal-Methode und seine Geschichte*" ("The Principle of the Infinitesimal Method and its History") (1883), he takes the concept of the "infinitely small," as it was established in the Leibnizian differential calculus and the Newtonian calculus of "fluxions," as "*the indispensable and basic intellectual means for any scientific cognition of "reality*."[44] The infinitesimal is emphatically not a thing (*Ding*), but a condition (*Bedingung*), a process or method through which we first discover and construct reality (*Wahrhaftes sein*).[45] For Hermann Cohen, "*Reality is never "given" in any sense, neither in sensation nor in mere intuition, but it must be produced by means of pure thought*." The infinitesimal method proves as the

---

40 Ibid., *Transcendentalism*, 2003 (1929), Volume 22, pp. 329–330 (405).

41 Immanuel Kant, *Kritik der reinen Vernunft*, S. 18 (B 17): "*Wenn die Anschauung sich nach der Beschaffenheit der Gegenstände richten müßte, so sehe ich nicht ein, wie man a priori von ihr etwas wissen könne; richtet aber der Gegenstand (als Objekt der Sinne) nach der Beschaffenheit unseres Anschauungsvermögens, so kann ich mir diese Möglichkeit ganz wohl vorstellen.*" Ibid., *Transcendentalism*, 2003 (1929) here: p. 330 (405).

42 Ibid., *Transcendentalism*, 2003 (1929), p(p). 330 (405–406).

43 Ibid., *Transcendentalism*, 2003 (1929), p. 331 (406).

44 Ernst Cassirer, *Neo-Kantianism*, The Encyclopedia Britannica. A New Survey of Universal Knowledge, Volume 16, 14th edition, London/New York, 1929, pp. 215–216, in: Ernst Cassirer, *Gesammelte Werke. Hamburger Ausgabe*, Volume 16, *Aufsätze und kleine Schriften. 1927–1931*, hrg. B. Recki, Meiner Verlag, Hamburg, 2003, pp. 308–315; here: p. 311 (215).

45 See: Ernst Cassirer, *Der kritische Idealismus und die Philosophie des 'Gesunden Menschenverstandes'*, Töpelmann, Gießen, 1906, p. 32, 1n; referred to by Moynahan,, 2003, p. 49.

centerpiece and ultimate methodological basis for the entire Kantian system purely as a matter of logic – as Cohen elaborates in his main systematic work in three volumes, "*The Logik der reinen Erkenntnis*" ("The Logic of Pure Thought") (1902), "*Ethik des reines Willens*" ("Ethics of Pure Will") (1904), and "*Aesthetik des reinen Gefühls*" ("The Aesthetics of Pure Feeling") (1912).[46] Together with Paul Natorp, Hermann Cohen pursued the transcendental task of "critical idealism" even further, when they founded the Marburg School of neo-Kantianism.[47] Subsequently, Hermann Cohen's insistence on the infinitesimal as the key to the transcendental method, as the centerpiece of Kantian philosophy, and as the ultimate method for all scientific philosophical inquiry; would have an even wider impact in the works of Cassirer.

Already in his *Substance and Function*, Cassirer adopts these central tenets of the philosophy of the Marburg School and emphasizes how the transformation of any perceptual or scientific fact in experience and knowledge is determined by the infinitesimal: "*The particular presentation reaches beyond itself, and all that is given* means *something that is not directly found in itself; but it has already been shown that there is no element in this 'representation' which leads beyond experience as a total system. Each particular member of experience possesses a symbolic character, insofar as the law of the whole, which includes the totality of members, is posited and intended in it. The particular appears as a differential that is not fully determined and intelligible without reference to its integral.*"[48] Similarly, in his philosophy of symbolic forms, in relation to the central concept of symbolic pregnance, because of which we have such thing as

---

46 Ernst Cassirer, *Neo-Kantianism*, The Encyclopedia Britannica. A New Survey of Universal Knowledge, Volume 16, 14th edition, London/New York, 1929, pp. 215–216; in Ernst Cassirer, *Gesammelte Werke. Hamburger Ausgabe*, Volume 16, *Aufsätze und kleine Schriften. 1927–1931*, hrg. B. Recki, Meiner Verlag, Hamburg, 2003, pp. 308–315; here: p(p). 311 (215–216).

47 Cf. Ernst Cassirer, *Von Hermann Cohens geistigem Erbe (1926)*, in: *Almanach des Verlages Bruno Cassirer*, Berlin, 1926, pp. 53–63, also in: Ernst Cassirer, *Gesammelte Werke. Hamburger Ausgabe*, Volume 16, *Aufsätze und kleine Schriften. 1927–1931*, hrg. B. Recki, Meiner Verlag, Hamburg, 2003, pp. 308–315.

48 See: Ernst Cassirer, *Substance and Function & Einstein's Theory of Relativity*, tr. W.C. Swabey and M.C. Swabey, Dover Publications, New York, 1953 (1910), p. 300; referred to by: Moynahan, 2003, pp. 35–75; here: p. 63.

meaningful experience in the first place, Cassirer writes: "*No conscious perception is merely given, a mere datum, which need only be mirrored; rather, every perception embraces a definite 'character of direction' by which it points beyond the here and now. As a mere perceptive differential it nevertheless contains within itself the integral of experience.*"[49] This process view or functional perspective of the nature of the conceptualization of perception or experience remains a constant throughout Cassirer's philosophic career. His theory of the functional concept, as developed in his four volume work on the problem of knowledge[50] and restated in his *Substance and Function*, constitutes the zenith of his scholarly contribution to the philosophy of the pre-First World War era, and stands as the foundation of his philosophy of symbolic forms (in four volumes).[51] With his philosophy of symbolic forms Cassirer moved beyond and above neo-Kantianism, and to a marked extent escaped the criticism with which neo-Kantianism was increasingly confronted. We now turn to the criticism raised against neo-Kantianism in the first half of the twentieth century, and give an assessment of that critique.

I. 3. What was the Critique Exerted upon Neo-Kantianism?

The end of the Wilhelmine Empire and the beginning of the Weimar era had marked a shift in culture as a whole.[52] As

---

[49] See: Ernst Cassirer, *The Philosophy of Symbolic Forms*, Volume 3, *The Phenomenology of Knowledge*, tr. R. Mannheim, Yale University Press, New Haven, 1957, p. 203; cited by: Moynahan, 2003, p. 67.

[50] For the fourth volume of Cassirer's problem of knowledge, see: Ernst Cassirer, *The Problem of Knowledge: philosophy, science, and biology since Hegel*, tr. W.H. Woglom and C.W. Hendel, Yale University Press, New Haven and London, 1950. The original German manuscript was first published in 1957, see: Ernst Cassirer, *Das Erkenntnisproblem in der Philosophie und Wissenschaft der neueren Zeit*, Volume 4, *Von Hegels Tod bis zur Gegenwart*, Kohlhammer, Stuttgart, 1957.

[51] For the fourth volume of Cassirer's philosophy of symbolic forms, see: Ernst Cassirer, *The Philosophy of Symbolic Forms*, Volume 4, *The Metaphysics of Symbolic Forms*, Krois, J.M. and Verene, D.P. (eds.), tr. Krois, J.M., Yale University Press, New Haven and London, 1996; first published as: Ernst Cassirer, *Zur MEtaphysik der symbolischen Formen,* hrsg. J.M. Krois, Nachgelassene Manuskripte und Texte, Volume 1, Meiner Verlag, Hamburg, 1995.

[52] Cf. Moynahan, 2003, pp. 35–75.

culture shifted its direction at the turn of the century, philosophy soon followed with its insistence on the immediate experience of life, the existential and sometimes the irrational, which gradually came to dominate the whole of cultural life in Germany. In philosophy this cultural turn was most prominently expressed by life philosophy. As every new era has to define itself by relating to the other, older one, so did the era that was characterized by life philosophy and existentialism. For many the old era was embodied by neo-Kantian philosophy. As Klaus Christiaan Köhnke has made clear in his authoritative work on neo-Kantian philosophy, in the nineteenth century and in the beginning of the twentieth century, there was barely any philosophical academic enterprise that did not one way or the other engage itself with the philosophy of Kant or did not react to the famous call by Otto Liebmann to go "*back to Kant*."[53] As Cassirer relates, "*In the first half of the nineteenth century all German philosophers were following the path that had been hewed by Kant and were attempting to complete his work*."[54]

For the first part of the twentieth century this was no different, according to Cassirer. The vehemence with which neo-Kantianism was attacked and rejected from all corners did not alter the fact that even in the first decades of the twentieth century the central tenet of German philosophical thought remained firmly tied to Kant.[55] As a result, the revolution that displayed itself in philosophy during the first half of the twentieth century was directed at and fought against neo-Kantianism. Although not apparent during the battle itself, when the revolutionary strain of thought in philosophy subsequently established itself, *i.e.*, when the revolution of life philosophy gradually acquired the form of an evolution, undeniably the self-image of life philosophy and that of existentialism was marked to a certain degree by this act of denial of the old era, *i.e.*, neo-Kantianism. Notwithstanding the denial of the legitimacy of the old strain of thought, the new strain of thought questioned the presuppositions of the old one, and attempted to redefine and improve these

---

[53] Köhnke, 1991; cf. Willey, 1978.

[54] See: Ernst Cassirer, *Hermann Cohen, 1842–1918*, Social Research, Volume 10, No. 2, May 1943, pp. 219–232; here: p. 223.

[55] See: Ernst Cassirer, *Neuere Kant-Literatur*, Theoria, Volume 6, 1940, pp. 87–100; here: p. 87.

presuppositions. With that, the philosophy of the new era, what we have termed life philosophy, brought itself to the fore as a development of the old one, so that any claim to the erasure of neo-Kantianism was bound to fail from the start.[56]

Much changed though, according to Cassirer, with the demise of the Weimar era. With the materialization of life philosophy in more and more cultural fields, including politics, the study of Kant in Germany came more or less to a stand-still, while it flourished in other parts of the world.[57] Cassirer (sometimes referred to as the last of the neo-Kantians), for his part, took this German neo-Kantian legacy with him on his odyssey. His continued indebtedness to neo-Kantianism, while developing and maintaining a philosophical position of his own, justifies exploring his relation to and subsequent disassociation with neo-Kantianism more fully in the following section.

What life philosophy objected to was the stress neo-Kantianism (purportedly) laid on logic and methodology, *i.e.*, that it left no space for satisfactory results that could be achieved through mysticism or oriental philosophy, for example. Furthermore, the complaints of life philosophy centered on the claim, that neo-Kantians reject metaphysics *in toto*, while Kant had only rejected scholastic metaphysics. The central objection of life philosophy was the extent to which neo-Kantianism had obsessively embraced the task of tackling the problem of knowledge or framing a philosophy of science. While neo-Kantianism sought to avoid falling back into German speculative idealism, which was discredited, especially since the revolution of 1848, it also tried strenuously to avoid unphilosophic forms of scientific materialism that characterized the latter half of the nineteenth century in Germany.[58]

At the root of the matter lies the distinction already introduced by Kant, between philosophy as a science, and

---

56 See: Sternberg, 1920, pp. 396–397.

57 See: Ernst Cassirer, *Neuere Kant-Literatur*, Theoria, Volume 6, 1940, pp. 87–100; here: pp. 88 ff., referring to the works of Paton (England), De Vleeschauwer (Belgium), and Marc-Wogau (Sweden).

58 See: Krois, 1987, p. 33; cf. Gregory, F., *Scientific Materialism in Nineteenth-Century Germany*, Studies in the History of Modern Science, Volume 1, D. Reidel, Dordrecht and Boston, 1977.

philosophy as a worldview (*Weltanschauung*).[59] In order to achieve this distinction, neo-Kantianism itself had to undergo a revolution, it had to reject the chaos produced by Hegelian speculative idealism, which had rendered the distinction between philosophy as science and as worldview obsolete, by directly going back to Kant's critical idealism. One of the driving forces behind the neo-Kantian movement was the opinion that philosophy had taken a wrong turn after Kant. Moreover, the metaphysical systems of the nineteenth century, according to the protagonists of the call to go "Back to Kant," proved insufficient in providing a philosophical framework that could come to grips with the recent achievements of science.[60]

While combating the false naturalism in science, neo-Kantianism experienced difficulty in fulfilling another duty, *i.e.*, avoiding any hypostatization of natural science, as was recognized especially by Hermann Cohen and the Marburg School.[61] In Wilhelmine Germany, though, natural science was the most acceptable channel of concern and enjoyed primacy above others. Before the First World War natural science was still "*the leading sector and most humane element of human thought*," and was imminently tied up with the hopeful future of Germany.[62] As a result, and, in retrospect, neo-Kantianism in its early naturalistic, scientific guise not only disputed the religious point of view, but expounded a scientific view of nature that bordered on the religious as to its claim of validity.[63]

However, what these objections forego is the degree to which neo-Kantianism could fulfill a completely different task, the degree to which it could take a normative stance and build up from it a comprehensive worldview. Sternberg, for example, makes this clear from a neo-Kantian perspective with respect to man's moral, religious, and legal life. While the religious must find its concretization in a moral life, Sternberg maintains that this does not render the religious dependent upon the moral.

---

59 See: Sternberg, 1920, p. 402.

60 Krois, 1987, pp. 33–34.

61 For the political significance of Cohen's and Cassirer's emphasis to avoid any form of objective as well as subjective dogmatism, see: Moynahan, 2003, pp. 61 ff.

62 Ibid., 2003, p. 69.

63 See: Renz, 2002, p. 20.

Likewise, law may draw its content from the moral, but it does not dissolve into morality. It is the task of philosophy to explicate the interdependence of these phenomena and place them on an equal footing vis-à-vis each other and allocate to each of them a place in culture. Especially for Hermann Cohen philosophy could not be a mere abstract system, a web of mere "speculative" concepts detached from culture. Rather, philosophy retains its substance and form from the "Faktum" of intellectual culture. "*It does not represent, as was assumed by dogmatic metaphysics, a distinct and separate realm of mind that could stand aside others, that could stand aside law and morality, aside art and religion.*"[64] The task of philosophy, according to Cohen, is to assess and express the particular direction or principle in which all these diverse intellectual forms converge. For Cohen that principle was the transcendental method, which, in this respect, related all of culture to science.

I. 4. What were Cassirer's Achievements above and beyond Neo-Kantianism?

In his philosophy of symbolic forms, Cassirer gives an explicit philosophical anthropological turn to the critical insights of the Marburg School, not only by fully embracing the symbol concept, but also by its explicit reference to the meaning perspective.[65] Therewith, as elaborated below, in significant respects, Cassirer's anthropological turn to the "critical idealism" of the Marburg School may be understood as an attempt to reconcile the thoughts of the Marburg School with the other main school of thought in neo-Kantianism, *i.e.*, the Baden or South-West School. Of course, Cassirer could not agree with the sharp distinction made by the Baden School between the "nomothetic" sciences and the "ideographic" science of culture;[66] because in the concept of the symbol he had found an instrument that was nomothetic and

---

[64] See: Ernst Cassirer, *Von Hermann Cohens geistigem Erbe (1926)*, in: *Almanach des Verlages Bruno Cassirer*, Berlin, 1926, pp. 53–63, also in: Ernst Cassirer, *Gesammelte Werke. Hamburger Ausgabe*, Volume 16, *Aufsätze und kleine Schriften. 1927–1931*, hrg. B. Recki, Meiner Verlag, Hamburg, 2003, pp. 308–315; here: pp. 482–483 (57).

[65] For a systematic elaboration, see: Chapter 5.

[66] Cf. Ankersmit, 1994, pp. 78–80.

idiographic at the same time, *i.e.*, that was applicable in the natural sciences as well as in the humanities, and hence precluded any sharp divide between the two. Nevertheless, the efforts of the Baden School did not remain unnoticed by Cassirer.[67]

While the Marburg School was praised and criticized at the same time for its scientific soundness and dedication, the Baden School foremost distinguished itself with its investigations into the realm of values. While rejecting the metaphysical premises of the Baden School as to the eternal nature of values, Cassirer, through the concept of the symbol, established a *via media* between the Marburg insistence on the scientific or symbolic foundation of culture on the one hand, and the Baden focus on the idiographic nature of culture on the other. His attempts at philosophical reconciliation (after the First World War), though, were overshadowed not only by methodological differences, but by intra-school and public complications as well. The relationship between the two Schools was downright bitter for the most part. Not the least responsible for that were racist anti-Semitic remarks by Kuno Fischer in relation to Hermann Cohen, the pronouncements by Bruno Bauch regarding the degree to which German culture was threatened by "Jewish alienation," but also the failure by Cohen to obstruct the promotion in Marburg of Ludwig Busse who was supported by Windelband in 1894, the rejection of the dissertation of Cassirer in Strasbourg because he was a Jew, and some literary and stylistic considerations.[68] No School, though, could have predicted the grim future that awaited neo-Kantianism, and history has made obsolete the question of what would have happened to neo-Kantianism if both Schools had sought greater cooperation. With the departure of Hermann Cohen from Marburg and the displacement of Cassirer, his chosen successor and closest disciple, from Cohen's chair in favor of the experimental psychologist Erich Jaens – the Marburg School soon bled to death.

---

[67] See: Ernst Cassirer, *Nature-Concepts and Culture-Concepts*, in: *The Logic of the Humanities*, (*Zur Logik der Kulturwissenschaften. Fünf Studien*, in: Göteborgs Högskolas Arsskrift, Volume 48, Heft 1, 1942, pp. 1–139), tr. C.S. Howe, Yale University Press, New Haven, 1961, pp. 117–158; cf. Paetzold, H., *Die Frage nach Ernst Cassirers Neukantianismus mit Blick auf Cohen und Natorp*, in: Krijnen, 1998, pp. 219–235; here: p. 234.

[68] See: Holzhey, 2004, pp. 39–40, 82n.

The same applies to the Baden School. Notwithstanding the fact that it saw no serious discontinuity until the end of the Weimar period, the Baden School did not manage to re-emerge after the Second World War, with its main exponents either dead or scattered around the world. In effect, neo-Kantianism was either silenced, as was the case with the Marburg School, or dead, as was the case with the Baden School. The only consolation is that we can get a glimpse of the original force of neo-Kantianism through the works of Cassirer.

Nevertheless, at the turn of the twentieth century, neo-Kantianism had established itself as the dominant philosophical school. However, as a result, an obvious gap had emerged between neo-Kantianism on the one hand, and speculative idealism on the other. While the early exponents of neo-Kantianism disassociated themselves completely from Hegel and his dialectic, later exponents sought to bridge the gap, which by then encompassed the whole period between Kant and Hegel.[69] One of the most comprehensive attempts to relate neo-Kantianism to Hegel, *i.e.*, to cover the epoch between Kant and Hegel with a philosophical investigation, was made by Ernst Cassirer.[70] But Cassirer accomplished even more, *i.e.*, more than merely explaining the development in philosophy post Hegel from a Kantian point of view. In his attempt to complement and think beyond the Marburg School of neo-Kantianism, to think beyond the transcendental method as understood by Cohen and Natorp, he drew on such wide sources as Cusanus, Leibniz, Hegel, von Humboldt, and Goethe.

What he accomplished, in this regard, was firstly a semiotic or linguistic transformation of the transcendental method as expressed by the transcendental idealism of the Marburg School. Most notably, for this transformation, Cassirer picked up and pursued the critical investigation of Wilhelm von Humboldt in the field of linguistics, and extrapolated from it a general scheme of cultural expressions, which he termed "the

---

69 Cf. Sternberg, 1920, pp. 396–426; here: pp. 403 ff.

70 Cf. Verene, 1969, pp. 33–46; cf. Ernst Cassirer, *The Problem of Knowledge: Philosophy, Science, and History since Hegel*, tr. W.H. Woglom and C.W. Hendel, Yale University Press, New Haven, 1950.

philosophy of symbolic forms."[71] He was furthermore unique in his insistence that "myth" was the matrix of culture and that it has a broader practical philosophical and political significance as well.[72] In addition, in lieu of the Kantian tripod of "knowledge, ethics, and aesthetics," which was still embraced by the Marburg School, Cassirer established a plurality of symbolic forms, without attributing primacy to the validity or value of the mathematical sciences. Next, while the paradigm of a *mathesis universalis* had significantly dominated modern philosophy from Descartes onwards to Leibniz, Spinoza, and Kant, and was eagerly adopted by the Marburg School, Cassirer replaced it with the dynamism of culture, *i.e.*, he transformed the critique of reason into the critique of culture.[73]

Moreover, whereas the Marburg School restricted its epistemological investigations mainly to mathematics and mathematical physics, Cassirer, with his introduction of the symbol concept, explored all the sciences, exact and cultural.[74] Heinz Paetzold elucidates this development by remarking, that "*Cassirer distances himself from the precepts of the neo-Kantianism of his academic teachers* [Hermann Cohen and Paul Natorp] *to the extent that symbolic thought becomes important for him.*"[75] With unparalleled eruditeness in the natural sciences as well as in the humanities, he set out to answer the all-encompassing question of how we understand meaning, *i.e.*, the meaning of meaning.[76] Cassirer no longer asks how "knowledge" is possible, rather he asks about the conditions of the possibility of how we understand the world and how we understand one another paradigmatically in

---

71 For Cassirer as a contributor to the semiotic or linguistic turn, see: Nöth, W., *Handbuch der Semiotik*, Metzler, Stuttgart, 1985, p. 9; referred to by: Soboleva, 2001, p. 281, 1n, with indebtedness to Heinz Paetzold.

72 See: Chapter 4.

73 See: Paetzold, H., *Die Frage nach Ernst Cassirers Neukantianismus mit Blick auf Cohen und Natorp*, in: Krijnen, 1998, p. 230.

74 For a systematic elaboration, see: Chapter 4.

75 See: Paetzold, H., *Die Frage nach Ernst Cassirers Neukantianismus mit Blick auf Cohen und Natorp*, in: Krijnen, 1998, p. 231.

76 Cf. Ogden, 2001 (1923), to which Cassirer refers in his *An essay on man* as the ultimate question he likewise wishes to address. Cf. also: Richards, 2001 (1936). For a contemporary jurisprudential orientation on "meaning", see: White, 2001; cf. White, 1990; and White, 1984.

language.[77] As John Michael Krois puts it, "*In all this Cassirer has transformed the theory of knowledge into the theory of the understanding of meaning.*"[78]

Finally, next to expanding the range within which the transcendental method could be applied, Cassirer also moved away from the Marburg School by narrowing and excluding its applicability to what he called with Goethe, *Urphänomene* (irreducible "primary or basis phenomena").[79] "*The fundamental reality, the Urphänomen, in the sense of Goethe, the ultimate phenomenon may, indeed, be designated by the term "life." This phenomenon is accessible to everyone; but it is incomprehensible in the sense that it admits of no definition, no abstract theoretical explanation. We cannot explain it, if explanation means the reduction of an unknown fact to a better known fact, for there is no better known fact.*"[80] With the Urphänomen Cassirer introduces a methodological solution or concept through which he expresses the most fundamental problem for the philosophy of symbolic forms. He searches for a concept to which every explanation of the world must ultimately return, *i.e.*, that admits of no further explanation and trumps infinite regress in representation and meaning. To basis phenomena the transcendental method obviously does not apply, because what makes them basis phenomena is the fact that they admit of no questioning about the conditions for their possibility.[81] They rather form the fundamental expression of the problem of transcendentalism. With Goethe's primary or basis phenomena, Cassirer complements his philosophy of symbolic forms.[82] "*The basis phenomena and that which reality in all its various forms, directions, and dimensions makes accessible to us; they are "the light and the way.*"[83]

---

77 See: Krois, 1992, pp. 437–453; here: p. 439.

78 Ibid., 1992, p. 440; for Cassirer's subsequent metaphysics of symbolic forms, see: Chapter 5

79 Ibid., 1992, p. 444.

80 Ibid., 1992, p. 444.

81 Cassirer mentions several other primary or basic phenomena. Next to life, the expressive function of meaning, the experience of the living human body, symbolic pregnance (*symbolische Prägnanz*), person, and time, are all referred to at various occasions as primary or basic phenomena; see: Krois, 1992, p. 445.

82 For an elaboration on Cassirer's indebtedness to Goethe, see: Chapter 5.

83 Referred to by: Naumann, 1999, p. 583.

II. CONCLUSION

In this chapter we have elaborated on the relation and subsequent disassociation between Cassirer's philosophy of symbolic forms and neo-Kantianism. We have focused specifically on the Marburg School, because Cassirer liberates himself from that School and progresses above and beyond neo-Kantianism in its Marburg formulation. Although his distance from the Baden School decreases, compared to his early Marburg standpoint, nevertheless, he cannot agree with the distinction between the natural sciences and the cultural sciences the Baden School introduced. With his symbol-concept he still embraces the transcendental method but gives to it a cultural or anthropological turn. Apart from broadening its range of applicability to all cultural forms, Cassirer restricts the applicability of the transcendental method by taking into consideration the so-called Goethean basis phenolmena. Within the latter the infinitesimal method and transcendentalism find their limit.

However, with his liberation from neo-Kantianism he, at the same time, escapes the criticism of life philosophy. In this respect, Cassirer was unique in his insistence on the philosophical study of mythical thought. As is explicated before, Cassirer does not reduce myth to sheer animistic imagery, but explains how myth also displays a particular mode of objectification and forms an expression of the human intellect, that is to say the symbolic capacities of man.

In the next chapter we focus more specifically on the practical significance of the philosophy of symbolic forms, by elaborating on Law as Symbolic Form, and in particular by explicating its relation to myth. Law, too, gives rise to "symbolic" perceptions and expectations – *his* or *her* rights make the citizen of a rule of law differ from that of a rule of men. A world without law or rights would be an entirely different one, and the loss or denial of rights, like the loss or withdrawal of the recognition of any other communal source of meaning, while disorienting, can in itself be a cause of "suffering," or of felt "injustice."[84] Law's

---

[84] Cf. Axel Honneth's "recognition-theoretical turn"; see: Honneth, A., *Redistribution or Recognition: A Response to Nancy Fraser*, in: Fraser, 2003, pp. 110–197; here: pp. 132–134. See also: Cahn, E.N., *The Sense of Injustice: An anthropocentric View of Law*, New York University Press, New York, 1949.

meaning has become part of our perception of the world and has its own particular "twist" to it. Law too has become a symbolic form, yet at another stage. Through law we seek to create a normative framework or a cosmos for our world of actions with a world of meaning and claims of truth of its own. As is shown in the following, it is through its contribution to culture as a whole, *i.e.*, through its progressive objectifications in the world of actions, that law attains its objective character and grounding. We now turn to the question of what is Law as Symbolic Form.

CHAPTER 7

LAW AS A SYMBOLIC FORM

I. INTRODUCTION

In this chapter we focus on why and how law is a symbolic form. We explain that law as a symbolic form is closely tied to Cassirer's intellectual and practical interest in the human rights tradition. Jurisprudence is the discipline that should provide a basis for the human rights tradition. Although Cassirer's interest in human rights reaches back to one of his earliest works, *i.e.*, his Leibniz book, he gives a systematic elaboration of jurisprudence first when he was in exile, and more explicitly during his period in Sweden. In Sweden he comes to the understanding that he should have spent more attention to human rights, and that he had not given jurisprudence its due in his philosophy of symbolic forms. Moreover, in his study and subsequent critique of the philosophy and jurisprudence of the Scandinavian Realists, in particular Axel Hägerström, Cassirer sheds important light on his own stance in ethics and jurisprudence. This is important because he rarely details his viewpoint on jurisprudence and ethics within his oeuvre.

In this chapter we explicate that law has become a symbolic system that sustains itself through its own conceptual rigor, *i.e.*, through the mutual reference of its key concepts. Furthermore, law escapes the pitfalls of a tautological nature, because of its relation and contribution to other fields of culture and culture taken as a whole, *i.e.*, through its particular mode of objectification in the sphere of actions. Law provides a framework through which we judge our actions, ourselves, and others. Human rights are essential for Law as Symbolic Form, because as normative standards of humanity they progressively inform legal systems to greater degrees of universality and objectivity. Their significance consists in the fact that they make clear to us that our representation of law, in positive law and concepts, can only be an approximation of law, never its fulfillment, and, accordingly, keep the legal system anthropocentric.

This chapter proceeds as follows. First, in Section I.1, we ask from where Cassirer's commitment toward jurisprudence or

Law as Symbolic Form stems. Furthermore, in Section I.2, we focus specifically on the question of what was Cassirer's critique of Scandinavian Realist jurisprudence; and thereby lay bare his own jurisprudential standpoint, as well as their underpinnings. Moreover, because every symbolic form is characterized by a triadic, logical structure, *i.e.*, the mythic or expressive, the mimetic or representative, and the symbolic sphere or the sphere of pure meaning, in Section I.3, we respectively ask "what is law" in the expressive, representative, and symbolic spheres.

We cannot attempt here to syllogistically subsume the phenomenon of law under the definition of symbolic form that we elucidated in Chapter 5, because that is not what interests us here, or what interested Cassirer in any single symbolic form. Such an objective would not give each symbolic form its due, that is to say, appreciate the way in which each symbolic form progressively contributes to the constitution of our objective world. Next to explicating the triadic development of law from the depths of archaic customs, the representation of law in positive acts and opinions, to the symbolic claims asserted by human rights, we are foremost interested in what way law manifests and maintains itself in the cultural sphere in general, and in our actual lives in particular. In addition, in Section I.4, we elaborate further on the symbolic sphere of law as signified by human rights, and in what sense Cassirer has offered a renewed philosophical justification of human rights through Law as Symbolic Form. Finally, in the conclusion we not only give an assessment of the results of this chapter, but also allude to the subject of the next chapter: the human promissory function that stands at the foundation of law.

I. 1. What Explains Cassirer's Engagement with Law as Symbolic Form?

Cassirer set course to Sweden after he had completed his one-year visiting appointment at All-Souls College, Oxford and after he had accepted a professorship at the University of Göteborg, in September 1935, but his decision to accept the new appointment was not easy.[1] It was becoming clearer to him that the mental distance between him and Germany was growing and that he needed to concentrate on a new generation of students. Cassirer, from his early writings displayed and explicated a steady concern for practical philosophy, *i.e.*, jurisprudence and ethics; for example, as we have witnessed when he publicly engaged himself with the polity of Weimar, in the Davos-encounter with Heidegger, in his study of the Cambridge Platonists, in his philosophical friendship with Schweitzer, and in his anticipation of Nazi ideology through the study of myth that later took the form of a political pathology; but especially during his period in Sweden this concern took a more explicit character. In a systematically significant work "*Axel Hägerström – eine Studie zur Schwedischen Philosophie der Gegenwart*" Cassirer set out to answer with all his intellectual weight the question that he asked in his inaugural lecture at the University of Göteborg in 1935, "*Are there general binding supra-individual, supra-state, supra-national ethical claims?*"[2]

Although Cassirer had never negated the tradition of inalienable human rights throughout his oeuvre, had stoutly defended them in Weimar despite strong protest and opposition, and had made the concept of individual freedom (especially in the form of the spontaneity of the individual mind, *i.e.*, transcendental freedom) central to his philosophy of symbolic forms, he felt he had not done enough. Even standing at the abyss separating humanity from barbarism, he did not give up believing in humanity, expressing his enthusiasm for the human rights tradition, and questioning himself for that purpose. In his

---

1 See: Ernst Cassirer, *The Concept of Philosophy as a Philosophical Problem (1935)*, in: Ibid., *Symbol, Myth, and Culture. Essays and Lectures of Ernst Cassirer 1935–1945*, edited by D.P. Verene, Yale University Press, New Haven and London, 1979, pp. 49–63; here: p. 63. For Cassirer's period in Sweden, see: Hanson, 2006. I would like to thank professor Nordin for the manuscript he sent in 2004.

2 See: Ernst Cassirer, *Axel Hägerström- eine Studie zur Schwedischen Philosophie der Gegenwart*, Göteborgs Högskolas Årsskrift, Elanders Boktryckeri Aktiebolag, Göteborg, 1939; ibid., *The Concept of Philosophy as a Philosophical Problem (1935)*, in: ibid., *Symbol, Myth, and Culture. Essays and Lectures of Ernst Cassirer 1935–1945*, edited by D.P. Verene, Yale University Press, New Haven and London, 1979, pp. 49–63; cf. Krois, 1987, p. 29.

inaugural lecture at the University of Göteborg, Cassirer contends that along with himself, all who have worked in the area of theoretical philosophy in the first half of the twentieth century deserve, in a certain sense, the reproach of Schweitzer. According to Schweitzer, the duty of philosophy "*would have been to admit to our world that the ethical ideals of reason would no longer find support*, as earlier, *in a total world view, but would be for the present dependent on themselves and would have to assert themselves in the world by their own inner force. It should have shown us that we have to struggle for the ideals on which our culture rests.*"[3]

Instead, says Cassirer, philosophy endeavored on behalf of the scholastic conception of philosophy, and all too frequently lost sight of the true connection of philosophy with the world, *i.e.*, human rights. "*But*," Cassirer admonishes, "*today we can no longer keep our eyes closed to the menacing danger. Today the urgency of the time warns us more strongly and more imperatively than ever that there is once again a question for philosophy which involves its ultimate goal and highest decisions. Is there really something like an objective theoretical truth, and is there something like that which earlier generations have understood as the ideal of morality, of humanity?*"[4] Henceforward, through his philosophy of symbolic forms, Cassirer more specifically and elaborately attempted to provide for a total worldview wherein the ethical ideals of reason, *i.e.*, human rights, would find support. But before answering the question of whether and why there are universally binding ethical claims, Cassirer first had to lay the groundwork for law as a symbolic form. Human rights as objective and valid claims are possible first when law itself stands for an autonomous phenomenon with independently objective and valid claims. Law, in this sense, is an autonomous functionality or medium of human consciousness that primarily finds support from its own symbolic and semiotic structures.

Cassirer first presents his view of law (*Recht*) and morality (*Ethik*) in his critical treatment of the jurisprudence of the

---

3 See: Ernst Cassirer, *The Concept of Philosophy as a Philosophical Problem (1935)*, in: Ibid., *Symbol, Myth, and Culture. Essays and Lectures of Ernst Cassirer 1935–1945*, edited by D.P. Verene, Yale University Press, New Haven and London, 1979, pp. 49–63; here: p. 60.

4 Ibid., 1979 (1935), pp. 60–61.

Uppsala School – also known as the Scandinavian Realists.[5] In this critique Cassirer takes the opportunity to grasp accurately and apply his basic view, as developed in his *Philosophy of Symbolic Forms*, to new fields, *i.e.*, jurisprudence and moral philosophy. Furthermore, Cassirer does not evade Hägerström's level of sophistication, but indeed tries to refute Hägerström's critical philosophy at his level of sophistication.[6] As a result, *Axel Hägerström* offers perspective to the following question: what is law according to Cassirer, *i.e.*, what is Law as Symbolic Form?

Notwithstanding the fact that Cassirer only gives a systematic elaboration of the symbolic forms of language, myth, and science, we extend Cassirer's investigation into symbolic forms to the discipline of jurisprudence as well, not only to fill up an apparent lacuna but, moreover, to give the systematic relevance and essential place of law in what Cassirer calls "the progressive development of human consciousness to higher degrees of objectivity" its due. In other words, we address in what sense law belongs to the "*humanitas ipsa,*" as Cassirer put it.[7] Law as Symbolic Form, in this respect, complements Cassirer's philosophy of symbolic forms from a systematic point of view, *i.e.*, it affects previous interpretations of the philosophy of symbolic forms, as we establish its practical significance.

For that purpose we have to continue our account of Cassirer's philosophy of symbolic forms, now to incorporate the field of jurisprudence into the general scheme of cultural expressions provided by Cassirer. As a result, we may refer to another common characteristic of symbolic forms, one which we had already considered. "*All symbolic forms,*" writes Cassirer, "*do not come to the fore as separate, independent and identifiable forms, but originate very gradually from the common matrix of Myth. All content of the mind, although we have to grant it an independent area and an autonomous principle, is factually first given to us only in this concatenation. The theoretical, the practical, and the aesthetic consciousness, the world of language and knowledge, of*

5 See: Ernst Cassirer, *Axel Hägerström- eine Studie zur Schwedischen Philosophie der Gegenwart*, Göteborgs Högskolas Årsskrift, Elanders Boktryckeri Aktiebolag, Göteborg, 1939.

6 Cf. Peczenik, 2003, p. 7.

7 See: Ernst Cassirer, *Vom Wesen und Werden des Naturrechts*, Zeitschrift für Rechtsphilosophie in Lehre und Praxis, Volume 6, No. 1, 1932, pp. 22–23.

art, of law and of ethics, the fundamental forms of society and that of the state," writes Cassirer, "(...) *they are all still originally connected to the mythico-religious consciousness.*"[8]

An independent form is first attained when it manages to cut itself loose from this layer and gradually go through the various stages of objectification, which are termed by Cassirer the three basic functions of consciousness, *i.e.*, the expressive function (or *Ausdrucksfunktion*), the representational function (or *Darstellungsfunktion*), and the significative function (or *Bedeutungsfunktion*), what Cassirer calls the purely "symbolic" sphere.[9] As they are not genetically autonomous creations (they rather originate from myth and stay interrelated to myth) and go through analogous stages of objectification in their logico-historical evolution, the various symbolic forms fulfill the model of a critically conceived universal history, and, in this respect, explicate the essential unity of human culture.[10] In the following section, we explain the place and function of law within human culture, by concentrating on Cassirer's critique of the jurisprudence of the Scandinavian Realists. Subsequently, in Section I.3, we consider law respectively at the mythical (or expressive), the representative, and the symbolic phase. In Section I.4, we explore the ethical import of the symbolic animal, by explicating Cassirer's renewed foundation of human rights, as well as its relevance for law.

I. 2. What is Cassirer's Critique of Scandinavian Realist Jurisprudence?

During his exile in Sweden, Cassirer encountered a jurisprudence that was underpinned by an epistemological philosophy that Cassirer had sought to overcome with his philosophy of symbolic

---

8 Ernst Cassirer, *Axel Hägerström – eine Studie zur Schwedischen Philosophie der Gegenwart*, Göteborgs Högskolas Årsskrift, Elanders Boktryckeri Aktiebolag, Göteborg, 1939, p. 85n; Sprache und Mythos, Leipzich, 1925, p. 37 f. The translation of Suzanne Langer contains an important omission, because it omits the translation of the words "law" and "ethics."

9 Verene, 1993, pp. 116–117.

10 Gadol, 1974, p. 224.

forms.[11] Furthermore, the nihilist account of practical philosophy given by the Scandinavian Realists, in particular by its founder Axel Hägerström (1868–1939), stood in stark contrast with the belief of Cassirer in absolute and objective values. However, most striking for Cassirer was a *prima facie* agreement that he actually perceived between his conception of the study of law and that of the Scandinavian Realists. Most significantly, Axel Hägerström too presumed the interconnectedness of myth and law. Nevertheless, Cassirer fundamentally disagreed with his premises, and it is this encounter with Hägerström which provides a general scheme for a Cassirerean jurisprudence, and an opportunity "*to grasp accurately and apply to new fields*," the basic view he developed in his philosophy of symbolic forms.[12]

For Cassirer, law is a symbolic form, and hence interconnected with myth.[13] However, this does not entail, as Hägerström contends, that law is composed of representations of superstition created by legal fantasy and carried over through the centuries. Hägerström demonstrates his position through the Roman conception of a contractual obligation, the oldest legal act of the world. To illustrate, in the case of a contractual obligation, the Romans presumed the existence of a real, albeit invisible, connection between two persons, which could be produced only through various strictly prescribed and almost ritualistic actions accompanied by verbal phrases. The problem is, of course, according to Hägerström, that no such relation exists in reality. Its significance is merely psychological for Hägerström. Likewise, the right of property is nothing but a mythical cloak for Hägerström and serves merely as the arrangement for the defense of established interests. As such they invoke objective forces that only impress us emotionally. Rights do not exist, for Hägerström, *i.e.*, they are illusory, because for them to be real they have to have

---

11 Krois, 1987, p. 154.

12 See: Ernst Cassirer, *Axel Hägerström – eine Studie zur Schwedischen Philosophie der Gegenwart*, Göteborgs Högskolas Årsskrift, Elanders Boktryckeri Aktiebolag, Göteborg, 1939, pp. 6–7.

13 See: Ernst Cassirer, *The Philosophy of Symbolic Forms*, Volume II, *Myth*, tr. R. Manheim, Yale University Press, New Haven, 1955 (1925), pp. 150 ff.

an empirical basis.[14] Cassirer agrees with Hägerström as to the genetic origins of law as a cultural datum, according to which, behind a façade of a rigid logical system of concepts, law contains a hidden layer of "magical" representations or fictions. However, for Cassirer that is not end, because these "fictions" still play an important function within law and make law for what it is, *i.e.*, something objective.

Hägerström is the geologist of law who searches for the deeper layers and ultimately for the deepest layer of law in order to give a formation plan of law. His formation plan concludes that the foundation of law does not lie in the immediate data given to us by the documents of law, but in order to comprehend the true meaning of these documents we have to go back to the mythical origins of these documents. Cassirer, as the cultural philosopher of law, on the other hand, is not satisfied with this single point of departure of law's concepts; he insists that we must grasp the *totality* of the possible meanings to be given to law's concepts, particularly considering their continuous reshaping and active motives. Of course, legal concepts first achieved their significance within the legal system they made up by way of mutual interaction and references. Nevertheless, they also display continuity from a genetic perspective, because they continue to be informed by mythical, religious, and ethical motives.[15]

Cassirer understands the genetic account of law in positive terms. There has not been a mere forgetting of the mythico-religious subsoil, but a transformation that has established a new form in place of the old. Whereas the concepts of law originate from the mythico-religious subsoil, for Cassirer, gradually they gain independence from myth, and maintain self-sufficient claims of their own. The development of Roman law demonstrates this thoroughly, according to Cassirer. The Romans thought of law as given and ordered by the gods and for them law could not be an autonomous phenomenon. All of *ius*, *i.e.*, law created by humans, ultimately has its origin in *fas*, *i.e.*, divine law.[16] Nevertheless, Cassirer maintains, that we can distinguish from the sheer

---

[14] See: Ernst Cassirer, *Axel Hägerström – eine Studie zur Schwedischen Philosophie der Gegenwart*, Göteborgs Högskolas Årsskrift, Elanders Boktryckeri Aktiebolag, Göteborg, 1939, pp. 99–100.

[15] Ibid., 1939, p. 90.

[16] Cf. Kaser, 1949, p. 28.

"animistic" imagery and sensational perceived by Hägerström, a theoretical core that was already present in pre-Socratic thought.[17]

Cassirer emphasizes that it was the essential achievement of pre-Socratic thought to have discovered the pure form of a theoretical, deductive science and gradually to have won field of myth. This universal struggle, initiated by the pre-Socratic philosophers in the form of replacing the power of myth (Mythos) by that of the force of reason (Logos), also affected law (Dike), the intellectual center and focus point of Greek thought.[18] While the classical tragedies of ancient Greek literature centered on the essential link between truth and law, they related them both to a common origin, *i.e.*, the cosmos, and, as a result, added to the notion of justice a universal and eternal propensity.[19] Accordingly, the development or transformation of Roman law from the initial narrowness of a local agrarian law to a more encompassing state law, and finally to that of a cosmopolitan account of law, according to Cassirer, was in fact no more than a synthesis and consistent pursuance of the Greek conception of natural law or *Dike*.[20] Moreover, by applying the methodology of Greek philosophy to jurisprudence, Roman lawyers created a jurisprudence subjected to the logical principles of identity and non-contradiction, thereby setting the foundations for jurisprudence as a systematic discipline. As a result of this process, Roman law gradually came loose from its mythical restraints by transcending archaic logic with its undifferentiated unity of speech and thought, and established in

---

17 See: Ernst Cassirer, *Axel Hägerström – eine Studie zur Schwedischen Philosophie der Gegenwart*, Göteborgs Högskolas Årsskrift, Elanders Boktryckeri Aktiebolag, Göteborg, 1939, pp. 91–95.

18 See: Jaeger, W., *Paideia. Die Formung des griechischen Menschen*, Walter de Gruyter & Co., Berlin, dritte Auflage, 1954, p. 96.

19 Ernst Cassirer, *Logos, Dike, Kosmos, In der Entwicklung der griechischen Philosophie*, Göteborgs Hogskolas Arsskrift, Volume 37, 1941: 6, Elanders Boktryckeri Aktiebolag, Göteborg, 1941, pp. 20–21. In his article *Logos, Dike, Kosmos* Ernst Cassirer stresses the importance of this link, first achieved firmly by early Greek thought, for the intellectual future of humankind and without which the subordination of the one or the many to a single other is soon due; cf. Chapters 3 and 4.

20 Cf. Chapter 3.

the practical world, the world of our actions – just as the Greeks accomplished for the theoretical world – a cosmos of law.[21]

To illustrate by contrast, primitive man still experiences his world as limited on all sides. Everywhere, there are, for primitive man, supernatural forces that keep him within fixed boundaries and that are capable of eliminating him. To achieve his goals, to ensure his well being, he must continuously please these supernatural forces and try to win their favor through prayers and sacrifices. However, primitive man is in even more of a difficult position, because the supernatural forces, which may be called demons or deities, are not subject to unchanging rules, rules that guide their conduct as well as that of men. Rather, the demonic forces that surround man and to which he is surrendered are endless in number and uncompromisingly treacherous and volatile.

In the polytheistic world the gods do not yet have a certain and determinable personality or character. To the contrary, they are thoroughly characterized by arbitrariness; in a sense they are free to do whatever they wish and, accordingly, push and pull man from one corner to the other with diametrically opposite claims. The contribution of the Romans consists precisely in the fact that with their systematic treatment of the law they want to reach beyond these oppositions. What makes their treatment of the law systematic is that they erected a totality of imperatives that at the least correlated with each other as to their primary intentions.[22] Therefore, also when we look at the edicts of the praetor, the edicts are not merely absorbed and registered; rather the dogmatists treat and examine them as to their consistency. They help make clear to what extent the edicts of the praetor can prejudge future cases, have value as precedent, or to put it otherwise, have a formative power in the cosmos of law.[23]

---

[21] See: Ernst Cassirer, *Axel Hägerström – eine Studie zur Schwedischen Philosophie der Gegenwart*, Göteborgs Högskolas Årsskrift, Elanders Boktryckeri Aktiebolag, Göteborg, 1939, pp. 92–93.

[22] For the development of the idea of justice in ancient Greek thought, see: Chapter 3.

[23] See: Ernst Cassirer, *Axel Hägerström – eine Studie zur Schwedischen Philosophie der Gegenwart*, Göteborgs Högskolas Årsskrift, Elanders Boktryckeri Aktiebolag, Göteborg, 1939, pp. 93–94.

Hägerström represents law as a totality of *heterogeneous* factors [*Kraftekonglomerat*], such as those of religious representations, the so-called consciousness of justice, class interests, and the general tendency to conform to existing relations, or the fear of anarchy; all cooperating with one another.[24] For Cassirer, though, this cannot be the *terminus ad quem* for jurisprudence. Jurisprudence instead has a duty to search for a solution to the fundamental problem of how the human intellect fuses these latter discords into some kind of unity. For the theoretical world, Kant had devised the concept of the "*unity of the plurality*" [*Einheit des Mannigfaltiges*].[25] The concepts of law, for Cassirer, have the same task of synthesis to fulfill as the Kantian "*pure concepts of the intellect*" [*reine Verstandesbegriffe*] or the "*categories*" [*Kategorien*]. For Kant, these were nothing more than a means of making us able to "*spell out representations and hence to be able to read them as experience*" [*Erscheinungen buchstabieren, um sie als Erfahrung lesen zu können*].[26] They represent the logical conditions for every synthesis of observation and form the means by which the latter first attains its objective meaning.

The concepts of law and that of nature may differ as to their proper object, *i.e.*, the former represents a unity of actions, while the latter represents a unity of observations, for Cassirer, they do not differ as to their content of truth or objective meaning. This insight of Cassirer, already formulated in his *Substanzbegriff und Funktionsbegriff*, entails that we must give up the copy theory of knowledge for a functional theory of

---

24 See: Bjarup, 1978, p. 136, for a full enumeration of these heterogeneous factors of Axel Hägerström.

25 See: Ernst Cassirer, *Axel Hägerström – eine Studie zur Schwedischen Philosophie der Gegenwart*, Göteborgs Högskolas Årsskrift, Elanders Boktryckeri Aktiebolag, Göteborg, 1939, pp. 95–96.

26 For a recent attempt of applying Kant's critical insights as to (transcendental) form in legal phenomena: cf. Summers, R.S., *On Giving Legal Form Its Due – A Sketch*, Associations, Volume 7, No. 1, Special Issue for The IVR 21st World Congress, 2003, p. 209: "*A phenomenon cannot be reduced, without remainder, to its parts. It is a fallacy to think that a legal phenomenon is a mere aggregation of parts. It is more. Its parts are organized into a whole that is unified.*"

knowledge.[27] As elaborated above,[28] according to the functional theory of knowledge, the objects do not determine the concepts they correspond to, but rather the concepts already contain certain questions directed to reality, and from the particular direction of these questions depends the answers we subsequently receive. This also applies to the concepts of law.[29]

In this regard, the concepts of law offer a new dimension next to the concepts of the natural sciences by bringing the real and possible acts of experience under a category (*sub specie*) of law.[30] The concepts of law direct themselves toward social experiences, for which they try to establish a logical scheme of order. In this scheme, Cassirer recognizes a progression from narrower to wider and finally to universal or ideal representations of unity,[31] *i.e.*, a movement from the mythical to the symbolical. "*Law is indeed, genetically viewed, interwoven with Myth; but it seems never to be wrapped in it entirely.*"[32] We now turn to the genetic account of law that can be given from the point of view of Cassirer's phenomenology.

I. 3. What are the Expressive, the Representative, and the Symbolic Phases in Law?

For Cassirer the Western conception of justice finds its origin in ancient Greek drama that introduces justice (that is always victorious over injustice) as a new theme.[33] Before this new theme in ancient Greek drama became of wider philosophical significance in the works of Plato, though, it first had to undergo

---

27 See: Ernst Cassirer, *Axel Hägerström – eine Studie zur Schwedischen Philosophie der Gegenwart*, Göteborgs Högskolas Årsskrift, Elanders Boktryckeri Aktiebolag, Göteborg, 1939, pp. 97–98.

28 See: Chapter 5.

29 See: Kelsen, H., *Das Verhältnis von Staat und Recht im Lichte der Erkenntniskritik*, Zeitschrift für öffentliches Recht, Volume 2, 1921, pp. 453–510, especially: pp. 464–467; reprinted in: Klecatsky, 1968, pp. 95–148, especially: pp. 105–108. See also: Marck, 1925.

30 See: Ernst Cassirer, *Axel Hägerström – eine Studie zur Schwedischen Philosophie der Gegenwart*, Göteborgs Högskolas Årsskrift, Elanders Boktryckeri Aktiebolag, Göteborg, 1939, pp. 97–98.

31 Ibid., 1939, p. 102.

32 Ibid., 1939, p. 102.

33 See: Chapter 3.

various transformations in ancient, Greek religious life. First when *Diké* established itself as the central guiding principle of Greek religious life, would Greek, philosophical thought take it up as its focus point. In this respect, there seems to be a law that precedes even our mere thoughts, just like the natural order exists independent from our senses and intellect and with its own configurations, fixed rules, and laws. As explicated before, the cosmos for the ancient Greeks is not created *ex nihilo*, but has been there always and unchanging, and cannot be questioned after its becoming. Likewise, law reigns as a cosmic phenomenon, as an eternal and unchanging force that rules over men as well as gods. The eternal character of law is best described by Sophocles: "*Not now and yesterday they have their being. But everlastingly, and none can tell the hour that saw their birth.*"[34] Antigone in her defiance of the decrees of Creon animates the same spirit when she appeals to ancient laws (*agropoi nomoi*) that cannot be overruled by any ruler divine or human. Moreover, it is precisely its arcane nature that renders law holy and makes it an object of veneration. Therefore, we cannot, and, indeed, we may not ask from where it comes or when it came about, because we can know only that it *is*.

Notwithstanding the latter, according to Cassirer, Greek philosophy did not confine itself to a merely heuristic role, but aspired to provide a justification of law, to be constitutive of it, precisely by questioning after the origins of law, *i.e.*, by asking about the true nature of law. It was the aim of ancient Greek philosophy not only to explain and respect the unchanging and eternal character of law, but also to rid it of all mythico-religious fetters and strongholds. It claimed to provide a justification of law, because ancient Greek philosophy, as the first in the history of humankind, sets out to free law from the fetters of myth in order to give law an independent footing and place.

According to Cassirer, the efforts of ancient, Greek philosophy would find their apex in the works of Plato. Plato gives us two answers to the question of the nature of law, *i.e.*, from the perspective of the Sophists and from the perspective of Socrates.

---

[34] Cited by: Ernst Cassirer, *Die Idee des Rechts und ihre Entwicklung in der modernen Philosophie*, Ernst Cassirer Papers, Essays and Lectures, Beinecke Rare Book & Manuscripts Library, Coll. No. GEN 98, Series No. II, Box No. 43, Folder No. 845, p. 15.

With that Plato introduces a dichotomy, according to Cassirer, that has held jurisprudence in its grips throughout the centuries, *i.e.*, the dichotomy between law as a mere technicality or outward cloak, an instrument of power and interests, and evaluated according to the measure of man, on the one hand, and law as an autonomous phenomenon, with independent meaning and claims of validity, and as a symbolic form, on the other.[35]

In this respect, we have already alluded to the development of Roman law in the previous section. If we look further in time, much further, in the modern period, for example, the initial concatenation of law and myth was perhaps expressed as no other by the jurisprudence of Sir Edward Coke (1552–1634), especially in his struggle for the principle that law is distinct from mere sovereign power. Sir Edward Coke referred to rights immemorial, that is to say rights based upon custom that predate any sovereign will. For that purpose he traced the fundamental law back even to the Saxon forests and the mythical Trojan settlers. Because if fundamental law is based on such mythical customs predating any authority of sovereign will, the fundamental law could not be repealed at the command of the sovereign.[36] Subsequently, Coke's successor, Sir Matthew Hale (1609–1676) took a further step by making clear that fundamental law could still prove an independent source of rights, even without referring to customs or rights of immemorial times.

The common law was continually changing and adapting, however, this was a steady change insensible by the subjects or the sovereign. The common law rather stood for the accumulated reason of many minds throughout many ages. Sir Matthew Hale advocated the reasonableness of experience and steady adaptation, and made clear that there was no need for the invocation of the authority of antiquity.[37] The same was already sufficiently represented by and could be perceived in the tenets of the common

---

[35] Cf. Ernst Cassirer, *Die Idee des Rechts und ihre Entwicklung in der modernen Philosophie*, Ernst Cassirer Papers, Essays and Lectures, Beinecke Rare Book & Manuscripts Library, Coll. No. GEN 98, Series No. II, Box No. 43, Folder No. 845, pp. 14–19.

[36] McConnel, 1998a, pp. 186–190. That rights are not secure if they were given by the grace of the sovereign – a Cokeian concern – was pursued to its end by the Founding Fathers, e.g. in the form of republicanism.

[37] Ibid., 1998, p. 188.

law. Even the king had no authority to change the law at his will, because the change came about insensibly, by the course of tradition. Law, Sir Matthew Hale maintained, exhibits a reasonableness of its own, and hence forms a limitation of the power of the sovereign, who, moreover, was commonly uneducated in legal reasoning. While we allude here to the inception of the idea of the rule of law, it is still a long road to what may be called law as a symbolic form, *i.e.*, law at the symbolic level, as signified paradigmatically by human rights.

But law establishes a gradual independence from myth, because at a certain moment of time, law necessarily enters the domain of language. Language, as a general form of intellectual expression or symbolic form, is a *conditio sine qua non* for law if it wishes to distinguish itself from mere habit or custom. In contrast to the (positive) enactments of the state, rights from custom or "accumulated reason" do not need an explicit formulation to have effect. Law takes on another form, reaches a new stage of objectivity and determinateness, when it is confronted by the demand that it should be written down or posited.[38] In this regard, Gnaeus Flavius' efforts are not in vain when he manages to retrieve the Law of the Twelve Tables. He makes them available to the general public, and readily accessible to all who wish to govern their lives according to their precepts. To a significant extent positive law ends indeterminacies that still prevail in the mythical sphere, and gives the individual a point of orientation. The representative form of law (and of government for that matter) reaches its apex when the claim establishes itself that only law that has been posited (by a democratically elected sovereign) deserves to be recognized as law.

In this respect, when law necessarily has to cloak itself in linguistic forms, the subordination of law to language supplants the dominion of myth. Moreover, when law enters the dominion of language and clothes itself in the forms of language, it has also achieved a new way or stage of objectification, because it receives

---

[38] For an exquisite explication of the significance of a written document for law and constitutionalism, see: Edmond Cahn, *Supreme Court and Supreme Law: An American Contribution*, in: Cahn, 1967, pp. 66–86.

a certain intellectual mark.[39] The demand of a written form of law not merely entails a form of revelation, as a result of which law may be presumed to be within the reach of every individual, but also involves the sharpening of the legal and auctorial senses. When the legislator produces a law he will attempt to give as precise and accurate a formulation as possible within his purview of the legal. This objectification is possible, first when we no longer perceive the essence of language in the "magical word," but in the *sentence*, *i.e.*, the provision of law.[40] The provisions of law display a degree of finality that renders a certain end to the plurality, variety and conflicts of individual interests. Therewith, it lays the foundation for something unique, characteristic only to human life.

In the provisions of statutes, judicial opinions, and treaties that confer specific legal rights to and prescribe concrete legal rules for the subjects of law we reach a new outlook and level of objectification. By bringing a certain social experience under a category of law we give shape to our future world of actions. Law, for Cassirer, just like language, possesses a typical function of *objectification*; it elevates man to a level of objective notion missing in the animal that lives in its immediate sense impressions.[41] The linguistic concepts of the field of actions, the concepts of law, attain a new meaning and task, because not only do they have the task of representing a given course of events, but also in a certain sense they have to grasp into another dimension of time, *i.e.*, the future. Accordingly, as speech directed toward the future becomes a "promise,"[42] and insofar as the legislator has a right to legislate for the people, the provisions of law become a powerful tool to order and manipulate society, albeit within the confines of its original right to legislate.

---

39 See: Ernst Cassirer, *Axel Hägerström – eine Studie zur Schwedischen Philosophie der Gegenwart*, Göteborgs Högskolas Årsskrift, Elanders Boktryckeri Aktiebolag, Göteborg, 1939, pp. 102–103.

40 Ibid., 1939, p. 103.

41 Ibid., 1939, pp. 105–106. Cf. Schwemmer, O., *Ernst Cassirer, Ein Philosoph der europäischen Moderne*, Akademie Verlag, Berlin, 1997, p. 154, 95n, makes clear that: "(...) Cassirer spielt hier auf Nietzsches Schrift *Zur Genealogie der Moral* an". This is also made clear by Cassirer's reference to Nietzsche in: Ernst Cassirer, *Vom Wesen und Werden des Naturrechts*, Zeitschrift fur Rechtsphilosophie in Lehre und Praxis, Volume 6, 1932, p. 22.

42 See: Chapter 8.

We can imagine a future course of action, among others by the limits we pose upon our actions through rules of law. In this respect, the rules of law are not merely constraining our future actions, but at the same time they are also *enabling* them. The rules of a base ball game not only constrain the actions of prospective players, they also make the game possible.[43] Accordingly, social life as we know it under the rule of law would dissolve into a less predictable conglomerate of actors if each actor was to postulate his own rule of law. By prescribing and proscribing certain courses of actions, not only do we avoid certain clashes of opposite expectations in respect of scarce goods, but by allocating them beforehand to their respective beneficiaries, by laying down rules for how we conduct ourselves vis-à-vis others, and by setting up exclusive arena to settle possible conflicts, we also relieve the social fabric of immense latent tension.[44] Social life becomes possible through the rule of law on a new level of determinateness and objectivity.

Moreover, through law we have a distinct point of view from which to judge our actions. Every action we undertake can be examined through the lens of the law. In this regard, whether we are conscious of it, whether we want it or not, we are all consumers of law or justice, in the positive sense – as when we construe and sign a contract – or in the negative – when we fall beyond the boundary of what is called legal or just.[45] In this respect, every object already carries with it a certain legal meaning, or symbolic pregnance as Cassirer would put it. The proverbial classroom chair that we grasp philosophically now can be the object of legal inquiry, just as everything else in the world. Is it legal to have the chair in the front of the emergency exit, who is the legal beneficiary of it, who has the intellectual property in respect of its design; are all questions we may ask and that immediately present themselves to us whenever we adopt a legal perspective. Our actions therefore are always accompanied by

---

[43] Cf. McConnell, M.W., *Textualism and Democratic Legitimacy: Textualism and the Dead Hand of the Past*, George Washington Law Review, Volume 66, 1998b, pp. 1127 ff. The example comes from Stephen Holmes.

[44] Cf. Ackerman, 1980.

[45] See: Cahn, E.N., *Law in the Consumer Perspective*, University of Pennsylvania Law Review, 112 (1963), in: Cahn, 1967, pp. 15–31; and, ibid., *The Consumers of Injustice* (1959), in: ibid., 1967, pp. 5–14.

legal significance or meaning, whether we relate to other humans or scarce objects. In this respect, whenever we engage in foundational legal interpretation or analysis we presume a basis phenomenon which we may call the basis phenomenon of Law, *i.e.*, the basic assumption that there is law, and without which assumption we could not start such legal analysis or even deny that there is such thing as law. As a result of the basis phenomenon of Law we have such thing as symbolic pregnance of law, hence legal meaning in whatsoever sense.

In addition, through law we have a particular understanding of ourselves.[46] We understand ourselves as a "we" under the rule of law. The "other" we regard as the other because he or she falls beyond the recognition or reach of the legal as we understand it.[47] These others may be members of another culture that we designate as evil, as unwilling or unable to underwrite the values we give expression to through the law. But they may also be nearby in geographical terms, as when we, to speak in Hegelian terms, reintegrate the villain or criminal within the legal order through our justice system, because through his or her conduct he or she has violated the law and thus put or regarded his or herself beyond the reach of the law. Law, in this regard, is a means through which we have a common world of meanings. These meanings are produced each time we materialize or bring to fruition the ideals for which law stands.

That is achieved every time a certain course of action fulfills or "falls under" a provision of law, and triggers so to speak a legal rule and therewith (insofar as necessary, directly or indirectly) the entire legal system. However, the legal system does not directly respond to a social constellation, but first grasps that social reality in its own terms, be it that of legal causality, or be it that of legal personality. Legal meaning is sustained by the mutual reference of legal concepts that reciprocally trigger each other, and, insofar as is necessary, the entire legal system. Legal acts that are accordingly created by the legal system are pure or symbolic acts, because for their "existence" they do not depend upon any empirical reality, but are entirely conditioned by the legal system. Legal concepts form a functional unity, because we

---

46 See: Kahn, 1997.

47 Cf. Fitzpatrick, 1992; and Fitzpatrick, 2001.

can no longer hold that legal concepts constitute or refer to certain substances. We "experience" them only when they stand in a relationship to other concepts and to the totality of law as a general system of legal concepts.[48] A legal act is said to exist only when supported by the legal system, or a sufficient nexus of concepts thereof.

It may be noted, that the different stages in the development of law correspond to different forms of reasoning in law. Syllogistic reasoning within law can be considered the first attempt to explain the fruition of legal concepts and rules in practical reality. However, syllogistic reasoning presumes a substantial unity between the triggering conditions set forth in a legal rule and the triggering events that satisfy the conditions. Syllogism does not merely require that the triggering events resemble the conditions of the rule, but that they are identical to those set forth in the conditions. In syllogistic reasoning, legal reality is set on a par with empirical reality. In analogical legal reasoning the demand that the triggering events are empirically identical to those set forth in the conditions of the rule is disavowed, and in lieu of a substantial unity between the conditions set forth in the legal rule and the actual triggering events, henceforth is placed the demand of resemblance or what may be called a sufficient degree of representation.[49] It is the contribution of legal reasoning by analogy that it acknowledges and makes clear, that the satisfaction of the triggering conditions set forth in the legal rule by the (triggering) events can only be an approximation, and not a complete substantiation.

Consistently pursued this insight leads to the employment of functional or relational reasoning within law.[50] The relational

---

48 Cf. Marck, 1925.

49 For analogy in legal reasoning, see: Weinreb, L.L., *Legal Reason: The Use of Analogy in Legal Argument*, Cambridge University Press, Cambridge, MA, 2005; cf. Brewer, S., *Exemplary Reasoning: Semantics, Pragmatics, and the Rational Force of Legal Argument by Analogy*, Harvard Law Review, Volume 109, No. 5, 1996, pp. 923–1028; and idem, *Scientific Expert Testimony and Intellectual Due Process*, Yale Law Review, Volume 107, No. 5, 1998, pp. 1535–1682; and Sunstein, C., *On Analogical Reasoning*, Harvard Law Review, Volume 106, 1999, pp. 741–791.

50 Cf. Ernst Cassirer, *Zur Logik der Symbolbegriffs*, Theoria, A Swedish Journal of Philosophy and Psychology, Volume 4, 1938, pp. 145–175, who distinguishes between "identity logic" and "relational logic."

function is already presupposed in analogical reasoning that demands a sufficient degree of similarity, because similarity, as Cassirer explains, depends upon an "*identity of reference, of point of view, under which the comparison takes place*." This identity of reference, or point of view, is described by Cassirer as a "*general law or rule*."[51] Moreover, in functional reasoning it becomes a basic principle that the mere satisfaction of a triggering condition by an event does not exhaust the legal rule, because its triggering conditions can never be fully satisfied. This is not to exclude the possibilities of syllogism and analogy within law, but to make clear that functionality is most characteristic for legal rules, as is paradigmatically expressed by the mathematical function or symbol of *f(x)*.

A triggering event of a legal rule is not merely subsumed, nor do we merely assume by analogy that a certain event sufficiently resembles the conditions mentioned in a legal rule, but we anticipate that event from the perspective of the legal rule and judge whether, and to what extent, the triggering event is covered by the rule, so as to put the event in a sequence of events that are directed into the direction expressed by the rule. Accordingly, conscious of the fact that the triggering conditions of a legal rule can never be completely satisfied, the legislator always legislates from a general perspective. The generality of a legal rule not only stems from the desire to defer the determination of whether the triggering conditions have been satisfied to the judicial branch, but, as Portalis already noted, also from the fact that it cannot possibly foresee every possible configuration it intends to cover by the rule. Yet by positing a legal provision as a general, functional rule the legislator is in the position to anticipate most, if not all, of them, because those events will already bear the mark of that rule insofar as it provides a question with which we already interpret those events, whether they be covered by the rule or whether they are deemed to be beyond its orbit. We now turn again to the characterization of law as a symbolic system.

---

[51] Referred to by: Krois, 1981, p. 100.

Although law as a universal referential system of (key) concepts has achieved the symbolic sphere,[52] law cannot maintain itself in the symbolic sphere without an ideal element that progressively spurs it to higher forms of generality or universality, and hence objectivity. Law is always in danger of degenerating into a mere formalistic regime that requires an almost ritualistic compliance of its provisions according to strict rules, *i.e.*, syllogistically, without which it will not be moved into action, and that also does not stand open to alternative solutions. Indeed, Cassirer writes, the further we go into the history of law, the more we see of this formalism that "works" only by strictly prescribed (verbal) actions, that albeit stands independent of social reality, but cannot satisfactorily address it with sufficient flexibility. "*Just as in the mythical and religious use of speech, as in the prayer and in the invocation of gods we find the rule in both that it works only when it is executed in strictly prescribed forms – as every omission or conversion of a word disturbs the power of the invocation, the same applies originally also for every legal act. It achieves its "binding" force first through the fact that it employs certain prescribed verbal phrases, and that it accompanies these with corresponding, strictly formulaic acts.*"[53] First when we recognize the ideal of human rights (as the universal demand of justice, hence the struggle against injustice) as a motivating factor for a legal system to progressively search for greater universality of its concepts, do we have a mechanism for law to maintain itself at the symbolic level. With higher degrees of universality law also achieves greater objectivity, because it becomes more encompassing in its range of applicability, and hence enlarges its potential formative effect in the sphere of meaning.[54]

In this respect, law need not continuously make itself felt present physically, because it endures in the sphere of meaning;

---

52 Cf. Kahn, P.W., *Comparative constitutionalism in a new key*, Michigan Law Review, Volume 101, Summer 2003, pp. 2677–2705; here: p. 2677.

53 See: Ernst Cassirer, *Axel Hägerström – eine Studie zur Schwedischen Philosophie der Gegenwart*, Göteborgs Högskolas Årsskrift, Elanders Boktryckeri Aktiebolag, Göteborg, 1939, p. 89.

54 See: Ernst Cassirer, *Was ist "Subjektivismus"?* (Vortrag gehalten im Philosophischen Verein in Stockholm am 23 Februar 1939), Theoria, A Swedish Journal of Philosophy and Psychology, Volume 5, Göteborg, 1939, pp. 111–140.

once established, law remains present by appealing through its meaning to the minds or symbolic life-worlds of people. To illustrate, criminalization by law too is an effort to bring under common categories certain forms of conduct deemed foreign or contrary to the values of a certain culture. Through law we seek to understand the other, try to come to terms with him, be it with compromises, be it imperialistically, or be it alternatively. We invite the other, sometimes under threat of punishment, to become part of this order of meaning we designate as law, by expecting from "newcomers" or outsiders who intend to interact with us (or vice versa) to understand that there is such thing as law and what it stands for or means. The meaning of law has become part of our lives and of the pattern of expectations in the daily interactions of people. We feel justified to be outraged or offended when our rights are transgressed, just as the religious man is offended when his holy places are treated with undue respect. The aura of sanctity surrounding law, as we understand it now, though, is not something religious. Rather religion too, as is the case with law, should be understood as constituted by the realm of meaning.[55]

Law viewed from the point of view of the philosophy of symbolic forms is law viewed from the meaning perspective. Rather than answering the question of what law is, *i.e.*, substantively, it tries to make clear how the law operates by establishing its presence in the sphere of meaning. This meaning ultimately is to be perceived by law's subjects. Law's meaning cannot be established by the sheer act of positing, for example by the proclamation or codification of a legislator. Nor can law have meaning without finding a concrete expression in what is regarded as "positive," be it in judicial opinions or legislative actions. Law as something ideal ultimately has to find its expression in some concrete positive act of the state (as the representative of the people) if it is to be perceived as law, *i.e.*, to have meaning as law. Conversely, that which rules, what ought to bind us as law, has to be related in some sense to law in an ideal sense. Judicial activity or review is characterized by expounding the meaning of law, and entails a prospective, retrospective, and

---

[55] I cannot elaborate here on the symbolic form of religion. For an elaboration of religion as a symbolic form, see: Richter, 2004; and Deuser, 2002.

an overall reflection on the meaning of law in every single case. Moreover, at a general level, the relationship between the ideal or universal and the positive or concrete may differ per legal culture, but what characterizes a legal culture is its claim on the actions of its subjects as being legitimate or persuasive, *i.e.*, as being the expression of the values to which its subjects can and ought to have assented to.[56] A legal culture that has given such an assent to human rights, commonly regarded as the highest ideal achievement of human civilization yet, we regard as embodying the rule of law.

We now turn to Cassirer's renewed foundation for human rights theory through the concept of *animal symbolicum*. Through the introduction of a concept that is more encompassing than previous definitions of human nature, and indeed purports to give a solution to the conflicting of the variety of ways human nature is allotted a certain and definite substantial feature; Cassirer underscores the universality of human rights with new force and sophistication. At the same time, though, as the following asserts, Cassirer's foundation of human rights escapes the criticisms that are most recently voiced in relation to the universality of human rights. The symbolic nature of man becomes both the fundamental problem of and the solution to the human predicament. Law's relevance for social life hinges upon this friction, by its constant effort to bring about more determinacy in human life.

I. 4. What is Cassirer's Philosophical Justification of Human Rights?

The idea of human rights can be traced back to the theory of natural rights as articulated by consecutive generations of natural lawyers. It has received its latest conceptual formulation, though, primarily after the Second World War, *i.e.*, after the Holocaust.[57] While, before the war, natural law was declared dead (as it had been declared before in earlier centuries, for example in the nineteenth century) and legal positivism reigned with full force, after the monstrosities of the war, natural law rose from its ashes

---

56 For the phenomenon of sacrifice as an essential feature of the political, see: Kahn, P.W., *The Question of Sovereignty*, Stanford Journal of International Law, Volume 40, Summer 2004, pp. 259–282; see also: Kahn, 2005.

57 See: Glendon, 2001.

and gave birth, so to speak, to the modern tradition of human rights, as something humans have by nature, by the sole fact that they are human. In the first years or decades after the war there seemed to be no direct need for any thoroughgoing philosophical justification of human rights, such as expressed by the Universal Declaration of Human Rights, proclaimed by the United Nations in 1948 with the experiences of the war still fresh in mind. Gradually though, with the sixties and seventies of the twentieth century, two sorts of criticisms were introduced with respect to the modern tradition of human rights.[58] While the one has focused on the subject of human rights, in the form of an internal critique of Western liberal and capitalistic culture, the other has focused on the external truth value or universal pretensions of the human rights tradition, in the form of cultural relativism. Both criticisms center on the claim to universality of the human rights tradition.

The following asserts that in the first part of the twentieth century Cassirer anticipated the criticism that rose against the human rights tradition, by giving a philosophical–anthropological justification of human rights. For this, he made clear, first, that law is a symbolic form and, second, that man is a symbolic being, an *animal symbolicum*. With respect to the former, Cassirer portrayed himself as an advocate of the natural law tradition, *i.e.*, as appreciative of the results it achieved with respect to the *a priori* nature of law. Cassirer's position in jurisprudence, although he is aware of the indebtedness of contemporary jurisprudence to that tradition, is not merely a restatement of the natural law tradition. For Cassirer natural law entails a fundamental and a constitutive moment for the concept of law, because it has managed to overcome two obstacles for jurisprudence. On the one hand, natural lawyers detached law from theological dogmatism – as initiated by Grotius, the Cambridge Platonists, and carried

---

58 See: Ansah, T., *Surprised by Sin: Human Rights and Universality*, Syracuse Journal of International Law and Commerce, Summer 2003, Volume 30, Issue 2, pp. 309–337. Cf. Milovanovic, D., *The Postmodernist Turn: Lacan, Psychoanalytic Semiotics, and the Construction of Subjectivity in Law*, Emory International Law Review, Volume 8, 1994, pp. 67–98. See also: Sen, A., *Elements of a Theory of Human Rights*, Philosophy and Public Affairs, Volume 32, No. 4, 2004, pp. 315–356.

further by others, such as Pufendorf[59] – on the other hand, they provided for the determination and marking out of the pure realm of law against the realm of state power or state absolutism – as embodied by Hobbes' Leviathan.[60] For Cassirer *law is a phenomenon distinct from religion and state power, i.e.*, as a particular symbolic form it exists, albeit interdependently, independent from other forms of objectification or having a world.

Primarily, law is not a means of legitimizing a certain entity, but functions as a mode by which humans give objective meaning or order to an otherwise less objective or orderly world. This ordering of the world through law, in its turn, reflects the meaning of law already present in the minds of the people. As a symbolic form, law expresses the "classifying instinct" of man; "*the desire of human nature to come to terms with reality, to live in an ordered universe, and to overcome the chaotic state in which things and thoughts have not yet assumed a definitive shape and structure.*"[61] Humans do this shaping and structuring as symbolic beings, by giving and expressing meaning, which is necessarily a normative matter, because it affects the way we relate to one another. Consequently, by considering the law or constitution in the minds of the people, the legislator or the magistrate renders law persuasive, and from its persuasiveness law finds its binding force.

In this sense, the concept of *animal symbolicum* becomes synonymous with the whole of humanity, and gives a philosophical anthropological justification of human rights. That is to say, the concept of the *animal symbolicum* determines the limits of the exercise of political power by considering the humanity of its actions, to which every individual has a right, by virtue of being human. The humanity that is involved here is the symbolic

---

59 See respectively: Grotius' famous statement in Prologomena 11 of his *De jure belli ac pacis libri tres* (1625) and for Pufendorf's separation of natural law and moral theology, see: Luig, K., *Samuel von Pufendorf, Über die Pflicht des Menschen und des Bürgers nach dem Gesetz der Natur*, Insel Verlag am Main und Leipzig, 1994.

60 Ernst Cassirer, *Vom Wesen und Werden des Naturrechts*, in: *Zeitschrift fur Rechtsphilosophie in Lehre und Praxis*, Volume 6, 1932, pp. 6–18; cf. Coskun, D., *De cultuur van mensenrechten*, Wolf Legal Publishers, Nijmegen, 2006.

61 See: Ernst Cassirer, *The Myth of the state*, Yale University Press, New Haven, 1946, pp. 15–17.

nature of the human being. The symbolic nature of the human being poses a limit upon state power, by its demand that state action must be accompanied by a sufficient level of persuasiveness. In the necessary validity of a norm of law, the individual takes itself not as an empirical thing, but as a free, self-determining, reasonable being,[62] but that is not satisfactory for the symbolic being. The symbolic nature of the human being demands that the particular application of a legal rule or the adoption of a legal rule takes into consideration that the human being is a meaningful being capable of independent and individual moral judgment and that such action is accompanied by persuasive arguments. A governmental action may be reasonable, yet it may fail to satisfy standards of persuasiveness,[63] which involves a reference to shared conceptions of justice or of right and wrong.[64]

The universality of human rights cannot be based upon any substantial definition of human nature, but can only refer to a functional common denominator. The functional definition of human nature brings a solution to the problem of the varying and contrary views on human nature depending on cultural or material contexts. Whether he or she is an aboriginal, a cosmopolitan, a villager, or an urban dweller, every human being lives by his or her symbols. In a negative sense, *i.e.*, from the point of view of negative liberty, we respect the symbols of one another because of the fact that we share the common knowledge that our symbols are precious or dear to us, and that, when the symbols have assumed a certain degree of relevance or meaning for us, we are prepared to fight for our symbols. To illustrate, most constitutions or national codes protect the integrity of the national flag, not to mention what we are prepared to do for our flag in the military context. In human lives, though, symbols assume a positive role as well. Symbols can be used to function as the

---

62 See: Ernst Cassirer, *Freiheit und Form. Studien zur deutschen Geistesgeschichte*, Gesammelte Werke Band 7, Felix Meiner Verlag, Hamburg, 1998 (1916); cited by: Moynahan, 2003, p. 63.

63 The level of scrutiny in the economic, transactional sphere is usually subject to a less stringent degree of scrutiny vis-à-vis the fundamental human and civil rights of the individual.

64 See: Edmond Cahn, *The Moral Decision: Right and Wrong in the Light of American Law*, Indiana University Press, Bloomington, IN, 1955.

center- or focus-point of our actions. Everything, hence everyone, can become a symbol, or function as a symbol.[65] The cruel and unjust treatment of a fellow citizen can simultaneously trigger the affection and reason of the entire populace. It is not necessary that one knows that other person personally or even distantly for such a person to become a symbol, what matters is that one can imagine that one could have been in his or her place; that in principle one human person *represents* humanity in its totality. It is from that principle that we derive the moral spirit to demand that every person should be treated as a meaningful being, and is equally worthy to pursue and experience happiness in life.

Of course, the possibility of happiness, the process of attaining to it, for the animal symbolicum, is more significant than the act of enjoyment itself. The impossibility of attaining to happiness, by contrast, seems much more unbearable than the sole state of misery. For the animal symbolicum there always seems to be a double layer to his experience of the world. This additional layer may be called the dimension of anticipation and prospection. Human experience is intensified (or when applicable chilled) by the anticipation of what is to come and the accumulation of what has been projected into the future. The web of symbolic meanings of the human animal seems doubly stronger than the non-human animals surround themselves with in terms of stimuli from the environment. Indeed, so important has the influence of symbols become for the human animal that he cannot fully experience the deep seated emotions within him without the proper symbols that accompany them. We cannot fully mourn our dead without a code of black garments, nor can we fully exclaim support for our nations without the invocation of our ancient heroes.

And, once we engage in these activities (of meaningful participation), it becomes clear to us that they are in fact inexhaustible; their ultimate goal seems unattainable. Whatever we do or say, our acts of meaningful expression seem never quite able to fully and definitely gain a hold on things. Our respect for the deceased can never fully be expressed, nor can we be patriotic enough in defending our nation, because there remain ever more ways of achieving the same and beyond. Disciplined self-restraint

---

65 Cf. Feige, 1999, pp. 141–168.

or moderation is reserved for the select few, but such prudence also seems to be a mere temporal solution. For the problem introduced by symbolism, that we never quite adequately get to the core and the end of matters, that when once the act of interpretation or meaning giving starts, there seems to be no end to it, because the end (or any prior contention) is always in dispute and its meaning contested; cannot be solved by mere self-restraint. Life would become a mere "volcano," waiting to erupt, and unknown in which direction it will explode, when its point of reference has receded. Ironically, the solution to symbolism is more symbolism.[66]

Law plays an important and constitutive role for the construction of social, hence individual reality. It helps to sustain, but at the same time law itself is dependent upon the individual "ego." Without an individual subject we cannot have a discourse wherein rights (or human rights) would make sense, *i.e.*, it has become a basis phenomenon for law. Therefore, when in the course of its development law identifies such thing as the "individual," it surrounds the individual with guarantees and conditions so as to cherish individuality. Law's "thriving," so to speak, depends upon the active participation of the individual into society, and its interactions with others. The individual can do so only when it is aware of its own individuality, and discovers its capacity of meaningful participation. Through law the individual attests to and sustains its individuality, because it is a channel or modus through which it relates to others, and renders the world comprehensible and (more) determinate for itself. Conversely, if it were not for the indeterminacies introduced by the symbolic nature of the human animal, *i.e.*, because of meaningful disagreement and the freedom involved with its symbolic nature, law would not have to progressively strive to bring an end to them, nor would the individual rise to an objective notion of self-awareness each time it makes its life more determinate through law.

---

66 I am indebted to Justice Breyer's statement, "*that the remedy for speech you don't like, is not less speech, it is more speech*". See: Supreme Court of the United States, Oral Argument in *Rumsfeld v. Forum for Academic and Institutional Rights*, No. 04-1152, http://www.supremecourtus.gov/oral_arguments/argument_transcripts/04-1152.pdf (last visited: September 18, 2006), p. 43.

II. CONCLUSION

Law has become a symbolic system that operates through functional concepts and rules, and foremost employs functional or relational reasoning. Law in the concrete is understandable only in the light of law as an ideal. However, there is no ultimate principle or rule through which we can derive the validity of the entire legal system. First, law is valid, is ruling, insofar as we can understand it, insofar as we can attach meaning to it as something to which one ought to adapt one's actions, *i.e.*, insofar as we find it persuasive that it is law.[67] The acts of representative government deserve a good measure of deference because in the legislative process the provisions of law will be evaluated as to its level of persuasiveness with the people. Furthermore, through judicial review, law in the concrete, for example as a statute, a judicial opinion, or an implemented treaty, is valid insofar as the judge understands it as the expression of law as an ideal. If not, within her array of responsibility, the judge will rule according to what she finds as having meaning in the sense of being the expression of what is considered to be law. Judicial review, in the light of law as an ideal, *i.e.*, in expounding the meaning of the constitution, and hence for example that of a statute, is not something subjective, rather it is the result of a prospective, retrospective, and overall reflection on the meaning of law.

Law as a symbolic system sustains itself by the mutual recognition of and reference between its (key) concepts. Law, therefore, has to be understood as a universal referential system. Once having established its autonomy from a genetic point of view, law escapes objections of being merely tautological in nature, hence of the impossibility of the objective grounding of it, by its interrelatedness to other cultural forms and by its relation vis-à-vis culture taken as a whole. In this respect, law sustains its own objective grounding through its progressive contribution to culture, *i.e.*, through its particular mode of objectification in the sphere of actions.

Furthermore, law's claims do not confine themselves within geographically demarcated boundaries, as recognized by law as a universal referential system. Law operates within and designates

67 I cannot elaborate here on the phenomenon of civil disobedience.

cultural boundaries. As Rawls, for example, illustrates in his the "Law of Peoples," the same normative framework that we set up for our world of actions, *i.e.*, the human rights tradition, we project into the rest of the world, so that, what we consider to be within our cultural horizon are those societies that adhere to some minimal fundamental norms of humanity.

Law starts at the mythological level by invoking rights from time immemorial (for example by Antigone, Sir Edward Coke, and so forth), but gradually overcomes the mythical stage by taking into consideration the force of language in its representative function. When law cloaks itself in sentences so as to produce provisions of law, those provisions, be they in legislative enactments, judicial opinions, or contracts, henceforth purport to represent law. When law sustains itself through its conceptual rigor it reaches the symbolic level, but it is also in danger of degenerating into mere strict legalism or formalism, when it places such value and significance to the sensory materialization of law so as to become a mere ritualistic matter. Statutes and judicial opinions merely represent or state the law as accurately as possible (hence deserve a good measure of interpretive deference), but they do not constitute law in all force and validity. Therefore, sheer legal formalism does not completely overcome the mythic stage in law, because it purports to present law, not to represent, or let alone functionalize it. Only in the symbolic phase law seems to have been cleansed of all mythic features.

Human rights signify law as a symbolic form paradigmatically. Indeed in the symbolic sphere, human rights claim validity, *i.e.*, have meaning as law, without any necessary connection to some concrete act of positing in a statute, opinion, or contract. In the form of human rights, the claims of law prevail even without being laid down in specific positive provisions. Human rights are different from natural rights or rights from time immemorial (as Coke has called them). Human rights are directed to the future, do not appeal to some ancient authority to voice their claim, and indeed have a radical, prophetic, or revolutionary import. Human rights progressively inform legal systems, because they function as an ideal to which every legal system as a rule of law strives. As normative standards of humanity within legal systems they spur the development of law toward greater degrees of universality and objectivity. Their significance consists in the fact that they make clear to us that our representation of law in positive law and concepts can only be an approximation of law, never its fulfillment. They keep the legal system focused on the fact that it ultimately has to deal with individuals, and that every individual carries with it a right to be considered as a morally and intellectually mature person, hence needs to be persuaded of the legitimacy of the actions of the polity. Justice therefore is something concrete and lively, because it sheds its light only within the practical workings of the law. It is our next task to consider the consequences of Law as Symbolic Form for social contract theory as an expressin of human, symbolic dignity.

CHAPTER 8

THE *LINGUISTIC TURN* OF SOCIAL CONTRACT THEORY

I. INTRODUCTION

In this chapter we examine Cassirer's approach to social contract theory. By reconstructing his theory of the social contract we answer the following two questions: First we ask what the social contract is according to Cassirer. Moreover, when we have established that the promise constitutes the core concept of social contract theory, we ask what the conditions for the possibility of a promise are for Cassirer. Accordingly, we first give a concise treatment of the history of social contract theory as conceived by Cassirer. Subsequently, we give an examination of how Cassirer, in the first half of the twentieth century, through his philosophy of symbolic forms gave a linguistic turn to social contract theory, by making reference to the unique symbolizing activity of the human being, paradigmatically in that of language. In line with the philosophy of language of Wilhelm von Humboldt, Cassirer holds that language has a decisively active or positive moment.

Language, when directed into the future takes the form of a promise: a recurring and fundamental element in any legal order, as already perceived by the natural lawyers, most notably Grotius. In this respect it is made clear that for Cassirer the human being is not merely an *animal rationale*, rather an *animal symbolicum*. By this conception of man, non-rational forms of human action are also taken into account, *in casu* by taking into consideration the concatenation of man's cultural life, *casu quo* law, language and morality, with its mythico-religious subsoil. Regard is given, furthermore, to Cassirer's treatment of the moral person, who by making and fulfilling promises engages in a symbolic, hence typically human activity, and thereby participates in its symbolically constituted humanity. Moreover, we explicate in what sense the human symbolic function is constitutive of human dignity, because it represents a sphere in which the participants reflect upon themselves as humans only by their interaction with one another. In effect, this chapter shows that, for Cassirer, the ideal of humanity and the specifically human sense of symbolic meaning are the conditions for the possibility of a promise.

This chapter proceeds as follows. First, in Section I.1, we answer the question of what was the social contract for Cassirer. Then, in Section I.2, we answer the question of what are the conditions for the possibility of a promise, according to Cassirer. Finally, in the conclusion we not only give an assessment of the results of this chapter, but also allude to the subject of the next part: Cassirer's position relative to neo-Kantian jurisprudence, in particular the jurisprudence (and social contract theory) of Hermann Cohen.

I. 1. What is the Social Contract for Cassirer?

That law and its force of validity are derived from the social contract by which law's subjects have bound themselves, *i.e.*, from the original autonomy of law's subjects, is, according to Cassirer, in modern philosophy first systematically taken into consideration by Nicholas von Cusa.[1] For Cusa all worldly powers were in their original constitution bound by the maxim, that the ruler does not have authority save that which arises from the ruler being the representative and administrator of the totality of wills, *i.e.*, the general will. According to Cusa worldly power was not derived from the pontiff but had independent origin, and, only independently conceived, could it perform its characteristic duties. This independent character was externally displayed, according to Cusa, in the establishment of annual meetings of the feudal parliaments, by the maintenance of a seated ruler, who was subject to the authority of the state, and by the reforms to the clerical jurisdiction.[2] It was only in modern

---

1 See: Ernst Cassirer, *Freiheit und Form. Studien zur deutschen Geistesgeschichte*, Gesammelte Werke Band 7, Felix Meiner Verlag, Hamburg, 1998 (1916), pp. 327–328 (488–489); cf. Cassirer, Erich, *Natur- und Völkerrecht im Lichte der Geschichte und der systematischen Philosophie*, C.A. Schwetschke & Sohn, Berlin, 1919, p. 71.

2 Cf. Lübbe, H., *Säkularisierung. Geschichte eines ideenpolitischen Begriffs.* 3. Um ein Nachwort erweiterte Neuausgabe, Verlag Karl Alber Freiburg, München, 2003, who explains that the term secularization denoted the process by which church properties were appropriated by the state.

times that Cusa's concepts of state autonomy and popular sovereignty came to the fore, when the natural law tradition developed into what we now know of as the rule of law. In this regard there has been a progressive liberation of law as a phenomenon distinct from religion and state power. As a result, ultimately humanity or human dignity is at the basis of law and state (cf. Article 1 of the German Constitution). As elaborated below, for Cassirer, this humanity cannot substantially be defined as rational, but only functionally as symbolic.

From the Renaissance onwards, the principle of rationality, as most notably exemplified in the mathematical sciences, became effective also in the other branches of science (natural sciences as well as in the humanities), a process termed by Cassirer as an intellectual process of liberation. Characteristic of this rationalism was "*the belief in the "autonomy of thought," i.e., the view that thought can discover by its own strength, without support from a supernatural revelation and without appeal to sense perception, a system of "eternal truths," a system presented to thought within its own realm and comprehended by thought as necessary.* (...) *The same is true also of practical consciousness.* (...) *there are ethical truths which can be comprehended with certainty as unconditional obligations or imperatives of action.*"[3] So we see Galileo advocating his theory of geometrical physics even against strong opposition of church and state, and Grotius declaring that the justification of law is independent of church and state.

For Cassirer, Grotius is not merely the founding natural lawyer, but also a great humanist. Grotius maintained that just as the human mind is, in and of itself, capable of creating quantities and numbers, the same creative nature is operative in the terrain of law. By abstracting from the given of the here and now, as the geometrician does, a whole system of law can be constructed out of the norms created by man himself. Law could no longer be founded on God's abundance of power as Calvin, who simultaneously elevated the Deity above all rules and norms, assumed. Grotius questioned the Calvinist dogma of predestination by defending the humanist idea of freedom

---

[3] Ernst Cassirer, *Encyclopaedia Britannica*, 14th edition, Volume 18: *Plants to Tripoli*, London/New York, 1929 (*Rationalism*), pp. 991–993; here: p. 991.

against the deterministic account of the will; that a will was not constitutive of law but pure reason. As a result, he also opposed, what Hobbes was later to call, the "mortal Deity" or Leviathan.[4] For Grotius law's validity was ultimately derived from natural law, from a principally supra- and ante-state law.[5]

Grotius, in contrast to the theories of Machiavelli and Bodin, took as the highest axiom that there is a law that antedates all human and divine sovereignty, which is, furthermore, independently valid from them. The validity of the "*lex* naturalis," according to Grotius, is constituted in that the legislator, when positing his single command, considers a norm that is simply of general applicability, that is paradigmatic and binding for his own as well as for any other individual will. As Cassirer writes: "*Undoubtedly* (...) *law poses a command, that is promulgated to the individual wills. But from this command does not originate the idea of law and justice, it rather lies behind this idea; it sets out its actual implementation, but this implementation must not be confused with the justification of the idea of law as such.*" Whereas sovereign will, be it human or divine, can be, in Fichte's words, "*ordo ordinatus*" or "ordered order," it cannot be "*ordo ordinans*" "ordering order."[6]

For Grotius the essence of the state was founded upon the concept of the social contract and therefore by nature the validity of this latter concept was inviolable. Moreover, the state was competent to create and to found rights, *i.e.*, to legislate insofar as it carried with it, and incorporated, an original right to legislate. With that Gorius was not introducing a new theory, nor did subsequent natural lawyers differ fundamentally from this basic insight. Whether natural law was derived from Divine

---

4 Cassirer conceives a similar "battle" or process in England by the "School of Cambridge"; cf. Ernst Cassirer, *Die Philosophie der Aufklärung*, J.C.B. Mohr Verlag (Paul Siebeck), Tübingen, 1932, esp. pp. 320 ff.; see also: idem, *The Platonic Renaissance in England* (Die platonische Renaissance in England und die Schule von Cambridge, Teubner, Leipzig and Berlin, 1932), tr. J.P. Pettegrove, University of Texas Press, Austin, 1953.

5 See: Ernst Cassirer, *Vom Wesen und Werden des Naturrechts*, Zeitschrift für Rechtsphilosophie in Lehre und Praxis, Volume 6, No. 1, 1932, p. 9.

6 See: Ernst Cassirer, *Die Philosophie der Aufklärung*, J.C.B. Mohr Verlag (Paul Siebeck), Tübingen, 1932, pp. 321–322; or ibid., *The Philosophy of the Enlightenment*, tr. F.C.A. Koelln and J.P. Pettigrove, Princeton University Press, NJ, 1951 (1932), p. 240.

will or human reason (participating in Divine), all natural lawyers agreed on the existence of a natural law (*lex naturalis*) that preceded the state and from which the state directly or indirectly receives its right to legislate. This original right for Grotius was derived from the social contract, by which the individuals tied and committed themselves reciprocally. This commitment or obligation was not first created by the state; it was rather the essential basis of it, its fundamental carrying principle. All validity of the "*lex civilis*" (law promulgated by the secular legislator), according to Grotius, would be crippled when this fundamental element was taken away from it, *i.e.*, when the premise that a once given promise has the force to oblige continuously no longer applies. "*This premise cannot itself be derived from any already available and given positive provisions, because rather it is the condition for its possibility, the condition sine qua non of every provision as such.*"[7] The state cannot, therefore, be thought of as the conglomeration of means of power and force. It is rather an ideal entity, whose condition is to be found in its sense and ideal purpose. And precisely this sense is implied in the contract as the product of free promising wills, as opposed to a necessitated, imposed, or forced obligation. As Cassirer remarks, the concept of man Grotius endorsed was, just as Nietzsche put it, that man is an animal that can promise.[8]

For Grotius society comes into existence by the motive or inclination of the human being to socialize. However, this inclination was for him not enough to explain a specifically human society, because the inclination toward socialization as such is common also in animal life. Unique for the human is that it gives its life a firm and enduring form by making him or herself objectively aware of life and, in this respect, becomes self-conscious in the idea of law as a binding and obligating norm. Accordingly, it was this form, Cassirer comments, not its usefulness for the sheer physical existence and the physical survival of human society that gave law its specific worth for Grotius. The capacity to elevate oneself to the pure idea of law and legal obligation, and the capacity to fulfill a promise once

---

7 See: Ernst Cassirer, *Vom Wesen und Werden des Naturrechts*, Zeitschrift für Rechtsphilosophie in Lehre und Praxis, Volume 6, No. 1, 1932, p. 9.

8 Of course, as Cassirer underlines, Nietzsche is otherwise at a great distance from the natural law tradition and, in fact, plainly rejects it.

given whatever its costs, was thereby the true origin and fundament of every specifically human society. For Grotius, as a result, law was not a coincidental human creation resulting from the sphere of the natural inclinations of human society; rather it was fundamental for the human being, a necessary precondition of the "*humanitas ipsa*."[9]

Subsequently, the problem of unity and plurality, the relationship between the totality of wills and the individual will was taken up by Leibniz, who held that we must go back analytically from the given and accomplished state to the individual will, wherein the former finds its actual constitutive element. This most fundamental justification of the state did not lie in providing for the physical protection or material promotion of the individual wills, but foremost in the personification and representation in all its historical existence of the union of the individual wills in one "intellectual republic" [*Geisterrepublik*]. In his struggle against slavery Leibniz was the first to advocate the theory of inalienable individual human rights. It is of paramount importance therefore for Leibniz that none of its members is excluded from the possibility to progressively elevate itself to independence of insight and determination of will, and that for that purpose education constitutes a basic right and a basic duty in any form of polity. No social contract or any other form of government can forego this claim of the individual, according to Leibniz, because the property that every reasoned sole [*vernünftige Seele*] owns over itself cannot be abandoned or transferred to another. It is in this sphere of natural and inalienable freedom, Cassirer agrees, that every absolute power finds its limit.[10]

In this respect, Cassirer writes, "*If a man could give up his personality he would cease being a moral being. He would become a lifeless thing – and how could such a thing obligate itself – how could it make a promise or enter into a social contract?* (...) *The contract of rulership which is the legal basis of*

---

[9] See: Ernst Cassirer, *Vom Wesen und Werden des Naturrechts*, Zeitschrift für Rechtsphilosophie in Lehre und Praxis, Volume 6, No. 1, 1932, pp. 22–23.

[10] See: Ernst Cassirer, *Freiheit und Form. Studien zur deutschen Geistesgeschichte*, Gesammelte Werke Band 7, Felix Meiner Verlag, Hamburg, 1998 (1916), p. 330 (pp. 491–492).

all civil power has, therefore, its inherent limits. There is no pactum subjectionis, no act of submission by which man can give up the state of a free agent and enslave himself. For by such an act of renunciation he would give up that very characteristic which constitutes his nature and essence: he would lose his humanity."[11] For Cassirer making and fulfilling a promise is a specifically human act; it is the participation of a moral person in his humanity.[12] At the same time, the human promissory function stands at the basis of the social contract. However, before examining the conditions for the possibility of the specifically human capacity to promise and making clear how the individual person as an *animal symbolicum* manages to shape its own future by making promises by virtue of the symbolic power of language, we first have to explain what Cassirer regards as the true contribution of the natural law tradition.

For Cassirer the social contract is made possible by virtue of the capacity of the human being to make use of language directed toward the future, that is to say symbolically and in the form of a promise. For Cassirer, the social contract is not merely a historical datum, but functions, in the sense of Kant, as a pure idea of the mind, that has a certain practical reality. The social contract as a mere historical datum, as a coalition of each particular and private will of a people in a general and public will, and into whose rights and duties we have entered as descendants, cannot insist that a people consider themselves as being bound by an already existing civil constitution.

This is established first when the social contract as a pure idea of the mind obliges every legislator that it legislates in such a way that it *could have had* originated from the united will of a whole people and that it views every subject not as a mere subject, but also as a citizen: the subject must be viewed as to have agreed with the general will.[13] Indeed, because in practice

---

11 Ernst Cassirer, *The Myth of the State*, Yale University Press, 1946, p. 288; cited by Krois, 1987, pp. 168–169.

12 Cf. Krois, 1987, pp. 156–157.

13 Immanuel Kant, *Über den Gemeinspruch: Das mag in der Theorie richtig sein, taugt aber nicht für die Praxis*, in: Werke, Bd. VI, S. 355–398: S. 380f. [Akad.-Ausg. VIII, 297]; see: Ernst Cassirer, *Freiheit und Form. Studien zur deutschen Geistesgeschichte*, Gesammelte Werke Band 7, Felix Meiner Verlag, Hamburg, 1998 (1916) p. 343 (pp. 509–509). cf. Ernst Cassirer, *Axel*

this claim is not fully accomplished or even accomplishable, one has to posit the claim for the greatest possibly unity of wills progressively.[14] Thus, for Cassirer, "*contract theory does not denote the historical past, to which the state ascribes itself and from which it derives its legitimacy, rather the future to which it strives.*"[15] As a result, the merits and plausibility of the natural law theory cannot be placed in the genetic explanation of the origin of law and society or in the social contract as a historical datum. That would be to supplant a symbolic act in the form of the social contract by a mere mythical reference.

The rule of law started on the mythical level, by its insistence on fundamental rights of time immemorial or natural rights.[16] The mythical stage is still operative when natural lawyers mention the phenomenon of the social contract merely as a historic occurrence to justify the fundamental rights of man. In the social contract, although we are directed not into an infinite mythical past, but are given a particular focus point in history, the claim of such a historic contract still emphasizes an original rendering of rights (by the people themselves) as a single occurrence, hence as something static, from which we can logically derive natural rights. However, natural law theory was not concerned primarily with how this or that natural right can be derived from a social contract *more geometrico*. The similarity that we may perceive between mathematics and law is not their supposed formalistic method; rather it is their common origin. Therefore, the question natural law was concerned with was that of the origin of law. It was concerned with digging up that area of origin from where the posited norms of law ultimately sprung up and from where they receive their continuing flow of inspiration. This area – and that is the fundamental thesis of

---

Hägerström- eine Studie zur Schwedischen Philosophie der Gegenwart, Göteborgs Högskolas Årsskrift, Elanders Boktryckeri Aktiebolag, Göteborg, 1939, p. 104.

14 Ibid., 1939, p. 79.

15 See: Ernst Cassirer, *Freiheit und Form. Studien zur deutschen Geistesgeschichte*, Gesammelte Werke Band 7, Felix Meiner Verlag, Hamburg, 1998 (1916), p. 343 (509).

16 See: Chapter 7; cf. Coskun, D., *Law as Symbolic Form. Ernst Cassirer and the Anthropocentric View of Law*, in: Bankowski, Z. (ed.), *Epistemology and Ontology*, IVR-Symposium Lund 2003, ARSP Beiheft 102, Steiner Verlag, Stuttgart, 2005, pp. 25–37.

natural law – is not situated outside, but inside, human intellect. The origin of law does not lie in convention or revelation, in whatever authoritative command, that addresses the individual from the exterior, but it is a characteristic and original way of reasoning or making sense of the world, a modus of the human intellect (*Geistigkeit*) that represents itself in the idea of law.[17]

The true contribution of the natural law tradition is, according to Cassirer, that is, by taking into consideration the promissory characteristic of man and declaring it as the highest principle, posed a true *philosophical problem*. Through the axiom of *pacta sunt servanda* the natural lawyers sought to found all law and society on the social contract. Although for Cassirer "*It is impossible to deduce from this or that original contract the substance of law or the content of positive provisions of law*";[18] and: "*a contract has meaning and force only within a state and a medium of laws,*"[19] it should be acknowledged that every rule of law for its existence is in the need of that characteristic *function* that the natural law tradition sought to accomplish through the concept of the contract.

The presupposition that a "*given word binds,*" "*that action is prescribed in a certain direction*" is "*a source and constantly recurring element*" in all consciousness and rule of law."[20] It is a *conditio sine qua non* for any rule of law to transcend its claim from the given of the here and now and to extend its provisions

---

17 See: Ernst Cassirer, *Vom Wesen und Werden des Naturrechts*, Zeitschrift für Rechtsphilosophie in Lehre und Praxis, Volume 6, No. 1, 1932, p. 5. The same intellectual process of liberation of that period also characterized the other branches of science (natural sciences as well as the humanities) not only theoretically, but also practically, as exemplified by Galileo's trial. Ibid., 1932, pp. 11–17. Cf. Sir Edward Coke's conflict with King James I and King Charles I, and Grotius' conflict with the Dutch Prince and Potentate of Orange.

18 See: Ernst Cassirer, *Axel Hägerström – eine Studie zur Schwedischen Philosophie der Gegenwart*, Göteborgs Högskolas Årsskrift, Elanders Boktryckeri Aktiebolag, Göteborg, 1939, p. 105.

19 See: Ernst Cassirer, *The Logic of the Humanities* (*Zur Logik der Kulturwissenschaften. Fünf Studien*, in: Göteborgs Högskolas Arsskrift, Volume 48, Heft 1, 1942, pp. 1–139), tr. C.S. Howe, Yale University Press, New Haven, 1961, p. 108.

20 See: Ernst Cassirer, *Axel Hägerström – eine Studie zur Schwedischen Philosophie der Gegenwart*, Göteborgs Högskolas Årsskrift, Elanders Boktryckeri Aktiebolag, Göteborg, 1939, p. 104.

into the future.[21] A rule of law, in the strict sense of the word, first comes into being when thought elevates itself in order to distance the posited of the here and now over the single moment of its positing, and to stretch it, in principle, across the future. "*The determinacy of the future by the present and the binding of the former to what the present has decided for the future is a moment that holds in any possible legislation.*" Law as a datum of culture [Kulturfaktum] finds its foundation upon this anticipation, on the prejudgment of the future by the present, without which anticipation, Cassirer emphasizes, no human rule of law or that of society is able to (continue to) exist.[22]

I. 2. What are the Conditions for the Possibility of a Promise?

We have seen that for Cassirer the human promissory function or capacity is a condition for the possibility of any rule of law or legal order. But this was not the ultimate question Cassirer sought to answer; it was rather more the question of the conditions for the possibility of a promise. In line with Kant, but also with the social contract theory of Rousseau, Cassirer writes: "*The social consciousness of man depends on a double act of identification and discrimination. Man cannot find himself, he cannot be aware of his individuality save through the medium of social life.*" Nevertheless, Cassirer maintains, "*But for man this medium is not merely an external determinative force. Man, like the animal, subjects itself to the rules of society, but, moreover, he has an active contribution in producing and an active capacity in changing the forms of social life.*"[23] The most effective tool

---

21 Cf. Finnis, J., *Revolutions and the Continuity of Law*, in: Simpson, A.W.B. (ed.), *Oxford Essays in Jurisprudence* (Second Series), Clarendon Press, Oxford, 1973, p. 65; Postema, G.J., *Law's Melody: Time and the Normativity of Law*, Associations, Volume 7, No. 1, Special Issue for The IVR 21st World Congress, 2003, pp. 232–235, 238.

22 See: Ernst Cassirer, *Axel Hägerström- eine Studie zur Schwedischen Philosophie der Gegenwart*, Göteborgs Högskolas Årsskrift, Elanders Boktryckeri Aktiebolag, Göteborg, 1939, p. 105.

23 See: Ernst Cassirer, *An Essay on Man. An Introduction to a Philosophy of Human Culture*, Yale University Press, New Haven, 1944, p. 223; cf. Ernst Cassirer, *Rousseau, Kant and Goethe*, tr. J. Gutmann, P.O. Kristeller, and J.H. Randall, Jr., Princeton University Press, Princeton, 1945; here: Chapter 1: Kant and Rousseau.

through which the human has an active share in social life is through language. Moreover, what distinguishes Cassirer's account of the social contract from previous philosophers is that he attempts to situate the origin of the social contract in that of language as a symbolic form, and makes it a *condition sine qua non* for any active participation in, and hence construction of social reality.[24] Therewith Cassirer effectuates a *linguistic turn* of social contract theory.

For Cassirer: "*Without speech there would be no community of men.*" But here too Cassirer is not interested in a substantial unity of language, rather in a functional unity: "*Two different languages may represent opposite extremes both with respect to their phonetic systems and to their parts-of-speech systems. This does not prevent them from accomplishing the same task in the life of the speaking community. The important thing here is not the variety of means but their fitness for and congruity with the end.*"[25] This unity of wills is not a completed fact for Cassirer, but a regulative idea that repeatedly has to be posited *ad infinitum* to the greatest extent possible, exactly because it is is generally acknowledged that the unity of wills can never be accomplished or is even accomplishable.[26] Furthermore, for Cassirer the communicative competence of language represents not merely a means of rhetoric or an instrument of consensus building, rather it harbors a more fundamental presumption, *i.e.*, the fact *that* one has engaged in communication or discourse, and has accepted the other as a partner of discourse on an equal and reciprocal footing, or at least the possibility thereof.[27] For every community or individual there might be different forms of

---

[24] See: Deacon, 1997, pp. 393–401; Oort, R. van, *Cognitive Science and the Problem of Representation*, Poetics Today, Volume 24, 2003, p. 277; cf. Ackerman, 1980, p. 5.

[25] See: Ernst Cassirer, *An Essay on Man. An Introduction to a Philosophy of Human Culture*, Yale University Press, New Haven, 1944, p. 130.

[26] See: Ernst Cassirer, *Axel Hägerström – eine Studie zur Schwedischen Philosophie der Gegenwart*, Göteborgs Högskolas Årsskrift, Elanders Boktryckeri Aktiebolag, Göteborg, 1939, *supra note* 5, p. 79; cf. Krois, J.M., *Aufklärung und Metaphysik*, Internationale Zeitschrift für Philosophie, Volume 1, 1992, pp. 284–285.

[27] Ibid., 1992, p. 285; cf. Krois, J.M., *Kultur als symbolischer Prozess. Philosophische Konsequenzen eines Paradigmenwechsels*, Deutsche Zeitschrift für Philosophie, 2001, pp. 373–375.

language respectively according to their identity and particularity, but nevertheless there can still be a unity of wills or societal engagement when there is the competence (hence the will) to communicate and enter into discourse with the other.

For Cassirer this is even inevitable, because the human no longer lives in a merely physical universe; the human lives in a symbolic universe. Although it is the human himself who creates this universe, he cannot but symbol.[28] "*Man has, as it were, discovered a new method of adapting himself to his environment. Between the receptor system and the effector system, which are to be found in all animal species, we find in man a third link which we may describe as the symbolic system. This new acquisition transforms the whole of human life. As compared with the other animals man lives not merely in a broader reality; he lives, so to speak, in a new* dimension *of reality.* (...) *Man cannot escape from his own achievement.* (...) *No longer can man confront reality immediately; he cannot see it, as it were, face to face.* (...) *Instead of dealing with the things themselves man is in a sense constantly conversing with himself. He has so enveloped himself in linguistic forms, in artistic images, in mythical symbols or religious rites that he cannot see or know anything except by this artificial medium.*"[29] The individual first in social life, and foremost through linguistic forms, discovers its true, *i.e.*, symbolic nature, because the symbolic as such excludes the merely subjective and includes the other.

In human life, we are not merely addressed or do we perceive merely alien forms of life, but we engage with it in a reciprocal connection – we enter into a debate with it [*wir setzen uns mit ihm "auseinander"*]. With animal, plant or other non-human physical life there is no such entering into a debate or discourse, but only a unilateral relationship. Although we may regard it as a part of life, we do not consider and claim that it knows and acknowledges us as life. This sphere is first achieved in the relation of person to person. The human being as a free

---

28 The expression "to symbol" or "symboling" is proposed by White, L.A., *Symboling: A Kind of Behavior*, Journal of Psychology, Volume 53, 1962, pp. 311–317.

29 See: Ernst Cassirer, *An Essay on Man. An Introduction to a Philosophy of Human Culture*, Yale University Press, New Haven, 1944, pp. 24–25.

personality not only addresses us, but we lay and make a claim to him or her – we consider him or her a member of the sphere of ends – as (s)he does to us. Here there is a pure reciprocity, a pure reversible relationship, where the recognition [*"Anerkennen"*] is mutual. This "giving and taking" is in the form of an ethical claim [*Ansprache*] and enunciation [*Aussprache*] – a discourse [*"Auseinandersetzung"*] between the I and the Other. This correlativity, reciprocity, or general correspondence [*respondere, Entsprechung*] is the basic form of an ethical community or society.[30]

Human life is, for Cassirer, thus, not characterized by a simple passive addressing, but by an active addressing, an active claiming that is hereby expressed. Along with the critical philosophy of language of Wilhelm von Humboldt Cassirer argues that language is an original and active medium, wherein thought first develops itself. Simultaneously language mediates between subject and object, between "I" and the world. The experience of the world and of the "I" first becomes as such in language; otherwise there are only undirected and diffuse flows of impressions. As Plato said, *"questioning and answering each other in discourse" is our only access to the world of the "idea."*[31] We do not first think and recognize, and subsequently clothe our thoughts in language – for example to convey thoughts to other human beings – rather through language we discover the unknown truth.[32] According to von Humboldt, language is not a

---

30 See: Ernst Cassirer, *Geschichte. Mythos. Mit Beilagen: Biologie, Ethik, Form Kategorienlehre, Kunst, Organologie, Sinn, Sprache, Zeit*, Nachgelassene Manuskripte und Texte, Band 3, Herausgegeben von K.C. Köhnke, H. Kopp-Oberstebrink und R. Kramme, Felix Meiner Verlag, Hamburg, 2003, pp. 198–199.

31 See: Ernst Cassirer, *The Logic of the Humanities* (*Zur Logik der Kulturwissenschaften. Fünf Studien*, in: Göteborgs Högskolas Arsskrift, Volume 48, Heft 1, 1942, pp. 1–139), tr. C.S. Howe, Yale University Press, New Haven, 1961, p. 113.

32 Ernst Cassirer, *Philosophie der symbolischen Formen. Die Sprache*, Volume 1, Bruno Cassirer, Berlin, 1923, p. 20 ff.; cf. Urban, W.M., *Cassirer's Philosophy of Language*, in Schilpp, P.A. (ed.), *Ernst Cassirer*, Library of Living Philosophers, Open Court Publishing Company, La Salle, Illinois (1949), 3rd print, 1973, pp. 281–315; Paetzold, H., *Sprache als symbolischen Formen. Zur Sprachphilosophie Ernst Cassirers*, Philosophisches Jahrbuch, Volume 88, 1981, p. 306.

"work" (*ergon*) but an activity (*energeia*); "*not anymore as the sheer description of a datum, but as a pure function, by which we construct our world from the inside out and give it a certain intellectual mark* [geistiger Prägung]."[33] Through language as a symbolic form we produce linguistic concepts and symbols with which we can relate to one another. Although symbols cannot be conceived without the giving of signs, they are distinct from signs.

Symbols constitute what may be called a mental content of meaning, whereas signs merely pertain to physiognomic qualities. Whereas the sign fades away when the physiognomic characteristics that make up a sign lose their force to appeal to the senses, symbols maintain their force in the sphere of meaning, irrespective of the diminishing quality of the sensory material that originally accompanied them. However, the sign for the philosophy of symbolic forms is never a mere cloak, an accidental and outward garment for thought, because when thought uses a sign it represents a basic tendency and form of thought.[34] The sign "*serves not merely to communicate a complete and given thought-content, but is an instrument, by means of which this content develops and fully defines itself.*" Accordingly, language does not enter an already existent objective world to give therein merely names to individual things, but it is itself a means, the most important of all, for the construction of an objective world, hence also, in its respect, for the formation of the future.[35] Animal life misses this dimension, because animal language is entirely subjective or emotional language as opposed to human language which, for Cassirer, is always propositional.[36]

Furthermore, the true definition of language can only be a genetic one:[37] we must go back from the product of language as a

---

33 See: Ernst Cassirer, *Idee und Gestalt. Goethe, Schiller, Hölderlin, Kleist*, B. Cassirer, Berlin, 1924, p. 68 ff.

34 See: Ernst Cassirer, *The Philosophy of Symbolic Forms*, Volume III, *Science*, tr. R. Manheim, Yale University Press, New Haven, 1957 (1929), p. 410.

35 Cf. Krois, 1981, p. 103.

36 See: Ernst Cassirer, *An Essay on Man. An Introduction to a Philosophy of Human Culture*, Yale University Press, New Haven, 1944, pp. 115–118.

37 See: Ernst Cassirer, *Philosophie der symbolischen Formen. Die Sprache*, Volume 1, Bruno Cassirer, Berlin, 1923, p. 104.

datum to the process of the becoming of language; from the *"forma formata"* to the "*forma formans.*"[38] As such this process of the symbolic form of language runs parallel to the development of other symbolic forms. "*All symbolic forms,*" writes Cassirer, "*do not come to the fore as separate, independent and identifiable forms, but originate very gradually from the common matrix of Myth. All content of the mind* (...) *is factually first given to us only in this concatenation.*"[39]

From the language pragmatic point of view, this is, of course, most apparent when there is no will to communicate, especially when there seems to be found no rational explanation for not entering into discourse with the other. Cassirer recognizes this dimension as the inherent mythical aspect of human culture. Myth, a symbolic form for Cassirer, is in the position of making rational discourse impossible in society, for example by bringing to the fore physiognomic qualities and emotions as obstacles for discourse.[40] As Cassirer remarks, there is no discourse or reasoning possible with myth, for example in the form of racism or hero- worship. For mythical thinking there is no distinction or distance between the real and the possible, between the actual and the ideal or symbolic. Therefore, for myth, there is no such thing as discursive understanding.[41] Also in social life, in the daily interactions of civilized men we cannot completely efface these data. Notwithstanding, it is clear for Cassirer that nevertheless

---

[38] See: Ernst Cassirer, *Symbol, Technik, Sprache. Aufsätze aus den Jahren 1927–1933,* E.W. Orth and J.M. Krois (Hrsg.), Meiner Verlag, Hamburg, (1932) 1985, p. 138.

[39] See: Ernst Cassirer, *Axel Hägerström- eine Studie zur Schwedischen Philosophie der Gegenwart,* Göteborgs Högskolas Årsskrift, Elanders Boktryckeri Aktiebolag, Göteborg, 1939, p. 85; cf. Ernst Cassirer, *Sprache und Mythos: ein Beitrag zum Problem der Götternamen,* in: Ibid., *Wesen und Wirkung des* Symbolbegriffs, Wissenschafliche Buchgesellschaft, Darmstadt, 1959 (urspr. Teubner, Leipzich, 1925), p. 112.

[40] Title 42, sections 1981 and 1982 of the United States Constitution, in this respect, respectively state that the competence and the capacity to contract, and that of the sale or lease of property shall not depend upon race (see: Jones v. Alfred H. Mayer Co., 392 U.S. 409 (1968); cf. Runyan v. McCrary, 427 U.S. 160 (1978); and cf. Goodman v. Lukens Steel (1987)); sections 1981 and 1982 may give rise to *dignitary damages.* See also: *Domino's Pizza Inc. v. McDonald,* 546 U.S. ___ (2006).

[41] See: Ernst Cassirer, *An Essay on Man. An Introduction to a Philosophy of Human Culture,* Yale University Press, New Haven, 1944, pp. 56–57.

we should search for the largest possible unity of wills and that this unity should serve as the cornerstone of our actions.[42] Moreover, it is the task of philosophy, Cassirer emphasizes, to attack not only the products and configurations of myth, but also its root, *i.e.*, its perception of expression.[43]

Myth does not perceive objectively, but only *physiognomic* characters: "*Mythical perception is always impregnated with these emotional qualities. Whatever is seen or felt is surrounded by a special atmosphere – an atmosphere of joy or grief, of anguish, of excitement, of exultation or depression.*"[44] The mythical world is at a much more fluid and fluctuating stage, and finds itself captured, as it were, by the actual sense impressions. This dependence upon the actual and superficial deeply influences its expressive capacities: "*Primitive man expresses his feelings and emotions not in mere abstract symbols but in a concrete and immediate way* (...)."[45] For mythical thought there is no distinction between the name of an object (the sign) and the meaning of the object (the symbol), and thus language does not represent a meaning but presents a given object. The representative function is absent in mythical thinking; the shaman who through strictly prescribed words invokes the powers of a certain demon or deity does not act in the name of, or represent, but rather is imbued by and embodies the demon or deity in full force and awe.

First when the power of the magical sense of the word is superseded by that of the sentence, when we differentiate between the sound (the sign) and the meaning of the word (the symbol) by contextualizing the word in the sentence, language adopts a representational function. Therewith, language not only overcomes the sphere of the mythical imagery, but also that of

---

[42] For a treatment of Ernst Cassirer's constitutional patriotism [*Verfassungspatriotismus*] see: Coskun, D., *Ernst Cassirer and European Constitutionalism*, in: Nergelius, J., Policastro, P., Urata, K. (eds.), *Form and Substance in Contemporary Constitutionalism*, Constitution and Multi-Level Democracy, Volume I, Ratio, Krakow, 2004.

[43] See: Ernst Cassirer, *The Logic of the Humanities* (*Zur Logik der Kulturwissenschaften. Fünf Studien*, in: Göteborgs Högskolas Arsskrift, Volume 48, Heft 1, 1942, pp. 1–139), tr. C.S. Howe, Yale University Press, New Haven, 1961, p. 94.

[44] See: Ernst Cassirer, *An Essay on Man. An Introduction to a Philosophy of Human Culture*, Yale University Press, New Haven, 1944, pp. 76–77.

[45] Ibid., 1944, p. 79.

the simple sensory presentation. Gradually, through the method of analogy or metaphor, we introduce the distinction between the meaning of a word and its sensory qualities, upon which any representation is still dependent. But when we pursue this distinction to its logical end, the way is opened for the realm of pure significative meaning, *i.e.*, the ideal or symbolic, where meaning is conceived and maintained independent of the object, as it was first represented to us and originally even presented or embodied by sensory signs. "*In language we can clearly discern the progression from the initial magical sense of the word to a pure function of representation, and thereby to an objective conception.*"[46]

Whereas the first phonetic expressions take place against the background of the affective, for example that discharges itself through the call; this is different in the representative function of language. The linguistically conceived and represented effect is not the same as it originally was, because it has undergone, as it were, a metamorphosis. "*The effect loses in that sense, that it learns to express itself and to conceive itself in this expression, that immediately mastering, that all-dominating and all-overturning power, that it exerts over the "I."* When it learns to reflect on itself in the linguistic expression, this reflection reacts upon the whole consciousness.

This becomes most apparent in the linguistic development of the child. The emotions and the immediate needs are the first and most important impulses to articulation as such. However, when more and more the symbolic consciousness gains ground, correlatively the pure effect retreats and loses its *despotic* hegemony.[47] "(...) *language awareness – the awakening symbol consciousness – impresses* its *stamp upon observation and perception in ever-increasing measure as it grows in strength and extends and clarifies itself. Both observation and perception become "objective" just to the degree that this linguistic energy succeeds in clarifying, differentiating, and organizing the mere*

---

46 See: Ernst Cassirer, *Axel Hägerström – eine Studie zur Schwedischen Philosophie der Gegenwart*, Göteborgs Högskolas Årsskrift, Elanders Boktryckeri Aktiebolag, Göteborg, 1939, p. 90.

47 Ernst Cassirer, *Symbol, Technik, Sprache. Aufsätze aus den Jahren 1927–1933*, E.W. Orth and J.M. Krois (Hrsg.), Meiner Verlag, Hamburg, 1985, pp. 135–142.

undifferentiated chaos of particular circumstances. Linguistic symbolism opens up an original phase of spiritual and intellectual life."[48] The life of mere impulses, of the here and now is thereby supplanted by a life of "meanings."[49]

When using ideal or symbolic language the human being is no longer bound solely to his immediate practical needs and sensory impressions, but has the ability to anticipate and determine the possible, hence his or her future. Linguistic concepts of the field of action, for example the concepts of law and morality, in this regard, attain their new meaning and task: "*Now they* [linguistic concepts] *not only have the task of representing a given course of events but, in a certain sense, they have to grasp another dimension of time. "Speech" should not solely hold fast to a constellation of facts given here and now and express it as such, but direct itself toward the future: it becomes a promise.*"[50] This direction to the future is a constructive moment in all human consciousness and characterized by Cassirer as the expression of the *will.* It arises with language in the symbolic sphere that transcends the immediately given of the here and now.

These linguistic concepts of the field of actions or performatives, as John L. Austin has called them, would seem to be invulnerable to mythological infiltration, because it makes use of language that performs an action rather than states (or asserts) anything. The latter is reserved for constative utterances as Austin has called them, because they "merely" describe or represent a given course of events.[51] Nevertheless, there is a chasm between these two fields, *i.e.*, the theoretical

---

48 See: Ernst Cassirer, *The Logic of the Humanities* (*Zur Logik der Kulturwissenschaften. Fünf Studien,* in: Göteborgs Högskolas Arsskrift, Volume 48, Heft 1, 1942, pp. 1–139), tr. C.S. Howe, Yale University Press, New Haven, 1961, p. 60.

49 Cf. Keller, 1954 (1902); and Lash, 1980.

50 See: Ernst Cassirer, *Axel Hägerström- eine Studie zur Schwedischen Philosophie der Gegenwart,* Göteborgs Högskolas Årsskrift, Elanders Boktryckeri Aktiebolag, Göteborg, 1939, p. 104.

51 See: McDonald, L.C., *Myth, Politics and Political Science,* The Western Political Quarterly, Volume 22, 1969, pp. 141–150; here: p. 141; Dinneen, J.A., *What Austin Does with Words,* Philosophy and Phenomenological Research, Volume 32, 1972, pp. 514–523; Austin, J.L., *How to Do Things with Words,* edited by J.O. Urmson, Harvard University Press, Cambridge, Massachusetts, 1962.

and the practical. Whereas the natural sciences have defeated mythological thought by making use of artificial or symbolic language and the method of rationalism, in the practical sphere man follows quite different rules. "*Scientific knowledge and technical mastery of nature daily win new and unprecedented victories. But in man's practical and social life the defeat of rational thought seems to be complete and irrevocable. In this domain modern man is supposed to forget everything he has learned in the development of his intellectual life. He is admonished to go back to the first rudimentary stages of human culture.*"[52] For man not to succumb to the powers of myth, not to lose thereby his or her freedom, every individual person has his or her own struggle.

The most important natural or human right for Cassirer is the right to develop freely one's own personality, which is explained below as symbolically constituted. By various examples, Cassirer makes clear the importance of the symbolic capacities of a person for his personality. Those who have lost some of their symbolic capacities, for instance that of speech in the case of aphasia, display a correlative deformation of their personalities. This consists among others of an impairment of the capacity to anticipate future events and in a complete dependence on actually given and presented things, because they are unable to "grasp" the possible. Moreover, our symbolic capacities provide us with our first access to the normative, again primarily through language. To illustrate, our first grasping at the correct meaning of words as a child, and our efforts to use the correct and appropriate words in the correct meaning, constitutes a first contact with the normative. In this sense, the development of one's symbolic personality is essential to participate in a social entity.

Finally, it is in the promise and its corollary of duty, in the capacity of ordering oneself, that the will first attain its ethical quality. Therefore, the anticipatory or future orientated direction of the symbolic function is, for Cassirer, constitutive for human

---

[52] Ernst Cassirer, *The Myth of the State*, Yale University Press, New Haven, 1945, pp. 1–2.

personality.[53] The will, through its temporal direction to a non-given, is no longer merely a mystic potency of man nor a simple fiction, but a "prospective intention"; an active formation of the "I" alien to mythical thought.[54] Through it the moral personality comes to the fore, what is called the unity, completeness, and inner consistency of a character. "*The basic claim the personality poses itself is the inner compliance of the conduct.*"[55] By posing tasks for ourselves and by making promises, to subsequently experience their fulfillment, we consequently become aware of our character and personality.

II. CONCLUSION

In this chapter we have examined the social contract theory of Cassirer. As a philosopher of culture Cassirer is not interested in the genealogical account natural law has to offer for the origin of law and society: the social contract as a historical datum has to be replaced by the social contract as a pure idea of the mind. This is not to discredit the achievements of natural law. In a sense every legislator still (necessarily) grasps at an ideal or symbolic dimension of law in order to legislate and it has to be clear for the legislator that there is a difference between the positing of the law and the origin of it, something already noticed by Grotius. But what interests Cassirer is that natural law has posed a real philosophical problem, *i.e.*, the problem of the promise. The promissory function is a constant and recurring element in every rule of law. Without it there would be no consciousness or rule of law and of society. Cassirer, in this respect, attributes a special role to the symbolic form of language, when he situates the origin of the social contract in a specifically active use of language. He thereby distinguishes himself from the natural lawyers and establishes a *linguistic turn* of social contract theory.

---

53 For the different degrees or phases in the development of the moral person from the perspective of the philosophy of symbolic forms, see: Krois, 1987, pp. 142–152.

54 See: Ernst Cassirer, *Axel Hägerström – eine Studie zur Schwedischen Philosophie der Gegenwart*, Göteborgs Högskolas Årsskrift, Elanders Boktryckeri Aktiebolag, Göteborg, 1939, p. 108.

55 Ibid., 1939, p. 67.

For Cassirer the human being is an *animal symbolicum*; man cannot but symbol. Man, as it were, has discovered and lives in a different dimension to animal life. He is not solely bound to his immediate sense impressions, but through the power of language manages to transcend the given of the here and now. Mythical thought is incapable of this, and only gradually, but not definitely, when the sentence supersedes the power of the word, and finally when it adopts meaning in the symbolic sense, language progressively manages to cut itself loose from the matrix of myth. What Cassirer makes clear is that before we can extend our linguistic concepts to the field of action (what Austin has called perfomatives) we have to overcome mythical thought, and push forward the distinction introduced by the representational function of language (what Austin has called constatives) between the object of our senses and the meaning of the object, to its conclusion by abstracting this meaning from the given course of events. Through language in the symbolic sphere man is able to direct his speech toward the future, and it becomes a promise. The linguistic sign serves not merely to convey a message, but has formative effect for the objective world of the individual, and commits him internally to this self-created world. To promise is a typically symbolic, hence human, activity which is not available to life that does not have developed symbolic functions. This basic direction toward the future is constitutive for the moral personality, which is characterized by a unity, completeness, and inner consistency.

By the continuing presence of mythical thought (in the practical sphere) it is clear that the unity of wills, Kant envisioned, is not always accomplished or even accomplishable. Cassirer therefore proposes to search for the greatest possible unity of wills. In this respect, it is essential that mythical thought should be dealt with at the roots, for it is impossible for myth to reach discursive understanding. Myth thinks in terms of collectivities instead of individual human persons, and in terms of good and evil instead of human dignity. The latter is related to the fundamental insight that by accepting the other into discourse we already presume the equality of that person on the symbolic level, *i.e.*, as capable of grasping and conveying meaning through symbolic forms. Therefore, for Cassirer language not merely has a pragmatic value, but stands at the core of an ethical (form) of life.

Moreover, it is constitutive for society, because in the form of an active addressing and responding it presumes the acceptance of the other as an end in itself, *i.e.*, as part of humanity. In addition, it presumes a shared and accessible conception of meanings on the symbolic level. These two elements, the symbolic nature of the human being, what we may call the principle of humanity, that is characterized by its direction through language toward the future, and the realm of symbolic meaning, that is accessible only to beings that exhibit the capacity to make use of symbols; constitute the conditions for the possibility of a promise. As is shown in the next chapter, Cassirer's theory of the symbolic (social) contract does not come out of the void, because for his view of the social contract Cassirer is indebted to Hermann Cohen. However, with his symbolic analysis of the social contract, Cassirer moves beyond the contract theory of Hermann Cohen, and neo-Kantian jurisprudence in general.

CHAPTER 9

CASSIRER'S POSITION IN RELATION TO NEO-KANTIAN JURISPRUDENCE

I. INTRODUCTION

In this chapter we provide the context for Cassirer's legal theory, in particular by explicating its indebtedness to the legal theory of Hermann Cohen. The Marburg School was the most proficient neo-Kantian School at engaging itself with practical philosophical investigations in the field of ethics and jurisprudence. Hermann Cohen's legal theory and ethical project, furthermore, constitutes the prevailing thesis around which other neo-Kantian jurisprudential endeavors center. Therefore, in this chapter, the divergence between Stammler's legal theory and that of Cohen, on the one hand, and Kelsen's critique of Marburg jurisprudence, on the other, together with Radbruch's critique of Kelsenian positivism, will represent the constellation into which we position Cassirer's legal theory.

In his epoch-making critique of neo-Kantian jurisprudence,[1] Erich Kaufmann states that German jurisprudence since the demise of Hegel's idealism, *i.e.*, since the second half of the nineteenth century, is in a genuine crisis.[2] The crisis in jurisprudence, according to Kaufmann, relates directly to the crisis in philosophy, and more broadly with the crisis in the intellectual life or culture of the era. Moreover, it is the distance which neo-Kantian jurisprudence had created for itself in respect of the social and the political, its insistence on its own autonomy of subject matter and method as distinct from other branches of science, and

1 I use the terms jurisprudence and the philosophy of law interchangeably. They both represent a systematic reflection on law and the study of law. The former is interconnected with the latter and is procured by it.

2 See: Kaufmann, 1964 (1921), pp. 1 ff.; cf. Smend, R., *Zu Erich Kaufmanns wissenschaftlichen Werk*, in: *Um Recht und Gerechtigkeit. Festgabe für Erich Kaufmann zu seinem 70. Geburtstag*, W. Köhlhammer, Stuttgart and Cologne, 1950, pp. 391–400; referred to by Paulson, 2005, pp. 540–541, 90 n. For a rebuttal of Kaufmann's criticism of neo-Kantian jurisprudence, see: Sauer, 1921, pp. 162–194.

the acceptance of a duality between the legal world and the "common" world (or the noumenal and the sensuous) that Kaufmann criticized. According to Kaufmann, Kant could not have agreed with the neo-Kantian representation of the phenomenon of law. Detached from the other sciences and incapable of addressing a real social and political issue, neo-Kantian jurisprudence was not in a position to offer a qualitative contribution, according to Kaufmann.

Instead, neo-Kantian jurisprudence, which was the prevalent strain of thought in German jurisprudence during the first half of the twentieth century, had focused on conceptual and scholarly intricacies, while it could have played a vital role in reconciling sheer power with law. For more than half a century, according to Kaufmann, German jurisprudence had not produced a single great work of jurisprudential scholarship. The end of German, speculative idealism seemed to have drained the inspirational well of German jurisprudence. The result was a shattered corpus of numerous strains of jurisprudential thought without an authoritative standing of their own, or a central question guiding them all in the same direction. To what extent was Kaufmann correct? Was neo-Kantian jurisprudence a folly deserving nothing but negative attention? What does neo-Kantian jurisprudence actually stand for? And why should we consider it for our present purposes? These issues come to the fore and are addressed in the following paragraphs.

At the turn of the twentieth century, many strains of thought in jurisprudence claimed to be critical or neo-Kantian by referring to Kant's critique. Furthermore, other schools came to the fore in reaction to neo-Kantian jurisprudence, for example in the form of the phenomenological school of jurisprudence, while the Hegel-Renaissance had inspired the rise of neo-Hegelian jurisprudence.[3] Gradually, though, neo-Kantian jurisprudence lost its privileged position as the prevailing jurisprudence in Germany, and had to make way for a jurisprudence that was most of all directed toward Hegel, that is, until Nazi ideology came to the fore and established its hegemony over jurisprudence as well.[4]

---

3 Cf. Pascher, 1992; Sauer, 1949, especially pp. 460–477; Sauer, 1923/24, pp. 284–313; and Wundt, 1926, pp. 372–375; here: p. 372.

4 Stolleis, 1999, p. 175 ff.

However, although criticized from diverse angles, neo-Kantian jurisprudence did have its merits, especially as it sought to move beyond mere legal positivism by seeing the need for and working toward a greater self-awareness in the study of law, without engaging in metaphysical ways of approaching law.[5]

While considering the merits of neo-Kantian jurisprudence, however, it must be made clear that the following does not offer a defense of neo-Kantian jurisprudence, nor does it attempt to enter into a debate with its critics. Neo-Kantian jurisprudence, in particular as it was inspired by the Marburg School, is relevant for our present purposes only insofar as it offers a context or constellation within which "Law as Symbolic Form" finds its historic positioning. Law as Symbolic Form finds its matrix in the philosophy of symbolic forms, while neo-Kantian jurisprudence was the prevailing philosophy in the study of law in the first half of the twentieth century that drew inspiration from the efforts of neo-Kantian philosophy in general, and, for our purposes, the Marburg School in particular.

The attempts of the neo-Kantians to create a truly scientific form of jurisprudence attracted great attention and grew in significance so as to become the prevailing strain of thought in jurisprudence in the first half of the twentieth century,[6] until the rise of (pre-pro) Nazi ideology. As a result, any jurisprudence emanating from that era that attempts to gain greater self-understanding, also has to understand its relation to or disassociation with neo-Kantian jurisprudence in particular, and neo-Kantian philosophy in general. Moreover, it is important to understand neo-Kantianism, as Cassirer would himself explain, because his early connections with and later departure from neo-Kantianism, in particular Hermann Cohen, provides the best context through which to understand his philosophy.[7] Accordingly, to put "Law as Symbolic Form" in its context means to explicate its relationship with, or, perhaps, its disassociation from, the themes developed in

---

5 See: Larenz, 1931, pp. 10–11.

6 Cf. Finnis, J.M., *Legal Enforcement of 'Duties to Oneself': Kant v. Neo-Kantians*, Columbia Law Review, Volume 87, 1987, pp. 433–456.

7 Toni Cassirer, 1981, p. 94: "*Now I will finally make clear for the others my relationship to Cohen, and I look forward to doing that. My tie to him and my later loosening from him – both are important*". Translated by Krois, 1992, pp. 437–453; here: p. 438, 1 n; cf. Moynahan, 2003, p. 40.

neo-Kantian philosophy in general, and neo-Kantian jurisprudence in particular. To what extent does Law as Symbolic Form address the same issues or problems as those addressed by neo-Kantian jurisprudence?

This chapter proceeds as follows. Firstly, in Section I.1, we answer the question of what was neo-Kantian jurisprudence. Next, in Section I.2, we focus more specifically on Marburg jurisprudence because it is most promising for our purposes, also for explicating Cassirer's inherited jurisprudential concerns, by answering the question of what was the jurisprudence of the Marburg School. Then, in Section I.3, we elaborate on Hermann Cohen's legal theory, and explicate why Cohen could not agree with Stammler's theory, and explain to what significant extent Cohen also disagreed with Kant's view of law. In addition, in Section I.4, we focus on Cohen's view of social contract theory. The concept of the contract for Cohen becomes a method through which he explains the ethical justification of the law, the state, the society, and the individual alike. Furthermore, in Section I.5, we address the basic objections raised against Marburg jurisprudence, especially by Hans Kelsen.

Finally, in the conclusion, we not only give an assessment of the results of this chapter, but also explain why Cassirer escapes the objections raised by Kelsen, and why his disagreement with Kelsen rests upon different grounds than the famous critique Radbruch raised against Kelsen. Cassirer fundamentally agrees with Cohen's ethical explanation of social life, but moves beyond it insofar as he gives a symbolic or semiotic turn to Cohen's view, by explicating the conditions for the possibility of the ethical form of social life and by introducing a plurality of symbolic forms to achieve and maintain an ethical life.

I. 1. What was Neo-Kantian Jurisprudence?

Neo-Kantian jurisprudence was the leading philosophy of law on the European continent during the first half of the twentieth century.[8] Its jurisprudence did not draw its inspiration directly

---

[8] See: Alexy, 2002; cf. Sauer, 1949, especially pp. 460–477; Sauer, 1923/24, pp. 284–313; and Sauer, 1921, pp. 162–194. Cf. Schmid, 1998, pp. 446–455; Pawlik, 1995, pp. 585–586; Gigliotti, G., *Ethik und das Faktum der*

from Kant's own jurisprudence, as developed by him in his Metaphysics of Morals and in his Metaphysics of Law, but rather was inspired by neo-Kantian philosophy, and in particular its methodology. The aim of neo-Kantian jurisprudence was analogous to that of neo-Kantianism in philosophy. The leading exponents of continental jurisprudence, Rudolf Stammler (1856–1938), Gustav Radbruch (1878–1949), and Hans Kelsen (1881–1973), were not only profoundly influenced by the works of neo-Kantian philosophers, but explicitly referred to their sources in neo-Kantian philosophy and sought to enter into a debate with them so as to achieve greater sophistication. Accordingly, neo-Kantian jurisprudence intended to provide a scientific foundation for law and jurisprudence by adopting therein the insights formulated by the neo-Kantians, who at their turn had applied Kant's conceptual–methodological determinations in his "Critique of Pure Reason" throughout the entire spectrum of the sciences, theoretical and practical.

After the second half of the nineteenth century, also known as the era of positivism, legal philosophy through neo-Kantian jurisprudence had found a new task for itself. While recognizing the significance of a coherent legal system consisting of empirical concepts, neo-Kantianism sought to go beyond mere positive law and positive concepts, without relapsing into absolute or intuitive phenomena such as natural law. In the hands of the neo-Kantian philosophers of law, the transcendental method proved fruitful in creating a jurisprudence that essentially entailed a philosophy of positive law as well as a science of positive law. According to neo-Kantian jurisprudence, some concepts were endowed with such a categorical form or character that they could legitimately be related to a unitary principle and could be of constitutive significance for any legal order. In his "Philosophy of Law" ("*Rechtsphilosophie*"), Gustav Radbruch voiced the neo-Kantian paradigm in a nutshell.[9] "*Later we will be vindicated* [in our beliefs] *that concepts such as the subject of law and the object of law, legal relationship and illegality, indeed the concepts of law*

Rechtswissenschaft bei Hermann Cohen, in: Holzhey, 1991, pp. 166–184; and Rudolph, 1999.

9 See: Kersting, W., *Neukantianische Rechtsbegründung. Rechtsbegriff und richtiges Recht bei Cohen, Stammler und Kelsen*, in: Alexy, 2002, pp. 23–68; here: pp. 30–31.

themselves, are not incidental features of a single or of all legal systems, but rather necessary presumptions to understand a legal system as a legal system."[10]

Neo-Kantian jurisprudence was not solely concerned with positive law and positive concepts and the logical ordering of them into a coherent system, but with the philosophical foundations of positive law. Historically as well as systematically it complements the so-called "jurisprudence of general concepts" ["*Allgemeine Rechtslehre*"] as it was developed by the Pandectists,[11] who were named so because of their teaching methods that were aligned to those of the Pandects in Roman jurisprudence.[12] Neo-Kantian jurisprudence does not attempt to establish a revolution in jurisprudence, because it remains indebted and tied to the tradition of the jurisprudence of general concepts that stood at the center of positivism in German jurisprudence.[13] Rather, what it attempts to do is to give a transcendental, hence scientific, dimension to the efforts of the so-called *Begriffsjurisprudenz* (conceptual jurisprudence) and *Konstruktionsjurisprudenz* (constructive jurisprudence) that flourished during the age of positivism and – as siblings of the jurisprudence of general concepts – were intrinsically bound with the works of Puchta, Windscheid (the early, pre-teleological) Jhering, Gerber, Laband, Von Gierke, and Jellinek.[14]

At the basis of this conceptual renaissance stood the endeavors of Friedrich von Savigny, who in his treatise on Roman law had first proposed a scientific and systematic, that is to say, a

---

10 See: Gustav Radbruch, *Rechtsphilosophie*, p. 110; referred to by: Kersting, W., *Neukantianische Rechtsbegründung. Rechtsbegriff und richtiges Recht bei Cohen, Stammler und Kelsen*, in: Alexy, 2002, pp. 23–68; here: p. 31.

11 The Pandectists were also of profound influence upon the theory of Wesley Hohfeld.

12 See: Lokin, 2001, p. 246.

13 Cf. Kennedy, 2001.

14 See: Kersting, W., *Neukantianische Rechtsbegründung. Rechtsbegriff und richtiges Recht bei Cohen, Stammler und Kelsen*, in: Alexy, 2002, pp. 23–68; p. 31; in the Netherlands especially J.P.H. Suijling seems to have been receptive to the jurisprudence of general concepts, but also the architect of the new Dutch Civil Code seems to have been profoundly influenced by conceptual jurisprudence; see: Meijers, E.M., *Algemene leer van het burgerlijk recht*, Volume 1, *De algemene begrippen van het burgerlijk recht*, Universitaire Pers Leiden, Leiden, 1948.

conceptual, syllogistic approach to law.[15] With neo-Kantian jurisprudence, the works of these great jurists would provide a matrix for developing a scientific approach to law, and in the works of Cohen, of ethics as well. However, at the turn of the twentieth century, the prevailing mood among jurists was far from optimistic that the study of law was scientific or could be compared to such a discipline as mathematics, and less remained of the logical–semantic optimism of the Pandectists or of the exponents of *Begriffsjurisprudenz* and *Konstruktionsjurisprudenz*.[16]

It was the time of the ascendancy of the "Free law movement" (*Freirechtsschule*) and that of its followers, the "interests jurisprudence" (*Interessenjurisprudenz*) and "value jurisprudence" (Wertungsjurisprudenz) who were inspired by the works of the later Jhering. What bound them together was a shared disbelief in conceptual jurisprudence in relation to its syllogistic approach to law's practice. Ironically, these critics of the jurisprudence of general concepts equally took the works of Friedrich von Savigny as their starting point.[17] Conceptual jurisprudence, according to the "Free law movement," proved inadequate in describing the practical workings of the law, because through its limited focus on statutory and customary law it neglected important determinative elements, such as economic factors, social utility, and the "*Rechtsgefühl*" of the people (literally: the people's feeling of the law).[18] Moreover, conceptual jurisprudence did not take into account the practical consequences that judicial decisions produced, *i.e.*, the relation between law and society. For that a new science was needed in the form of the sociology of law that would explicate the relations between law and society on the one hand, and the cultural values of law on the other.[19] At the beginning of the twentieth

---

15 Cf. Lokin, 2001, pp. 243–244.

16 Cf. Pihlajamäki, 2004, pp. 469–487; here: p. 474.

17 I would like to thank Corjo Jansen (Nijmegen) for his insightful remarks on this subject.

18 Cf. Pihlajamäki, 2004, pp. 469–487; here: pp. 474–475: the "Free law movement" had a profound influence on the development of legal realism in America and Scandinavia.

19 See: Kantorowicz, H., *Der Kampf um die Rechtswissenschaft* (1906), in: ibid., *Rechtswissenschaft und Soziologie: Ausgewählte Geschriften zur Wissenschaftslehre*, Müller, Karlsruhe, 1962, pp. 17–21; referred to by Pihlajamäki, 2004, pp. 469–487; here: p. 474, 19 n.

century, conceptual jurisprudence was discredited by the "Free law movement" and the sociology movement, and saw a growing decline in support among legal scholars and legal philosophers.

Nevertheless, in another respect and form, conceptual jurisprudence would prove very fruitful again, because it was to become an important ingredient for the rise of neo-Kantian jurisprudence in the first half of the twentieth century, especially through the efforts of Hermann Cohen. Relying on the conceptual rigor and systematic elaboration of the conceptual jurists, Cohen in his "Ethics of the Pure Will" gave an important impetus for the rise of neo-Kantianism in jurisprudence. He moved to give jurisprudence as it was developed by the conceptualists an important position in his ethical theory by considering jurisprudence as the factum of science for ethics. He declared: "*The law has its roots in ethics, so it must be possible to determine and constitute ethics in jurisprudence.*"[20] Ethics was to be a science, and, accordingly, jurisprudence the factum of the science for ethics. With that he gave jurisprudence, as it was first developed by conceptual jurisprudence, a new scientific perspective and task. At the start of the twentieth century, Stammler was the first legal philosopher and jurist to pick up and pursue systematically the Marburg neo-Kantian initiative in jurisprudence, and to move beyond the strict, positivist jurisprudence that was inspired by the historical school of Savigny, and had received a first mature formulation by Puchta and Windscheid.[21] *Through the works of the neo-Kantian philosophers of law in the twentieth century the age of positivism received a constructive pursuance and critical depth.*

Neo-Kantian jurisprudence was foremost the result of lawyerly efforts and dedication.[22] However, not only through individual jurists engaged in legal philosophy through the perspective and intellectual tools offered by neo-Kantianism, but also within the different neo-Kantian Schools themselves,

---

[20] Hermann Cohen, *Ethik des reinen Willens*, p. 227; cited by Kersting, W., *Neukantianische Rechtsbegründung. Rechtsbegriff und richtiges Recht bei Cohen, Stammler und Kelsen*, in: Alexy, 2002, pp. 23–68; here: p. 32.

[21] See: Sauer, 1949, p. 463.

[22] See: Kersting, W., *Neukantianische Rechtsbegründung. Rechtsbegriff und richtiges Recht bei Cohen, Stammler und Kelsen*, in: Alexy, 2002, pp. 23–68; here: p. 24.

considerable energies were devoted to the study of law.[23] To some extent, therefore, it should not come as a surprise that neo-Kantian jurisprudence reflected the same attitude toward the tendencies that had led to the neo-Kantian synthesis in philosophy, as the latter sought to avoid doctrinal metaphysics on the one hand, and strict positivism (in the form of scientific materialism) on the other.[24] By the same token, one of the central tenets of neo-Kantian jurisprudence became its attempt to find a way between strict empirical positivism on the one hand, and a metaphysical natural law theory that elevated values into absolute legal norms on the other. What it attempted was to upgrade jurisprudence to a scientific level, and therewith to bridge the classical gap in jurisprudence between positivism and natural law theory. The scientific optimism, *i.e.*, the strong belief in the fruitfulness of the transcendental method, was another characteristic the neo-Kantian philosophers of law held in common with their counterparts in neo Kantian philosophy.[25] In the following paragraphs, we further explore neo-Kantian jurisprudence, specifically as it was developed by the Marburg School, not only because it was foremost the Marburg School that engaged in the study of jurisprudence, but also because Cassirer was closest to and most informed by Marburg jurisprudence than any other legal philosophical endeavor. Therewith, we can discern more to the full Cassirer's relation to or disassociation with Marburg, neo-Kantian legal theory.

I. 2. What was the Jurisprudence of the Marburg School?

It was through the work of the Marburg School that the practical philosophy of Immanuel Kant gained new significance.[26] Whereas Kant had restricted his transcendental method to the

---

[23] See especially: Lask, E., *Rechtsphilosophie*, in: idem, *Gesammelte Schriften*, hrsg. E. Herrigel, Volume 1, Mohr (Paul Siebeck), Tübingen, 1923, pp. 277–331.

[24] See: Chapter 6.

[25] See: Kersting, W., *Neukantianische Rechtsbegründung. Rechtsbegriff und richtiges Recht bei Cohen, Stammler und Kelsen*, in: Alexy, 2002, pp. 23–68.

[26] Ibid., 2002, p. 24; cf. Sprenger, G., *Die Wertlehre des Badener Neukantianismus und ihre Austrahlungen in die Rechtsphilosophie*, in: ibid., 2002, pp. 157–177; here: p. 169.

mathematical sciences and decided to approach practical or moral philosophy not through the transcendental method but through "common sense,"[27] the Marburg School undertook its own course. The Marburg School undertook to pursue the insights Kant formulated in his "Critique of Pure Reason," most notably the transcendental method, consistently throughout Kant's entire critique, including the "Critique of Practical Reason." Accordingly, in his search for the factum of science for ethics to critically investigate the conditions of its possibility, Hermann Cohen turned to jurisprudence as the factum of ethics and took critical philosophy to a new level.[28] Therewith, the stage was set for neo-Kantian jurisprudence, which from then on saw as its general task to give a scientific foundation of law and jurisprudence, by drawing inspiration from the efforts of the neo-Kantians to explain the foundations of the mathematical natural sciences from the perspective of the "Critique of Pure Reason."[29] This does not mean, though, that neo-Kantian jurisprudence could be brought under one conceptual and theoretical denominator. Not only did the philosophical methods differ from one school to another, but also between individual legal philosophers viewpoints were incommensurable, hence were a cause of discord, for example between Kelsen and Stammler, and Stammler and his Marburg teacher Cohen.[30] As to the latter relationship, whereas both recognized the importance of approaching law from the Kantian transcendental perspective, so as to lead jurisprudence into the path of a science, the actual results they arrived at differed significantly. In fact, the conclusion Stammler reached in his jurisprudence seemed so grave a mistake for Cohen that he called it a "defection" ("Abfall").

Nevertheless, through the works of Cohen, Natorp and Stammler, the Marburg School formulated a jurisprudence that viewed the philosophy of law as a truly ethical discipline. It was their aim to explain the relationship between the individual and

---

[27] This is different for positive, statutory law, according to Kant; see: Lisser, 1922, pp. 15 ff.

[28] Ibid., 1922, p. 3.

[29] See: Kersting, W., *Neukantianische Rechtsbegründung. Rechtsbegriff und richtiges Recht bei Cohen, Stammler und Kelsen*, in: Alexy, 2002, pp. 23–68; here: p. 27.

[30] Ibid., 2002, p. 27.

society, however, not by considering the socio-juridical meaning of a community, but by considering its scientifically constituted form. This scientific form, according to the Marburg School, was imprinted in a community through jurisprudence, which fulfills the constitutional task of forming a societal unity guided by laws. Jurisprudence by the Marburg School was regarded primarily as a science – in the broad meaning of the term – or a theory of legislating and of legal hermeneutics. Jurisprudence, according to the Marburg School, had a dual task. First, it has a systemizing task of ordering the multifarious legal experiences of the past into a systemized order of positive law. Second, jurisprudence is a theory of legislating, which has the duty of adapting positive law to ethical laws and guiding the system of positive law toward its ethical goal.[31] While agreeing on these dual tasks of jurisprudence, Cohen and Stammler differed in their views as to the relationship between the systematic task of jurisprudence in logical ordering, and the more normative task of recognizing the ethical import of a legal system and the need for striving toward its actualization.

Whereas Cohen insisted on the connection between ethical and legal problems at the methodological as well as the practical level, Stammler not only methodologically distinguished between legal philosophy and social philosophy, but as to subject matter also inserted a methodological separation between the concept of law and the idea of law.[32] Law as an idea, for Stammler, is different from law as a concept. For Stammler, *"The law* [as an idea] *is a mode of human volition."*[33] As an idea, law functions as a pole star that integrates the various distinct wills of individuals into a single societal will. The idea of law explicates the purpose of the law as: "*the society of free willing*

---

31 Müller, 1994, pp. 179–180.

32 Ibid., 1994, pp. 180–182; cf. Müller's conclusion that the dichotomy between natural law theory and positivism proves insufficient in explaining the jurisprudence of the Marburg School, because the concept of law of the Marburg School is not a substantive concept, but a functional concept, at pp. 181 ff.

33 Stammler, R., *Das Recht im Zusammenhang mit der Kulturentwicklung* (1914), in: Stammler, 1970, pp. 27–38; here: pp. 34 ff.

humans."[34] Accordingly, while the concept of law gives a logical ordering and systematization to our legal experiences, the idea of law determines the direction in which the various individual wills converge into a societal will.[35] As such, law is a precondition, a condition for the possibility of a society that is held together by laws, *i.e.*, not on an ad hoc basis, but objectively or scientifically. The direction law takes the way in which it lays down the objectives of a society, is objective and good in itself, according to Stammler, because it is context-dependent.[36] "*Law*," according to Stammler, "*is the coercive effort toward the good.*"[37] In this regard, the judiciary is not supposed to engage in subjective, free considerations, but in objectively "right" judgments, which can be deduced logically from the objective good of the social ideal.[38]

In his so-called "good law" thesis ("*richtiges Recht*"), Stammler claimed that the idea of law was distinct from the concept of law, because the former was purposively informed by the struggle for survival of a people and the means they use to survive materially. The idea of law is materially conditioned or context-dependent, and belongs to the proper domain of natural law, according to Stammler, because it deals with substantive issues.[39] However, the inner tendency of law toward the good has no effect on the validity of positive law. "*It does not yet contradict the concepts of law, when a social norm stipulates bigamy, widow-burning, slavery, the expulsion of weak children. An insincere friend is sure enough a contradiction; nothing different from a triangular circle; but there can be an unjust judge, just as an ill or criminal human being still can be*

---

34 Stammler, R., *Begriff und Bestimmung der Rechtsphilosophie* (1914), in: Stammler, 1970, pp. 1–26; here: p. 16.

35 Ibid., 1970 (1914), pp. 18–19.

36 Ibid., 1970 (1914), p. 9.

37 Stammler, R., *Die Bedeutung des Deutschen Bürgerlichen Gesetzsbuch für den Fortschritt der Kultur* (1900), in: Stammler, 1970, p. 54; cited by: Kersting, W., *Neukantianische Rechtsbegründung. Rechtsbegriff und richtiges Recht bei Cohen, Stammler und Kelsen*, in: Alexy, 2002, pp. 23–68; here: p. 51.

38 See: Jansen, 1993, pp. 191–205; here: p. 200.

39 Stammler, R., *Begriff und Bestimmung der Rechtsphilosophie* (1914), in: Stammler, 1970, pp. 1–26; here: p. 5.

subsumed under the concept of human being."[40] Equally, law, according to Stammler, is a predicate attributed to certain social norms without regard to their content, *i.e.*, they are morally neutral. The concepts of law are the *a priori* elements of legal judgment, because they first make any contingent, material provision of law a form of law. They cannot be determined by natural law, but are the proper concern of jurisprudence, according to Stammler. This view of Stammler, especially his distinction between the morally neutral concept of law and the inherently and objectively good idea of law, differed markedly from Cohen's standpoint in legal philosophy. We now turn to the legal philosophy of Cohen, and subsequently contrast it with other neo-Kantian legal philosophers, so that we can position Cassirer's legal theory in this reconstructed legal philosophical constellation.

I. 3. What was the Jurisprudence Hermann Cohen Envisioned?

As opposed to Stammler, Cohen could not envision a jurisprudence that was indifferent to or that maintained a neutral stance toward ethical norms, not even at the conceptual level.[41] Cohen maintained, "*Whosoever sees in the achievements of ethical culture only instinct and the lust for power ... frankly, he cannot be brought to ethical knowledge.*"[42] Stammler's "good law"-thesis or for that matter his "natural law with changing contents" stood in sharp contrast with the ethical jurisprudence Cohen envisioned. In his jurisprudence, Cohen presupposes a unity between law and morality and explains that he disagrees with Kant's concept of law, because it assumes physical characteristics. According to Cohen, the divide between morality and law was initiated by Thomasius and Kant, and springs forth from their physical

---

40 Rudolf Stammler, *Die Lehre von dem richtigen Recht*, p. 56; cited by: Kersting, W., *Neukantianische Rechtsbegründung. Rechtsbegriff und richtiges Recht bei Cohen, Stammler und Kelsen*, in: Alexy, 2002, pp. 23–68; here: p. 53.

41 Ibid., 2002, pp. 27–28.

42 Hermann Cohen, *Ethik des reinen Willens*, p. 420; cited by: Lisser, 1922, p. 50.

explanation of the concept of force.[43] Kant's concept of law shows an obvious methodological flaw, according to Cohen, because it is not inspired by the so-called transcendental freedom. Cohen refers here to the dual explanation of the concept of human freedom Kant maintained in his *Groundwork of the Metaphysics of Morals* (1785) on the one hand, and his *Metaphysics of Morals* (1797) on the other. Whereas in the *Groundwork of the Metaphysics of Morals* Kant had focused his investigations on the subject who imposes an obligation, in the *Metaphysics of Morals* Kant concentrated on the subject upon whom obligations or constraints are imposed. Whereas the former, for Kant, stands for a pure form of human freedom, the latter refers to our capacity of free choice in actions, *i.e.*, when practical reason is "*putting itself under obligation.*"[44]

With the latter, though, we also enter into a completely different sphere, *i.e.*, into the sphere of coercion or force.[45] The concept of force in Kant's doctrine of rights actually becomes an important conceptual element for it. Whereas for the concept of moral duty, according to Kant, it is important to investigate not only the action, but also its subjective maxims and motives, the concept of right abstracts from every subjective consideration and aspires to evaluate actions merely with respect to its "*objective circumstances and execution.*"[46] Legality, according to Kant, is not concerned with the motives of an action, *i.e.*, whether it is motivated out of duty, but only with the agreement or disagreement of an action with the laws. In this respect, legality may not only *command*, but also *demand* a certain course of actions, because it is, strictly viewed, concerned only with the external enforceability of actions. "*Right in its strict sense*," according to Kant, must "*be envisaged as the possibility*

---

43 For the development of the idea of law in the jurisprudence of Thomasius and Kant, see: Coskun, D., *De cultuur van mensenrechten*, Wolf Legal Publishers, Nijmegen, 2006, Chapter 3.7.8.

44 See: Immanuel Kant, *The Metaphysics of Morals*, 1797 (ed. M. Gredor), Cambridge, p. 235; referred to by: Ward, 1997, p. 27.

45 Cf. Ernst Cassirer, *Kant's Life and Thought* (B. Cassirer, Berlin, 1921) tr. J. Haden, intr. by S. Körner, Yale University Press, New Haven and London, 1981, pp. 397–398.

46 Ibid., 1981 (1921), p. 398.

of a general and reciprocal coercion consonant with the freedom of everyone in accordance with universal laws."[47]

Kant's doctrine of rights is concerned with the just ordering of society, or with what he terms "*whether the action of one can be united with the freedom of the other in accordance with a universal law.*"[48] It entails that the freedom of one person can be restricted only when he or she infringes upon the freedom of another. Right in that instance becomes identical to an authorization to coerce someone, who infringes upon the freedom of another, to refrain from doing so, and to act according to the universal law. We put ourselves under a universal obligation, according to Kant, when our actions are informed by the universal obligation, either out of duty, which renders such action ethical and legal at the same time; or out of incentive from coercion, which renders such action merely legal. The coercion of a person's freedom of action in such a way that it no longer infringes upon the freedom of another, *i.e.*, the production of lawful conduct in accordance with the universal law, is asserted by the legislator. Neither is lawgiving that is directed toward achieving lawful conduct necessarily ethically inspired, that is to say, spurred by duty. "*That lawgiving which makes an action a duty and also makes this duty the incentive is ethical. But that lawgiving which does not include the incentive of duty in the law and so admits an incentive other than the Idea of duty itself is juridical.*"[49] When Kant introduces the concept of coercion or force as the incentive other than duty, accordingly henceforward it becomes an essential element for any juridical right: "(...) *thus right and the authority to apply coercion mean one and the same thing.*"[50]

---

47 Immanuel Kant, *Metaphysical Elements of the Theory of Right*, introduction, para. E (VII, 33 t.) (*Ak.* VI, 232 f.); cf. introduction, III (VII, 19) (*Ak.* VI, 218); cited by: Ernst Cassirer, *Kant's Life and Thought* (B. Cassirer, Berlin, 1921) tr. J. Haden, intr. S. Körner, Yale University Press, New Haven and London, 1981, p. 399.

48 See: Immanuel Kant, *The Metaphysics of Morals*, 1797 (ed. M. Gredor), Cambridge, p. 46; referred to by: Ward, 1997, p. 27. Cf. Cassirer's legislative maxim in Chapter 1.

49 See: Immanuel Kant, *The Metaphysics of Morals*, 1797 (ed. M. Gredor), Cambridge, p. 46; referred to by: Ward, 1997, p. 27.

50 Immanuel Kant, *Metaphysical Elements of the Theory of Right*, introduction, para. E (VII, 33 t.) (*Ak.* VI, 232 f.) cf. introduction, III (VII, 19)

However, the force Kant recognizes is an external one, and directed toward the regulation of conduct proper, as distinct from the act of free choice itself. "*It* (...) *depends* (...) *on the principle of the possibility of an external coercion which can exist with the freedom of everyone in accordance with universal laws.*"[51] As indicated earlier, Cohen does not follow Kant in this. The inner freedom of choice as an ethical maxim, and the constraint of our actions for the purposes of universal freedom Kant distinguished from that inner freedom; are intertwined for Cohen. Cohen acknowledges the importance of constraint or force upon our actions, but the force he recognizes is an inner force of the human being, *i.e.*, the force to legislate for oneself and to act according to a law that is legislated by one's own choice and to which one feels bound to abide. Cohen distinguishes himself from Kant, exactly at this point. Kant relates the binding nature of law to an external force, whereas Cohen makes clear that the binding nature of law resides within its persuasive power to make people act accordingly. It is reasonable self-constraint ("*Selbstzwang*") or reasonable "self-coercion" ("*Selbstnötigung*"), rather than sheer obedience to an external authority. *Law for Cohen is the reign of persuasion rather than the reign of force.*[52]

Cohen's jurisprudence is wholly intertwined with his ethics. An ethics without jurisprudence, according to Cohen, would be incomprehensible, *i.e.*, it would either vanish in the "*psychological quicksand of the subjective arbitrary,*" or would suffocate in the "*dogmatic dungeons of religion.*"[53] Jurisprudence, foremost through its conceptual conciseness and precision, fulfills the role of a mathematical system in the ethical theory of Cohen, analogous to the natural sciences. "*Ethics can be approached as the logic of the humanities* [Geisteswissenschaften]. *It has as its*

(*Ak.* VI, 218) referred to by Ernst Cassirer, *Kant's Life and Thought* (B. Cassirer, Berlin, 1921) tr. J. Haden, intr. S. Körner, Yale University Press, New Haven and London, 1981, p. 399.

51 Ibid., 1983 (1921), p. 399.

52 Cf. Winter, 1980, pp. 352 ff.; on the concept of law as the reign of persuasion, see: Edmond Cahn, *The Binding of Isaac: A Case Study*, in: Cahn, 1967, pp. 232–240; especially: pp. 239–240; cf. his famous expression: "*the very first place for grace to shine is within the practical workings of the law*" at p. 240.

53 See: Kersting, W., *Neukantianische Rechtsbegründung. Rechtsbegriff und richtiges Recht bei Cohen, Stammler und Kelsen*, in: Alexy, 2002, pp. 23–68; here: p. 32.

main problem the concepts of the individual, the totality, as well as the will and the action. All philosophy is dependent upon the factum of the sciences. This dependency upon the factum of the sciences counts for us as the eternal in Kant's system. The analog to mathematics is represented by jurisprudence [Rechtswissenschaft]. *It can be described as the mathematics of the humanities, and principally so for ethics.*"[54] The transcendental method provides that philosophy can begin its investigation first when knowledge has become a scientific fact. Equally, because the Marburg School maintains the transcendental method in the practical sphere as well, practical philosophical investigations in the field of ethics also have to depart from scientific facta, and for Cohen these are provided by jurisprudential concepts.

However, the facta of ethics, according to Cohen, are not constituted by valid, positive laws as such, but can be reached only through an analysis of jurisprudence, *i.e.*, an analysis into its "*clearest and scientific, constitutive* [*i.e.*, transcendental] *elements, and pivotal concepts.*" The ethical principles that thereby come to the fore represent at the same time the foundations of law and state for Cohen. What was previously termed natural law, henceforward is described by Cohen as "the law of law" ("*Recht des Rechtes*") or "the ethics of law" ("*Ethik des Rechts*"), explicating the interconnectedness of ethics and law,[55] paradigmatically in the (functional) concept of the social contract.[56]

As a result, while ethics finds its transcendental foundation in jurisprudence, conversely, jurisprudence and the other cultural sciences find their transcendental foundation in ethics, but principally so for jurisprudence, because it is conceptually most advanced, according to Cohen.[57] The interconnectedness of ethics and jurisprudence, especially considering the famous phrases of

---

54 Hermann Cohen, *Ethik des reinen Willens*, p. 66; cited by Kersting, W., *Neukantianische Rechtsbegründung. Rechtsbegriff und richtiges Recht bei Cohen, Stammler und Kelsen*, in: Alexy, R., 2002, pp. 23–68; here: p. 32.

55 Ibid., 2002, pp. 33–34.

56 For an elaboration of Cohen's view of the concept of the contract, see the next section.

57 Hermann Cohen, *Ethik des reinen Willens*, p. 227; referred to by: Lisser, 1922, p. 51.

Cohen that "*the law of law is the ethics of law*" and that "*ethics must be pursued as a jurisprudence,*" may pose a danger to jurisprudence so as to render it a mere technicality. However, jurisprudence distinguishes itself as an autonomous discipline or science through its conceptual discipline. Jurisprudence is a methodological system of self-created concepts, according to Cohen, and, furthermore, distinguishes itself from other cultural fields through its conceptual clarity and definiteness. Jurisprudence is constituted by "*its own corpus and framework of concepts. Therewith a technique, which merely applies given concepts, differs from a method, which creates its own concepts.*"[58] Jurisprudence derives its concepts from transforming ethical principles into the principles of a legal system, but a legal system is never a mere static thing, something given, or organically growing in the sense of the Historical School, because it is to be understood as an ongoing task of progressively systematizing our legal experiences.[59] This comes very close to Law as Symbolic Form.

I. 4. What is the Social Contract Theory of Hermann Cohen?

Central to Cohen's legal and ethical theory is the concept of action.[60] The human reveals himself through his actions, according to Cohen.[61] We can know another human being only through his actions, and, accordingly, law judges the individual only by his actions that have legal significance. Action in the legal sense of the term is not an empirical or psychological concept, according to Cohen, but a *pure* concept.[62] As pure concepts they exist only through the recognition of the legal system, that is to say, independent from psychological and physiological factors, and as the expression of the *pure will.* Therefore, because all legal acts are essentially conditioned concepts, they are pure concepts. Cohen considers the primary advantages of law above such phenomena as religion or biology,

---

[58] Hermann Cohen, *Ethik des reinen Willens*, p. 604; cited by: Lisser, 1922, p. 52.

[59] Müller, 1994, p. 190.

[60] Pascher, 1992, p. 44.

[61] Hermann Cohen, *Ethik des reinen Willens*, p. 74; cited by: Lisser, 1922, p. 54.

[62] Pascher, 1992, p. 45.

that law considers the individual only to the extent in which he is a subject of law.[63] However, as a subject of law the individual is never an isolated being for Cohen, because there cannot be an individual in the ethical sense of the term without a legal order already recognizing him as such and wherein his actions are displayed and have formative effect.[64] Moreover, legal actions presuppose at least two acting subjects who stand in a relation to one another. The form that the relation between subjects of law assumes is that of the *contract*, according to Cohen. The contract is constituted by the expression of distinct legal wills, which are pure speech acts recognized by the legal system. Accordingly, because every legal act presupposes legal subjects that stand in a relation to one another in the form of (speech acts expressing the pure will and reciprocally constituting) a contract, Cohen concludes, that "*all law* [can be] *related back to the contract*."

The contract is the ethical justification of the law, the state, the society, and the individual alike for Cohen.[65] Conceptually the contract not only poses the contracting parties as ends in themselves, but also presupposes the intention to bind each other reciprocally according to the law of the contract (*lex contractus*). The reciprocal obligation of the contractual parties, moreover, presupposes the recognition of the other as a free and equal person. Cohen explains how only through the recognition of the individual in an ethical community (as constituted by laws through the concept of the contract) the individual attains to its individuality. "*The contract in effect renders from the appeal a claim. And therefrom the "Other" transforms itself from an "I" into a "Thou." A "Thou" is not a "He." The "He" was an "Other." The "He" is in danger of also being treated as an "It." "Thou" and "I" virtually belong to another. I cannot say "Thou" without relating you to me; without uniting you with the "I" in this relationship. But therein at the same time resides the augmented assertion: that I cannot think of an "I," without thinking of a "Thou." In that way the "Other" in self-awareness*

---

63 Moynahan, 2003, pp. 35–75; here: p. 61.

64 Cf. Hermann Cohen, *Ethik des reinen Willens*, p. 225: "*kein Individuum im ethischen Sinn ohne Rechtsgemeinschaft*"; referred to by: Pascher, 1992, p. 40.

65 Winter, 1980, p. 327.

has at the same time transformed itself into the flipside of the "I." When self-consciousness has to mean the unity of the will, then it must represent the union of the "I" and "Thou." The will *unites me and you; you and me. This union entails the task of self-consciousness.*"[66] The contract is not an experiment or an arbitrary action, but rather more fundamentally underlies every act of self-consciousness, and represents an ethical process for Cohen.

It is a precondition for the individual to attain to self-consciousness by relating himself to the other, and thereby becoming conscious of its own individuality only through its relation to the other, *i.e.*, the "Thou" that becomes an "I." The contract therefore is a transcendental concept and represents a process through which different individuals relate to one another and progressively achieve their individuality in the ethical sense of the term. Because the contract is a legal construct that first attains its significance within a context of a legal system, accordingly, a subject of law who establishes himself as an individual by relating to the other through contract is at the same time an ethical being, according to Cohen.[67] Cohen vindicates his position that subjects of law are fundamentally ethical by referring to entities such as legal persons, corporations and the state that come into existence through contractually informed relations, and provide stable or default relational settings for such contracting.[68] What makes them ethical entities, according to Cohen, is that they "exist" through their own legislative efforts, *i.e.*, to the extent of their legislative enactments and actions inspired or guided by laws pursuant to their constitution or corporate charter.[69] The self in the ethical and legal sense of the term, according to Cohen, is never a given thing but an unending task that must be realized. Ethical and legal subjects "exist"

---

66 Hermann Cohen, *Ethik des reinen Willens*, p. 235; cited in German by: Winter, 1980, p. 328.

67 Ibid., 1980, p. 329.

68 I am indebted to William Allen for this insight. The main economic justification for legal entities lies in the fact that they significantly reduce transaction costs.

69 Hermann Cohen, *Ethik des reinen Willens*, pp. 341–342; referred to by: Lisser, 1922, p. 55.

(under law) to the extent that they act. *Ethicality for Cohen is the process through which the "I" progressively relates to a "Thou."*[70]

Therewith, Cohen's method attains new significance in the domain of ethics as well. Cohen's engagement with Kantian ethics did not entail a mere representation of Kant's ideas but an explicit refinement and systematic continuation of Kant's basic ethical ideas.[71] Especially, in relation to the core Kantian concept of autonomy, Cohen formulated an original interpretation of Kantian ethics. The ethical subject acts not out of freedom, but rather toward freedom, according to Cohen. The idea of autonomy becomes "autotely": "*ethically self-dependent and worthy is only such action that is directed to the realization of a society, in which the single individual that belongs to it is "always simultaneously an end in itself, never a mere means.*"[72] Freedom is a regulative idea for Cohen. It is an unending task for the individual; in order to have it the individual must create it for himself through his own actions, *i.e.*, by working toward a society or context wherein he is, foremost, an end in himself. Cohen's Marburg colleague Paul Natorp expresses this social(istic[73]) turn of Kantian ethics in more pregnant terms. "*Mere will-less obedience and service is not a virtue of men but of things, and above all to degrade a whole class of people [...] to a class of will-less subservients, means to strip them of their ethical character completely and therewith to abdicate them of the morality of the community as such.*"[74] Most significantly, for the Marburg School, only in an ethical community guided and constituted by laws, can the individual find its determination as an individual.[75]

---

70 Herewith is explained at the same time the origin of the ethical import of Cassirer's philosophy of symbolic forms. Because symbolic forms are modes through which humans give meaning to their world and understand one another by conveying meaning, *i.e.* relate to one another, they explicate the ethical structures of our universe.

71 See: Ernst Cassirer, *Hermann Cohen und die Erneuerung der Kantischen Philosophie*, Kantstudien, Band 17, Berlin, 1912, pp. 252–273; here: p. 268.

72 Ibid., 1912, p. 269.

73 Cf. Holzhey, 1991.

74 Paul Natorp, *Sozialpädagogik: Theorie der Willenserziehung auf der Grundlage der Wissenschaft*, Fromman, Stuttgart, 1898, p. 184; cited by: Müller, 1994, pp. 187–188.

75 Cf. Derbolav, 1983, p. 78.

Ethics and jurisprudence that converge with one another in the concept of the contract, are essentially concerned with the scientific constitution of society. However, ethics and jurisprudence, according to Cohen, pursue their investigations and direct their concepts not into nature or natural concepts – analogous to the natural sciences – but only into culture and cultural concepts. The precepts of ethics and of positive law clearly distinguish them from the laws of nature or scientific laws in that the former are directed primarily and foremost into the future.[76] It is characteristic for the law that it relates itself to future conduct, according to Cohen.[77] In most legal systems the futurity of the law is expressed through the principle of legality, or the prohibition of retroactive laws,[78] but more fundamentally, every legal system, if it is to exist as a legal system, must display an orientation toward the future or future conduct. Ethical and legal norms do not purport to describe a real occurrence, *i.e.*, they do not try to explain what has happened or what has yet to happen, but only prescribe or postulate a certain course of action that should (or should not) occur. Furthermore, while it is essential for a natural law that occurrences that have been predicted or explained by it actually (have) occur(ed) as was predicted or explained, for legal rules it does not matter as to their validity whether individuals have acted pursuant to or in contradiction with the rule of law.

The normative meaning of the rule of law is not offended by the factual circumstances, because the focus of a norm is always directed toward the future.[79] The orientation to the future is a precondition for any legal or ethical norm, because, as it deals with our conduct, and intends to determine it into a

---

[76] Hermann Cohen, *Ethik des reinen Willens*, p. 283 cited by Lisser, 1922, p. 51.

[77] See: Winter, 1980, p. 365 ff.; cf. Cohen's treatment of the concepts of ethical futurity and Jewish messianism, at pp. 367 and 385 ff. See also: Cohen, 1972.

[78] For a comprehensive overview of the history of the principle of legality in the common law, see: *Stogner v. California*, 539 U.S. 607 (2003); for the dilemma the principle of legality poses for issues relative to transitional justice, see: the case of the German "wall shooters," e.g. in: *Streletz, Kessler and Krenz v. Germany* (Applications nos. 34044/96, 35532/97 and 44801/98), ECHR, Strasbourg, 22 March 2001.

[79] Winter, 1980, pp. 368–369.

certain direction, it can do so only by focusing on the future. Only in the future the possibilities appear to us to act in a certain way. A rule of law that is directed toward the past, which has formative effect for the past, is something *prima facie* incomprehensible. Our rules of law cannot have any meaning for the past, for what has been before, but only for the future, for what has yet to come. When a natural law has been discredited through an occurrence which was said to be impossible by the natural law *ex ante*, this renders the natural law invalid not only for the future, but in respect of the past it will be considered as if in reality it did not have any validity at all in the first place.[80] Moreover, by contrast, amendments to current legal or ethical laws or breaches of them do not render them invalid for the past; their validity is not dependent on what has happened in the past, because it is only concerned with what should happen. To illustrate, in the case of rules of law that have been repealed or superseded by new laws, we are not concerned with their past validity, but only with their validity in the future, and accordingly, how we should evaluate their past claims in our present and futurable judgments.[81] While we have herewith explicated the legal theory of the main and single most important representative of Marburg jurisprudence, it is our subsequent task to consider the criticism that it had to face, especially from who has been called the greatest continental jurist of the twentieth century, *i.e.*, Hans Kelsen.

Therefore, before we turn to an assessment of Cassirer's legal theory it may be helpful first to elaborate on other representatives of neo-Kantian jurisprudence, who also took the transcendental method as their starting point, so as to compare the particular directions they took and the results they arrived at. For that, the following will be attempted. First, we elaborate on the jurisprudence of Hans Kelsen and his indebtedness and subsequent critique of the jurisprudence of the Marburg School, *viz.* his critique that the legal theories of Hermann Cohen and

---

80 Ibid., 1980, pp. 370–371.

81 For a discussion of the futility of legislative attempts to burden the futurity of legislative orientation, *i.e.* by claiming eternal validity or an express repeal of past legislation for new legislation to have effect, see: (especially) the concurring opinion of Justice Scalia, in: *Lockhart v. United States*, 546 U.S.__ (2005). Cf. Rubenfeld, 2001.

Rudolf Stammler fail to avoid the pitfalls of natural law theory. Furthermore, we address the criticism of Gustav Radbruch in respect of legal positivism and Hans Kelsen in particular through his injustice thesis. Finally, in the conclusion, we make clear how Cassirer's legal theory escapes the criticisms voiced by Kelsen to the address of Marburg jurisprudence, and explicate in what way Cassirer's jurisprudence distinguishes itself from that of Kelsen, Radbruch, and the Marburg School. Therewith, we give a historical and systematical positioning of Cassirer's legal theory vis-à-vis neo-Kantian jurisprudence, and provide perspective for Law as Symbolic Form.

I. 5. What were the Basic Objections Raised against Marburg Jurisprudence?

Kelsen's basic objection to the Marburg jurisprudence was that it represented a form of natural law theory and, especially relative to Cohen, that he accordingly was unwilling to forego the ethico-metaphysical postulates behind his pure concepts.[82] Because both Hermann Cohen and Rudolf Stammler were familiar with the pitfalls of natural law theory and yet both refrained from explicating their support for some natural law theory in particular, or claimed to voice a natural law theory themselves[83] – they rather sought, as did Kelsen, a *via media* between natural law theory on the one hand and positivism on the other – it is clear that Kelsen objects to features of Marburg jurisprudence that apparently had not overcome natural law theory as Kelsen found critical. Kelsen's pure theory of law was greatly influenced by Kantian, or as was rather more the case, neo-Kantian thought.[84] We cannot enter here into the debate which School, the Baden or the Marburg School, was most influential for the

---

82 See: Kelsen, H., *The Pure Theory of Law, 'Labandism', and Neo-Kantianism. A Letter to Renato Treves*, in: Paulson, 1998, pp. 169–175; here: pp. 173–174.

83 Cf. Willey, 1964, p. 133.

84 See: Edel, G., *The* Hypothesis *of the Basic Norm: Hans Kelsen and Hermann Cohen*, in: Paulson, 1998, pp. 195–219; here: p. 196.

development of Kelsen's thought.[85] Our ambition is to explicate his relationship to the Marburg School, because that is most promising for our present purposes as to why Cassirer escapes Kelsen's criticism to the address of the Marburg School.

In relation to the influence of Hermann Cohen, Kelsen writes "*What is essential is that the theory of the basic norm arises completely from the Method of* Hypothesis *developed by Cohen.*"[86] Kelsen's Pure Theory of Law is thus significantly indebted to Cohen's theoretical philosophy. "*A point of special significance is,*" writes Kelsen, "*that just as Cohen understood Kant's* Critique of Pure Reason *(Kritik der reinen Vernunft) as a theory of experience, so likewise I seek to apply the transcendental method to a theory of positive law.*"[87] Both Cohen and Kelsen sought to find an *a priori* concept (generated or "originated" from thought) through which to lay a foundation for their theory of law. Kelsen embraces Cohen's transcendental method,[88] however, he cannot profess his allegiance to Cohen's particular application of the transcendental method in the field of law, and therefore he has to reject Cohen's entire ethical framework as well.[89]

Kelsen's pure theory is pure in two respects. It is pure as to the subject matter of law and it is pure as to the methodology of law. Jurisprudence, as subject matter, is concerned only with the cognition of the validity of positive law, with demonstrating the necessary transcendental presuppositions on which the claim to validity of the positive law rests.[90] Law, according to Kelsen, should be explained only through its own precepts. However, jurisprudence in remaining pure as to its subject matter, must also remain pure in its method. Legal theory, according to Kelsen, enquires transcendentally into the presuppositions and

---

85 Especially Stanley Paulson has been proficient in explicating that Kelsen was probably much more indebted to the Baden School than the Marburg School, although Kelsen himself seems to refer foremost to the latter factor.

86 See: Kelsen, H., *The Pure Theory of Law, 'Labandism', and Neo-Kantianism. A Letter to Renato Treves*, in: Paulson, 1998, pp. 169–175; here: p. 174.

87 Ibid., 1998, p. 171.

88 See: Paulson, S., *Einleitung*, in: Alexy, 2002, pp. 11–21; here: p. 17.

89 See: Edel, G., *The* Hypothesis *of the Basic Norm: Hans Kelsen and Hermann Cohen*, in: Paulson, 1998, pp. 195–219; here: pp. 209–210.

90 Ibid., 1998, p. 219.

foundations of the claim of the positive law to validity, and remains pure only insofar as the transcendental explanation of the validity of positive law is drawn exclusively from the positive law itself.[91] Law, according to Kelsen, is to be considered exclusively in terms of the law; "*for to cognize something legally or to understand something juridically means nothing other than to understand it as law.*"[92] Consequently, jurisprudence as method, in explicating the skeleton of normativity upon which the validity of positive law rests, and especially its "spine" in the form of the basic norm, is only concerned with what the positive law *is*, not how it *ought* to be.[93]

Kelsen maintains that all legal norms can be related back to an ultimate, basic norm, which we presuppose every time we understand something as law. Kelsen maintains that there is a first legislator who has lent his power to actually enforce the coercive character of a norm, and it is from that hypothesis (that an authority has lent his power to enforce the norms of a legal system), according to Kelsen, that we can take notice of the basic norm.[94] It is the basic norm that gives any legal act objective validity and normativity as being law. Law for Kelsen becomes a meaning perspective, because everything to which the basic norm applies can be considered to be within the realm of law.[95] However, properly speaking (sic), the basic norm is not a norm at all, because it only introduces normativity into the legal system grammatically, just as in a language game in the Wittgensteinian sense of the term; it is only meant as a hypothesis and is completely a functional concept.[96]

Kelsen disagrees with the legal theory (hence the ethics) of Hermann Cohen, because it does not overcome natural law

---

91 Ibid., 1998, p. 211.

92 Ibid., 1998, pp. 197 and 211, 38 n.

93 Ibid., 1998, p. 219.

94 Ibid., 1998, pp. 218–219.

95 On the perspectival dimension of Kelsen's basic norm, see: Roermund, B. van, *Instituting Authority. Some Kelsenian Notes*, Ratio Juris, Volume 15, No. 2, 2002, pp. 206–218; especially: pp. 214 ff.; cf. Roermund, B. van, *Authority and Authorisation*, Law and Philosophy, Volume 19, 2000, pp. 201–222, especially: pp. 211–212; and Roermund, 1997.

96 See: Kersting, W., *Neukantianistische Rechtsbegründung. Rechtsbegriff und richtiges Recht bei Cohen, Stammler und Kelsen*, in: Alexy, 2002, pp. 23–68; here: pp. 61–62.

theory according to Kelsen, that is to say, because it presupposes substantive (or metaphysical) ethical norms. Kelsen may be right that Cohen's legal theory has features that can justifiably be related to the rationale of natural law theory, especially his insistence that law is necessarily informed by ethical norms. However, Kelsen does not do justice to Cohen on the conceptual level or in relation to the *a priori* understanding of law. Kelsen contends that the characteristic difference between his legal theory and that of Cohen is, "*that Cohen lacked the courage to draw from the Kantian transcendental philosophy ultimate conclusions in the field of social reality* (...). *He was unable to forego the assumption of a contentually constituted, materially determined* a priori. *With reference to those positive norms determining social life, he could not rest content with purely formal categories of* a priori *validity. For that would have inevitably led to ethical relativism, something that Cohen – exactly like Kant on this point – was not prepared to accept, if only because of his religious convictions. Thus, the Cohennian legal philosophy, like Stammler's, is a theory of natural law, not a theory of positive law* (...)."[97] What Kelsen did not take into account, though, was that a theory of natural law could nevertheless still simultaneously be a theory of positive law – because such was one of the aims of Marburg jurisprudence, *i.e.*, to provide a theory and science of positive law for the scientific constitution of society.[98] However, more importantly also in a different respect, Kelsen does not give Cohen's theory its due.

When Cassirer's well-known book *Substance and Function* appeared Cohen praised Cassirer for its scholarly achievement. Cohen regarded this fundamental work of Cassirer as the fulfillment of the philosophy of the Marburg School, and even contended he could not imagine a better representation of the theory of the Marburg School; he could now retire in peace, Cohen stated. Cohen expressed strong agreement with Cassirer that concepts could only be functional (progressively produced by thought) and never substantive (standing in itself or as such). It is striking, though, that Kelsen refers to Cassirer to vindicate his

---

97 Kelsen, H., *The Pure Theory of Law, 'Labandism', and Neo-Kantianism. A Letter to Renato Treves*, in: Paulson, 1998, pp. 169–175; here: p. 173.

98 See: Chapters 9.1–9.4.

theoretical position that the concepts of law have become functional concepts (instead of substantive concepts), while at the same time he contends that Cohen makes use of substantive concepts.[99] Cassirer was only translating (and vindicating) the theoretical views of the school of Cohen in the light of contemporary achievement in science (*i.e.*, the relativity theory of Einstein; and the quantum mechanics of Planck). Kelsen misunderstands Cohen's conceptual theory, while Cassirer and Cohen could only have agreed with Kelsen's propagation of the theory of functional concepts in relation to legal phenomena, of course, to the extent it was properly applied. Just as we know now that atoms do not have a tangible core, but consist of waves, which we can know of (or explain their "existence") only by the laws or relations that guide and determine them; so can neither positive law refer to tangible, substantive concepts, but have significance only in the interrelatedness between themselves and with the legal system as a whole.

Kelsen disagrees with the results of Cohen's legal theory, because it does not appear to exclude ethics completely from the realm of law, which Kelsen considers critical. Kelsen's theory is concerned with the cognition of law as law, however, the concept of force Kelsen adopts for that purpose (to instigate or trigger the so-called hypothetical basic norm) assumes a physical character-ristic (as is the case with Kant). Law is assumed to be law (with an independent claim of validity) through the basic norm, because of the expression of the intent of an original authority to enforce law's normative claims. It is ultimately power that guides law, and law that follows the developing scenes of power.[100] Therewith, Kelsen has intentionally introduced a

---

99 See: Kelsen, H., *Das Verhältnis von Staat und Recht im Lichte der Erkenntniskritik*, Zeitschrift für öffentliches Recht, Volume 2, 1921, pp. 453–510, especially: pp. 464–467; reprinted in: Klecatsky, 1968, pp. 95–148, especially: pp. 105–108; cf. Kelsen, H., *The Pure Theory of Law, 'Labandism', and Neo-Kantianism. A Letter to Renato Treves*, in: Paulson, 1998, pp. 169–175; here: p. 174. See also: Marck, 1925, who achieved different results from Kelsen, while also taking Cassirer's *Substance and Function*-book as his conceptual starting-point. Cf. the law and morality chapter of Krois, 1987.

100 See: Kersting, W., *Neukantianistische Rechtsbegründung. Rechtsbegriff und richtiges Recht bei Cohen, Stammler und Kelsen*, in: Alexy, 2002, pp. 23–68; here: p. 63. Roermund, 2002, argues that the supreme norm sets a norm for norm-setting, and that the former cannot be done without the

volitional component to his theory of law,[101] and created a new problem, *i.e.*, the problem of distinguishing the power of an authority (necessary to experience law as law according to Kelsen) from the phenomenon of law itself. With the new problem Kelsen therewith (unavoidably) introduces, he might cut the proverbial Gordian knot, but as a result he does not satisfactorily address the problem of the relation between law and ethics, between positive law and the ideals of law. The question Cohen asked and with which Cassirer also engaged himself was rather: What is the persuasive character of law so as to induce us to act accordingly and willingly? Only the persuasive character of law explains the binding force of law and makes law a viable and attractive alternative to sheer force. If law was not accompanied by the power of persuasion and was not an essential element of it, law would not only be indistinguishable from sheer external force to make us act as commanded by a sovereign, as the legal positivist thinker John Austin famously contended, but, strictly logically speaking, the sovereign would also have to commit himself to the difficult if not impossible task of constantly enforcing and threatening to enforce its commands. Law as the reign of persuasion in this regard is not only more economical for the sovereign, but, moreover, it is also more responsive to the subjects of law as autonomous or intellectually and morally mature persons.

Cassirer could not have agreed with Kelsen's pure theory of law or with Kelsen's representation of Cohen's legal theory,

---

simultaneous exercise of legal reasoning; the basic norm is a form of focusing, rather than cutting off legal argumentation. This line of argument comes very close to Cassirer's position relative to his employment of the basis phenomenon. However, the act of setting the supreme norm, for Kelsen, is reserved only for an authority that expresses its intent to use force, and is directed mainly to legal officials. What Roermund calls à la Panofsky (1991) the problem of "the vanishing point of law," we have anticipated as the functional nature of law, and have expressed the problem (of the infinite questionability of law) most fundamentally in the Goethean basis phenomenon, *i.e.* the basis phenomenon of Law.

101 For the radical decisionist character of Kelsen's legal hermeneutics, which in essence is characterized by an arbitrary act, *i.e.* as a volitional and not a cognitive, act for Kelsen, see: Brugmans, E., *Rechterlijke ongehoorzaamheid als norm. Kelsens visie op de taak van de rechter*, in: De Groot-van Leuwen, 2006, pp. 269–289; here: pp. 286 ff.

but on different grounds than (the later) Gustav Radbruch would disagree with Kelsen.[102] Radbruch criticized the positivist theory of law in the Kelsenian sense of the term by claiming that positivist theory had rendered jurists vulnerable and defenseless to an authoritarian regime. While before the Nazis came to power Radbruch had given prevalence to legal determinacy as essential for legality, after the Second World War, Radbruch experienced an about-face and asserted that justice was the prime element of legality. As a result, he formulated the so-called injustice thesis, which basically entails that a grave injustice of a law renders such law invalid as law.[103] A law that is at such apparent and grave conflict with the principles of justice and the normative demands of humanity looses, according to Radbruch, its validity.[104] Law enacted by the sovereign legislator enjoys some *prima facie* deference as to its validity even when it does not do justice or benefits (part of) the populace, however, there is a limit to what the people may endure because of the injustice of a statute, according to Radbruch. When "*the conflict between statute and justice reaches such an intolerable degree* (...), *the statute, as 'flawed law' ('unrichtiges Recht'), must yield to justice.* (...) *Where there is not even an attempt at justice, where equality, the core of justice, is deliberately betrayed in the issuance of positive law, then the statute is not merely 'flawed law', it lacks completely the very nature of law.*"[105] Radbruch's about-face is often explained as a turn toward natural law theory away from positivism;[106] however, more modest interpreters have stressed

---

[102] The following does not purport to give an exhaustive treatment of the legal theory of Radbruch or of his critique of positivism, in particular in the Kelsenian mold. It merely sets the stage for a possible critique from a Cassirerean perspective, by traversing roads already paved.

[103] Edmond Cahn in his *The Sense of Injustice* would not go so far as to deny legal validity to an unjust law.

[104] See: Radbruch, G., *Five Minutes of Legal Philosophy* (1945), Oxford Journal of Legal Studies, Volume 26, 2006, pp. 13–15; and idem, *Statutory Lawlessness and Supra-Statutory Law* (1946), Oxford Journal of Legal Studies, Volume 26, 2006, pp. 1–11.

[105] Cited by: Paulson, 2006, p. 26.

[106] This reading has importantly been encouraged by Herbert Hart's Oliver Wendell Holmes Lecture at Harvard Law School, April 30, 1957; see:

the claim that Radbruch was much more convinced of and concerned with the normative claims of human rights.[107] As is asserted below, Cassirer would have agreed with Radbruch's concern in relation to the normative claim of human rights, but, moreover, he would make that concern into the very driving forces of law.[108]

II. CONCLUSION

Cassirer also enters into the debate about the relation between morality and law. However, in contrast to neo-Kantian jurisprudence, he maintained that the dichotomy between positive law and legal values, ideals, or principles – what could be called here normative demands of humanity – could not be brought to a conclusion, not even through the transcendental method. The antithesis between written law and unwritten law was one of the driving forces of law as early as Plato's Republic, according to Cassirer.[109] For Cassirer the antithesis rather epitomizes the infinite task of jurisprudence to bring the tension between these both indispensable and unavoidable elements of law, the positive and the ideal or the particular and the universal of law, more comprehensible and their synthesis more intelligible. Law is a symbolic form insofar as it expresses or posits the ideals of law in some concrete act of positing. Law as an ideal necessarily has to find expression in something concrete, for example a statute or a judicial opinion, to have a formative effect on the cosmos or universe of law. Conversely, positive law distinguishes itself from mere (state) power with autonomous claims of its own only insofar

---

Paulson, 2006, p. 18. This view is still wide-spread and little contested among legal scholars; see, e.g. Horwitz, 1997, p. 582.

[107] Cf. Paulson, 2006, pp. 39–40; Paulson, 1995, pp. 489–500; Mertens, 2003, especially pp. 283–286; and Jansen, C.J., *Gustav Radbruch*, in: Cliteur, 1992, pp. 71–89; especially: pp. 81–83.

[108] For Radbruch's position vis-à-vis Kelsen, another aspect of the constellation, see Haldemann, 2005.

[109] See: Ernst Cassirer, *Die Idee des Rechts und ihre Entwicklung in der modernen Philosophie*, Ernst Cassirer Papers, Essays and Lectures, Beinecke Rare Book & Manuscripts Library, Coll. No. GEN 98, Series No. II, Box No. 43, Folder No. 845, p. 35.

as it is able to persuade us that it reflects our own ethical maxims and principles about what the law ought to demand and what it accordingly may expect from us.

Eliminating the dichotomy between positive law and the ideals of law would not only render the philosophy of law obsolete and our experience of law (as being just or unjust, effective or ineffective for the cause of justice, and so forth) less meaningful, but it would also trump the development of law into higher levels of objectivity and universality. Cassirer does not contend to have solved the millennial question of the conceptual separation of law and morals. If he has a solution, it is only to recognize that the divide between law and ethics is not to be considered as a mere gap between the symbolic forms of law and ethics. He agrees with the positivists that law and ethics are two separate, autonomous realms. However, the distance between the two fields does not consist of a vacuum or a clear neutral line; rather there exists a constant tension and competition between the two fields to cover as many cultural phenomena as possible. Law and ethics are separate realms, but they interact with one another, because both claim their validity upon the individual in its own way. The tension between the various symbolic forms, for example law and ethics, are resolved only in the concrete acting individual, and those actions are evaluated differently by each symbolic form. Moreover, the tension between positive law on the one hand and ethical claims on the other is an issue that gives contemporary jurisprudence its *raison d'être*. While law is the prime academic concern of jurisprudence it has also to investigate its relationship with ethics to explain its autonomous view of the world. *While religion posed the greatest challenge for the autonomy of law since the classical and traditional natural law era, and history dominated the minds of the nineteenth-century positivists, the twentieth century has put to the fore ethics or morality as the main challenge to jurisprudence.*

Law as symbolic form does not answer the question of whether the injustice of a law renders such law invalid legally. That is a matter of judicial review, which is resolved within the practical workings of the law. Rather what it attempts to portray is that in the case of an injustice (a discrepancy with the ethical claims or the demands of humanity) of a legal system, the laws of such a legal system lose their meaning as being law in terms of what they ought to represent of ethical principles and maxims from the perspective of its subjects. In the face of an injustice, real or perceived, the subject of law will no longer find law sufficient for explaining his world, and he will look for alternative ways of making sense of his world. Some will look into history, others will find inspiration in poetry, and yet another will find support in morality to voice his opposition.[110] Law stands at the center of culture; in a sense it is the culmination of culture, *i.e.*, when it voices the highest standards and normative claims of culture. Ethical principles are external to law and, although they are important for the development of law, cannot render law invalid. At most, they can make law less appealing as a symbolic form, because of incongruencies with ethical developments, and induce it to reformulate itself. On the flip side, though, when law loses its meaning and force as a symbolic form, this cannot diminish our ethical responsibilities, because ethics for Cassirer is an autonomous form of its own.

In addition, Cassirer does not ground law and state on a social contract, but rather recognizes that as to the problem of the social contract, especially natural law theory had explicated what is at the root of the binding character of law, *i.e.*, that we consider ourselves bound to (spoken or written) language. With the help of language in the symbolic sense, with the objectifying function of language, the human overcomes the mythical aspects of life. Symbolic language itself becomes the most important cause of how, what the natural lawyers would have said, the human overcomes the state of nature, by creating a cosmos out of a chaos. In a similar way, out of the chaos of possible actions in human life through law we create a world of actions, and constitute social life that progressively achieves higher levels of determination.

Finally, social life is never a mere given, but achieved only by the active participation of its members. In social participation, in the active involvement of the "I" with a "Thou," the "I" first reaches its individuality. Cassirer fundamentally

---

110 I cannot elaborate here on the phenomenon of civil disobedience.

agrees with Cohen's understanding of the ethical form of (social) life, but he also goes further by exploring not only the conditions for the possibility of the ethical form of social life – that Cassirer localizes in the symbolic nature of the human being – but also by explicating how the "I" progressively relates to a "Thou" in a plurality of symbolic forms. The road to freedom for the individual is opened when the individual sets out to traverse all the configurations life has to offer.

CONCLUSION TO PART II

In this part we have elaborated on Law as Symbolic Form. For that purpose we have first given an elaboration and interpretation of the philosophy of symbolic forms. We concluded that the philosophy of symbolic forms constitutes an ethical project, and insofar as we can take ethics as the discipline that investigates and prescribes rules for how one ought to act to one another, that the philosophy of symbolic forms investigates the conditions for the possibility of ethicality. Through the philosophy of symbolic forms Cassirer makes clear how the "I" progressively relates to a "Thou" through the various symbolic forms. Through symbolic forms we create distinct worlds for ourselves in which we can interchange and maintain common meanings with one another. In the recognition of the other as a meaningful being, we come to understand our own individual humanity. Individuality therefore can never be a form of self-proclaimed importance or an exaltation of the ego, but is always the product of interaction with others, and can be grasped only as in a "snapshot."

By considering the humanity of another person, we discover our own individual humanity. Human dignity is not something beyond our comprehension, because it consists of the fact that we relate to one another as human beings (through various symbolic forms). This is best expressed whenever we enter into a debate with one another. The process of progressively relating to another person can be disrupted, though, by mythical perceptions that stress physiognomy and emotionality. First when we manage to overcome our mythical perception of the world are we in the position to raise ourselves to the specifically human symbolic level, and engage in activities such as promising. Symbolical language directed to the future is an essential factor (as well) for any form of constitutional and legislative activity.

Law is a symbolic form, and accordingly starts at the mythical level, but reaches to the representative stage when it discovers the sentence as its most sophisticated form of expression, and finally finds its symbolic expression paradigmatically in human rights (as safeguarded by the courts). Law as a symbolic system sustains itself through its own conceptual rigor, but if it does not want to degenerate into a mere formalistic system it must progressively seek higher forms of universality and objectivity. Human rights keep a legal system anthropocentric, and compel a legal system to take into consideration that it ultimately has to persuade *individual* subjects, and therefore make explicit that it is always in need of arguments or justification for that purpose.[1] Human rights are a bulwark for a legal system to treat its subjects as individuals, because the law ultimately always concerns the concrete and active individual. The idea of human rights stands as a pole star, so to speak, and inspires legal systems to consider fundamental norms of humanity.

We have explained humanity not as a substantial entity that holds together all human beings in some concrete bond with one another, but as a functional unity. All human beings display the capacity of symbolization, *i.e.*, they understand and create meaning. Legislative, executive, and judicial action therefore must always be accompanied by a degree of persuasiveness, which poses a limitation on state power and action. The degree in which the subjects of a polity are treated as symbolic beings that are capable of independent and individual moral judgment, at the same time signifies the democratic maturity of such a polity. The rule of law is only another expression of the same moral spirit that demands that a democracy is strong because of its persuasive power and not persuasive because of its material force.[2] Conversely, it demands from individuals a unity, completeness, and inner consistency of character. Not only does that entail that the individual must demand that nothing should be done in its name that could not withstand the scrutiny of its individual reason and moral convictions, but also that in dealing with private parties the individual takes into consideration the symbolic nature of the other. That has pragmatic but also fundamentally ethical significance.

We have explained the concept of law as a legal function. The legislator acts in such a way that it demands from the totality of the people nothing more than that the people could have demanded from itself out of ethical principles and maxims. The

---

1 The level of judicial scrutiny required in the non-economic, individual sphere is usually higher than in the economic sphere of voluntary transactions.

2 Cf. Cahn, E.N., *The Democratic Resolution*, in: Cahn, 1967, pp. 462–465; here: p. 465.

legislator envisions not a single event or a class of events, but foremost a series of events that it intends to cover with the legal rule or function. Even in analogical reasoning in law the legal function operates as the measure by which we compare the similarity of various cases. Legal rules set standards to which one could and ought to have assented to, or, in other words, for how one should act. Legal validity accrues from an inner act of persuasion that something is law, *i.e.*, something to which one ought to abide by. This process of extolling the meaning of law (as being law), we have explained through Cassirer's notion of symbolic form. Legal meaning is not merely imposed from without or above, but it is produced by an inner energy of the mind as a result of which we adhere internally to the meaning accompanying a legal act, and is expressed by our outward actions. To explain this process we have alluded to the concept of symbolic pregnance in law, and furthermore, the basis phenomenon of Law, *i.e.*, the basic assumption that there is such thing as law as a unitary phenomenon – but only so if we further explore the symbolic or meaning structures underlying law.

In addition, in this part we have focused on Cassirer's relation to neo-Kantian jurisprudence. We have explicated the interconnectedness of his philosophy with neo-Kantian philosophy and maintained that Cassirer moved above and beyond neo-Kantianism with his symbolic theory of culture and man. We have seen that with his theory of the symbol he distinguishes himself from neo-Kantian philosophy, and with his theory of the symbolic nature of man distinguishes Law as Symbolic Form from neo-Kantian jurisprudence in general and the legal philosophy of Hermann Cohen in particular.

The inevitable futurity of legal rules Cohen acknowledged, giving Cassirer the opportunity to formulate his so-called linguistic concepts of the field of actions. Just as the infinitesimal method results in the functional theory of knowledge for Cassirer, now, in the field of jurisprudence, it leads to the insight that legal concepts and rules are characterized foremost by functionality. The legal rule is a function that takes the form of a question directed into the future that already anticipates its triggering events. In this respect it is not merely coincidental that ethics and law converge with one another, because the formulation of the legal rule or function is informed by ethical motives, and accordingly, when law transforms ethical claims into a legal function, the ambit of that function will be determined by its formulation, *i.e.*, when we anticipate, determine and assess what it intends to cover.

Moreover, Law as Symbolic Form provides a basis for human rights because of its autonomous position and independent claims of validity. Law derives its binding force from its reasonableness or rather its persuasive character, an insight developed by Hermann Cohen and carried further by Ernst Cassirer. As we saw, Cassirer searches for a symbolic explanation of the persuasive character of law. The answer may seem obvious, that the persuasiveness of the phenomenon of law depends upon the fact that we can understand its meaning, but only so if we disregard the many hurdles, such as physiognomic and emotional factors, the mythic perception of expression poses. Moreover, through his philosophy of symbolic forms Cassirer explains how we can attach meaning to something as law, *i.e.*, internally adhere to it as law. Equally, Cassirer takes up the theory of the social contract, as it was developed by Hermann Cohen, and gives it a symbolic dimension, not only to lay bare the conditions for the possibility of the contractual obligation and method, but also to elucidate its connection to human dignity.

Cassirer cannot agree with Kelsen's foundation of law in a basic norm. Kelsen's basic norm, as a result of which we regard something as law, is ultimately related to a physical notion of force. Cassirer is rather interested in a moral notion of force, or, how he would term it through his philosophy of symbolic forms, how we are made to internally adhere to the meaning of law (as law). It requires a mental activity and entails an act of inner persuasion, because it is brought about by man himself. For that purpose we have finally and foundationally ultimately referred to the Goethean unitary concept of the basis phenomenon in relation to law, *i.e.*, the basis phenomenon of Law. Whenever we engage in legal work, *i.e.*, expound the meaning of law, by adhering to, interpreting or rejecting it, we necessarily presuppose the basis phenomenon of Law. From the presupposition that there is such thing as law, to which we may relate all concrete legal provisions and cases, we derive the possibility of legal meaning. It is only by further analysis that we may discern more to the full in what sense some concrete act of the legislator or judiciary constitutes law. When we engage in such analysis we necessarily presuppose a notion of law as a basis phenomenon, and are in the position to encounter upon or call to our attention to such thing as law because of the basis phenomenon of Law.

Jurisprudence, according to Cassirer, is not merely the systematic, conceptual pursuance of ethics. They are separate domains for Cassirer, and both direct their claims differently on the individual. Whereas ethics concerns the motives of the individual, law ultimately achieves a cosmos for our world of outward actions. However, they are not separated by a neutral line or a vacuum. For law to have effect as a symbolic form it is necessary that it reflects the law in the mind of people, *i.e.*, that one could and ought to have assented to it out of ethical principles and maxims. The conceptual analysis of law goes hand to hand with its genetic account. Both ethics and law are products of, spring forth from the formative or symbolic powers of man, and although, as any other symbolism, they might confront us as something objective, *i.e.*, as part of reality that is beyond our immediate reach, ultimately we must always bring them to account to their very source: our independent and individual moral judgment.

PRIMARY LITERATURE

Ernst Cassirer

Leibniz' System in seinen wissenschaftlichen Grundlagen, Gesammelte Werke, Band 1, Felix Meiner Verlag, Hamburg (1902) 1998.

Der kritische Idealismus und die Philosophie des gesunden Menschenverstandes, philosophische Arbeiten, Volume 1, 1906.

Hönigswald, Richard, Dr. Phil. Et med. Beiträgezur Erkenntnistheorie und Methodenlehre (Rezension), Kanststudien, Volume 14, 1909, pp. 91–98.

Aristoteles und Kant, Kantstudien, Volume 16, 1911, pp. 431–447.

Freiheit und Form. Studien zur deutschen Geistesgeschichte, Gesammelte Werke Band 7, Felix Meiner Verlag, Hamburg (1916) 1998.

Hölderlin und der deutsche Idealismus, Logos, Internationale Zeitschrift für Philosophie der Kultur, Band 7, 1917/18, pp. 262–282.

Hölderlin und der deutsche Idealismus II, Logos, Internationale Zeitschrift für Philosophie der Kultur, Band 8, 1918/19, pp. 262–282.

Hermann Cohen und die Erneuerung der Kantischen Philosophie, Kantstudien, Bol. 17, Berlin, 1912, pp. 252–273.

The Philosophy of Symbolic Forms, Volume I, Language, tr. R. Manheim, Yale University Press, New Haven, 1953 (1923).

The Philosophy of Symbolic Forms, Volume II, Myth, tr. R. Manheim, Yale University Press, New Haven, 1955 (1925).

The Philosophy of Symbolic Forms, Volume III, Science, tr. R. Manheim, Yale University Press, New Haven, 1957 (1929).

Paul Natorp, Kantstudien, Volume 30, 1925, pp. 18–298.

Die Philosophie der Griechen von den Anfängen bis Platon, in: Dessoir, M., Lehrbuch der Philosophie, IM Verlag Ullstein, Berlin, 1925, pp. 7–139.

Individuum und Kosmos in der Philosophie der Renaissance (1927) 2, unveränderte Auflage, Wissenschatliche Buchgesellschaft, 1963.

Die Idee der republikanischen Verfassung, Rede zur Verfassungsfeier am 11. August 1928, Friederichsen, De Gruyter & Co. M.B.H., Hamburg, 1929.

Leibniz und Jungius, in: Meyer, A., Beiträge zur Jungius-Forschung, Paul Hartung Verlag, Hamburg, 1929, pp. 21–37.

Encyclopaedia Britannica, 14th edition, London/New York 1929. Volume 16, pp. 215–216 (Neo-Kantianism); Volume 18, pp. 991–993 (Rationalism); Bd. 21, pp. 500–502 (Substance); Volume 22, pp. 405–406 (Transcendentalism); Volume 22, pp. 522–524 (Truth).

Wandlungen der Staatsgesinnung und der Staatstheorie in der deutschen Geistesgeschichte, in: Enge Zeit. Spuren Vertriebener und Verfolgter der Hamburger Universität im Auditorium Maximum der Universität, Von-Melle-Park 23. Februar – 4. April 1991, Hg. von Angela Bottin unter der Mitarbeit von Rainer Nicolaysen, Hamburg, 1991.

Vom Wesen und Werden des Naturrechts, Zeitschrift für Rechtsphilosophie in Lehre und Praxis, Volume 6, No. 1, 1932, pp. 1–27.

Psychologie und Philosophie, Bericht über den XII. Kongreß der Deutschen Gesellschaft für Psychologie in Hamburg vom 12. – 16. April 1931, Jena, 1932, pp. 73–76.

Kant and the Problem of Metaphysics: Remarks on Heidegger's Interpretation of Kant, in: Gram, M.S. (ed. and tr.), Kant: Disputed Questions, Quadrangle Books, Chicago, 1967, pp. 131–157.

Die Sprache und der Aufbau der Gegenstandswelt, Bericht über den XII. Kongreß der Deutschen Gesellschaft für Psychologie in Hamburg vom 12. – 16. April 1931, Hrs. Gustav Kafka, Jena, 1932, pp. 134–145.

Die Philosophie der Aufklärung, J.C.B. Mohr Verlag (Paul Siebeck), Tübingen, 1932.

Formen und Formwandlungen des philosophischen Warheitsbegriff, in: Ernst Cassirer, Geist und Leben. Schriften zu den Lebensordnungen von Natur und Kunst, Geschichte und Sprache, Orth, E.W. (ed.) Orth, Reclam, Leipzig, 1993.

Le Lange et La Construction du Monde des Objets, Journal de Psychologie Normale et Pathologique, Volume 30, Paris, 1933, pp. 18–44.

Symbol, Technik, Sprache. Aufsätze aus den Jahren 1927–1933, Herausgegeben von E.W. Orth und J.M. Krois, Felix Meiner Verlag, Hamburg, 1985.

Inhalt und Umfang des Begrifss, Bemerkungen zu Konrad Marc-Wogau: Inhalt und Umfang des Begriffs, Theoria, A Swedish Journal of Philosophy and Psychology, Volume 2, 1936, pp. 206–232.

Naturalistische und humanistische Begründung der Kulturphilosophie, Göteborgs Kungl. Vetenskaps – och Vitterhets – Samhälles Handlingar. Femte foljden, Ser. A, Bd. 7, Nr. 3, 1939, pp. 1–28.

Zur Logik der Symbolbegriffs, Theoria, A Swedish Journal of Philosophy and Psychology, Volume 4, 1938, pp. 145–175.

Axel Hägerström – eine Studie zur Schwedischen Philosophie der Gegenwart, Göteborgs Högskolas Årsskrift, Göteborgs Högskolas Årsskrift, Elanders Boktryckeri Aktiebolag, Göteborg, 1939.

"Review of A. Cornelius Benjamin's An Introduction to the Philosophy of Science. New York: Macmillan, 1937," Lychnos. Upsala/Stockholm (1938), pp. 456–461.

Descartes. Lehre – Persönlichkeit – Wirkung, Bermann-Fischer Verlagm, Stockholm, 1939.

Die Philosophie im XVII. Und XVIII. Jahrhundert, Actualités Scientifiques et Industrielles 841, Philosophie Chronique Annuele publiée par L'Institut International de Collaboration Philosophique V, Paris, 1939.

Was ist "Subjektivismus?" (Vortrag gehalten im Philosophischen Verein in Stockholm am 23 Februar 1939), Theoria, A Swedish Journal of Philosophy and Psychology, Volume 5, Göteborg, 1939, pp. 111–140.

William Stern (Gestorben in Durham, North Carolina, am 27. März 1938), Zur Wiederkehr seines Todestages, Acta Psychologica, Amsterdam, 1940, pp. 1–15.

Neuere Kant-Literatur, Theoria, Volume 6, 1940, pp. 87–100.

William Stern. Zur Wiederkehr seines Todestages, Acta Psychologica, Volume 5, 1940, pp. 1–15.

Thorild und Herder, Theoria, A Swedish Journal of Philosophy and Psychology, Volume 7, Göteborg, 1941, pp.75–92.

Logos, Dike, Kosmos in der Entwicklung der Griechischen Philosophie, Göteborgd Högskolas Arsskrift, Volume 47:6, 1941.

The Logic of the Humanities (Zur Logik der Kulturwissenschaften. Fünf Studien, in: Göteborgs Högskolas Arsskrift, Volume 48, Heft 1, 1942, pp. 1–139), tr. C.S. Howe, Yale University Press, New Haven, 1961.

The Influence of Language upon the Development of Scientific Thought, The Journal of Philosophy, Volume 39, No. 12, 1942, pp. 309–3327.

Giovanni Pico della Mirandola, A Study in the History of Renaissance Ideas, Journal of the History of Ideas, Volume 3, 1942, pp. 123–144; 319–346.

Galileo: A New Science and a New Spirit, The American Scholar, Volume 12, No. 1, 1942–1943, pp. 5–19.

Some Remarks on the Question of the Originality of the Renaissance, Journal of the History of Ideas, Volume 4, 1943, pp. 49–56.

Newton and Leibniz, The Philosophical Review, Volume 52, 1943, pp. 366–391.

Hermann Cohen, 1842–1918, Social Research, Volume 10, No. 2, May 1943, pp. 219–232.

Force and Freedom: Remarks on the English Edition of Jacob Burckhardt's "Reflections on History," The American Scholar, Volume 13, No. 1, 1943–1944, pp. 407–417.

An essay on man: an introduction to a philosophy of human culture, Yale University Press, New Haven, 1944.

Galileo's Platonism, in: Ashley Montagu, M.F. (ed.), Studies and Essays in the History of Science and Learning, offered in homage to George Sarton on the Occasion of his Sixtieth Birthday 31 August 1944, H. Schumann, New York, 1946, pp. 279–297.

The Concept of Group and the Theory of Perception, Philosophy and Phenomenological Research, Volume 5, 1944–1945, pp. 1–35.

Rousseau, Kant and Goethe, tr. James Gutmann, Paul Oskar Kristeller, and John Hermann Randall, jr., Princeton University Press, Princeton, 1945.

Ficino's Place in Intellectual History (Book Review), Journal of the History of Ideas, Volume 6, 1945, pp. 483–501.

Structuralism in Modern Linguistics, Word, Journal of the Linguistic Circle of New York, devoted to the study of linguistic science in all its aspects, Volume 1, No. 2, 1945, pp. 99–120.

The Myth of the State, Yale University Press, New Haven, 1945.

Thomas Manns Goethe-Bild, Eine Studie über Lotte in Weimar, The Germanic Review, Volume 20, 1945, pp. 167–194.

Albert Schweitzer as Critic of Nineteenth-Century Ethics, in: Roback, A.A., The Albert Schweitzer Jubilee Book, Sci-Art Publishers, Cambridge, Massachusetts, 1946, pp. 241–257.

Wesen und Wirkung des Symbolbegriffs, Bruno Cassirer, Oxford, 1956.

Über die Wurde des Menschen von Pico della Mirandola, in: Agora. Eine humanistische Schriftenreihe. Die Schriftenreihe erscheint in Verbindung mit dem Ludwig-Georgs-Gymnasium, Darmstadt. Jg. 5. Nr. 12 (Juni 1959), pp. 48–61.

Philosophie und exakte Wissenschaft. Kleine Schriften, eingeleitet und erläutert von W. Krampf, Vitorio Klosterman, frankfurt am Main, 1969.

Mythic, Aesthetic and Theoretical Space, translated by D.P. Verene and L.H. Foster, Man and World, Volume 2, 1969, pp. 3–17.

Symbol, Myth, and Culture. Essays and Lectures of Ernst Cassirer 1935–1945, edited by D.P. Verene, Yale University Press, New Haven and London, 1979.

Kant's Life and Thought (B. Cassirer, Berlin, 1921) translated by J. Haden, introduction by S. Körner, Yale University Press, New Haven and London, 1981.

The Philosophy of Symbolic Forms, Volume 4, The Metaphysics of Symbolic Forms, Krois, J.M. and Verene, D.P. (eds.), tr. Krois, J.M., Yale University Press, New Haven and London, 1996.

SECONDARY LITERATURE

Adams, D., Metaphors for Mankind: The Development of Hans Blumenberg's Anthropological Metaphorology, Journal of the History of Ideas, Volume 52, 1991, pp. 152–166.

Adriaanse, H.J., De uitstraling van Hermann Cohen in het interbellum: Cassirer, Rosenzweig, Scholem, Nederlands Theologisch Tijdschrift, Volume 47, 1993, pp. 292–302.

Ankersmit, F.R., Ernst Cassirer als Cultuurfilosoof, Groniek, Volume 27, 1994, pp. 67–80.

Bast, R.A., Cassirers Rousseau-Interpretation, Romanistische Zeitschrift für Literaturgeschichte (Cahiers d'Histoire des Littératures Romanes), Volume 15, 1991, pp. 352–385.

Bauch, B., Cassirer, Ernst, Der kritische Idealismus und die Philosophie des, "Gesunden menschenverstandes" (Recension), Kant-Studien, Volume 11, 1906, pp. 463–466.

Baumgardt, D., Ernst Cassirer und die moderne Wissenschaftslage, Zeitschrift für Religions – und Geistesgeschichte, Volume 11, 1959, pp. 275–279.

Bayer, T.I., Socratic Self-Knowledge and the Philosophy of Symbolic Forms, http://www.pdcnet.org/pdf/bayer.pdf (last visited: September 18, 2006).

Bellquist, J.E., Mythic Consciousness: Cassirer's Theories and Strindberg's Practice, Mosaic, Volume 20, 1987, pp. 71–81.

Bidney, D., Human Nature and the Cultural Process, American Anthropologist, New Series, Volume 49, 1947, pp. 375–399.

Bidney, D., Myth, Symbolism, and Truth, The Journal of American Folklore, Volume 68, 1955, pp. 379–392.

Blumenberg, Wirklichkeiten, in denen wir leben: Aufsätze und eine Rede, Reclam, Stuttgart, 1981.

Brameld, T., Philosophical Anthropology: The Educational Significance of Ernst Cassirer, Harvard Educational Review, Volume 26, 1956, property, pp. 207–232.

Brandis, C., Bakhtin, Cassirer and Symbolic Forms, Radical Philosophy, Volume 85, No. 8, 1997, pp. 20–27.

Brandis, C., Two Routes "to Conreteness" in the Work of the Bakhtin Circle, Journal of the History of Ideas, Volume 63, 2002, pp. 521–537.

Braun, H.J., Holzhey, H., Orth, E.W., Über Ernst Cassirers Philosophie der symbolische Formen, Suhrkamp, Frankfurt am Main, 1988.

Breckon, G.L., Cassirer's Genealogy of the "I," Idealistic Studies, Volume 1, 1971, pp. 278–291.

Buesch, Th.A., The Literary Genre as Symbolic Form, The Journal of Aesthetics and Art Criticism, Volume 31, 1973, pp. 525–530.

Bundgaard, P.F., Ernst Cassirer's Theory of Perception – Toward a Geometry of Experience, in: Foss, G., Kasa, E. (eds.), Forms of Knowledge and Sensibility – Ernst Cassirer and the Human Sciences, Nordic Academic Press, Kristiansand, 2002.

Cahoone, L.E., The Interpretation of Galilean Science: Cassirer Contrasted with Husserl and Heidegger, Studies in History and Philosophy of Science, Volume 17, 1986, pp. 1–21.

Cassirer, T., Mein Leben mit Ernst Cassirer, Gerstenberg Verlag, Hildesheim, 1981.

Cohen, R.A., Humanism and Anti-Humanism: Levinas, Cassirer and Heidegger, Conférence au Còngres Emmanuel Levinas à Jérusalem, 20–23 mai 2002.

Conley, P., Das mythische Denken bei Ernst Cassirer nach der "Philosophie der symbolischen Formen", Abschlußarbeit zur Erlangung des Magister Artium im Fachbereich Philosophie, Universität Franfurt, August 1993.

Corver, G., Een moment uit de geschiedenis van de wijsgerige antropologie der 20e eeuw, Kant-Studien, Volume 38, 1984, pp. 105–111.

Cristaudo, W., Heidegger and Cassirer: Being, Knowing and Politics, Kant-Studien, Volume 82, 1991, pp. 469–483.

Deuser, H., Moxter, M. (Hrsg.), Rationalität der Religion und Kritik der Kultur: Hermann Cohen und Ernst Cassirer, Religion in der Moderne Bd. 9, Echter, Würzburg, 2002.

Dews, P., Imagination and the Symbolic: Castoriadis and Lacan, Constellations, An International Journal of Critical and Democratic Theory, Volume 9, No. 4, December 2002, pp. 516–521.

Dosch, H.G., Ernst Mach und Ernst Cassirer, Internationale Zeitschrift für Philosophie, 1997, pp. 189–204.

Doyon, S., Joël Gaubert, La Science politique d'Ernst Cassirer. Pour une refondaton symbolique de la raison pratique contre le mythe politique contemporarain (Recension), Laval théologique et philosophique, Volume 54, 1998, pp. 199–200.

Dreher, J., The Symbol and the Theory of the Life-World: "The Transcendence of the Life-World and Their Overcoming by Signs and Symbols", Human Studies, Volume 26, 2003, pp. 141–163.

Eekert, G. van, 'Synthesis Speciosa' en de taak van de filosofie. Cassirer en Heidegger voor het tribunaal van de Kritik der reinen Vernunft, in: B. Raymaekers (ed.), Gehelen en fragmenten. De vele gezichten van de filosofie. Acta van de veertiende filosofiedag te Leuven, Universitaire Pers, Leuven, 1993, pp. 230–234.

Eekert, G. van, Ernst Cassirer. Philosophie der symbolischen Formen, Hermeneutische vernieuwing als voortzetting van de kritisch-idealistische traditie, in: Boey, K., Cools, A., Leilich, J., Oger, E. (eds.), Ex Libris van de filosofie in de 20ste eeuw. Deel 1: Van 1900 tot 1950, Acco, Amersfoort, 1997, pp. 125–144.

Erickson, S.A., Cassirer's Dialectic. A Critical Discussion, Idealistic Studies, Volume 4, 1974, pp. 251–266.

Ettelt, W., Der Mythos als symbolische Form. Zu Ernst Cassirers Mythosinterpretation, Philosophische Perspektiven, Volume 4, 1972, pp. 59–70.

Eubanks, C.L., Petrakis, P.A., Reconstructing the World: Albert Camus and the Symbolization of Experience, The Journal of Politics, Volume 61, 1999, pp. 293–312.

Feige, M., Rescuing the Person from the Symbol: "Peace Now" and the Ironies of Modern Myth, History and Memory, Volume 11, 1999, pp. 141–168.

Ferrari, M., Cassirer und der Raum. Sechs Variationen über ein Thema, Internationale Zeitschrift für Philosophie, 1997, pp. 167–188.

Ferrari, M., Ernst Cassirer. Stationen einer philosophischer Biographie. Von der Marburger Schule zur Kulturphilosophie. Aus dem Italienischen übersetz von M. Lauschke, Felix Meiner Verlag, Cassirer–Forschungen, Bd. 11, Hamburg, 2003.

Fetz, R.L., Genetische Semiologie? Symboltheorie im Ausgang von Ernst Cassirer und Jean Piaget, Freiburger Zeitschrift für Philosophie und Theologie, 28. Band, 1981, pp. 434–470.

Fetz, R.L., Whitehead, Cassirer, Piaget. Drei Denker – ein gemeinsames Paradigma, Salzburger Theologische Zeitschrift, Volume 3, 1999, pp. 145–168.

Fischer, P., Empfindungsausdrücke verstehen. Konvergenzen in den Ansätzen von Cassirer und Wittgenstein, Dialektik, 2001, No. 1, pp. 33–51.

Flitner, W., Bötticher, E., Ernst Cassirer zum Gedächtnis. Rede auf Ernst Cassirer, Im Selbstverlag der Universität Hamburg, 1955.

Franke, W., Metaphor and the Making of Sense: The Contemporary Metaphor Renaissance, Philosophy and Rhetoric, Volume 33, 2000, pp. 137–153.

Frede, D., Schmücker, R. (Hrsg.), Ernst Cassirers Werk und Wirkung. Kultur und Philosophie, Wissenschaftliche Buchgesellschaft, Darmstadt, 1997.

Friedman, M., Language and Living Speech, Philosophy Today, Volume 13, 1969, pp. 43–46.

Friedman, M., A Parting of the Ways. Carnap, Cassirer, and Heidegger, Open Court, Chicago and La Salle, Illinois, 2002.

Friedman, M., Carnap, Cassirer, and Heidegger: The Davos Disputation and Twentieth Century Philosophy, European Journal of Philosophy, Volume 10, No. 3, December 2002, pp. 263–271.

Friedman, M., Ernst Cassirer and the Philosophy of Science, www.nd.edu/~hps/Friedman=Cassirer.doc, 2002 (last visited: September 18, 2006).

Frohss, R., Bemerkungen zur philosophisch-idealistischen Sprachauffassung Cassirers, Zeitschrift für Phonetik, Sprachwissenschaft und Kommunikations-Forschung, Volume 29, 1976, pp. 526–528.

Gadol, E.T., The Idealistic Foundations of Cultural Anthropology: Vico, Kant and Cassirer, Journal for the History of Philosophy, Volume 12, 1974, pp. 207–225.

Gay, P., The Social History of Ideas: Ernst Cassirer and After, in: Wolff, K.H. and Moore, B., Jr. (eds.), The Critical Spirit, essays in honor of Herbert Marcuse, Beacon Press, Boston, 1967, pp. 106–120.

Gay, P., Weimar Culture. The Outsider as Insider, Secker & Warburg, London, 1968.

Gilliam, H., The Dialectics of Realism and Idealism in Modern Historiographic Theory, History and Theory, Volume 15, 1976, pp. 231–256.

Glenn, J.D. Jr., Kant's Theory of Symbolism, in: Andrew, J.R. (ed.), Knowledge and Value. Essays in Honor of Harold N. Lee, Tulane Studies in Philosophy, Volume 21, 1972, pp. 13–21.

Goudsblom, J., Elias and Cassirer, Sociology and Philosophy, Theory, Culture & Society, Volume 12, 1995, pp. 121–126.

Gordon, P.E., Science, Finitude, and Infinity: Neo-Kantianism and the Birth of Existentialism, Jewish Social Studies, Volume 6, 1999, pp. 30–53.

Gram, M.S. (ed. and tr.), Kant: Disputed Questions, Quadrangle Books, Chicago, 1967.

Grassi, E., Can Rhetoric Provide a New Basis for Philosophizing? The Humanist Tradition, Philosophy and Rhetoric, Volume 16, 1983, pp. 1–18, and pp. 75–97.

Gross, S.W., Felix Aestheticus und Animal Symbolicum. Alexander G. Baumgarten – die "vierte Quelle" der Philosophie Ernst Cassirers? Deutsche Zeitschrift für Philosophie, Volume 49, 2001, pp. 275–298.

Grube, G., Repräsentation. Skizze für einen relationalen Repräsentationsbegriff unter kritischer Bezugnahme auf Ernst Cassirer und Nelson Goodman, www.dissertation.de, Berlin, 2002.

Gumpel, L., The Essence of 'Reality' as a Construct of Language, Foundations of Language, Volume 11, 1974, pp. 167–185.

Günzler, C., Späte Begegnung: Ernst Cassirer und Albert Schweitzer. Biographische Anmerkungen zur deutschen Kulturphilosophie, Zeitschrift für philosophische Forschung, Volume 49, 1995, pp. 312–319.

Gusfield, J.R., Michalowicz, J., Secular Symbolism: Studies of Ritual, Ceremony, and the Symbolic Order in Modern Life, Annual Review of Sociology, Volume 10, 1984, pp. 417–435.

Haaksma, H.W.H., Cassirer als filosoof van de techniek, Filosofie, Volume 8, 1998, No. 5, pp. 36–43.

Habermas, J., Die befreiende Kraft der symbolischen Formgebung. Ernst Cassirers humanistische Erbe und die Bibilothek Warburg, in: Ibid., Vom sinnlichen Eindruck zum symbolischen

Ausdruck. Philosophische Essays, Suhrkamp Verlag, Franfurt am Main, 1997, pp. 9–40.

Hackenesch, C., Selbst und Welt. Zur Metaphysik des Selbst bei Heidegger und Cassirer, Cassirer–Forschungen, Band 6, Meiner Verlag, Hamburg, 2001.

Hamburg, C.H., Kant, Cassirer and the concept of space, Tulane Studies in Philosophy, Volume 3, 1964, pp. 89–111.

Hamburg, C.H., A Cassirer–Heidegger Seminar, Philosophy and Phenomenological Research, Volume 25, 1964, pp. 208–222.

Hanson, J., Nordin, S., Ernst Cassirer: The Swedish Years, Peter Lang, Bern [et al.], 2006.

Hartshorne, C., Freedom requires indeterminism and universal causality, Journal of Philosophy, Volume 55, 1958, pp. 793–811.

Hendel, C.W., Ernst Cassirer, Man and Teacher, Philosophy and Phenomenological Research, Volume 6, 1945, pp. 156–159.

Heusen, B. van, Jakob von Uexküll and Ernst Cassirer, Semiotica, Volume 134, 2001, pp. 275–292.

Ihmig, K.-N., Cassirers Begriff von Objektivät im Lichte der Wissenschaftsauffasungen des ausgehenden 19. Jahrhunderts, Philosophia Naturalis, Volume 30, 1993, pp. 28–62.

Innis, R.E., Perception, Interpretation and the Signs of Art, The Journal of Speculative Philosophy, Volume 15, 2001, pp. 20–32.

Itzkoff, S., The Sources of Cultural Pluralism, Eductional Theory, Volume 26, 1976, pp. 231–232.

Itzkoff, S.W., Ernst Cassirer: Scientific Knowledge and the Concept of Man, University of Notre Dame Press, Notre Dame and London, 1971.

Jenkins, I., Logical Positivism, Critical Idealism, and the Concept of Man, The Journal of Philosophy, Volume 47, 1950, pp. 677–695.

Kaegi, D., Cassirer wider die Idealisten, Internationale Zeitschrift für Philosophie, 1997, pp. 313–322.

Kaegi, D., Rudolph, E. (Hg.), Cassirer–Heidegger, 70 Jahre Davos Disputation, Cassirer–Forschungen, Bd. 9, Felix Meiner Verlag, Hamburg, 2002.

Kaplan, B., An Approach to the Problem of Symbolic Representation: Nonverbal and Verbal, The Journal of Communication, Volume 11:2, 1961, pp. 52–62.

Kassab, E.S., Phenomenologies of Culture and Ethics: Ernst Cassirer, Alfred Schutz and the Tasks of a Philosophy of Culture, Human Studies, Volume 25, 2002, pp. 55–88.

Kautz, T., Ernst Cassirer und die Ethik. Eine Studie zur Philosophie der symbolischen Formen, Diss. Heinrich-Heine-Universität Düsseldorf, Dissertations Druck, Darmstadt, 1990.

Klein, K.L., What Was the Linguistic Turn? (Review Article), Clio. A Journal of Literature, History and the Philosophy of History, Volume 30, 2000, pp. 70–90.

Klibansky, R., Leroux, R. (eds.), Erinnerungen an ein Jahrhundert: Gespräche mit Georges Leroux, trans. By Petra Willim, Insel-Verlag, Frankfurt am Main, 2001.

Kniesche, H., Ernst Cassirer (1874–1945), in: M. Dascal, D. Gerhardus, K. Lorenz, G. Meggle (eds.), Sprachphilosophie. Ein internationales Handbuch zeitgenössischer Forschung, Volume 1, Walter de Gruyter, Berlin, New York, 1992, pp. 524–550.

Koehl, R., Cassirer's View of Myth and Symbol, The Monist, Volume 50, 1966, pp. 553–625.

Koestler, A., The Act of Creation, Pan Books LTD, London, 1966 (1964).

Kohn, H., The Study of Man. The Myth of the State. Examined in the Light of Recent History, Commentary; A Jewish Review, Volume 4, 1947, pp. 80–82.

Köhnke, K.C., The Rise of Neo-Kantianism. German Academic Philosophy between Idealism and Positivism, tr. R.J. Hollingdale [Entstehung und Aufstieg des Neukantianismus] Cambridge University Press, Cambridge, 1991.

Kraft, J., Cassirer. Die Philosophie der Aufklärung, Zeitschrift für öffentliches Recht, Volume 14, 1934, pp. 662–663.

Krois, J.M., Der Begriff des Mythos bei Ernst Cassirer, in: Poser, H. (Hrsg.), Philosophie und Mythos, De Gruyter, Berlin, 1979, pp. 199–217.

Krois, J.M., Peirce and Cassirer: The Philosophical Importance of a Theory of Signs, Proceedings of the C.S. Peirce Bicentennial International Congress, Graduate Studies Texax Tech University. No. 23, 1981, pp. 99–104.

Krois, J.M., Cassirer's Unpublished Critique of Heidegger, Philosophy and Rhetoric, Volume 16, No. 1, 1983, pp. 147–159.

Krois, J.M., Cassirer. Symbolic Forms and History, Yale University Press, New Haven, 1987.

Krois, J.M., Cassirer, Neo-Kantianism and Metaphysics, Revue de Metaphysique et de Morale, Volume, 97, 1992, pp. 437–453.

Krois, J.M., A Note about Philosophy and History: The Place of Cassirer's Erkenntnisproblem, Science in Context, Volume 9, 1996, pp. 191–194.

Krois, M., Aufklärung und Metaphysik. Zur Philosophie Cassirers und der Davoser Debatte mit Heidegger, Internationale Zeitschrift für Philosophie, 1997, pp. 273–289.

Krois, J.M., Ernst Cassirer's Idea of the Renaisance and the Beginnings of Modernity, in: Rudolph, E. (Hg.), Die Renaissance und ihr Bild in der Geschichte. Die Renaissance als erste Auklärung III, Mohr Siebeck, Tübingen, 1998, pp. 181–187.

Krois, J.M., Kultur als symbolischer Prozess. Philosophische Konsequenzen eines Paradigmenwechsels, Deutsche Zeitschrift für Philosophie, 2001, pp. 367–375.

Krois, J.M., What are images and what are they for? Museumspädagogischer Dienst Berlin, September 14, 2001, <http://www.kunst-als-wissenschaft.de/multimedia/KroisEn.pdf> (last visited: September 18, 2006).

Küker, A., Transformation, Reflexion und Heterogentität. Eine Untersuchung zu den Deutungsperspektiven der Kunst in der Philosophie Ernst Cassirers, Wissenschaftliche Buchgesellschaft, Darmstadt, 2002.

Kuypers, K., Ernst Cassirer (1874–1945), Algemeen Nederlands Tijdschrift voor Wijsbegeerte en Psychologie, Volume 48, 1956, pp. 177–184.

Langer, S.K., Philosophy in a New Key. A study in the Symbolism of Reason, Rite, and Art, 3rd print, Harvard University Press, Cambridge, Mass., 1960 (1942).

Lenneberg, E.H., A Note on Cassirer's Philosophy of Language, Philosophy and Phenomenological Research, Volume 15, 1954–1955, property, pp. 512–522.

Lipton, D.R., Ernst Cassirer. The Dilemma of a Liberal Intellectual in Germany 1914–1933, University of Toronto Press, Toronto, 1978.

Lübbe, H., Cassirer und die Mythen des 20. Jahrhunderts, Vanderhoeck & Ruprecht, Göttinge, 1975.

Lüddecke, D., Staat – Mythos – Politik, Überlegungen zum politischen Denken bei Ernst Cassirer, Spektrum Politikwissenschaft Bd. 22, Ergon, Würzburg, 2003.

Luft, E. von der, Cassirer's Dialectic of the Mythical Consciousness, Reports on Philosophy, Volume 8, 1984, pp. 3–13.

Lunau, H., Ernst Cassirer: Axel Hägerström, Eine Studie zur schwedischen Philosophie der Gegenwart (Review), Theoria, Volume 5, 1939, pp. 215–218.

Lüth, E.H., Ernst Cassirer und eines seiner letzten Werke, Zeitschrift für philosophische Forschung, Volume 1, 1946, pp. 598–602.

Lynch, D.A., Ernst Cassirer and Martin Heidegger: The Davos Debate, Kant-Studien, Volume 81, 1990, pp. 360–370.

Makkreel, R.A., Vico and some kantian reflections on historical judgment, Man and World, Volume 13, 1980, pp. 99–120.

Mann, F., Ernst Cassirer and "Primeval Stupidity", Terra Libra Holdings, 2002, <www.buildfreedom.com/tl/tl071.html> (last visited: March 8, 2006).

Marck, S., Substanz- und Funktionsbegriff in der Rechtsphilosophie, J.C.B. Mohr (Paul Siebeck), Tübingen, 1925.

Marcondes, D., Language and Knowledge in Cassirer's Philosophy of Symbolic Forms, Internationale Zeitschrift für Philosophie, 1997, pp. 250–260.

Marc-Wogau, K., Der Symbolbegriff in der Philosophie Ernst Cassirers, Theoria, A Swedish Journal of Philosophy and Psychology, Volume 2, 1936, pp. 279–332.

Margreiter, R., "... auf vulkanischem Boden": Geschichte, Kontingenz und Normativität bei Ernst Cassirer, in: Hegel-Jahrbuch, 1996, Berlin, 1997, pp. 252–258.

Marx, W., Cassirers Symboltheorie als Entwicklung und Kritik des Neokantischen Grundlagen einer Theorie des Denkens und Erkennens, Archiv für die Geschichte der Philosophie, Volume 57, 1975, pp. 188–206 and pp. 304–339.

McCoy, C.N.R., The Turning-Point in Political Philosophy, The American Political Science Review, Volume 44, 1950, pp. 678–688.

Menzel, L., Ordnungsrelationen und Mundus Sensibilis. Eine auseinandersetzung mit Ernst Cassirer, Kant-Studien, Volume 59, 1968, pp. 230–239.

Merker, B., Was ist der Mensch? Anthropologie als Transzendentalphilosophie, Internationale Zeitschrift für Philosophie, 1997, pp. 323–331.

Möckel, C., Symbolische Prägnanz – ein phänomenologiscger Begriff? Zum Verhältnis von Ernst Cassirers Philosophie der symbolischen Formen und Husserls Phänomenologie, Deutsche Zeitschrift für Philosophie, Volume 40, 1992, pp. 1050–1063.

Möckel, C., "Leben" als Quell symbolischer Formen. Eine Auseinandersetzung Cassirers mit Simmel und Scheler, Logos, Volume 5, 1998, pp. 355–386.

Morgan, J.H., Religious Myth and Symbol: A Convergence of Philosophy and Anthropology, Philosophy Today, Volume 18, 1974, pp. 68–84.

Mormann, Th., Idealistische Häresien in der Wissenschaftsphilosophie: Cassirer, Carnap und Kuhn, Journal for General Philosophy of Science, Volume 30, 1999, pp. 233–271.

Moynahan, G.B., Hermann Cohen's Das Prinzip der Infinitesimalmethode, Ernst Cassirer, and the Politics of Science in Wilhelmine Germany, Perspectives on Science, Volume 11, 2003, pp. 35–75.

Müller-Strömsdörfer, I., Der Mensch innerhalb der Grenzen der symbolischen Vernunft. Zur ernst Cassirers 'Was ist der Mensch?' Philosophische Rundschau, 1962, pp. 208–224.

Naumann, B., The Genesis of Symbolic Forms: Basis Phenomena in Cassirer's Works, Science in Context, Volume 12, Issue 4, 1999, pp. 575–584.

Naumann, B., Recki, B. (eds.), Cassirer und Goethe. Neue Aspekte einer philosophisch-literarischen Wahlverwandtschaft, Studien aus dem Warburg-Haus, Band 5, Akademie Verlag, Belin, 2002.

Neumann, K., Ernst Cassirer: Das Symbol, in: Josef Speck (ed.), Grundprobleme der grossen Philosophen: Philosophie der Gegenwart, Volume 2, Göttingen: Vandenhoech & Ruprecht, 1972, pp. 102–145.

Noack, H., Ernst Cassirer. Zur Würdigung seines Werkes anläßlich der 80. Wiederkehr seines geburtstages am 28. Juli

1954, Zeitschrift für philosophische Forschung, Volume 8, 1954, pp. 446–455.

Ogden, C.K. and Richards, I.A., The Meaning of Meaning. A Study of the Influence of Language upon Thought and of the Science of Symbolism, Selected Works 1919–1938, J. Constable (ed.), Routledge, London and New York, 2001 (1923).

Oort, R. van, Cognitive Science and the Problem of Representation, Poetics Today, Volume 24, 2003, pp. 237–295.

Orth, E.W., Der Begriff der Kulturphilosophie bei Ernst Cassirer, in: Brackert, H., Wefelmeyer, Fr. (eds.), Bestimmungen im 20. Jahrhundert, Suhrkamp, Frankfurt am Main, 1990, pp. 156–191.

Orth, E.W., Philosophische Anthropologie als Erste Philosophie. Ein Vergleich zwischen Ernst Cassirer und Helmuth Plessner, Dilthey-Jahrbuch, Volume 7, Vandenhoeck & Rupprecht, Göttingen, 1990–1991, pp. 250–274.

Orth, E.W., Martin Heidegger und der Neukantianismus, Man and World, Volume 25, 1992, pp. 421–441.

Orth, E.W., Interkulturalität und Inter-Intentionalität. Zu Husserls Ethos der Eneuerung in seinen japanischen Kaizo-Artikeln, Zeitschrift für philosophische Forschung, Volume 47, 1993, pp. 333–351.

Orth, E.W., Ist der Neukantianer Ernst Cassirer ein Nominalist? Verlegenheiten der Substanzkritik, Internationale Zeitschrift für Philosophie, 1997, pp. 261–272.

Paetzold, H., Sprache als symbolischen Formen. Zur Sprachphilosophie Ernst Cassirers, Philosophisches Jahrbuch, Volume 88, 1981, pp. 301–315.

Paetzold, H., Ernst Cassirer und die Idee einer transformierten Transzendentalphilosophie, in: Kuhlmann, W., Böhler, D., Kommunikation und Reflexion. Zur Diskussion der Transzendentalproblematik. Antworten auf Karl-Otto Appel, Suhrkamp, Frankfurt am Main, 1982, pp. 124–156.

Paetzold, H., Mythos als symbolische Form. Zu Ernst Cassirers philosophischer Deutung des Mythos, Neu Zeitschrift für systematische Theologie und Religionsphilosophie, Volume 23, 1983, pp. 224–243.

Paetzold, H., Ernst Cassirer zur Einführung, Junius Verlag, Hamburg, 1993.

Paetzold, H., Die Realität der symbolischen Formen. Die Kulturphilosophie Ernst Cassirers im Kontext, Wissenschaftliche Buchgesellschaft, Darmstadt, 1994.

Paetzold, H., Ernst Cassirer. Von Marburg nach New York. Eine philosophische Biographie, Wissenschaftliche Buchgesellschaft, Darmstadt, 1995.

Paetzold, H., Die Bedeutung von Kants Dritter Kritik für die Politische Philosophie in der Postmoderne, in: Franke, U. (Hg.), Kants Schlüssel zur Kritik des geschmaks. Ästhetische Erfahrung heute – Studien zur Aktualität von Kants "Kritik der Urteilskraft", Sonderheft des Jahrgangs 2000 der Zeitschrift für Ästethik und Allgemeine Kunstwissenschaft, Felix Meiner Verlag, Hamburg, 2000, pp. 189–208.

Pätzold, D., Ernst Cassirers begrip van de techniek, Filosofie, Volume 8, No. 5, 1998, pp. 44–47.

Perpeet, W., Ernst Cassirers Kulturphilosophie, Zeitschrift für philosophische Forschung, Volume 36, 1982, pp. 252–262.

Piaia, G., Cassirer, Historiker der Renaissancephilosophie, in: Rudolph, E. (Hg.), Die Renaissance und ihr Bild in der Geschichte. Die Renaissance als erste Auklärung III, Mohr Siebeck, Tübingen, 1998, pp. 167–180.

Poole, B., Bakhtin and Cassirer. The Philosophical Origins of Bakthin's Carnival Messianism, South Atlantic Quarterly, Volume 97, No. 3/4, 1998, pp. 537–578.

Price, K.B., Ernst Cassirer and the Enlightenment¸ Journal of the History of Ideas, Volume 18, 1957, pp. 101–112.

Pulkkinen, J., Russel and the Neo-Kantians, Studies in History and Philosophy of Science, Volume 32, 2001, pp. 99–117.

Randall, J.H., The Career of Philosophy, Volume 3, Philosophy after Darwin and Other Essays, B.J. Singer (ed.), Columbia University Press, New York, 1977.

Recki, B., Ernst Cassirer in Hamburg, Porträt, Information Philosophie, Juni 2000, pp. 80–86.

Recki, B., Cassirer über Geist und Bewusstsein, in: Schumacher, R. (Hrsg.), Idealismus als Theorie der Representätion? Mentis, Paderborn, 2001, pp. 271–284.

Recki, B., Das Ethos der Freiheit. Ernst Cassirers ungeschriebene Ethik und ihre Postulatenlehre, in: Bermes, C. Jonas, J., Lembeck, K.-H., Die Stellung des Menschen in der Kultur. Festschrift für Ernst Wolfgang Orth zum 65.

Geburtstag, Königshausen & Neumann, Würzburg, 2002, pp. 271–293.

Recki, B., Kultur als Praxis. Eine Einführung in Ernst Cassirers Philosophie der symbolischen Formen, Deutsche Zeitschrift für Philosophie, Sonderband 6, Akademie Verlag, Berlin, 2004.

Regelmann, J.-P., Die Stellung der Biologie in den neukantianistischen Systemen von Ernst Cassirer und Nicolai Hartmann, Acta Biotheoretica, Volume 28, 1979, pp. 217–233.

Renz, U., Die Rationalität der Kultur. Zur Kulturphilosophie und ihrer transzendentalen Begründung bei Cohen, Natorp und Cassirer, Cassirer–Forschungen, Band 8, Meiner Verlag, Hamburg, 2002.

Richards, I.A., The Philosophy of Rhetoric, Selected Works, J. Constable (ed.), Routledge, London and New York, 2001 (1936).

Richter, C., Die Religion in der Sprache der Kultur: Schleiermacher und Cassirer: kulturphilosophische Symmetrien und Divergenzen, Mohr Siebeck, Tübingen, 2004.

Rudolph, E., Einleitung: Wußte die Renaissance, daß es sie gab? Elemente einer vormodernen Geschichtsphilosophie in der Renaissance, in: Rudolph, E. (Hg.), Die Renaissance und ihr Bild in der Geschichte. Die Renaissance als erste Auklärung III, Mohr Siebeck, Tübingen, 1998, pp. 1–15.

Rudolph, E. (Hg.), Cassirers Weg zur Philosophie der Politik, Cassirer–Fortschungen Band 5, Felix Meiner Verlag, Hamburg, 1999.

Rudolph, E., Küppers, B.-O., Kulturkritik nach Ernst Cassirer, Cassirer–Forschungen; Bd. 1, Felix Meiner Verlag, Hamburg, 1995.

Rudolph, E., Sandkühler, H.J. (eds.), Symbolische Formen, mögliche Welten – Ernst Cassirer, Dialektik, Volume 1, Meiner Verlag, Hamburg, 1995.

Ruesch, J., The Social Control of Symbolic Systems, The Journal of Communication, Volume 17:4, 1967, pp. 276–301.

Sandkühler, H.J., Wissenskulturen, Pluralismus und Recht, Dialektik, Zeitschrift für Kulturphilosophie, 2002/2, pp. 41–52.

Sandkühler, H.J., Paetzold, D., Kultur und Symbol. Handbuch zu Ernst Cassirer, Metzler Verlag, Stuttgart, 2003.

Schalow, F., Imagination. Heidegger's Retrieval of the Kantian Ethic, University Press of America, Lanham, 1986.

Scherer, M., Vom Apriori der Prägnanz. Vortheoretische Sinnersclossenheit als zentrales Motiv der kulturphilosophie Ernst Cassirers, inaugural Dissertation an der Ludwig-Maximilian-Universität zu München, Dissertations Druck, Darmstadt, 1996.

Schilpp, P.A., The Philosophy of Ernst Cassirer, Open Court Publishing Company, La Salle, Illinois (1949), 3rd print, 1973.

Schmidt, J., The Legacy of the Enlightenment, Philosophy and Literature, Volume 26, 2002, pp. 432–442.

Schrag, C.O., Heidegger and Cassirer on Kant, Kant-Studien, Volume 58, 1967, pp. 87–100.

Schrems, J.J., Ernst Cassirer and Political Thought, Review of Politics, Volume 29, 1967, pp. 180–203.

Schulz, B., Philosophie und Politik. Die Davoser Disputation zwischen Ernst Cassirer und Martin Heidegger in der Retroperspektive, Internationale Zeitschrift für Philosophie, 1997, pp. 290–312.

Schürmann, V., Die Substanz der Relation. Notizen zu Ernst Cassirer, Zeitschrift für philosophische Forschung, Volume 48, 1994, pp. 104–116.

Schweitzer, A., The Philosophy of Civilization, tr. C.T. Campion, University Press of Florida, Tallahassee, 1981 (1923) or Prometheus Books, Buffalo, NY, 1987 (1923).

Schwemmer, O., Über das Verstehen das Fremden, Information Philosophie, Volume 1, 1995, pp. 5–19.

Schwemmer, O., "Moralisierung" durch "Kultivierung"? Über den Zusammenhang zwischen wissenschaftlichen Verstehen und moralischer Kultur, Jahrbuch für Wissenschaft und Ethik, Volume 2, 1997, pp. 55–73.

Schwemmer, O., Der Werkbegriff in der Methaphysik der symbolische Formen. Zu Cassirers Konzeption eines vierten Bandes der Philosophie der symbolische Formen, Internationale Zeitschrift für Philosophie, 1997, pp. 226–249.

Schwemmer, O., Ernst Cassirer. Ein Philosoph der europäischen Moderne, Akademie Verlag, Berlin, 1997.

Skidelsky, E., From epistemology to cultural criticism: Georg Simmel and Ernst Cassirer, History of European Idean, Volume 29, 2003, pp. 365–381.
Skinner, Q., Meaning and Understanding in the History of Ideas, History and Theory, Volume 8, 1963, pp. 3–53.
Smart, H.R., Cassirer versus Russel, Philosophy of Science, Volume 10, 1943, pp. 167–175.
Snethlage, J.L., De zekerheid der geschiedenis vergeleken met die der natuurweteschap (Cassirer, Huizinga, Romein), Algemeen Nederlands Tijdschrift voor Wijsbegeerte en Psychologie, Volume 34, 1941, pp. 125–140.
Soboleva, M., Zur philosophischen Hermeneutik Ernst Cassirers, Phänomologische Forschungen, 2001, pp. 281–294.
Stark, Th., Symbol, Bedeutung, Transzendenz. Der Religionsbegriff in der Kulturphilosophie Ernst Cassirers, Religion in der Moderne; Bd. 2, Echter, Würzburg, 1997.
Sternberg, K., Der Neukantianismus und die Forderungen der Gegenwart, Kant-Studien, Volume 25, 1920, pp. 396–426.
Strenski, I., Ernst Cassirer's Mythical Thought in Weimar Culture, History of European Ideas, Volume 5, 1984, pp. 363–383.
Sundaram, K., Kant or Cassirer: A Study in Complementarity, Zeitschrift für allgemeine Wissenschaftstheorie, Volume 3, 1972, pp. 40–48.
Sundara Rajan, R., Cassirer and Wittgenstein, International Philosophical Quarterly, Volume 7, 1967, pp. 591–610.
Switalski, W., Ernst Cassirer. Substanzbegriff und Funktionsbegriff (Literaturbericht), Zeitschrift für Psychologie und Physiologie der Sinnesorgane, Volume 64, 1913, pp. 304–306.
Taubald, B., Mediale Öffentlichkeit und Moral. Notizen zur Hermeneutik der Massenmedien in modernen Gesellschaften, Jahresbericht der societas ethica, 2001, <http://homepage.univie.ac.at/Benjamin.Taubald/medmoral.pdf> (last visited: March 8, 2006).
Troeltsch, E., Humanismus und Nationalismus in unserem Bildungswesen, in: Ibid., Deutscher Geist und Westeuropa, H. Baron (ed.), Scientia Verlag, Aalen, 1966, pp. 231–235.
Universität Hamburg, Hamburger Universitätsreden Neue Folge I, Herausgegeben von der Pressestelle der Universität Hamburg, Zum Gedenken an Ernst Cassirer (1874–1945),

Ansprachen auf der Akademischen Gedenkfeier am 11. Mai 1999, Dölling und Galitz Verlag, 1999.
Verene, D.P., Kant, Hegel, and Cassirer: The Origins of the Philosophy of Symbolic Forms, Journal of the History of Ideas, Volume 30, 1969, pp. 33–46.
Verene, D.P., Cassirer's Concept of Symbolic Form and Human Creativity, Idealistic Studies, Volume 8, 1978, pp. 14–32.
Verene, D.P., Cassirers Kultuphilosophie, Allgemeine Zeitschrift für Philosophie, Volume 9, 1984, pp. 1–18.
Verene, D.P., Metaphysical Narration, Science, and Symbolic Form, The Review of Metaphysics, Volume 47, 1993, pp. 115–132.
Vergely, B., Cassirer. La Politique du juste, Édition Michalon, 1998.
Waite, G., On Esotericism. Heidegger and/or Cassirer at Davos, Political Theory, Volume 26, 1998, pp. 603–651.
Wells, R., Philosophy of Language, in: R. Klibansky (ed.), Philosophy in the Mid-Century: A Survey, Volume II, La Nuvoa Italia, Florence, 1958, pp. 139–145.
White, L.A., The Concept "Social": A Critical Note, Social Forces, Volume 4, 1925–1926, pp. 72–74.
White, L.A., The Symbol: The Origin and Basis of Human Behavior, Philosophy and Science, Volume 7, 1940, pp. 451–463.
White, L.A., Symboling: A Kind of Behavior, Journal of Psychology, Volume 53, 1962, pp. 311–317.
Wiegerling, K., Prozeßdenken in Cassirers Philosophie der symbolischen Formen. Der Prozeßcharakter der naturwissenschaftlichen Erkenntnis und die symbolische Erkenntnis des Prozesses, in: Bucher, A.J., Peters, D.S., Evolution im Diskurs. Grenzspräche zwischen Naturwissenschaft, Philosophie und Theologie, Friedrich Pustet Verlag, Regensburg, 1998, pp. 305–316.
Wiegerling, K., The Superfluous Body: Utopias of Information and Communication Technology, Concilium, 2002–2001, pp. 19–28.
Wildgen, W., The genres of semiosis (symbolic forms, generalized media) and cultural evolution, contribution to the Syposium, The Migration of genres, Urbino, 9–11 July 2001 (<http://www.fb10.uni-bremen.de/homepages/wildgen/pdf/evolutionofgenresurbino.pdf>) (last visited: September 18, 2006).

Willey, T.E., Back to Kant. The Revival of Kantianism in German Social and Historical Thought, 1860–1914, Wayne State University Press, Detroit, 1978.

Winter, E., Ethik und Rechtswissenschaft. Eine historisch-systematische Untersuchung zur Ethik-Konzeption des Marburger Neukantianismus im Werke Hermann Cohens, Schriften zur Rechtstheorie, Heft 92, Duncker & Humblot, Berlin, 1980.

Wisner, D.A., Ernst Cassirer, Historian of the Will, Journal of the History of Ideas, Volume 58, 1997, pp. 145–161.

Witte, B., Dahnke, H.-D., und Otto, R. (Hrg.), *Goethe Handbuch*, Band 4/2, *Personen, Sachen, Begriffe L-Z*, Metzler, Stuttgart, 1998.

Wolandt, G., Cassirers Symbolbegriff und die Grundlegungsproblematik der Geisteswisschenschaften, Zeitschrift für philosophische Forschung, Volume 18, 1964, pp. 614–626.

Zaner, R.M., An Approach to a Philosophical Anthropology, Philosophy and Phenomenology Research, Volume 27, 1966, pp. 55–68.

Zill, R., Gebrochene Strahlen, zersplitterte Spiegel. Zur Partikularisierung der Weltbetrachtung, in: Rohbeck, J. (Hg.), Philosophie und Weltanschauung, Dresdner Hefte für Philosophie, Heft 1, Thelem bei w.e.b. Univ.-Verl., Dresden, 1999, pp. 179–196.

SECONDARY READING

Ackerman, B.A., Social Justice in the Liberal State, Yale University Press, New Haven and London, 1980.

Albert, K., *Lebensphilosophie. Von den Anfängen bei Nietzsche bis zu ihrer Kritik bei Lukács*, K. Alber, Freiburg/München, 1995.

Aleinikov, A., Constitutional Law in the Age of Balancing, The Yale Law Journal, Volume 96, 1987, pp. 943–1005.

Alexy, R., A Defence of Radbruch's Formula, in: Freeman, M.D.A. (ed.), Lloyd's Introduction to Jurisprudence, 7th edition, Sweet and Maxwell, London, 2001, pp. 374–391.

Alexy, R., Meyer, L.H., Paulson, S.L., Sprenger, G. (Hrsg.), Neukantianismus und Rechtsphilosophie, Interdisziplinäre Studien zu Recht und Staat, Band 25, Nomos Verlagsgesellschaft, Baden-Baden, 2002.

Amrine, F., Zucker, F.J., and Wheeler, H., Goethe and the Sciences: A Reappraisal, D. Reidel Publishing Company, Dordrecht, 1987.

Apelt, W., Geschichte der Weimarer Verfassung, Biederstein Verlag, München, 1946.

Atiyah, F.B.A., Promises, Morals, and Law, Clarendon Press, Oxford, 1981.

Aul, J., Aspekte des Universalisierungspostulats in Kants Ethik, Neue Hefte für Philosophie, Volume 22, 1983, pp. 62–94.

Austin, J.L., How to Do Things with Words, J.O. Urmson (ed.), Harvard University Press, Cambridge, Massachusetts, 1962.

Badmington, N., Theorizing Posthumanism, Cultural Critique, Volume 53, 2003, pp. 10–27.

Balkin, J.M., Cultural Software. A Theory of Evolution, Yale University Press, New Haven and London, 1998.

Baumgardt, D., Über einige Hauptmethodenfragen der modernen Ethik (Von Kant bis zur Gegenwart), Logos, Volume 19, 1930, pp. 376–403.

Baumgardt, D., Unlösbare moralische Konflikte. Ihre Auslegung im Judentum, Christendum und der Existentialphilosophie, Zeitschrift für Religions- und Geistesgeschichte, Volume 11, 1959, pp. 297–314.

Baumgardt, D., Natural Right Valid in Itself and Allegedly Relativistic Eudaemonism, in: Hook, S. (ed.), Law and Philosophy. A Symposium, New York University Press, New York, 1964, pp. 172–176.

Baumgardt, D., Rationalism and the Philosophy of Despair: Pre-Nazi German Ethics, 1913–1933, The Sewanee Review, Volume 55, 1947, pp. 223–237.

Binder, J., Der Wissenschaftskarakter der Rechtswissenschaft, Kant-Studien, Volume 25, 1920, pp. 321–365.

Bjarup, J., Skandinavischer Realismus, Verlag Karl Alber, Freiburg-München, 1978.

Boldt, H., Das Erbe Weimars: Die Relativität der Dinge, ZiF: Mitteilungen 3/2003, http://www.uni-bielefeld.de/ZIF/Publikationen/ 03-3-Boldt.pdf (last visited: September 18, 2006).

Brenner, M., The Renaissance of Jewish Culture in Weimar Germany, Yale University Press, New Haven and London, 1996.

Burrow, J.W., The Crisis of Reason. European Thought, 1848–1914, Yale University Press, New Haven and London, 2000.

Caenegem, R.C. van, An Historical Introduction to Western Constitutional Law, Cambridge University Press, Cambridge, 1996.

Cahn, E.N., Confronting Injustice, The Edmond Cahn Reader, Norman Redlich and Lenore L. Cahn (eds.), introduction by Hugo L. Black, Little, Brown, 1967.

Carstens, U., Schlüter-Knauer, C., Der Wille zur Demokratie. Traditionslinien und Perspektiven, Duncker & Humblot, Berlin, 1998.

Cassirer, Erich, Natur- und Völkerrecht im Lichte der geschichte und der systematischen Philosophie, C.A. Schwetschke & Sohn, Berlin, 1919.

Chomsky, N., On Nature and language: with an Essay on "The Secular Priesthood and the Perils of Democracy", Adriana Belletti and Luigi Rizzi (eds.), Cambridge University Press, Cambridge, 2002.

Cliteur, P.B., Loth, M.A., *Rechtsfilosofen van de twintigste eeuw*, Gouda Quint B.V., Arnhem, 1992.

Cobb, S.H., The Rise of Religious Liberty in America: A History, Burt Franklin, New York, 1970 (1902).

Coelho. L.F., A Contribution to a Critical Theory of Law, Legal Philosophy: General Aspects, ARSP Beiheft 82, Franz Steiner Verlag, Stuttgart, 2002, pp. 85–98.

Cohen, H., Religion of Reason, Out of the Sources of Judaism, tr. S. Kaplan, introd. L. Strauss, Frederick Ungar Publishing Co., New York, 1972.

Colie, R.L., Light and Enlightenment: A Study of the Cambridge Platonists and the Dutch Arminians, Cambridge University Press, New York, 1957.

Craemer, Ruegenberg, I., Logische und andere Eigenschaften des kategorischen Imperativs, Neue Hefte für Philosophie, Volume 22, 1983, pp. 45–61.

Cragg, G.R., The Cambridge Platonists, Oxford University Press, New York, 1968.

Deacon, T.W., The Symbolic Species: the Co-evolution of Language and the Brain, Norton, New York, 1997.

Derbolav, J., Abriss europäischer Ethik. Die Frage nach dem Guten und ihr Gestaltwandel, Königshausen & Neumann, Würzburg, 1983.

Deringil, S., Turkey's Foreign Policy during the Second World War: An 'Active' Neutrality, Cambridge University Press, Cambridge, 1989.

Dinneen, J.A., What Austin Does with Words, Philosophy and Phenomenological Research, Volume 32, 1972, pp. 514–523.

Dreier, R., Neues Naturrecht oder Rechtspositivismus? Rechtstheorie, Volume 18, 1987, pp. 368–385.

Dreier, R., Rechtsphilosophie und Diskurstheorie. Bemerkungen zur Habermas' "Faktizität und Geltung", Zeitschrift für philosophische Forschung, Volume 48, 1994, pp. 90–103.

Dworkin, R., The Threat to Patriotism, The New York Review of Books, Volume 49, No. 3, 2002, <http://www.nybooks.com/articles/15145> (last visited: September 18, 2006).

Eliade, M., The Holy and the Profane; the Nature of Religion, tr. W.R. Trask, Harbourt, Brace Jovanovic, New York, 1959.

Elon, A., The Pity of it All: A History of Jews in Germany, 1743–1933, Metropolitan Books, New York, 2002.

Evans, R.J., The Coming of the Third Reich, Allen Lane, London, 2003.

Everson, M., Strong Evaluations, Self Interpretation and Constitutional Patriotism. Comments on John Erik Fossum, 'Charters and Constitution Making', ARENAs European Conference, 2002, Democracy and European Governance, <http://www.arena.uio.no/events/Conference2002/Papers.html> (last visited: September 18, 2006).

Eyck, E., Geschichte der Weimarer Republik, Erster Band, Von Zusammenbruch des Kaisertums bis zur Wahl Hindenburgs, Eugen Rentsch Verlag, Erlenbach-Zürich und Sturrgart, 1957.

Fellmann, F., *Lebensphilosophie. Elemente einer Theorie der Selbsterfahrung*, Rowohlt, Reinbek bei Hamburg, 1993.

Fitzpatrick, P., The Mythology of Modern Law, Routledge, London, 1992.

Fitzpatrick, P., Modernism and the Grounds of Law, Cambridge University Press, Cambridge, 2001.

Fleisner, P., Von der Stammesgemeinschaft zur Globalgesellschaft – und zurück? <http://21st.century.phil-inst.hu/ktar/fleissner.htm> (last visited: September 18, 2006).

Föllmer, M., Graf, R. (Hg.), Die >>Krise<< der Weimarer Republik. Zum Kritik eines Deutungsmusters, Canysus Verlag, Frankfurt und New York, 2005.

Forschner, M., Reine Morallehre und Anthropologie. Kritische Überlegungen zum Begriff eines a priori gültigen allgemeinen praktischen Gesetzes bei Kant, Neue Hefte für Philosophie, Volume 22, 1983, pp. 25–44.

Fraser, N., and Honneth, A., Redistribution or Recognition?: A Political–Philosophical Exchange, translated by J. Golb [et al.], Verso, London and New York, 2003.

Fullinwider, S.N., Hermann von Helmholtz: The Problem of Kantian Influence, Studies in History and Philosophy, Volume 21, 1990, pp. 41–55.

Gigliotti, G., Ethik und das Faktum der Rechtswissenschaft bei Hermann Cohen, in: Holzhey, H. (Hg.), Ethischer Sozialismus. Zur politischen Philosophie des Neukantianismus, Suhrkamp, Frankfurt am Main, 1991, pp. 166–184.

Glendon, M.A., *A World Made New, Eleanor Roosevelt and the Universal Declaration of Human Rights*, Random House, New York, 2001.

Goodstein, E., Style as Substance. Georg Simmel's Phenomenology of Culture, Cultural Critique, Volume 52, 2002, pp. 209–234.

Greiff, Pablo de, Habermas on Nationalism and Cosmopolitanism, Ratio Iuris, Volume 15, 2002, pp. 418–439.

Groot, A.G.G. de, Der skandinavische Realismus und seine Bedeutung für die rechtliche Grundlagenforschung, Diss. Universiteit Utrecht, Utrecht, 1997.

De Groot-van Leeuwen, L.E. de, Van den Bossche, A.M., Buruma, Y., *De ongehoorzame rechter. Rechters versus andere rechters, de wetgever, de bevolking en het Europees recht*, Serie Rechtspleging RU, Kluwer, Deventer, 2006.

Grossheim, M., *Von Georg Simmel zu Martin Heidegger. Philosophie zwischen Leben und Existenz*, Bouvier Verlag, Bonn-Berlin, 1991.

Grossheim, M., *Ludwig Klages und die Phänomenologie*, Akademie Verlag, Berlin, 1994.

Grusswald Curran, V., Racism's Past and Law's Future, Vermont Law Review, Volume 28, 2004, pp. 683–712.
Gusy, C. (Hrsg.), Demokratisches Denken in der Weimarer Republik, Interdisziplinäre Studien zu Recht und Staat Bd. 16, Nomos Verlag, Baden-Baden, 1994.
Haag, J., *The Spann Circle and the Jewish Question*, Yearbook of the Leo Baeck Institute, Volume XVIII, 1973, pp. 93–126.
Habermas, J., A Postscript to "Knowledge and Human Interests", Philosophy and the Social Sciences, Volume 3, 1973, pp. 157–189.
Habermas, J., Reconciliation Through the Public Use of Reason: Remarks on John Rawls's Political Liberalism, The Journal of Philosophy, Volume 92, 1995, pp. 109–131.
Habermas, J., From Kant to Hegel: On Robert Brandom's Pragmatic Philosophy of Language, European Journal of Philosophy, Volume 8, 2000, pp. 321–355.
Habermas, J., Why Europe Needs a Constitution, New Left Review, Volume 11, 2001, pp. 5–26.
Habermas, J., Constitutional Democracy. A Paradoxical Union of Contradictory Principles? Political Theory, Volume 29, 2001, pp. 766–781.
Habermas, J., Intolerance and Discrimination, International Journal of Constitutional Law, Volume 1, 2003, pp. 2–12.
Habermas, J., On Law and Disagreement. Some Comments on "Interpretative Pluralism", Ratio Iuris, Volume 16, 2003, pp. 187–194.
Hackeschmidt, J., The Torch Bearer: Norbert Elias as a Young Zionist, Yearbook of the Leo Baeck Institute, Volume XLIX, 2004, pp. 59–74.
Haldemann, F., Gustav Radbruch vs. Hans Kelsen: A Debate on Nazi Law, Ratio Iuris, Volume 18, No. 2, 2005, pp. 162–178.
Hannover, H.E., Politische Justiz 1918–1933, Fischer Bücherei, Hamburg, 1966.
Hartung, G., Zur Genealogie des Schuldbegriffs: Friedrich Nietzsche und Max Weber im Vergleich, Archiv für Geschichte der Philosophie, Volume 76, 1994, pp. 302–318.
Hartung, G., Nietzsches Genealogie der Moral. Eine Herkunfts – und Destruktionsgeschichte des Sinnhorizonts moderner Kultur, in: Junge, M. (Hrsg.), Macht und Moral. Beiträge zur

Dekonstruktion von Moral, Westdeutscher Verlag, Wiesbaden, 2003, pp. 41–59.

Hartung, G., Zur Genealogie des Versprechens. Ein Versuch über die begriffsgeschichtlichen und anthropologischen Voraussetzungen der modernen Vertragstheorie, in: Schneider, M. (Hg.), Die Ordnung des Versprechens. Naturrecht – Institution – Sprechakt, Wilhelm Fink Verlag, München, 2005.

Hauser, M.D., The Evolution of Communication, The MIT Press, Cambridge, Massachusetts, London, England, 1996.

Hauser, M.D., Konishi, M. (ed.), The Design of Animal Communication, The MIT Press, Cambridge, Massachusetts, London, England, 1999.

Hertzberg, A., *A Reminiscence of Ernst Cassirer*, Yearbook of the Leo Baeck Institute, Volume XV, 1970, pp. 245–246.

Hiden, J.W., The Weimar Republic, 2nd edition, Longman, London and New York, 1996.

Hofman, H., Geschichlichkeit und Universalitätsanspruch des Rechtsstaats, Universitas, Volume 9, 1995, pp. 841–857.

Holzhey, H. (Hg.), Ethischer Sozialismus. Zur politischen Philosophie des Neukantianismus, Suhrkamp, Frankfurt am Main, 1991

Holzhey, H., und Röd, W., Die Philosophie des ausgehenden 19. und des 20. Jahrhunderts. 2 Neukantianismus, Idealismus, Realismus, Phänomenologie, Geschichte der Philosophie, hrgs. W. Röd, Band XII, Verlag C.H. Beck, München, 2004.

Horkheimer, M. and Adorno, T.W., Dialectic of Enlightenment, tr. J. Cumming, Continuum, New York, 1972 (1944).

Horwitz, M.J., Why is Anglo-American Jurisprudence Unhistorical? Oxford Journal of Legal Studies, Volume 17, 1997, pp. 551–586.

Hunt, R.N. (ed.), The Creation of the Weimar Republic. Stillborn Democracy? D.C. Heath and Company, Lexington, Massachusetts, 1969.

Hyder, D., Foucault, Cavaillès, and Husserl on the Historical Epistemology of the Sciences, Perspectives on Science, Volume 11, 2003, pp. 107–129.

Jacobsen, A.J., Schlink, B., Weimar. A Jurisprudence of Crisis, translated by Belinda Cooper (a.o.), University of California Press, Berkeley [a.o.], 2000.

Jaeger, W.W., Paideia: The Ideals of Greek Culture, Volume I, Archaic Greece, The Mind of Athens, translated from the Second German Edition by Gilbert Highet, Basil Blackwell, Oxford, 1943.

Jaeger, W.W., Paideia: The Ideals of Greek Culture, Volume II, The Search for the Divine Centre, translated from the Second German Edition by Gilbert Highet, Basil Blackwell, Oxford, 1944.

Jaeger, W., Paideia: the Ideals of Greek Culture, Volume III, The Conflict of Cultural Ideals in the Age of Plato, translated from the Second German Edition by G. Highet, Basil Blackwell, Oxford, 1945.

Jansen, C.J., Poortinga, E., *Het onderwijs in de rechtsfilosofie van Paul Scholten*, Recht en Kritiek, Volume 19, 1993, pp. 191–205.

Jasper, G., Der Schutz der Republik. Studien zur Staatlichen Sicherung zur Demokratie in der Weimarer Republik 1922–1930, J.C.B. Mohr (Paul Siebeck), Tübingen, 1963.

Kahn, P.W., Reason and Will in the Origins of American Constitutionalism, Yale Law Journal, Volume 98, 1989, pp. 449–517.

Kahn, P.W., The Reign of Law. Marbury v. Madison and the Construction of America, Yale University Press, New Haven and London, 1997.

Kahn, P.W., The Cultural Study of Man. Reconstructing Legal Scholarship, Chicago University Press, Chicago and London, 1999.

Kahn, P.W., Putting Liberalism in Its Place, Princeton University Press, Princeton, NJ, 2005.

Kahn, P.W., After Eden. Adam and Eve and the Problem of Evil, Princeton University Press, Princeton and Oxford, 2007.

Kantorowicz, E.H., The King's Two Bodies: A Study in Mediaeval Political Theology, Princeton University Press, Princeton, 1957.

Kaser, M., Das altrömische Ius. Studien zur Rechtsvorstellung und Rechtsgeschichte der Römer, Vandenhoeck & Ruprecht, Goettingen, 1949.

Karpat, K.H., The Politicization of Islam: Reconstructing Indentity, State, Faith, and Community in the Late Ottoman State, Oxford University Press, New York, 2001.

Kaufmann, E., Kritik der neukantischen Rechtsphilosophie. Eine Betrachtung über die Beziehungen zwischen Philosophie und Rechtswissenschaft, Scientia Verlag, Aalen, 1964 (1921).

Keller, H., The Story of My Life, Double Day & Company, Inc., Garden City, New York, 1954 (1902).

Kelsen, H., Der soziologische under der juristische Staatsbegriff: kritische Untersuchung des Verhältnisses von Staat und Recht, 2nd, J.C.B. Mohr (Paul Siebeck), Tübingen, 1922.

Kelsen, H., Hauptprobleme der Staatsrechtslehre entwickelt aus der Lehre vom Rechtssatze, 2nd, J.C.B. Mohr (Paul Siebeck), Tübingen (1911) 1923.

Kelsen, H., The Pure Theory of Law, 2nd edition, tr. M. Knight, University of California Press, Berkeley and Los Angeless, 1967.

Kennedy, D., Legal Formalism, in: Neil J. Smelser & Paul B. Baltes (eds.), The International Encyclopedia of the Social and Behavioral Sciences, Volume 13, 2001, pp. 8634–8638.

Kirste, S., The Temporality of Law and the Plurality of Social Times. The Problem of Synchronizing Different Time Concepts through Law, Legal Philosophy: General Aspects, ARSP Beiheft 82, Franz Steiner Verlag, Stuttgart, 2002, pp. 23–44.

Klecatsky, H. et al. (eds.), Die Wiener rechtstheoretische Schule. Schriften von Hans Kelsen, Adolf Merkel, Alfred Verdross, Volume 1, Europa Verlag, Vienna, 1968.

Kohler, J., Nietzsche and die Rechtsphilosophie, Reprint from ARSP Volume 1 (1907/08), Nietzsche und das Recht, ARSP Beiheft 77, Franz Steiner Verlag, Stuttgart, 2001, pp. 263–268.

Kolb, E., The Weimar Republic, 2nd edition, tr. P.S. Falla and R.J. Park, Routledge, London and New York, 2005.

Kronman, A.T., The Lost Lawyer: Failing Ideas of the Legal Profession, Belknap Press, Cambridge, Massuchusets, 1995.

Lash, J.P., *Helen and Teacher, The Story of Helen Keller and Anne Sullivan Macy*, Seymour and Merloyd Lawrence, New York, 1980.

Larenz, K., Rechts- und Staasphilosophie der Gegenwart, Junker und Dünnhaupt Verlag, Berlin, 1931.

Liebeschütz, H., Jewish Thought and Its German Background, Yearbook of the Leo Baeck Institute, Volume I, 1956, pp. 217–236.
Liebeschütz, H., *The Relevance of the Middle Ages for the Understanding of Contemporary Jewish History*, Yearbook of the Leo Baeck Institute, Volume XVIII, 1973, pp. 3–25.
Lindahl, H., 'Vorst, op God na'. Politieke macht en de symbolisering van soevereiniteit, Nederlands Tijdschrift voor Rechtsfilosofie en Rechtstheorie, Volume 26, 1997, pp. 122–136.
Lindahl, H., Sovereignty and Symbolization, Rechtstheorie, Volume 28, 1997, pp. 347–371.
Lindahl, H., Democracy and the Symbolic Constitution of Society, Ratio Iuris, Volume 11, 1998, pp. 12–37.
Lindahl, H., De Staten-Generaal vertegenwoordigen het gehele Nederlandse volk: Over representatie als rechtsfilosofisch probleem, Nederlands Tijdschrift voor Rechtsfilosofie en Rechtstheorie, Volume 28, 1999, pp. 8–29.
Lindahl, H., Authority and Representation, Law and Philosophy, Volume 19, 2000, pp. 223–246.
Lindahl, H., Rechtsvorming als politieke representatie: de kwestie van constitutionele toetsing, in: Broerse, E.-J., Klink, B. van, De rechter als rechtsvormer, Boom, Den Haag, 2001, pp. 173–196.
Lindahl, H., Sovereignty and the Institutionalization of Normative Order, Oxford Journal of Legal Studies, Volume 21, 2001, pp. 165–180.
Lindahl, H., Gadamer, Kelsen and the Limits of Legal Interpretation, Phenomenologische Forschungen, 2002, pp. 27–49.
Lindemans, B., Methode en interpretatie van het oorspronkelijke contract, in: Tinnevelt, R., Verschraegen, G. (red.), Rawls. Een inleiding in zijn werk, Pelckmans, Kapellen [a.o.], 2002, pp. 53–69.
Lisser, K., Der Begriff des Rechts bei Kant. Mit einem Anhang über Cohen und Görland, Kant-Studien, Ergänzungshefte, No. 58, Reuther & Reichard Verlag, Berlin, 1922.
Lokin, J.H.A., Lex Semper Loquitur. Over wetgeven en rechtspreken, in: Groninger Opmerkingen en Mededelingen, Stichting "Het Groningsch Rechtshistorisch Fonds", Groningen, 1984, pp. 1–50.

Lokin, J.H.A., and Zwalve, W.J., Hoofdstukken uit de Europese Codificatiegeschiedenis, 3rd, Kluwer, Deventer, 2001.
Lübbe, H., Säkularisierung. Geschichte eines ideenpolitischen Begriffs. 3. Um ein Nachwort erweiterte Neuausgabe, Verlag Karl Alber Freiburg, München, 2003.
Luig, K., Samuel von Pufendorf. Über die Pflicht des Menschen und des Bürgers nach dem Gesetz der Natur, Insel Verlag am Main und Leipzig, 1994.
Lukács, G., Die Zerstörung der Vernunft, 3. Auflage, Berlin/ Weimar, 1984.
Lytton, T.D., "Shall not the Judge of the Earth Deal Justly?": Accountability, Compassion, and Judicial Authority in the Biblical Story of Sodom and Gomorrah, The Journal of Law and Religion, Volume 18, 2002-2003, No. 1, pp. 31–55.
MacCormick, N., Time, Narratives, and Laws, in: Bjarup, J., Blegvad, M. (eds.), Time, Law, and Society, Franz Steiner Verlag, Stuttgart, 1995, pp. 111–125.
Mainzer, K., Thinking in Complexity. The Complex Dynamics of Matter, Mind, and Mankind, Third Revised and Enlarged Edition, Springer, Berlin, 1997.
Mango, A., Atatürk, John Murray, London, 1999.
Mann, G. [et al.], Universele wereld geschiedenis, deel 9, De twintigste eeuw, tr. I.J. Brugmans [et al.] (Propyläen Weltgeschichte, Band 9, Das zwanzigste Jahrhundert, 1960), Uitgeverij Scheltens & Giltay N.V., Den Haag, 1974.
Mann, G., Deutsche Geschichte 1919–1945, Fischer Bücherei, Frankfurt am Main, 1961.
Marcuse, H., One Dimensional Man. Studies in the Ideology of Advanced Industrial Society, Routledge & Kegan Paul Ltd., London, 1964.
Martin, C.G., "Boundless The Deep": Milton, Pascal, and the Theology of Relative Space, English Literary History, Volume 63, 1996, pp. 45–78.
McConnell, M.W., Comment: Institutions and Interpretation: A Critique of City of Boerne v. Flores, Harvard Law Review, Volume 111, 1997, pp. 153–196.
McConnel, M.W., David C Baum Memorial Lecture: Tradition and Constitutionalism before the Constitution, University of Illinois Law Review, Volume 1998a, pp. 173–198.

McConnell, M.W., Textualism and Democratic Legitimacy: Textualism and the Dead Hand of the Past, George Washington Law Review, Volume 66, 1998b, pp. 1127 ff.

McConnell, M.W., Establishment and Disestablishment at the Founding, Part I: Establishment of Religion, William and Mary Law Review, volume 44, 2003, pp. 2105–2208.

McDonald, L.C., Myth, Politics and Political Science, The Western Political Quarterly, Volume 22, 1969, pp. 141–150.

Meerloo, J.A.M., The Rape of the Mind: The Psychology of Thought Control, Menticide, and Brainwashing, World Pub. Corp., Cleveland, 1956.

Meerloo, J.A.M., Creativity and Eternization: Essays on the Creative Instinct, Humanities Press, New York, 1968.

Meerloo, J.A.M., Delusion and Mass-Delusion, Johnson Reprint Corp., New York, 1968.

Mertens, Th., Nazism, Legal Positivism and Radbruch's Thesis on Statutory Injustice, Law and Critique, Volume 14, 2003, pp. 277–295.

Mertens, Th., Kant in Weimar, Inaugurele Rede, Kluwer, Deventer, 2000.

Morris-Reich, A., Simmel's and Lacan's Ethics of the Exception, Telos, Volume 18, 2002, pp. 131–148.

Mosse, G.L., German Jews beyond Judaism, Indiana University Press, Bloomington, 1985.

Meyer, J.C., Church and State in Massachusetts from 1740 to 1833, Western Reserve University, Cleveland, 1930.

Mommsen, H., The Rise and Fall of Weimar Democracy, tr. E. Forster and L.E. Jores, The University of North Carolina Press, Chapel Hill and London, 1996.

Müller, C., Die Rechtsphilosophie des Marburger Neukantianismus. Naturrecht und Rechtspositivismus in der Auseinandersetzung zwischen Hermann Cohen, Rudolf Stammler und Paul Natorp, J.C.B. Mohr (Paul Siebeck), Tübingen, 1994.

Murphy, W.F., Tanenhaus, J., Comparative Constitutional Law. Cases and Commentaries, MacMillan, London, 1977.

Neocleous, M., Fascism, University of Minnesota Press, Minneapolis, 1997.

Norton, A., Transubstantiation: The Dialectic of Constitutional Authority, The University of Chicago Law Review, Volume 55, 1988, pp. 458–472.

Oehler, K., Zur Logik einer Universalpragmatik, Semiosis, Volume 1, 1976, pp. 14–23.

Ormond, Th., Richterwünde und Regierungstreue. Dienstrecht, politische Betätigung und Disziplinierung der Richter in Preußen, Baden und Hessen, 1866–1918, Klostermann, Frankfurt am Main, 1994.

Otto, R., The Idea of the Holy: An Inquiry in the Non-Rational Factoring the Idea of the Divine and Its Relation to the Rational, tr. J.W. Harvey, Oxford University Press, New York, 1950.

Owen, D., The Contest of Enlightenment. An Essay on Critique and Genealogy, Journal of Nietzsche Studies, Volume 25, 2003, pp. 35–57.

Panofsky, E., Perspective as Symbolic Form, tr. C.S. Wood, Zone Books, New York, 1991.

Pascher, M., Hermann Cohens Ethik als Gegenentwurf zur Rechtsphilosophie Hegels, Verlag des Instituts für Sprachwissenschaft der Universität Innsbruck, Innsbruck, 1992.

Paulson, S.L., Radbruch on Unjust Laws: Competing Earlier and Later Views? Oxford Journal of Legal Studies, Volume 15, No. 3, 1995, pp. 489–500.

Paulson, S.L., Litschewski Paulson, B. Normativity and Norms: Critical Perspectives on Kelsenian Themes, Clarendon Press, Oxford, 1998.

Paulson, S.L., The Theory of Public Law in Germany 1914–1945, Oxford Journal of Legal Studies, Volume 25, 2005, pp. 525–545.

Paulson, S.L., On the Background and Significance of Gustav Radbruch's Post-War Papers, Oxford Journal of Legal Studies, Volume 26, No. 1, 2006, pp. 17–40.

Peczenik, A., Leon Petrazycki and the Post-Realistic Jurisprudence, in: Gorecki, J., Sociology und Jurisprudence of Leon Petrazycki, University of Illinois Press, Urbana [a.o.], 1975, pp. 83–105.

Peczenik, A., Introduction, Associations, Volume 7, No. 1, Special Issue for The IVR 21st World Congress, 2003.

Pihlajamäki, H., Against Metaphysics in Law: The Historical Background of American and Scandinavian Legal Realism Compared, The American Journal of Comparative Law, Volume 52, 2004, pp. 469–487.

Postel, D., Letter to America: An Interview with Jürgen Habermas, The Nation, December 16, 2002.
Povinelli, E.A., The Cunning of Recognition. Indigenous Alterities and the Making of Australian Multiculturalism, Duke University Press, Durham and London, 2002.
Purcell, E.A., The Crisis of Democratic Theory: Scientific Naturalism and the Problem of Value, University Press of Kentucky, Lexington, 1973.
Rasch, W., Human Rights as Geopolitics. Carl Schmitt and the Legal Form of American Supremacy, Cultural Critique, Volume 54, 2003, pp. 120–147.
Raulff, U., Blick in den Giftschrank. Ernst Cassirers Verfassungspatriotismus und die Politik der Weimarer Republik, Frankfurter Allgemeine Zeitung, 2. September 1992, S. N 5.
Redlich, N., Comments on the Constitutional Counter-Revolution, presented on September 13, 2002, at University of District of Columbia School of Law.
Ricœur, P., Can Fictional Narrative be True? The Phenomenology of Man and of the Human Condition. Analecta Husserliana, Volume 14, 1977, pp. 3–19.
Riekkinen, P., The Power of the Supreme Court and the Death Sentence: "The mystical foundation of the authority", Challenges to law at the end of the 20th century: Law, Justice and Culture, ARSP Beiheft 68, Franz Steiner Verlag, Stuttgart, 1998, pp. 162–179.
Ringer, F.K., The Decline of the German Mandarins. The German Academic Community, 1890–1933, Harvard University Press, 1969.
Robinson, W.P., Language in Social Worlds, Blackwell Publishing, Oxford, 2003.
Roermund, B. van, Het verdwijnpunt van de wet. Een opstel over symboolwerking van wetgeving, W.E.J. Tjeenk Willink, Deventer, 1997.
Roermund, B. van, Authority and Authorisation, Law and Philosophy, Volume 19, 2000, pp. 201–222.
Roermund, B. van, Instituting Authority. Some Kelsenian Notes, Ratio Juris, Volume 15, No. 2, 2002, pp. 206–218.
Rotenstreich, N., Schematism and Freedom, Revue internationale de philosophie, Volume 110, 1974, pp. 464–474.

Rubenfeld, J., Freedom and Time: A Theory of Constitutional Self-Government, Yale University Press, New Haven and London, 2001.

Sauer, W., Neukantianismus und Rechtswissenschaft in Herbststimmung. Eine Antikritik, Logos, Internationale Zeitschrift für Philosophie und Kultur, 1921, pp. 162–194.

Sauer, W., Übersicht über die gegenwartigen Richtungen in der deutschen Rechtsphilosophie. Zum 200. Geburtstag Kants, Archiv für Rechts- und Wirtschaftsphilosophie, Volume 17, 1923–1924, pp. 284–313.

Sauer, W., System der Rechts – und Sozialphilosophie: Vorlesungen zugleich über allgemeine Philosophie und Soziologie, Verlag für Recht und Gesellschaft, Basel, 2nd, 1949.

Scheuerman, W.E. (ed.), The Rule of Law under Siege. Selected Essays of Franz L. Neumann and Otto Kirchheimer, University of California Press, Berkeley [a.o.], 1996.

Schnädelbach, H., Philosophie in Deutschland 1831–1933, Suhrkamp, Frankfurt am Mein, 4th print, 1991.

Schoordijk, H.C.F., De privaatrechtelijke rechtscultuur van de twintigste eeuw in context, Koninklijke Nederlandse Akademie van Wetenschappen, Amsterdam, 2003.

Schrems, J.J., Revolutionary Theology and Political Thought, The Thomist, Volume 46, 1982, pp. 347–369.

Schulze, H., Weimar. Deutschland 1917–1933, Die Deutschen und ihre Nation, Severin und Siedler Verlag, Berlin, 1982.

Schwemmer, O., Die praktische Ohnmacht der reinen Vernunft. Bemerkungen zum kategorischen Imperativ Kants, Neue Hefte für Philosophie, Volume 22, 1983, pp. 1–24.

Searle, J.R., The Construction of Social Reality, Penguin Books, London, 1996.

Shaw, S.J., Turkey and the Holocaust: Turkey's Role in Rescuing Turkish and European Jewry from Nazi Persecution, 1933–1945, New York University Press, New York, 1993.

Shaw, J., Postnational Constitutionalism in the European Union, Journal of European Public Policy, Volume 6, 1999, pp. 579–597.

Shaw, J., Relating Constitutionalism and Flexibility in the European Union, in: Búrca, G. de, Scott, J., Constitutional

Change in the EU From Uniformity to Flexibility?, Hartland Publishing, Oxford – Portland Oregon, 2000, pp. 337–358.

Siltala, R., Whose Justice, Which Ideology? Ratio Juris, Volume 16, 2002, pp. 123–130.

Simmel, G., The Philosophy of Money, Routledge, London, 1990 (1900).

Smith, C.E., Feit en rechtsnorm, Shaker Publishing, Maastricht, 1998.

Sommer, M., Mit dem Zufall leben. Überlegungen zu Kants Moralphilosophie, Neue Hefte für Philosophie, Volume 22, 1983, pp. 95–112.

Sontheimer, K., Antidemokratisches Denken in der Weimarer Republik. Die politischen Ideen des deutschen Nationalismus zwischen 1918 und 1933, Nymphenburger Verlagshandlung, München, 1962.

Sprenger, G., Recht als kulturerscheinung, Deutsche Rechts- und Sozialphilosophie um 1900, ARSP Beiheft 43, Franz Steiner Verlag, Stuttgart, 1991, pp. 134–153.

Stammler, R., Rechtsphilosophische Abhandlungen und Vorträge, Volume 2, 1914–1924, Scientia Verlag, Aalen, 1970.

Stewart, I., Kelsen Tomorrow, Current Legal Problems (Legal Theory at the End of the Milennium), Volume 51, 1998, pp. 181–204.

Stolker, C.J.J.M., 'Ja, geléérd zijn jullie wel!' Over de status van de rechtswetenschap, Nederlands Juristenblad, Volume 78, 2003, pp. 766–778.

Stolleis, M., Geschichte des öffentlichen Rechts in Deutschland. 3. Band. Staats- und Verwaltungsrechtswisenschaft in Republik und Diktatur 1914–1945, C.H. Beck Verlag, München, 1999.

Stolleis, M., Judicial Review, Administrative Review, and Constitutional Review in the Weimar Republic, Ratio Iuris, Volume 16, 2003, pp. 266–280.

Stone, J., Human Law and Human Justice, Stanford University Press, Stanford, California, 1965.

Strasser, M., The Image of Man, Legal Philosophy: General Aspects, ARSP Beiheft 82, Franz Steiner Verlag, Stuttgart, 2002, pp. 13–22.

Struchiner, N., The Meaning of Justice. The Need of a New Paradigm of Law, Legal Philosophy: General Aspects, ARSP Beiheft 82, Franz Steiner Verlag, Stuttgart, 2002, pp. 78–84.

Sunstein, C.R., Naked Preference and the Constitution, Columbia Law Review, Volume 84, 1984, pp. 1689–1732.

Sunstein, C.R., The Second Bill of Rights. FDR's Unfinished Revolution And Why We Need it More Than Ever, Basic Books, New York, 2004.

Taylor, C. [et al.], Multiculturalism. Examining the Politics of Recognition, Edited and Introduced by A. Gutmann, Princeton University Press, Princeton, NJ, 1994.

Thüring, H., Das Gedächtnis als Grund und Abgrund des Rechts bei Friedrich Nietzsche. Eine Erwägung zur Genealogie, Nietzsche und das Recht, ARSP Beiheft 77, Franz Steiner Verlag, Stuttgart, 2001, pp. 57–76.

Unger, R.M., What Should Legal Analysis Become? Verso, London and New York, 1996.

Vos, K.D., The Contribution of Edmond Cahn, H. Richard Niebuhr, and John MacMurray to the Ethics of Responsibility, Columbia University, Ph.D., 1972, UMI Dissertation Services, Ann Arbor, Michigan, 2003.

Vries, S. de, Winkler Prins. Grote Wereldgeschiedenis. Schouwspel van zestig eeuwen menselijke beschaving. Deel 6: De twintigste eeuw, Elsevier, Amsterdam en Brussel, 1976.

Ward, I., Kantianism, Postmodernism and Critical Legal Thought, Kluwer Academic Publishers, Dordrecht, Boston, and London, 1997.

Weber, F.G., The Evasive Neutral: Germany, Britain, and the Quest for a Turkish Alliance in the Second World War, University of Missouri Press, Columbia, 1979.

Weinberger, O., The Language of Practical Philosophy, Ratio Iuris, Volume 15, 2002, pp. 283–93.

White, J.B., When Words Lose Their Meaning: Constitutions and Reconstitutions of Language, Character, and Community, The University of Chicago Press, Chicago and London, 1984.

White, J.B., Justice as Translation: An Essay in Cultural and Legal Criticism, The University of Chicago Press, Chicago and London, 1990.

White, J.B., The Edge of Meaning, The University of Chicago Press, Chicago and London, 2001.

White, L.A., Individuality and Individualism. A Culturological Interpretation, International Journal of Comparative Sociology, Volume 4, 1963, pp. 31–49.

Wiegerling, K., Medienethik, Metzler, Stuttgart, 1998.
Wundt, M., Julius Binder, Philosophie des Rechts, Berlin 1925, Logos, Internationale Zeitschrift für Philosophie und Kultur, Volume 15, 1926, pp. 372–375.
Yack, B., The Longing for Total Revolution. Philosophic Sources of Social Discontent from Rousseau to Marx and Nietzsche, Princeton University Press, Princeton, New Jersey, 1986.
Zimmerman, M., Blind in the Right Eye: Weimar as a Test Case, Israel Law Review, Volume 32, 1998, pp. 395–406.

BOOK REVIEWS

Bayer, T.I., Book Review, Ernst Cassirer, The Logic of the Cultural Sciences: Five studies, translated by S.G., Lofts, Yale University Press, New Haven, 2000, Journal of the History of Philosophy, Volume 39, 2001, pp. 451–543.
Pawlik, M., Claudius Müller, Die Rechtsphilosophie des Marbuger Neukantianismus. Naturrecht und Rechtspositivismus in der Auseinandersetzung zwischen Hermann Cohen, Rudolf Stammler und Paul Natorp, ARSP, Volume 91, 1995, pp. 585–586.
Pranger, R.J., The Politicization of Islam: Reconstructing Identity, State, Faith, and Community in the Late Ottoman State (Book Review), Mediterranean Quarterly, Volume 13, 2002, pp. 135–138.
Schmid, P.A., Neue Forschungen zum Marburger Neukantianismus, Philosophisches Jahrbuch, Volume 105, 1998, pp. 446–455.
Weatherston, M., Frank Schalow, The Renewal of the Heidegger–Kant Dialogue: Action, Thought, and Responsibility (Book Review), Man and World, Volume 28, 1995, pp. 449–450.

INDEX

Law and Philosophy Library

1. E. Bulygin, J.-L. Gardies and I. Niiniluoto (eds.): *Man, Law and Modern Forms of Life*. With an Introduction by M.D. Bayles. 1985 ISBN 90-277-1869-5
2. W. Sadurski: *Giving Desert Its Due*. Social Justice and Legal Theory. 1985 ISBN 90-277-1941-1
3. N. MacCormick and O. Weinberger: *An Institutional Theory of Law*. New Approaches to Legal Positivism. 1986 ISBN 90-277-2079-7
4. A. Aarnio: *The Rational as Reasonable*. A Treatise on Legal Justification. 1987 ISBN 90-277-2276-5
5. M.D. Bayles: *Principles of Law*. A Normative Analysis. 1987 ISBN 90-277-2412-1; Pb: 90-277-2413-X
6. A. Soeteman: *Logic in Law*. Remarks on Logic and Rationality in Normative Reasoning, Especially in Law. 1989 ISBN 0-7923-0042-4
7. C.T. Sistare: *Responsibility and Criminal Liability*. 1989 ISBN 0-7923-0396-2
8. A. Peczenik: *On Law and Reason*. 1989 ISBN 0-7923-0444-6
9. W. Sadurski: *Moral Pluralism and Legal Neutrality*. 1990 ISBN 0-7923-0565-5
10. M.D. Bayles: *Procedural Justice*. Allocating to Individuals. 1990 ISBN 0-7923-0567-1
11. P. Nerhot (ed.): *Law, Interpretation and Reality*. Essays in Epistemology, Hermeneutics and Jurisprudence. 1990 ISBN 0-7923-0593-0
12. A.W. Norrie: *Law, Ideology and Punishment*. Retrieval and Critique of the Liberal Ideal of Criminal Justice. 1991 ISBN 0-7923-1013-6
13. P. Nerhot (ed.): *Legal Knowledge and Analogy*. Fragments of Legal Epistemology, Hermeneutics and Linguistics. 1991 ISBN 0-7923-1065-9
14. O. Weinberger: *Law, Institution and Legal Politics*. Fundamental Problems of Legal Theory and Social Philosophy. 1991 ISBN 0-7923-1143-4
15. J. Wróblewski: *The Judicial Application of Law*. Edited by Z. Bańkowski and N. MacCormick. 1992 ISBN 0-7923-1569-3
16. T. Wilhelmsson: *Critical Studies in Private Law*. A Treatise on Need-Rational Principles in Modern Law. 1992 ISBN 0-7923-1659-2
17. M.D. Bayles: *Hart's Legal Philosophy*. An Examination. 1992 ISBN 0-7923-1981-8
18. D.W.P. Ruiter: *Institutional Legal Facts*. Legal Powers and their Effects. 1993 ISBN 0-7923-2441-2
19. J. Schonsheck: *On Criminalization*. An Essay in the Philosophy of the Criminal Law. 1994 ISBN 0-7923-2663-6
20. R.P. Malloy and J. Evensky (eds.): *Adam Smith and the Philosophy of Law and Economics*. 1994 ISBN 0-7923-2796-9
21. Z. Bańkowski, I. White and U. Hahn (eds.): *Informatics and the Foundations of Legal Reasoning*. 1995 ISBN 0-7923-3455-8
22. E. Lagerspetz: *The Opposite Mirrors*. An Essay on the Conventionalist Theory of Institutions. 1995 ISBN 0-7923-3325-X

Law and Philosophy Library

23. M. van Hees: *Rights and Decisions*. Formal Models of Law and Liberalism. 1995 ISBN 0-7923-3754-9
24. B. Anderson: "*Discovery*" *in Legal Decision-Making*. 1996 ISBN 0-7923-3981-9
25. S. Urbina: *Reason, Democracy, Society*. A Study on the Basis of Legal Thinking. 1996 ISBN 0-7923-4262-3
26. E. Attwooll: *The Tapestry of the Law*. Scotland, Legal Culture and Legal Theory. 1997 ISBN 0-7923-4310-7
27. J.C. Hage: *Reasoning with Rules*. An Essay on Legal Reasoning and Its Underlying Logic. 1997 ISBN 0-7923-4325-5
28. R.A. Hillman: *The Richness of Contract Law*. An Analysis and Critique of Contemporary Theories of Contract Law. 1997 ISBN 0-7923-4336-0; 0-7923-5063-4 (Pb)
29. C. Wellman: *An Approach to Rights*. Studies in the Philosophy of Law and Morals. 1997 ISBN 0-7923-4467-7
30. B. van Roermund: *Law, Narrative and Reality*. An Essay in Intercepting Politics. 1997 ISBN 0-7923-4621-1
31. I. Ward: *Kantianism, Postmodernism and Critical Legal Thought*. 1997 ISBN 0-7923-4745-5
32. H. Prakken: *Logical Tools for Modelling Legal Argument*. A Study of Defeasible Reasoning in Law. 1997 ISBN 0-7923-4776-5
33. T. May: *Autonomy, Authority and Moral Responsibility*. 1998 ISBN 0-7923-4851-6
34. M. Atienza and J.R. Manero: *A Theory of Legal Sentences*. 1998 ISBN 0-7923-4856-7
35. E.A. Christodoulidis: *Law and Reflexive Politics*. 1998 ISBN 0-7923-4954-7
36. L.M.M. Royakkers: *Extending Deontic Logic for the Formalisation of Legal Rules*. 1998 ISBN 0-7923-4982-2
37. J.J. Moreso: *Legal Indeterminacy and Constitutional Interpretation*. 1998 ISBN 0-7923-5156-8
38. W. Sadurski: *Freedom of Speech and Its Limits*. 1999 ISBN 0-7923-5523-7
39. J. Wolenski (ed.): *Kazimierz Opalek Selected Papers in Legal Philosophy*. 1999 ISBN 0-7923-5732-9
40. H.P. Visser 't Hooft: *Justice to Future Generations and the Environment*. 1999 ISBN 0-7923-5756-6
41. L.J. Wintgens (ed.): *The Law in Philosophical Perspectives*. My Philosophy of Law. 1999 ISBN 0-7923-5796-5
42. A.R. Lodder: *DiaLaw*. On Legal Justification and Dialogical Models of Argumentation. 1999 ISBN 0-7923-5830-9
43. C. Redondo: *Reasons for Action and the Law*. 1999 ISBN 0-7923-5912-7

Law and Philosophy Library

44. M. Friedman, L. May, K. Parsons and J. Stiff (eds.): *Rights and Reason*. Essays in Honor of Carl Wellman. 2000 ISBN 0-7923-6198-9
45. G.C. Christie: *The Notion of an Ideal Audience in Legal Argument*. 2000 ISBN 0-7923-6283-7
46. R.S. Summers: *Essays in Legal Theory*. 2000 ISBN 0-7923-6367-1
47. M. van Hees: *Legal Reductionism and Freedom*. 2000 ISBN 0-7923-6491-0
48. R. Gargarella: *The Scepter of Reason*. Public Discussion and Political Radicalism in the Origins of Constitutionalism. 2000 ISBN 0-7923-6508-9
49. M. Iglesias Vila: *Facing Judicial Discretion*. Legal Knowledge and Right Answers Revisited. 2001 ISBN 0-7923-6778-2
50. M. Kiikeri: *Comparative Legal Reasoning and European Law*. 2001 ISBN 0-7923-6884-3
51. A.J. Menéndez: *Justifying Taxes*. Some Elements for a General Theory of Democratic Tax Law. 2001 ISBN 0-7923-7052-X
52. W.E. Conklin: *The Invisible Origins of Legal Positivism*. A Re-Reading of a Tradition. 2001 ISBN 0-7923-7101-1
53. Z. Bańkowski: *Living Lawfully*. Love in Law and Law in Love. 2001 ISBN 0-7923-7180-1
54. A.N. Shytov: *Conscience and Love in Making Judicial Decisions*. 2001 ISBN 1-4020-0168-1
55. D.W.P. Ruiter: *Legal Institutions*. 2001 ISBN 1-4020-0186-X

Volumes 56–63 were published by Kluwer Law International.

56. G. den Hartogh: *Mutual Expectations*. A Conventionalist Theory of Law. 2002 ISBN 90-411-1796-2
57. W.L. Robison (ed.): *The Legal Essays of Michael Bayles*. 2002 ISBN 90-411-1835-7
58. U. Bindreiter: *Why Grundnorm?* A Treatise on the Implications of Kelsen's Doctrine. 2002 ISBN 90-411-1867-5
59. S. Urbina: *Legal Method and the Rule of Law*. 2002 ISBN 90-411-1870-5
60. M. Baurmann: *The Market of Virtue*. Morality and Commitment in a Liberal Society. 2002 ISBN 90-411-1874-8
61. G. Zanetti: *Political Friendship and the Good Life*. Two Liberal Arguments against Perfectionism. 2002 ISBN 90-411-1881-0
62. W. Sadurski (ed.): *Constitutional Justice, East and West*. 2002 ISBN 90-411-1883-7
63. S. Taekema: *The Concept of Ideals in Legal Theory*. 2003 ISBN 90-411-1971-X
64. J. Raitio: *The Principle of Legal Certainty in EC Law*. 2003 ISBN 1-4020-1217-9

Law and Philosophy Library

65. E. Santoro: *Autonomy, Freedom and Rights*. A Critique of Liberal Subjectivity. 2003 ISBN 1-4020-1404-X
66. S. Eng: *Analysis of Dis/agreement – with particular reference to Law and Legal Theory*. 2003 ISBN 1-4020-1490-2
67. D. González Lagier: *The Paradoxes of Action*. (Human Action, Law and Philosophy). 2003 ISBN Hb-1-4020-1661-1
68. R. Zimmerling: *Influence and Power*. Variations on a Messy Theme. 2004 ISBN Hb-1-4020-2986-1
69. A. Stranieri and J. Zeleznikow (eds.): *Knowledge Discovery from Legal Databases*. 2005 ISBN 1-4020-3036-3
70. J. Hage: *Studies in Legal Logic*. 2005 ISBN 1-4020-3517-9
71. C. Wellman: *Medical Law and Moral Rights*. 2005 ISBN 1-4020-3751-1
72. T. Meisels: *Territorial Rights*. 2005 ISBN 1-4020-3822-4
73. G.W. Rainbolt: *The Concept of Rights*. 2005 ISBN 1-4020-3976-X
74. O. Ezra: *Moral Dilemmas in Real Life*. Current Issues in Applied Ethics. 2006 ISBN 1-4020-4103-9
75. N.T. Casals: *Group Rights as Human Rights*. A Liberal Approach to Multiculturalism. 2006 ISBN 1-4020-4208-6
76. C. Michelon Jr.: *Being Apart from Reasons*. The Role of Reasons in Public and Private Moral Decision-Making. 2006 ISBN 1-4020-4282-5
77. A.J. Menendez and E.O. Eriksen (eds): *Arguing Fundamental Rights*. 2006 ISBN 1-4020-4918-8
78. J. Stelmach and B. Brozek: *Methods of Legal Reasoning*. 2006 ISBN 1-4020-4936-6
79. M. La Torre: *Constitutionalism and Legal Reasoning*. A New Paradigm for the Concept of Law. 2007 ISBN 1-4020-5594-3
80. P. Costa and D. Zolo (eds.): *The Rule of Law*. History, Theory and Criticism. 2007 ISBN 978-1-4020-5744-1
81. H. Avila: *Theory of Legal Prinicíples*. 2007 ISBN 978-1-4020-5878-3
82. D. Coskun: *Law as Symbolic Form*. Ernst Cassirer and the Anthropocentric View of Law. 2007 ISBN 978-1-4020-6255-1